T0371624

GATT and Global Order in the Postwar Era

After the Second World War, the General Agreement on Tariffs and Trade (GATT) promoted trade liberalization to help make the world prosperous and peaceful. Francine McKenzie uses case studies of the Cold War, the creation of the EEC and other regional trade agreements, development, and agriculture to show that trade is a primary goal of foreign policy, a dominant (and divisive) aspect of international relations, and a vital component of global order. She unpacks the many ways in which trade was politicized and the layers of meaning associated with trade; and trade policies, as well as disputes about trade, communicated ideas, hopes, and fears that were linked to larger questions of identity, sovereignty, and status. This study reveals how the economic and political dimensions of foreign policy and international engagement intersected, showing not only that trade was instrumentalized in the service of particular policies but also that trade was an essential aspect of international relations.

Francine McKenzie is a professor at the University of Western Ontario. She is an international historian who has published extensively on international cooperation, trade, and global order. Her publications include *Redefining the Bonds of Commonwealth, 1939–1948* (2002), *A Global History of Trade and Conflict since 1500* (2013), and *Dominion of Race: Rethinking Canada's International History* (2017).

GATT and Global Order
in the Postwar Era

Francine McKenzie

University of Western Ontario

CAMBRIDGE
UNIVERSITY PRESS

University Printing House, Cambridge CB2 8BS, United Kingdom

One Liberty Plaza, 20th Floor, New York, NY 10006, USA

477 Williamstown Road, Port Melbourne, VIC 3207, Australia

314–321, 3rd Floor, Plot 3, Splendor Forum, Jasola District Centre,
New Delhi – 110025, India

79 Anson Road, #06–04/06, Singapore 079906

Cambridge University Press is part of the University of Cambridge.

It furthers the University's mission by disseminating knowledge in the pursuit of
education, learning, and research at the highest international levels of excellence.

www.cambridge.org
Information on this title: www.cambridge.org/9781108494892
DOI: 10.1017/9781108860192

First published 2020

Printed in the United Kingdom by TJ International Ltd, Padstow Cornwall

A catalogue record for this publication is available from the British Library.

ISBN 978-1-108-49489-2 Hardback

For my teachers: Bob McKenzie, Bob Bothwell,
David Fieldhouse

Contents

Figures

Tables

Acknowledgements

After many years of work, it is with relief, anticipation, and some disbelief that I am writing the acknowledgements for this book. I have benefited from the support, generosity, and assistance of many people throughout this project. Sometimes help was easily given – sharing a contact, telling me about relevant publications, or providing information about a source – and sometimes there was a big commitment of time and effort. Regardless of the size of the favour, I could not have completed *GATT and Global Order in the Postwar Era* without it.

Librarians and archivists around the world have assisted me with research. They explained the workings of their archives, tracked down elusive texts, and pointed me to collections I probably would not have found on my own. Thanks to Ryan Toohey for talking to me about doing research in India. As I travelled to archives, I was lucky to have friends who put me up: Fern Roberts, Michael Bing, Mary Gooderham, Andrew Cohen, and Henrietta Harrison. I am also grateful to Chris Tait and Mike Aloisio, research assistants who helped me to figure out the complicated workings of GATT. Jessi Gilchrist has provided great help in preparing the manuscript for publication. On my travels, I spoke to officials who had been involved in GATT as negotiators, members of the secretariat, and national policy-makers. Their involvement with GATT goes back to the Geneva conference of 1947 and the original secretariat. They were valuable sources from whom I learned a lot. David Lee, Andrew Needs, Ian Hill, and David Elder helped connect me to some of these people.

Over the last decade, colleagues and friends have read parts of the manuscript. Their intellectual generosity and critical feedback influenced the final product in many ways. Thanks to Lucia Coppolaro, Beth Fischer, Sue Howson, Daniel Manulak, Robert McKenzie, Kathy Rasmussen, Charles Roger, Rogerio de Souza Farias, Terry Sicular, Mike Szonyi, Richard Toye, Todd Weiler, and Tom Zeiler. I am also indebted to the two anonymous reviewers for their serious and sustained attention to my book. Sjrdan Vucetic and Charles Roger have steered me to relevant literature in political science.

I am grateful for support from various granting agencies, including the Social Science and Humanities Research Council. My home university – the University of Western Ontario – also provided generous funding for this project.

My family has always encouraged me in my work. They have been especially supportive and patient with this project. When I began working seriously on it, my kids (Bobby and Katie) were too young to understand what it meant to write a book and they had no idea what GATT was. They now have a good sense of what is involved in producing a work of this size and scope and they can tell you more about GATT than they ever wanted to know. My spouse, Mike Szonyi, has been golden throughout this process. He persuaded me to stick with GATT when I wanted to abandon it; he helped me to think about the ways in which history connects to conditions today; he read the manuscript more than once, providing thoughtful, constructive, and critical feedback; he managed everything on the home front when I was in archives and at conferences.

Although I am not always easy to teach, I have had wonderful teachers throughout my life. I have dedicated this book to three of them. When I was in grade school, my father – Bob McKenzie – used to ask me what I had learned in my history classes. When I told him what I had been taught, he always replied: 'They left out the most interesting parts.' He would then supplement what I had learned with knowledge he had acquired over a lifetime of assiduous reading, always stressing the human side of history. He sustained my interest in history when I was young and supported my ongoing education by giving me works of history for the rest of his life. Bob Bothwell encouraged me to believe I could become a historian. He is an inspiring teacher and a generous mentor. Over lunch one day, he suggested that I should write a history of GATT. It might have been a passing remark, but I took it seriously! David Fieldhouse was a sympathetic, supportive, and awe-inspiring supervisor. He showed me how important economic topics were to political and international history. He also encouraged me to think for myself. To this day, I pass on some of his best advice to my own graduate students.

Abbreviations

AOT	associated overseas territory
CAP	common agricultural policy
CET	common external tariff
CG18	Consultative Group of Eighteen
CMEA	Council for Mutual Economic Assistance
DREE	Direction des relations économiques extérieures (France)
EC	European Community
ECOSOC	Economic and Social Council
ECSC	European Coal and Steel Community
EEC	European Economic Community
EFTA	European Free Trade Association
EU	European Union
FAO	Food and Agriculture Organization
FNSEA	Fédération nationale des syndicats d'exploitants agricoles (France)
GSP	Generalized System of Preferences
ICC	International Chamber of Commerce
ICITO	Interim Commission for the International Trade Organization
ICU	International Commercial Union
IOS	Investors Overseas Service
IMF	International Monetary Fund

ITO	International Trade Organization
LAFTA	Latin American Free Trade Association
LTA	Long-Term Arrangement on International Trade in Cotton Textiles
MFA	Multifibre Arrangement
MFN	Most Favoured Nation
MITI	Ministry of International Trade and Industry
NATO	North Atlantic Treaty Organization
NIEO	New International Economic Order
NTB	non-tariff barrier
OECD	Organization for Economic Cooperation and Development
OEEC	Organization for European Economic Cooperation
OTC	Organization for Trade Cooperation
PRC	People's Republic of China
ROC	Republic of China
RTAA	Reciprocal Trade Agreements Act
TEA	Trade Expansion Act
UN	United Nations
UNCTAD	United Nations Conference on Trade and Development
UNRRA	United Nations Relief and Rehabilitation Administration
USTR	United States trade representative
VER	voluntary export restraint
WHO	World Health Organization
WTO	World Trade Organization

Introduction
GATT in World Affairs

No one expected that the end of hostilities in 1945 would automatically mean the return of peace. Officials who thought about the postwar period thought in terms of a peace that had to be won or else it might be lost. They tried to understand the causes of conflict and identify the conditions for stability, security, and well-being so that they could construct a new and viable global order. Their plans brought together rules, norms, nations, and international organizations to manage and contain conflict, and to build a new foundation of understanding and cooperation across people and nations. The United Nations (UN) was at the centre of this reconstructed postwar architecture, but it could not be expected to uphold peace on its own. Wartime blueprints mapped out a host of specialist international organizations that would tackle specific elements of international order and disorder. The planning of these agencies revealed a complex understanding of the causes of conflict and of the necessary ingredients for peace. There was widespread belief that the condition of the world economy, as well as economic relations between states, would be critically important to the postwar order. A peaceful world had to be prosperous; at the very least, economic instability, poverty, and the gap between have and have-not states would have to be alleviated. Officials in the United States and Britain designed three organizations that were intended to stabilize currencies, promote industrial development, and liberalize world trade as interconnected parts of a secure and expanding global economic order: the International Monetary Fund (IMF), the International Bank for Reconstruction and Development (usually referred to as the World Bank), and the International Trade Organization (ITO). The IMF and the World Bank emerged from the Bretton Woods conference of 1944, but negotiations to establish the ITO carried on into the postwar period. The delay proved terminal. Alone among these new international organizations, the ITO was never established. Instead, its role was fulfilled by the General Agreement on Tariffs and Trade (GATT), a contractual agreement negotiated by twenty-three countries in 1947 which bound them to liberalize trade by lowering tariffs. Eric Wyndham White, GATT's first executive

Table 0.1 *Rounds of GATT negotiations*

1947	Geneva round
1949	Annecy round
1950–1951	Torquay round
1956	Geneva round
1960–1961	Dillon round
1964–1967	Kennedy round
1973–1979	Tokyo round
1986–1994	Uruguay round

secretary, described it as the 'Cinderella of international organizations': it arrived late on the scene of postwar global governance and had almost no institutional resources.[1] Although GATT was supposed to be a temporary measure, it oversaw and encouraged trade liberalization for almost half a century through eight rounds of discussion and activity (see Table 0.1). This book tells the institutional and international history of GATT, the least well known of the three international economic organizations.

GATT was one of many international organizations established to restore and maintain order in the postwar era. The prominence and responsibilities of international organizations prompted the establishment of a new journal, *International Organization*, in 1947. The journal's first editor anticipated that international organizations would be 'an increasingly important part of the study and understanding of international relations'.[2] But historians, at least, did not rush to study these organizations. This was partly because diplomatic historians at the time were focused on explaining the start of the Second World War and later the causes of the Cold War. Conflicts, rivalry, and the pursuit of power defined the boundaries of worthwhile subjects for diplomatic historians. International organizations were relegated to a minor role, with the possible exception of the United Nations.[3] Since the end of the Cold War, conceptions of global affairs have changed[4] and the range of historical subjects studied has expanded. International historians are asking

[1] 'The Achievements of the GATT', address by Eric Wyndham White at the Graduate Institute of International Studies, Geneva, December 1956 (Geneva: WTO Archives).
[2] H. Bundy, 'An Introductory Note', *International Organization* 1 (1) (1947), 1.
[3] Even the historical literature on the UN has been slim until recently. The UN Intellectual History Project produced fifteen volumes between 2001 and 2010, although they were not all written by historians. The seventieth anniversary of the UN in 2015 was the theme of numerous conferences which have generated more published studies.
[4] Iriye has been at the forefront of major shifts in the field, including the approach to diplomatic history from the perspective of intercultural relations. He also challenges the logic of the nation-state as the primary actor or framework in which to situate international

new questions and exploring new subjects, including manifestations of internationalist thinking;[5] cooperation at multiple levels; the values, norms, and priorities of the global community; the authority of nation-states; the activities of transnational actors; the rise of experts; and conceptions of world order.[6] This new scholarship also explores the agency and impact of international organizations as creators of norms, intermediaries between nations, and forums that reduced tensions and facilitated cooperation. While our understanding of international organizations is still developing and debates about their agency and autonomy continue, studies

---

history. See *Global and Transnational History: The Past, Present and Future* (Basingstoke: Palgrave Macmillan, 2013), 2.

[5] Sluga and Clavin write that until recently, 'the theme of internationalism . . . could rarely be heard as more than a whisper in narratives of the past'. G. Sluga and P. Clavin (eds.), *Internationalisms: A Twentieth Century History* (Cambridge: Cambridge University Press, 2017), 3. Also see S. Jackson and A. O'Malley (eds.), *The Institution of International Order: From the League of Nations to the United Nations* (London and New York: Routledge, 2018) for a discussion about the many forms of internationalism.

[6] Recent histories of the League of Nations are evidence of this redirection of historical interest. See P. Clavin, *Securing the World Economy: The Reinvention of the League of Nations, 1920–1946* (Oxford: Oxford University Press, 2013) and S. Pedersen, *The Guardians: The League of Nations and the Crisis of Empire* (New York: Oxford University Press, 2015). Scholars have produced many studies of postwar international organizations over the last twenty years: see A. van Dormael, *Bretton Woods: Birth of a Monetary System* (London: Macmillan, 1978); R. Gardner, *Sterling–Dollar Diplomacy in Current Perspective: The Origins and Prospects of Our International Economic Order* (New York: Columbia University Press, 1980); L. S. Pressnell, *External Economic Policy Since the War, Vol. I: The Post-War Financial Settlement* (London: Her Majesty's Stationery Office, 1986); G. Schild, *Bretton Woods and Dumbarton Oaks: American Economic and Political Postwar Planning in the Summer of 1944* (New York: St. Martin's Press, 1995); T. W. Zeiler, *Free Trade, Free World: The Advent of GATT* (Chapel Hill: University of North Carolina Press, 1999); M. A. Glendon, *A World Made New: Eleanor Roosevelt and the Universal Declaration of Human Rights* (New York: Random House, 2001); P. J. Hearden, *Architects of Globalism: Building a New World Order during World War II* (Fayetteville: University of Arkansas Press, 2002); S. C. Schlesinger, *Act of Creation: The Founding of the United Nations: A Story of Superpowers, Secret Agents, Wartime Allies and Enemies and Their Quest for a Peaceful World* (Boulder, CO: Westview Press, 2003); A. L. S. Sayward, *The Birth of Development: How the World Bank, Food and Agriculture Organization, and World Health Organization Changed the World, 1945–1965* (Kent, OH: Kent State University Press, 2006); D. A. Irwin, P. C. Mavroidis, and A. O. Sykes, *The Genesis of the GATT* (New York and Cambridge: Cambridge University Press, 2008); G. Sluga, 'UNESCO and the (One) World of Julian Huxley, *Journal of World History*, 21 (3) (September 2010), 393–418; D. Mackenzie, *ICAO: A History of the International Civil Aviation Organization* (Toronto: University of Toronto Press, 2010); J. Reinisch, 'Internationalism in Relief: The Birth (and Death) of UNRRA', *Past & Present*, 201 (6) (January 2011), 258–289; B. Steil, *The Battle of Bretton Woods: John Maynard Keynes, Harry Dexter White, and the Making of a New World Order* (Princeton and Oxford: Princeton University Press, 2013); S. Kott, 'Fighting the War or Preparing for Peace? The ILO During the Second World War', *Journal of Modern European History* 12 (3) (August 2014), 359–376; O. Rosenboim, *The Emergence of Globalism: Visions of World Order in Britain and the United States, 1939–1950* (Princeton: Princeton University Press, 2017); A. L. Sayward, *The United Nations in International History* (London and New York: Bloomsbury, 2017).

of the international community and international relations that exclude international organizations are at best incomplete and at worst misleading.

Situating GATT in the international community and within the global governance structure is a challenge. There is a vast literature on GATT written by economists, lawyers, political scientists, historians, policy-makers, GATT officials, and activists. Scholars have written extensively about rounds of trade negotiations because they were GATT's raison d'être. Such accounts usually focus on the Kennedy round (1964–1967) and the Uruguay round (1986–1994), arguably the two most important rounds of negotiations. Studies have also examined specific sectors of trade (for example, agriculture or intellectual property), trade practices (such as anti-dumping), or cross-cutting issues with links to trade (including the environment and sovereignty). Some scholars have written about GATT in relation to a single country's overall trade policy. But it is not clear what these various aspects of GATT add up to. The variety of ways in which scholars characterize GATT has occluded our understanding of what it was, how it functioned, and what effect it had: it has been defined as a regime, a contract, an inter-governmental treaty, a body of law, a legal framework, a set of guidelines, a club, a forum, an instrument of US interests, or, more broadly, the interests of industrial countries, a consumers' union, and a political agency. Those scholars who identify it as an international organization variously describe it as a de facto organization, an obscure organization, an informal organization, and an organization lacking both muscle and universality. Characterizations such as these reinforce the view of GATT as improvisational, incomplete, ineffective, and unknown.

While most studies of GATT adopt a technical approach and focus on specific rounds of trade negotiations or specific trade practices, this study considers international trade as an essential component of global politics. GATT's history is an ideal venue to explore quotidian international relations and to re-examine our understanding of the nature, dynamics, drivers, and priorities of post-1945 international relations and the liberal international order. This study also unpacks the many ways in which trade was politicized. Trade policies, trade negotiations, and disputes about trade communicate ideas, hopes, and fears that are linked to larger questions of identity, sovereignty, and status. This study shows how economic and political factors and goals are integrated into foreign policy, how trade is instrumentalized in the service of particular policies or relations, and how it is a distinct aspect of international relations. As Richard Cooper put it many years ago, 'trade policy *is* foreign policy'.[7]

---

[7] R. N. Cooper, 'Trade Policy is Foreign Policy', *Foreign Policy* 9 (1972/73), 18–36. Italics added.

The history of GATT can also help us refine our understanding of the nature of international organizations. When national representatives convened in GATT, an international space was created where national trade goals were promoted in a dynamic that was competitive and cooperative. But this study shows that GATT was more than a meeting point for national representatives. It had its own normative authority and agency. Its authority initially stemmed from the Depression and the Second World War, events which gave rise to the institutional internationalism of GATT. Its internationalism was communicated through the promotion of trade liberalization: lower tariffs (and later the removal of other kinds of trade barriers) and open markets – which would, in theory, make all countries more prosperous and the world more stable, possibly even more peaceful – and adherence to rules in defining trade policies and practices. GATT's secretariat actively upheld its internationalist philosophy by promoting ever more liberalization, although it sometimes obscured its activism and influence to pre-empt concerns about encroachment on the sovereign authority of governments over trade policy. As members participated in rounds of negotiations and held national trade policies to the standard of GATT rules and sanctioned practices, the internationalist contributions and soundness of those members were assessed in an international forum. However, the secretariat did not single out members when they deviated from GATT rules and norms. Political realities meant that compromise and flexibility were needed to keep members committed to a common cause even though they all strayed from the liberalization path some of the time. The need for diplomatic deftness and the search for compromise was also made necessary by concerns about institutional survival. Pushed too far, members might quit. Many threatened to withdraw; few followed through. In fact, GATT membership increased steadily, with a flood of new applicants in the 1990s, which reinforced its normative authority – although that still had to be discharged carefully.

Close study of GATT's operations raises questions about the workings of the liberal international order, starting with claims about US leadership and hegemony. Although GATT members (properly called contracting parties, but I usually refer to them as members) often complained about the absence of US leadership, the history of the organization reveals multilateralism in action, with opportunities for many nations to advance new ideas and priorities. While concerns about power and security run through the book, by bringing such topics as agriculture and protectionism to the fore this study redraws conventional international fault lines and revises our understanding of global priorities. Most importantly, a history of GATT demonstrates the presence of competing and co-existing conceptions of world order in which rules, power, and individual and collective interests were valued and observed to different degrees. It also exposes unspoken assumptions, unacknowledged goals, and (perhaps) unintended consequences that force a rethinking of the liberal international project. Today many scholars endorse the liberal order that succeeded the Second World War because it has sustained security, stability, and prosperity. They warn that its destruction will lead to chaos.[8] Some question whether this confidence is misplaced. The liberal order may not have been 'the nirvana that people now suggest', and faith in its merits and achievements may be a result of nostalgia and dubious historical reasoning.[9] This study produces fine-grained historical evidence about how GATT worked, who benefited from it, who supported it and why, what faults its critics identified, and whether the organization could adapt to new conditions; all of these questions should inform discussions about the past, present, and future of the global order.

My approach is historical, synthetic, and empirical. To explain GATT's evolution and operations as well as relations among its members requires detailed information about daily activities, from multiple perspectives, and on many issues. I include rounds of trade negotiations, but they are not as central here as they are in other studies. Instead, I devote more space to exploring what happened between rounds of negotiations; the activities and initiatives of the secretariat, particularly the directors-general; and the formulation of trade policies in national capitals. Recent developments in international history[10] and new historical studies of international organizations have informed my methodology, including

---

[8] Petition: Preserving Alliances, https://docs.google.com/forms/d/e/1FAIpQLSesHdZWx pp13plS4nkLOSMHv4Dg1jaksBrCC6kWv6OfVAmO5g/viewform. The petition appeared in the *New York Times* on 27 July 2018. The arguments behind support for the postwar order are developed more fully in D. Deudney and G. J. Ikenberry, 'Liberal World: The Resilient Order', *Foreign Affairs* 97 (4) (July/August 2018), 16–24. For a recent collection of essays that consider Trump's impact on the liberal order, see R. Jervis et al. (eds.), *Chaos in the Liberal Order: The Trump Presidency and International Politics in the Twenty-First Century* (New York: Columbia University Press, 2018).

[9] S. M. Walt, 'Why I Didn't Sign Up to Defend the International Order', *Foreign Policy* (1 August 2018), https://foreignpolicy.com/2018/08/01/why-i-didnt-sign-up-to-defend-the-international-order/. See also G. Allison, 'The Myth of the Liberal Order: From Historical Accident to Conventional Wisdom', *Foreign Affairs* 97 (4) (July/August 2018), 124–133; S. Wertheim, 'Paeans to the "Postwar Order" Won't Save Us' (6 August 2018), War on the Rocks website, https://warontherocks.com/2018/08/paeans-to-the-postwar-order-wont-save-us/.

[10] Finney observes that international history is a moving target, continually expanding and redefining itself. Nonetheless, he notes that there is a common interest in 'profound structural forces, the formulation as well as the execution of policy, a wider range of actors and a host of new thematic concerns'. P. Finney, *Palgrave Advances in International History* (Basingstoke and New York: Palgrave Macmillan, 2005), 7.

multinational archival research; attention to ideas and motivations behind policies, interests, and objectives; examination of state and non-state actors; and a focus on attempts to cooperate. National actors and the pursuit of power and security also figure prominently. The result is a series of detailed thematic chapters that explain how GATT functioned over almost fifty years.

I have been working on the history of GATT for a long time. When I began this research, I needed to explain and justify why I was adopting an institutional and politico-diplomatic approach. Today, when long-standing international trade agreements are being jettisoned and relations between states are thus being destabilized, when trade policy is openly used to promote national power, when the usefulness and legitimacy of the World Trade Organization (WTO) are called into question, and when many of the so-called architects of the liberal trade order reject its pre-mises and purposes in favour of mercantilist reasoning, this approach seems self-evident. In fact, it would always have made sense. Many current trends are consistent with the longer history of trade policies and practices rather than a sudden departure or an unprecedented chal-lenge. The belief in liberal trade as a condition of a stable and prosperous world was questioned and challenged throughout the twentieth century, but it now seems more tenuous than ever. The history of GATT shows how a balance was struck between individual and collective interests, between short- and long-term thinking, and between adherence to rules and the flexing of national muscle. GATT's history should reinforce confidence about the resilience of the global trade order; it has survived many assaults and challenges. But there is also cause for concern because the default internationalism that restrained members from sabotaging the organization seems sorely lacking today.

Trade, International Politics, and Global Order

Trade has long been one of the main forms of contact between peoples and nations.[11] According to Robert Gilpin, trade is 'the oldest and most important nexus among nations ... trade along with war has been central to the evolution of international relations'.[12] It seems axiomatic that GATT should be historically examined as a site of international contact where conflicts emerged and where efforts to cooperate were pursued. The challenge in connecting what happened in GATT with relations

---

[11] K. Pomeranz and S. Topik, *The World that Trade Created: Society, Culture, and the World Economy, 1400 to the Present* (Armonk and London: M. E. Sharpe, 1999).

[12] R. Gilpin, *The Political Economy of International Relations* (Princeton: Princeton University Press, 1990), 171.

between peoples, governments, and countries is that there was an unspoken agreement that politics should not enter into GATT's business or at least not be openly acknowledged as influencing trade liberalization. It is no surprise that some officials who represented their countries in GATT admitted to being unaware of international political forces and foreign policy objectives and goals, although others acknowledged these openly.[13] Perhaps because of the convention of talking about trade as a technical subject, some scholars assert that GATT was largely impervious to political pressures and interests.[14] For example, Gerard and Victoria Curzon describe GATT's history as politically 'uneventful' because members were like-minded and kept political issues outside of GATT.[15] Many presume this depoliticization was a virtue.

This study treats trade practices – such as preferential tariffs, dumping, import quotas, and voluntary export restraints – and economic debates, such as whether or not regional trade blocs are trade creating or trade diverting, as fundamentally political activities. Both domestic and international political interests and goals have informed trade policy. Decisions about the substance of trade negotiations, in particular what sectors could be liberalized and which ones required protection, have prioritized competing domestic interests and have meant weighing domestic and international priorities against one another. As Gilbert Winham puts it, political leaders decide 'what *can* be done' and technical experts determine 'what *will* be done'.[16] States have also used trade policy to serve specific political purposes, although they have not always acknowledged this. Lucia Coppolaro makes this point in her recent study of the European Economic Community (EEC) during the Kennedy round. As she explains in relation to a dispute over chickens

[13] Author interview with Richard Nottage, Wellington, New Zealand, 18 July 2005; author interview with Simon Reisman, Ottawa, Canada, 17 May 2005; author interview with Jake Warren, Ottawa, 18 May 2005; author interview with Julio Lacarte, 20 May 2005.
[14] Kock concedes that the effects of the Cold War could not be entirely avoided. K. Kock, *International Trade Policy and the GATT, 1947–1967* (Stockholm: Almqvist and Wiksell, 1969), 73. Preeg also notes that GATT members were mostly like-minded and therefore they avoided 'serious political frictions'. E. H. Preeg, *Traders and Diplomats: An Analysis of the Kennedy Round of Negotiations under the General Agreement on Tariffs and Trade* (Washington, DC: Brookings Institution, 1970), 24. Zacher and Finlayson also claim the GATT depoliticized international trade; J. A. Finlayson and M. W. Zacher, 'The GATT and the Regulation of Trade Barriers: Regime Dynamics and Functions' in S. D. Krasner (ed.), *International Regimes* (Ithaca, NY: Cornell University Press, 1983), 314.
[15] G. Curzon and V. Curzon, 'GATT: A Trader's Club' in R. W. Cox and H. K. Jacobson (eds.), *The Anatomy of Influence: Decision Making in International Organization* (New Haven, CT, and London: Yale University Press, 1974), 328.
[16] G. R. Winham, *International Trade and the Tokyo Round Negotiation* (Princeton: Princeton University Press, 1986), 377.

(but which is generally applicable), 'behind an apparently minor and arcane issue lay important political and commercial questions'.[17] The instrumentalization of trade gave new meaning to trade practices and trade negotiations. Political motivations and decisions became more conspicuous as trade moved from the low to high policy realm in the 1960s, when trade came under the watch of senior political figures and became a dominant issue in relations between states. Discussions of trade policies and practices in GATT should not be understood primarily as a debate about economic doctrine. Paul Krugman explains that the logic behind GATT – which he labels 'GATT-think' – is 'a simple set of principles that are entirely consistent ... but makes no sense in terms of economics'. He concludes that GATT was 'not built on a foundation laid by economic theory'. But he also acknowledges that the legal-political process resulted in more trade liberalization than could ever have been achieved by 'the lecturing of economists on the virtues of free trade'.[18]

Even more startling than Krugman's claim that the work of GATT makes no sense as applied economics is Susan Strange's assertion that GATT was largely irrelevant to the growth of global trade. In 1985, by which time the organization had existed for almost forty years, she wrote that 'the overnight disappearance of the GATT beneath the waters of Lac Leman would hardly be noticed in the world of commerce'.[19] Strange is not alone in denying or downplaying GATT's relevance to the growth of global trade. Andrew Rose finds that membership in GATT and the WTO did not affect the volume or flow of trade.[20] Soo Yeon Kim

[17] L. Coppolaro, *The Making of a World Trading Power: The European Economic Community (EEC) in the GATT Kennedy Round Negotiations (1963–67)* (Farnham: Ashgate, 2013), 86. P. Low states that we cannot fully understand GATT unless we take into account the 'political realities that intervene to shape the system', although the point about rules is to make the system less susceptible to political forces. P. Low, *Trading Free: The GATT and US Trade Policy* (New York: Twentieth Century Fund Press, 1993), 21–22.

[18] P. Krugman, 'Does the New Trade Theory Require a New Trade Policy?' *World Economy* 15 (4) (July 1992), 429–430. Krugman defines GATT-think as a form of 'enlightened mercantilism' in which exports are good and imports are bad. He asserts that the logic is wrong, but the results are 'mostly right'.

[19] S. Strange, 'Protectionism and World Politics', *International Organization* 39 (2) (Spring 1985), 259. Strange stresses the importance of the security and monetary/credit systems to the growth of trade, although she asserts that GATT and its rules had the effect of increasing confidence, which, combined with other factors, did contribute to the growth of trade.

[20] A. K. Rose, 'Do We Really Know that the WTO Increases Trade?' *American Economic Review* 94 (1) (March 2004), 98–114. His analysis provoked a reaction and a correction, although Rose was not persuaded that his analysis was wrong. See M. Tomz, J. L. Goldstein, and D. Rivers, 'Do We Really Know that the WTO Increases Trade? Comment', *American Economic Review* 97 (5) (December 2007), 2005–2018, and A. K. Rose, 'Do We Really Know that the WTO Increases Trade? A Reply', *American Economic Review* 97 (5) (December 2007), 2019–2025.

calculates that GATT had a 'large, positive, and significant impact' for only five of GATT's members, among the largest and most developed: Britain, the USA, Canada, France, and Germany.[21] Douglas Irwin demonstrates that the average tariff rate in the United States fell by roughly two-thirds between 1945 and 1967 and inflation was responsible for three-quarters of the drop; tariff negotiations were not primarily responsible for lowering tariff rates.[22] Many scholars do credit GATT and trade liberalization as causes for the expansion of trade. It makes sense that lowering tariffs, and later removing other kinds of barriers, would increase global trade. Certainly, the value of world trade grew almost every year between 1948 and 1994. But when one considers that many areas of trade lay outside GATT's purview, including arms and oil; that other areas such as agriculture and textiles – two of the largest sectors of global trade – were protected despite GATT's efforts to liberalize these areas; and that as tariff barriers were incrementally lowered, new forms of restriction were introduced; then the sceptics' interpretation has merit. If GATT *had*, however, been swallowed up by Lac Leman, it *would* have been noticed in the world of global governance.

This book is a work of international history that borrows from political science without being committed to a single theory. The goals of theorists – in service to paradigms that can predictably explain types of events – derive from generalizations with which historians often find fault.[23] The aims of political scientists and historians might be complementary, but their methodologies are distinct: classification as opposed to causation; patterns and predictability versus individual meaning. As Miriam Fendius Elman explains, a historical case study might substantiate a theory after the fact, but 'the forces allegedly driving the events that political scientists see as inevitable may not have been those that mattered to the decision-makers involved'.[24] Nonetheless, the work of political scientists in four areas – leadership and hegemony, the impact of trade interdependence on inter-state relations, the overlap between domestic and international spheres, and the function of international

---

[21] S. Y. Kim, *Power and the Governance of Global Trade: From the GATT to the WTO* (Ithaca, NY: Cornell University Press, 2010), 88.

[22] D. A. Irwin, *Clashing over Commerce: A History of US Trade Policy* (Chicago: University of Chicago Press, 2017), 484–486. He points out that the data isn't available for other countries and GATT never made such calculations.

[23] P. W. Schroeder, 'International History: Why Historians Do It Differently than Political Scientists' in D. Wetzel, R. Jervis, and J. S. Levy (eds.), *Systems, Stability and Statecraft: Essays on the International History of Modern Europe* (Basingstoke and New York: Palgrave Macmillan, 2004), 287–289.

[24] M. Fendius Elman, 'International Relations Theories and Methods' in P. Finney (ed.), *Palgrave Advances*, 145.

organizations – informs this study by identifying critical issues and unresolved debates.

Scholars from many disciplines have long treated US hegemony in the origins of GATT as revealed truth. The legal scholar Kenneth Dam explains the creation of GATT as a product of US planning and a reflection of American ideas.[25] Economist Karin Kock describes the early trade and employment proposals that preceded GATT as 'an American document not only in form but, to a great extent, in its aims and content'.[26] Many political scientists support this interpretation. For example, Kevin Buterbaugh and Richard Fulton maintain that US hegemony was essential to the international cooperation attained in GATT, the IMF, and the World Bank and that cooperation has been 'fundamentally the product of American diplomacy'.[27] Judith Goldstein puts it even more starkly: 'The GATT was the creation of the United States.'[28] The importance that scholars attach to the USA's power and direction in the postwar trade system has not diminished over time. William J. Bernstein, a financial expert, characterizes the early drafts of what would become the GATT/ITO as 'nothing more and nothing less than a road map for the new commercial Pax Americana'.[29] Soo Yeon Kim also identifies the USA as the 'principal architect' of GATT, exercising the 'greatest influence' on its norms and structure.[30] Douglas Irwin, Petros Mavroidis, and Alan Sykes identify Cordell Hull, the US secretary of state from 1933 to 1944, as 'the most important individual responsible for what ultimately became the GATT', although they also acknowledge the importance of Anglo-American cooperation to its establishment.[31] Others agree that joint Anglo-American support was behind the establishment of GATT. For example, Ernest Preeg identifies 'a willful and paternalistic United States with strong United Kingdom support' as the main forces behind GATT.[32] Even though there is some nuance to the hegemonic

---

[25] K. W. Dam, *The GATT: Law and International Economic Organization* (Chicago: University of Chicago Press, 1970), 10.

[26] Kock, *International Trade Policy*, 29.

[27] K. Buterbaugh and R. Fulton, *The WTO Primer: Tracing Trade's Visible Hand through Case Studies* (Basingstoke: Palgrave Macmillan, 2007), 6.

[28] J. Goldstein, 'The United States and World Trade: Hegemony by Proxy?' in T. C. Lawton, J. N. Rosenau, and A. C. Verdun (eds.), *Strange Power: Shaping the Parameters of International Relations and International Political Economy* (Aldershot and Burlington: Ashgate 2000), 255.

[29] W. J. Bernstein, *A Splendid Exchange: How Trade Shaped the World* (New York: Atlantic Monthly Press, 2008), 356–357.

[30] Kim, *Power and the Governance of Global Trade*, 10 and 26. See Kim's chapter 1 for her larger argument.

[31] Irwin, Mavroidis, and Sykes, *The Genesis of the GATT*, 12.

[32] Preeg, *Traders and Diplomats*, 13.

explanation, most studies continue to underline the importance of the USA's support and power to the creation and operations of GATT and indeed the entire postwar liberal order.[33] Daniel Sargent's comparison of the United States in the 1940s with Atlas, assuming godlike responsibilities to ensure the well-being of the world, is evidence of the resilience of this view.[34]

There is no question that without US involvement, GATT would not have got off the ground. But neither GATT's establishment nor its subsequent operations can be satisfactorily explained in terms of US hegemony. Not only did GATT not function as US officials had expected, but there were instances when the USA failed to impose its will on GATT members and when other states played various leadership roles. John Ruggie suggests that while hegemony might explain the structure of a regime, it reveals little about its nature and workings.[35] Volker Rittberger and Bernhard Zangl note that the hegemonic theory does not explain why GATT persisted even after the USA began to decline.[36] Keohane adds that according to hegemonic stability theory, the trade regime should have eroded as the USA's hegemonic position crumbled. He admits there was some erosion, but there were also 'intensive efforts at cooperation'.[37] David Deese usefully sets hegemonic theory aside in his study of leadership in GATT.[38] In my analysis, I ask how and when US leadership was exercised, and with what effect, rather than presuming that US hegemony explains how GATT arose and functioned.

[33] Ikenberry explains how US leadership and influence defined the postwar order in which institutions were one of the dominant features. These institutions 'lock[ed] in' an order that was in the interest of the USA but that also required the USA to agree to some constraints on its actions. Although the USA emerged from the war as the 'preeminent power', Ikenberry asserts that US hegemony was open, as well as reluctant, and this allowed European states to have influence and strengthened the legitimacy of the liberal order. See G. J. Ikenberry, *After Victory: Institutions, Strategic Restraint, and the Rebuilding of Order After Major Wars* (Princeton and Oxford: Princeton University Press, 2001), chapters 1 and 6.
[34] He writes: 'The United States bestrode the world in 1945, supreme in military capabilities, serene in geopolitical security, and unrivaled in economic productivity. Confident in their power, American leaders intended to remake the international order, expecting to assume "the responsibility which God Almighty intended," as President Truman put it, "for the welfare of the world"'. D. J. Sargent, *A Superpower Transformed: The Remaking of American Foreign Relations in the 1970s* (Oxford: Oxford University Press, 2015), 1, 19.
[35] J. G. Ruggie, 'International Regimes, Transactions, and Change: Embedded Liberalism in the Postwar Economic Order' in S. Krasner (ed.), *International Regimes*, 197–199.
[36] V. Rittberger, B. Zangl, and M. Staisch, *International Organization: Polity, Politics and Policies*, translated by A. Groom (Basingstoke: Palgrave Macmillan, 2006), 212.
[37] R. O. Keohane, *After Hegemony: Cooperation and Discord in the World Political Economy* (Princeton and Oxford: Princeton University Press, 1984), 213.
[38] D. Deese, *World Trade Politics: Power, Principles and Leadership* (London and New York: Routledge, 2008), 5.

A sceptical approach to the assumption of US hegemony allows other GATT members, including Australia, Brazil, Canada, Czechoslovakia, India, Mexico, Nigeria, and Uruguay, among many others, to come to the fore. They showed initiative and exerted leadership at various times and across many issues. As Roger de Souza Farias points out, developing countries were more than 'mere extras in the great drama of post-war diplomacy'.[39] This insight applies to all the 'non-great' powers. GATT's history should be told as that of an ensemble rather than a one-man show. Focusing on smaller states and their experiences in GATT reveals the multiplicity of voices and perspectives in a global dynamic and shows how GATT worked in ways that cannot be explained simply in terms of power balances. Patricia Clavin describes the League of Nations as a multiverse in which 'a plurality of views about global and regional coordination and cooperation were generated, and where they could be compared and could compete'.[40] The same possibilities of the multiverse were also evident in GATT. The multilateral approach, which still leaves ample room for the USA, the EEC, and other powerful members of GATT, explains why an organization that generated little enthusiasm among its members and the wider global public nonetheless had legitimacy. It was a legitimacy born out of economic and political disasters of the past, sustained by the organization's relentless quest to have a universal membership and relevance, and upheld by the support of its small-power members.

The connection between liberal trade and global peace was a mantra within GATT from beginning to end. In 1948, Wyndham White explained that without 'conditions of well-being and prosperity' there would be no hope of 'attaining the prize of enduring peace'.[41] Fifty years later, Renato Ruggiero, the director-general of the WTO, credited 'the multilateral system' for being 'a force not only for economic growth but also for more stable and cooperative international relations'.[42] President Bill Clinton of the United States likewise praised 'a far-sighted generation of leaders who acted on the bitter lessons of protectionism, devastating depression and war' and created GATT, as well as the IMF and the World Bank, because they believed that 'growing economic interdependence would lead to

[39] R. de Souza Farias, 'Brazil and the Origins of the Multilateral Trading System', *International History Review* 37 (2) (March 2015), 315.
[40] Clavin, *Securing the World Economy*, 7.
[41] E. Wyndham White, 'The International Trade Organization and the Future Pattern of World Trade', Speech to the Annual Convention of the National Association of Credit Men, Cleveland, Ohio, 18 May 1948, WTO.
[42] WT/Fifty/3/19 May 1998/Statement by the Director-General, H. E. Mr. Renato Ruggiero, WT/Fifty/1–3/H/ST/1–17/INF/1–14/ST1-2, WTO.

greater peace among nations'.[43] The link between trade liberalization – often misleadingly called free trade – and a stable, interdependent, multilateral global order was an article of faith, reinforced by
the fears of liberal trade advocates about the consequences that
would follow from protectionism: cut-throat competition, lawless-
ness, a return to depression conditions, and possibly war.[44] Their
understanding was that trade would promote international order and
cooperation just as eating well is associated with good physical
health. The connection between liberal trade and international stability was invoked as the main line of defence against those who
proposed alternatives to GATT and the principles of reciprocity,
non-discrimination, and the Most Favoured Nation (MFN) principle.

Many political scientists have examined the link between trade and
peace. Han Dorussen and Hugh Ward conclude that if two countries are
connected through trade then 'their relations should be more peaceful'.[45]
Not all agree with this finding. Strange doubts the link between trade and
peaceful relations: she calls this the 'quite unwarranted belief ... that
protectionism jeopardizes peace and that world order at the political
level may be directly threatened if the multilateral trade order is allowed
to crumble'.[46] Katherine Barbieri's research adds to the doubt that trade
leads to peaceful relations between states.[47] Along the same lines, Robert
Gilpin argues that it is not possible to generalize about 'the relationship of
economic interdependence and political behavior'.[48]

Rather than use the history of GATT to test how the volume and
nature of trade affects political relationships, I ask why this association
has been made so often. The association of trade with peace reveals a lot

---

[43] WT/Fifty/H/ST/8/18 May 1998: Statement by H. E. Mr. William J. Clinton, WTO.

[44] Krugman refers to it as a leap of faith, cited in G. Dunkley, *The Free Trade Adventure: The
WTO, the Uruguay Round and Globalism – A Critique* (London and New York: Zed Books,
2000), 145. Gilpin claims that beliefs in any economic ideology, whether liberal, nationalist, or Marxist, were all 'acts of faith'. *The Political Economy of International Relations*, 41.
Kirshner also describes the conviction that an open world economy would promote peace
and prosperity as a belief 'rooted in the founders' faith in classical liberal economics'.
Kirshner, 'Introduction', in Kirshner (ed.), *The Bretton Woods-GATT System*, x.

[45] H. Dorussen and H. Ward, 'Trade Networks and the Kantian Peace', *Journal of Peace
Research* 47 (1) (January 2010), 29.

[46] Strange, 'Protectionism and World Politics', 244–245.

[47] K. Barbieri, *The Liberal Illusion: Does Trade Promote Peace?* (Ann Arbor: University of
Michigan Press, 2002).

[48] He is only willing to go this far: 'What can be said with some justification is that trade is
not a guarantor of peace. On the other hand, the collapse of trade has frequently led to the
outbreak of international conflict ... '. Gilpin, *Political Economy of International Relations*,
58. Also see F. McKenzie, 'Introduction' in L. Coppolaro and F. McKenzie (eds.),
A Global History of Trade and Conflict since 1500 (Basingstoke: Palgrave Macmillan,
2013), 2–3.

about the strengths and weaknesses of GATT as an institution and of the strategies used to shore up its relevance when it came under attack or to galvanize the momentum behind trade liberalization when it slowed. It is also telling of the way some people made sense of trade, viewed their connection to the rest of the world, valued the consequences that flowed from global commercial exchange, and thought about the aims and priorities of national involvement in world affairs. What this association – between a liberal trade order and global peace – reveals and symbolizes is relevant to this study; measuring the impact of interdependence on the condition of international relations is not.

International trade is not simply international. Trade cuts across domestic and international spheres. Decisions in one realm have consequences in the other. Domestic considerations were often factored into trade policy at the national level and subsequently defined international negotiating strategies and aims. Decisions made in international negotiations – such as lowering tariffs – intensified competition, with the result that consumers had more choices and at cheaper prices, but people employed in affected sectors might also lose their jobs. Although the dynamics of trade policy flow in both directions, some scholars assert that trade is a product of domestic forces. According to Goldstein, 'Trade policy has always been, and will always be, a hostage to domestic politics.'[49] This claim is too categorical and yet it is widespread. Thomas Oatley faults studies that focus exclusively on domestic considerations and set international factors aside. He acknowledges that a reductionist methodology aims at more robust findings, but it skews results by explaining foreign economic policy solely in terms of domestic politics.[50] Older approaches that examine the interaction of domestic and international contexts and factors remain useful. Robert Putnam highlights the way domestic political structures and actors (such as political parties, interest groups, public opinion, legislators, and election cycles) shaped the goals of, and possibilities for, international trade negotiations and how tensions at one or the other level make international agreement more or less likely. Domestic and international goals and priorities can align or be at odds with one another. In many cases, there is a tension between the two levels and the challenge for governments and officials is to resolve the tension, securing domestic

---

[49] J. Goldstein, 'Trade Liberalization and Domestic Politics' in A. Narlikar, M. Daunton, and R. M. Stern (eds.), *The Oxford Handbook on the World Trade Organization* (New York: Oxford University Press, 2012), 80.

[50] T. Oatley, 'The Reductionist Gamble: Open Economy Politics in the Global Economy', *International Organization* 65 (2) (Spring 2011), 317–319.

well-being without compromising international cooperation.[51] Ruggie's theory of embedded liberalism helps to explain the link between domestic and international economic interests, in particular the need to protect jobs and provide social welfare at home to enable the promotion of trade liberalization internationally.[52]

The history of GATT provides considerable evidence about how the domestic and international realms overlap and interact. The dynamic was not always conflictual, and tension between advocates and opponents of trade liberalization and protection does not easily map onto a domestic–international schema. However, this volume does not include many detailed accounts of the ways in which trade policies were developed nationally. I am indebted to other scholars whose work focuses on domestic policy-making. I focus on how domestic decisions played out internationally, their consequences for relations between states, and the implications for global order. I build on studies that connect trade negotiations in GATT to international relations. Such studies typically focus on trade negotiations between the USA and the EEC. For example, some studies of the Kennedy round explain it in terms of an attempt by the USA to forge closer relations with western Europe or as the moment when the EEC was raised to eye level with the USA, becoming a leader in GATT.[53] This book considers the implications of trade negotiations for many GATT members, large and small, developed and developing, leaders and followers, allies and rivals, like-minded and ideologically distinct.

Finally, this study considers whether GATT was an independent actor or the instrument of state interests.[54] Many assume that the small size of the secretariat and the tenacity with which governments insisted on

[51] R. D. Putnam, 'Diplomacy and Domestic Politics: The Logic of Two-Level Games', *International Organization* 42 (3) (Summer 1988), 432–434, 459–460.

[52] Ruggie, 'International Regimes, Transactions, and Change', 208, 215.

[53] Preeg, *Traders and Diplomats*; P. Winand, *Eisenhower, Kennedy, and the United States of Europe* (Basingstoke: Macmillan, 1993); Coppolaro, *The Making of a World Trade Power*; S. Dryden, *Trade Warriors: USTR and the American Crusade for Free Trade* (New York: Oxford University Press, 1995); T. W. Zeiler, *American Trade and Power in the 1960s* (New York: Columbia University Press, 1992); N. P. Ludlow, 'The Emergence of a Commercial Heavy-Weight: The Kennedy Round Negotiations and the European Community of the 1960s', *Diplomacy & Statecraft* 18 (2) (July 2007), 351–368.

[54] Oestreich discusses competing views of international organizations, in particular the realist view that they are forums where national actors meet and act, the liberal view that they are producers of norms, and the constructivist view that they are principal agents, meaning independent actors who serve their own interests. See J. E. Oestreich, 'Introduction' in J. E. Oestreich (ed.), *International Organizations as Self-Directed Actors: A Framework for Analysis* (Abingdon: Routledge, 2012), 1–8. Rittberger and Zangl describe the realist, neo-institutionalist and social constructivist views of international organizations. See Rittberger et al., *International Organization*, 14–24. Barnett and Finnemore claim international organizations have independent authority, have their own agendas, and can disseminate norms. M. N. Barnett and M. Finnemore, 'The

national sovereignty meant that the secretariat had little ability to act independently or to take initiatives.[55] One might reasonably expect that the GATT secretariat was further limited by the meagerness of its resources. Despite its shortcomings, the secretariat, led originally by the committed, energetic, and effective Eric Wyndham White, devised bureaucratic means to keep its growing membership on the liberal trade path. This was not easily done. Domestic and international pressures and developments revived support for protectionist and discriminatory approaches to trade. Moreover, the secretariat's influence was often understated and its agency masked. The last thing an organization as vulnerable as GATT could tolerate was a backlash from members who feared that the organization was too powerful: that it encroached on their sovereignty and overrode domestic priorities. There were numerous attempts made to strengthen GATT and they invariably failed because some members, especially the USA, did not want it to become too autonomous. Against a backdrop in which members fiercely protected their individual interests, and therefore pushed against the collective approach of GATT, the secretariat had to downplay its influence, autonomy, and initiatives.

The organization that came to life on 1 January 1948 changed over fifty years. GATT evolved in response to the ebbs and flows of global international relations. These included Cold War rivalry, détente, decolonization, tensions between industrial countries and the global south, the formation of the European Economic Community, and the rise of new centres of power such as Brazil, India, and Japan. International developments were both challenge and opportunity. In many cases, concerns for institutional legitimacy and survival shaped the secretariat's position rather than strict adherence to its liberalizing mandate. The literature emphasizes the importance of compromise, flexibility, and pragmatism for GATT's successful operations, no doubt important, but this characterization glosses over the organization's ability to adapt while remaining steadfast in its commitment to trade liberalization.

GATT was a product of the entangled and competing forces of nationalism and internationalism, worldviews that existed in a fluid dynamic. In exchanges between national representatives at GATT, one can see a nationalist–internationalist tension.[56] Like the UN and the other

Politics, Power, and Pathologies of International Organizations', *International Organization* 53 (4) (Autumn 1999), 699, 706, 713.

[55] R. Blackhurst, 'The Role of the Director-General and the Secretariat' in Narlikar et al. (eds.), *The Oxford Handbook on the World Trade Organization*, 149.

[56] Amrith and Sluga situate this tension at 'the very heart of the UN's intellectual history'. S. Amrith and G. Sluga, 'New Histories of the United Nations', *Journal of World History* 19 (3) (September 2008), 273.

specialized agencies, GATT's mission rested on universalistic claims about a common good. Its core prescriptions – that trade should be open, multilateral, and non-discriminatory – were economic expressions of a liberal political ideal, a view that was widely accepted during and immediately after the war, but that was subsequently contested and criticized for being exclusive, favouring some members and disadvantaging others, extending the USA's influence, transgressing national sovereignty, and causing domestic economic suffering. The shift towards protectionist trade policies and the establishment of regional trade blocs, especially after 1970, were interpreted as threats to that universalist and internationalist ideology; they challenged GATT's legitimacy and relevance. A history of GATT allows us to gauge the strength of internationalist ideology and convictions and draws out competing views about whether the international community should be governed by power or rules.[57] It permits a study of competing norms and worldviews, as well as the limits and possibilities of international cooperation. The result is a detailed study of global governance on a day-to-day basis.[58]

Chapter Summaries

This study is organized around four themes that were central to postwar international relations and that were major challenges to GATT: the Cold War, regionalism, development, and agriculture. They can be thought of as fault lines that divided GATT members into various groups. The alignments that emerged revealed transnational communities of interest (for example, among efficient exporting farmers and among subsidized exporting farmers), competing economic ideologies (liberal trade and protectionism), alternative forms of economic association (regionalism versus globalism) and rival interests, dynamics, and communities that also defined the unfolding and contested global order.

Each thematic chapter covers the period of GATT's existence from 1948 to 1994, when the WTO was established and GATT was subsumed within it (although the discussion of regionalism is divided into two chapters). To avoid repetition and stay on track, the chapters discuss recurring issues and specific moments or events in relation to each chapter's theme. For example, the Kennedy round is discussed in Chapters 2,

---

[57] J. H. Jackson makes this point about the WTO, which he sees as an ideal case study for 'the concept of "rule orientation" compared to "power orientation"'. 'The Case of the World Trade Organization', *International Affairs* 84 (3) (May 2008), 439.

[58] Oestreich identifies the 'quotidian world of IOs' (international organizations) as needing further study and in turn being related to 'larger questions of international theory'. *International Organizations as Self-Directed Actors*, 5.

3, 5, and 6 in relation to the Cold War, European integration, development, and agriculture, respectively. The chapters do not all cover the
entire period with equal weight. During the Cold War, covered in
Chapter 2, ideological pressures were felt most strongly in the early
years of GATT, revived in the 1960s over the question of admitting
communist countries as members, and then faded until the question of
Chinese and Soviet membership was taken up in the 1980s.

For all four themes, the late 1960s was a time of transition in global
economics and politics and for GATT. From 1948 to the late 1960s,
national economies recovered from the devastation of the war, standards
of living rose, currencies stabilized, and the global economy expanded.
The rate of growth slowed in the late 1960s, followed by two decades of
economic volatility, high rates of inflation, and floating exchange rates.
The late 1960s also marked a time when Cold War issues began to
attenuate within GATT (as members had largely finished grappling
with the question of the admission of communist countries), the effects
of decolonization turned development into a higher priority, and the
consolidation of the EEC sparked a proliferation of regional trade
arrangements. There was a shift from the early postwar certainties to
a time of uncertainty, when it was not clear what form the global order
would take.[59]

The late 1960s also separates two stages in GATT's institutional
development: an initial era of consolidation and a later era of crisis. By
the end of the 1960s, GATT was well established as an international
organization. It had a permanent home in Villa le Bocage and a more
reliable revenue stream than in its early days, and its work was evolving
and expanding to remain relevant to changing international economic
conditions. The term of the first executive secretary of GATT, Eric
Wyndham White, who is credited (when he is acknowledged) with
GATT's success and survival, came to an end in 1968. Beginning in the
late 1960s, GATT was under more or less constant siege, linked to the
appeal of protectionism and regionalism. These trends had never been
entirely absent, but they were resurgent. GATT's efforts to liberalize
international trade faced stiffer opposition and more obstacles. The belief
in trade liberalization as the way to promote global prosperity and peace

---

[59] C. S. Maier, "'Malaise": The Crisis of Capitalism in the 1970s' in N. Ferguson, et al.
(eds.), *The Shock of the Global: The 1970s in Perspective* (Cambridge, MA: Belknap Press of
Harvard University Press, 2010), 26. As Iriye puts it, 'during the 1970s so many drastic
changes occurred that the decade may be said to have marked the beginning of a new
period of world affairs'. I. Iriye, *Global Community: The Role of International Organizations
in the Making of the Contemporary World* (Berkeley: University of California Press, 2002),
126. See also R. Gilpin, *Political Economy of International Relations*, 3.

was increasingly contested. Freer trade came to be associated with unemployment, corporate dominance, inequality, injustice, and environmental degradation. GATT also ceased to be an institution that flew below the radar of public opinion, becoming the object of organized protests in the 1980s and 1990s. Public and political debates about GATT and trade liberalization became sharper and GATT turned into a besieged international organization, a holdout of liberal ideas and ideals that received uneven support from members and was denounced by special interest groups. Although GATT officials tried to explain that trade liberalization was in the best interests of all, this argument had little traction.

This book begins with a background chapter that describes the international, economic, and political environment of the 1940s. It explains GATT's accidental origins and briefly describes international negotiations during and immediately after the war that ultimately ended in the demise of the ITO, leaving GATT as the centre of a liberal trade order. It examines the internationalist ideals associated with liberal trade and identifies the earliest GATT officials who embodied that internationalist spirit and ideology. It explains the relationship between supporters of freer trade and advocates of protectionism, with the latter group well represented but temporarily marginalized in the postwar international climate. It also outlines GATT's early institutional capabilities and authority.

Histories of the Cold War rarely mention GATT, and histories of GATT rarely refer to the Cold War. Chapter 2 explains the link between them. The Cold War could be considered a midwife to GATT because the bipolar conflict compelled founding members to overcome disagreements, which were especially sharp between the USA and the UK, and identify a common interest, without which there would not have been a final agreement. Because only one of the original members was from the eastern bloc – Czechoslovakia joined before the coup of June 1948 – GATT developed into a forum of the western alliance rather than an inclusive global organization.[60] Subsequent successful applicants had to be either western-oriented or useful to the ongoing economic rivalry with the Soviet bloc. In this way, GATT became a buttress to the western alliance, but in restricting membership it belied its commitment to universal representation. It was no surprise that the Soviet Union criticized GATT at the United Nations and called for the creation of a truly inclusive trade organization. GATT could not escape the polarization

---

[60] R. Toye, 'Developing Multilateralism: The Havana Charter and the Fight for the International Trade Organization, 1947–1948', *International History Review* 25 (2) (June 2003), 282–305.

and competition of the Cold War. As détente set in during the mid-1960s, the United States and other members used GATT to build bridges to communist countries with the twin aims of enhancing cooperation between East and West and weakening the communist bloc.[61] In the 1980s, the Soviet Union and the People's Republic of China (PRC) pursued the possibilities of membership; neither was concluded by the time the WTO came into being in 1995. With the end of the Cold War, GATT's mission was briefly marked by a triumphalist tone, especially pronounced when former Soviet bloc countries applied for membership. The rhetoric about GATT's mission echoed that of 1945, emphasizing peace and stability. However, the ideological triumph of liberal trade did not put GATT on a secure footing.

Arthur Dunkel, director-general from 1980 to 1993, observed that the main source of GATT's insecurity came from its own members and their pursuit of individual interests above all.[62] Chapters 3 and 4 explore the commitment of members to the organization by looking at their involvement in regional trade agreements. Chapter 3 focuses on the creation of the European Economic Community (EEC). The General Agreement permitted the establishment of regional trade blocs as long as they contributed to the growth of global trade and advanced the goal of trade liberalization. The Treaty of Rome contradicted several of GATT's core principles. Concerned GATT members as well as the secretariat protested that the EEC should accommodate GATT, instead of GATT accommodating the EEC. EEC members resisted. France emerged as a determined challenger to and central player in GATT, a posture encouraged by the foreign policy aims of President de Gaulle and a Gaullist bureaucracy. Although the six founding members of the EEC resented being subjected to interrogation by GATT, they were active and influential members of the organization and they became a new centre of power alongside the United States.[63] Their impact on GATT was mixed. They promoted and stifled liberalization; they encouraged and blocked GATT's evolution; they upheld and disregarded GATT norms and rules. In this they were both typical and singular, and the EEC case makes clear how serious the internal challenge was to GATT.

---

[61] L. H. Haus, *Globalizing the GATT: The Soviet Union's Successor States, Eastern Europe, and the International Trading System* (Washington, DC: Brookings Institution, 1992).

[62] Speech by Dunkel in Tokyo, 'Will the multilateral trading system cope with the challenges of a rapidly changing world?' 13 June 1990, GATT/1483, GDL.

[63] Coppolaro, *The Making of a World Trade Power*. Ludlow, 'The Emergence of a Commercial Heavy-Weight'. Deese suggests that the EEC only had power to block the USA. He also notes that the EEC's involvement in GATT in the 1960s and 1970s was crucial to its ability to act as a great power. See *World Trade Politics*, 58, 86.

Many regional agreements were concluded after the Treaty of Rome. Chapter 4 examines the proliferation of regional agreements and their implications for the commitment to and belief in a multilateral and liberal trade system. The EEC contributed to the proliferation through the expansion of EEC membership and by negotiating agreements with countries outside the EEC. But the EEC was not alone; eventually, almost every GATT member participated in some kind of regional trade agreement. While many scholars flag the US decision to conclude regional agreements in the 1980s as the start of a regional alternative to GATT, this chapter suggests a different periodization – the regional challenge was evident throughout the 1960s and 1970s – and a different explanation about how regional trade undermined GATT. While regional trade arrangements were permissible under GATT, there was debate about whether such agreements promoted or obstructed the growth of trade and whether they propelled or blocked liberalization. Although the debate continues to this day, the GATT secretariat saw regional agreements as a threat to their core principles and to the organization as a whole. Regionalism was associated with an international community in which rules were bypassed in favour of national interests, rights trumped obligations, and spheres of power undercut the commitment to inclusive well-being. GATT could not function in such a world. Concerns about relevance and legitimacy escalated to the point that some predicted the demise of GATT. Attempts to scrutinize or oversee such agreements revealed the limits of the organization's authority and its inability to enforce its rules. Nonetheless, members registered regional trade agreements with GATT and in doing so they acknowledged the legitimacy of GATT and of their obligations to it, accepted accountability, and upheld the necessity of a multilateral and liberal approach to trade.

As the pace of decolonization accelerated in the late 1950s, former colonies of contracting parties were automatically admitted to GATT. Their economic priorities related to development. As Chapter 5 explains, development had appeared on the earliest GATT agendas, mostly in relation to reconstruction after the war. At the 1947–1948 conference in Havana, representatives of developing countries contested the liberal axioms and priorities of the ITO. By the end of the conference, the revised charter of the ITO made development the top priority. The change was indicative of a different way of thinking about global trade and its uses, but the demise of the ITO downgraded the development function of global trade. It was not until newly independent countries became GATT members in the late 1950s and early 1960s that the role of trade as an engine of economic development was taken up again. But renewed interest in the developing world did not translate into meaningful action in GATT. The main obstacles to improving market access for the exports of developing countries lay in the domestic sphere of developed countries, linked to concerns about economic inefficiency and rising unemployment. Double standards were evident. Rules were applied inconsistently to developed and developing countries, and in industrial countries arguments about domestic well-being overrode commitments to the international goals of the organization. In frustration, developing members of GATT supported the establishment of the United Nations Conference on Trade and Development (UNCTAD), which both criticized and threatened to replace GATT. Although an awkward partnership eventually developed between GATT and UNCTAD, the movement for a New International Economic Order (NIEO) in the 1970s renewed demands for the global trade system to cease to be an instrument of injustice and exploitation. The challenge for GATT was to respond to the changed circumstances of the global order and refute a counternarrative in which liberal trade was an instrument of oppression. Attempts to redefine and broaden GATT's scope reveal the discrepancy of power between north and south, developed and developing, as well as the limited capacity of newly established and economically weak states to wield power. GATT's inability to serve the trade interests of developing members also undermined its credibility and exposed the ways in which the liberal promise was not fulfilled. Even though overcoming the north–south divide was a goal of GATT, it was not effective in promoting development through trade.

Chapter 6 is a study of the contest between those wanting to liberalize trade in agriculture and those wanting to protect it. Although agricultural products were originally included in GATT's mission, they were gradually exempted. The USA's actions were critical. In 1955, the USA requested a waiver that effectively removed agriculture from GATT's reach. The creation of the EEC's Common Agricultural Policy (CAP) a few years later expanded the practice of protectionism in agricultural commodities. Developing members of GATT insisted that freedom in trade should extend to agricultural goods, which constituted many of their exports. But this was not primarily a fight between industrialized and agricultural countries or between developed and developing countries; such neat divisions are rare. It was a dispute that pitted efficient and inefficient farmers against one another. It also became a dispute between the USA and the EEC. Liberalizing trade in agriculture became a test of the contracting parties' commitment to GATT and revealed how difficult it was to promote national and domestic interests without jeopardizing collective international well-being. The debate was also inextricably linked to national values and identities, showing how trade was invested with meaning that had no reference to economic logic. Agriculture was situated at a hotly contested point of intersection between social-domestic and international-political priorities and perspectives. The GATT secretariat appealed to consumers, its natural constituency, to oppose protectionism. But consumers did not rally to GATT's defence. The project of liberalizing trade in agriculture was almost certainly GATT's greatest challenge and without a doubt its greatest failure.

Over almost fifty years, GATT pushed trade liberalization forward, despite significant opposition and hesitation. It had to continually justify its existence against critics from all corners. It often conjured up scenarios of conflict and suffering – such as depression and war – to push back against critics and to invigorate supporters. It was both embattled and effective. Understanding how GATT navigated opposition and obstruction tells us about the scope, possibilities, and influence of international institutions in the postwar international order. Many people regard GATT as a highly successful organization. The concluding chapter of this book identifies key elements of its success, including its adaptability to a changing global environment; its reliance on strong members as well as small and mid-sized states, which seized their chances to lead and whose engagement shored up the legitimacy of the organization; a proactive – albeit discreet – secretariat; and an impressive but imperfect record in relation to the liberalization of global trade.

GATT was a do-gooding international organization. As Ben Shephard – the historian of the United Nations Relief and Rehabilitation Administration (UNRRA), another do-gooding international organization – points out, the subject matter is less sexy than tales of malice, devastation, conflict, and human suffering.[64] The work that people did in GATT involved talking rather than fighting; they traded concessions rather than blows (although arguments were constant); they made decisions through compromise rather than outright victory. Robert Samuelson observed in the *Washington Post* that it is easy to be bored by GATT.[65] In fact, its history was punctuated by achievement and defeat, activity and paralysis, enthusiasm and disdain, calm and crisis. Despite and because of its overall success in liberalizing world trade, GATT was constantly subjected to criticism and opposition. Throughout its history, proposals were advanced to reform GATT, supplement it, circumvent it, and replace it entirely. In 1990, the dean of the MIT Sloan School of Management,

---

[64] B. Shephard, *The Long Road Home: The Aftermath of the Second World War* (New York: Alfred A. Knopf, 2011), 8.
[65] R. Samuelson, 'Why GATT Isn't Boring', *Washington Post* (22 December 1993), A21.

Lester Thurow, went so far as to pronounce GATT dead.[66] International trade negotiations were characterized by crises and acrimony, as we see vividly today. Trade is a subject about which governments and people feel strongly because they experience directly the consequences of trade policies and patterns, whether in the kind of job they have (or lose), the range and price of consumer items they can choose from, or how they spend their leisure time (watching Hollywood blockbusters or nationally produced films). Given what people, governments, and countries stand to lose and gain from global trade, it could not be otherwise.

[66] L. C. Thurow, 'Gatt is Dead; the World Economy as We Know It is Coming to an End, Taking the General Agreement on Tariffs and Trade With It', *Journal of Accountancy* 170 (3) (September 1990), 36–39.

1 Accidental Organization
Origins and Early Years of GATT

Both the establishment and the mandate of the General Agreement on Tariffs and Trade were products of global conflict and cooperation. GATT's purpose was defined by a belief in trade's dual capacity to engender cooperation and to incite discord among peoples and nations. Its challenge was to prevent disagreement and clashes sparked by trade while also facilitating the growth of global trade to increase prosperity and, so the thinking went, promote peace and stability. Conflict and cooperation were also essential ingredients in the emergence of a consensus in support of a liberal trade order. It took the Second World War to consolidate the belief that liberal trade was essential to economic growth and international stability. This made it possible for governments to endorse a liberal trade order, even though trade was inherently competitive and trade policies were typically framed to promote national interests first and foremost.

This chapter explains the historical development of an internationalist philosophy of trade liberalization and shows how that understanding became widespread during the Second World War. It describes briefly the negotiations from 1941 to 1947 that culminated in the General Agreement and explains government and public reactions to GATT. Finally, it examines the early years of the organization, explaining its initial and limited capabilities and the conduct of its proactive secretariat. This chapter also begins to explore the many meanings of and ideas about trade. Many scholarly accounts of trade are technical. But questions of trade bear on issues about which passions are easily roused: national identity, status, and sovereignty, as well as job security and local traditions and practices. Attitudes about trade can be polarizing. Governments and individuals have believed that trade could make the world a better place and that trade could inflict damage akin to a natural disaster. Understanding these contrary views, which persisted throughout GATT's existence, is essential to understanding what GATT could and could not do.

The Internationalism of Liberal Trade

GATT rested on the belief in the interconnectedness of peace, prosperity, and trade. The first two components – peace and prosperity – had long been associated in art, literature, politics, and philosophy. Adam Smith justified free trade as the best way to increase individual and national well-being. In *Wealth of Nations*, Smith described an ideal market as one in which people pursued their self-interest with minimal government intervention. International trade was consistent with, and conducive to, liberalism because it reinforced key features of the free market: specialization, competition, and efficiency.[1] But Smith also drew a link between trade and the state of political relations. Smith observed that illiberal trade practices corroded relations between states. Resentment arose, and even worse, 'revenge' was taken against protected domestic producers. This had been evident in the dispute between France and the Netherlands, which led to war in 1672. According to Smith, a 'spirit of hostility has subsisted between the two nations ever since'.[2]

In the mid-nineteenth century, Richard Cobden drew out the implications of free trade for foreign policy and domestic reform in the campaign to repeal the Corn Laws in England. Cobden insisted that free trade was both means and end to make England more egalitarian and democratic; it went hand in hand with a host of social reforms including land ownership, widening the franchise, and the abolition of slavery. Codben's endorsement of free trade also had implications for British foreign policy. He argued that the guiding principle should be non-intervention; that would 'give a guarantee for peace'.[3] Cobden also believed that free trade agreements would improve relations between nations. He characterized the Cobden–Chevalier treaty with France in 1860 as a step in 'transforming fundamental political and economic relationships'.[4] Cobden was also involved in the burgeoning European peace movement of the nineteenth century. He understood peace and free trade to be mutually reinforcing, as in their shared support for disarmament. But Cobden stopped short of claiming that free trade created peace.[5]

---

[1] A. Smith, *Wealth of Nations: An Inquiry into the Nature and Causes of the Wealth of Nations* (Oxford: Oxford University Press, 1996). See also D. A. Irwin, *Against the Tide: An Intellectual History of Free Trade* (Princeton: Princeton University Press, 1996), 75–86, for a succinct explanation of Smith's ideas about trade.

[2] Smith, *Wealth of Nations*, 295–296.

[3] N. C. Edsall, *Richard Cobden, Independent Radical* (Cambridge, MA: Harvard University Press, 1986), 242.

[4] Ibid., 64, 341.

[5] M. Ceadal, 'Cobden and Peace' in A. Howe and S. Morgan (eds.), *Rethinking Nineteenth-Century Liberalism: Richard Cobden Bicentenary Essay* (Aldershot and Burlington: Ashgate, 2006), 192, 200, 203–206. Edsall points out that the closest Cobden came to linking trade

The Economist magazine, founded in 1843, also made the case for free trade as the way to eradicate strife within nations, especially class conflict, as well as strife between nations.[6] The association of free trade with harmonious relations between states was a recurring promise of economic internationalism. This equation lifted trade above the merely technical and, according to Mark Mazower, invested economic practices and commercial exchange with 'noble ideas'. The supporters of free trade looked at tariffs as 'a step toward isolation and belligerence', whereas an open economy was 'the prerequisite for both prosperity and global harmony'.[7] Free trade was imbued with a righteousness based on claims that it fostered conditions of equality, social justice, and domestic and international goodwill. Its advocates, then and throughout the twentieth century, would repeat these claims, which were also attached to GATT.

In the early twentieth century, Norman Angell refined the argument for free trade and the interdependence of nations. He repudiated the social Darwinist conception of international relations, in which strong nations sought to dominate weaker ones and all were engaged in a struggle for survival, as a 'desperately dangerous misconception'. Instead, he made a case that economic interdependence maximized conditions of prosperity. Shared economic interests upheld peace among nations.[8] But, as the First World War revealed, the fact that the nations of Europe were deeply entwined economically did not prevent them going to war.

Although Angell was awarded the Nobel peace prize in 1933, such realist thinkers as E. H. Carr repudiated the internationalist logic that Angell espoused. Carr traced the origins of Angell's ideas to Adam Smith. He conceded that Smith's ideas about free trade might once have been valid, but the conditions that allowed all to benefit from the ongoing expansion of trade had ended, replaced by conditions of scarcity. Carr dismissed Angell as an unrealistic utopian.[9]

---

and peace was when he noted that the workings of the modern economy prevented 'those traditional demonstrations of armed force, upon which peace or war formerly depended'. Edsall, *Richard Cobden*, 261–262.

[6] As James Wilson, the first editor of *The Economist*, put it: restrictions on trade engendered 'jealousies, animosities and heartburnings between individuals and classes in this country, and again between this country and all others'. See R. D. Edwards, *The Pursuit of Reason: The Economist 1843–1993* (London: Hamish Hamilton; New York: Penguin Books, 1993), 19.

[7] M. Mazower, *Governing the World: The History of an Idea* (New York: Penguin Press, 2012), 39.

[8] N. Angell, *The Great Illusion: A Study of the Relation of Military Power to National Advantage* (London: Heinemann, 1912), vii, ix, 30–31.

[9] J. Weiss, 'E. H. Carr, Norman Angell, and Reassessing the Realist-Utopian Debate', *International History Review* 35 (5) (August 2013), 1160–1161.

The trade policies that Angell had prescribed – and the interdependence that liberal trade policies created – were cast aside during the Great Depression as governments around the world introduced protectionist policies to shut out exports in the hope of stimulating domestic economic activity and reducing unemployment. Efforts to devise an international and coordinated solution to the Depression failed, most strikingly at the 1933 World Economic Conference.[10] Economic fragmentation, beggar-my-neighbour policies, and zero-sum attitudes had their parallel in international relations, characterized by naked lies, unfulfilled promises, crassly self-interested deals, and the betrayal of principles. Even though liberal trade had not engendered cooperative international relations before the First World War, the flip side was evident in the 1930s when economic ill-will spilled into the political realm. Protectionist and autarkic measures contributed to the deterioration of international relations. J. B. Bridgen of Australia, like many policy-makers around the world, believed that the Depression had given rise to Hitler and many other social disorders.[11] This kind of thinking validated the liberal approach to trade and elicited support for trade liberalization. As Jagdish Bhagwati put it, the Depression 'helped to stack the cards in favour of pro-trade forces, providing the ideological momentum for liberal trade'.[12]

In the United States, support for trade liberalization centred on the State Department and its secretary from 1933 to 1944, Cordell Hull. Hull was deeply committed to the cause of *freer* trade. He recorded in his memoirs that as early as 1916 he had realized the connection between trade and international conditions: 'unhampered trade dovetailed with peace; high tariffs, trade barriers, and unfair economic competition, with war'.[13] He championed liberal trade from the start of his political career in the House of Representatives (1907–1921). As secretary of state, he put his beliefs into practice with the passage of the Reciprocal Trade Agreements Act (RTAA) in 1934. Under the RTAA, the executive had authority to negotiate bilateral trade agreements without requiring

---

[10] P. Clavin, *The Great Depression in Europe, 1929–1939* (Basingstoke: Macmillan Press, 2000), chapter 6.

[11] Memo by J. B. Bridgen from Australian Embassy, Washington, re Australian International Economic Policy, March 1947, A1068/ER47/70/1, AA. Skidelsky also observes that people associated Hitler's rise with the Depression. It was 'an extreme reaction to the extreme effect of the great depression on Germany', reinforcing the conviction that there would be no peace without economic reform. R. Skidelsky, *John Maynard Keynes, Vol. III: Fighting for Britain 1937–1946* (Basingstoke: Macmillan, 2000) 179.

[12] J. Bhagwati, *Protectionism* (London and Cambridge, MA: MIT Press, 1988), 22.

[13] C. Hull, *The Memoirs of Cordell Hull, Vol. 1* (New York: Macmillan Co., 1948), 81.

Congressional ratification as long as no tariff was reduced by more than 50 per cent. The goal was to conclude as many bilateral trade agreements as possible in the hope that this would create conditions of economic interdependence and reverse the deterioration of international relations. By the time the war began in 1939, nineteen such agreements had been negotiated. Despite the start of the war, Hull was convinced that the RTAA had been the right idea; it simply had not had enough time to stabilize international relations.

There were other proponents of liberal trade and the logic of economic internationalism in the 1930s. The experts of the Economic and Financial Section of the League of Nations remained steadfast in their belief that liberal policies and an open global economy were the best way to combat depressions. They were to some extent fatalistic about the recurrence of depressions, but deeply optimistic about the ability to offset the effects of economic downturn through the international coordination of policies. Many officials who assumed prominent roles in shaping national postwar economic policies during and after the war, such as James Meade in Britain, Leo Pasvolsky in the United States, and Louis Rasminsky in Canada, had previously worked for the Economic and Financial Section of the League of Nations.[14] In fact, it was Meade who drafted the first version of what would eventually become GATT. The Depression was a formative experience for the architects of the early GATT, and the shadow of another depression hovered throughout its existence. Officials justified their work in terms of preventing another depression which in turn conjured up the nightmare of global war.

The International Chamber of Commerce (ICC) was another bastion of economic liberalism in the interwar years. This transnational group of businesspeople promoted world trade as the means to realize peace and prosperity, which they asserted were 'one and indivisible'.[15] The ICC's members regarded the removal of barriers to trade as a form of economic disarmament.[16] In 1937, members gathered for their annual meeting in Berlin. Hitler himself welcomed the delegates and congratulated them on their effort to promote peace through trade. Afterwards they listened to Hermann Goering

---

[14] P. Clavin, *Securing the World Economy: The Reinvention of the League of Nations 1920–1946* (Oxford: Oxford University Press, 2013), 218, 230. See Clavin generally for the link between League economic experts and their impact on national trade policies.

[15] G. L. Ridgeway, *Merchants of Peace: Twenty Years of Business Diplomacy Through the International Chamber of Commerce 1919–1938* (New York: Columbia University Press, 1938), 7.

[16] 'Its creed, like Cobden's, coupled international trade with international peace.' Ridgeway, *Merchants of Peace*, 3, 6.

extol the virtues of Nazi economic policies whose core principles were autarchy, nationalism, rearmament, and expansion.[17] Undaunted by the strength of the nationalist, expansionist, racist, and militaristic economic doctrine then flourishing in Germany, ICC members clung to their faith. As Thomas Watson, chair of IBM and president of the ICC, declared: 'world trade is the surest road to world peace.'[18] Eric Wyndham White, who would become GATT's first executive secretary (this was the title used in GATT until 1965, when it was replaced with director-general), attended the ICC meeting in Berlin. Despite pockets of liberals who believed that economic internationalism remained a valid policy option in the 1930s, protectionism held much appeal and was widely practised.

It took the Second World War to entrench the belief that open markets were essential for peace and beneficial for all.[19] Liberal trade came to be accepted as the best practice, if not the only defensible policy. The circumstances of the war were needed to overcome anxiety about the future and curb an instinct to protect national interests and sovereignty above all. Unless trade among nations was fundamentally cooperative, even if still competitive, the postwar peace would be undermined. As Harry Hawkins, one of the leading economic planners in the US State Department, put it in 1944: 'Nations which are economic enemies are not likely to remain political friends for long.'[20] While prosperity might not be a sufficient condition for peace, it was widely believed to be a necessary condition. As Hull explained, 'a revival of world trade [was] an essential element in the maintenance of world peace. ... I do not mean ... that flourishing international commerce is of itself a guaranty of peaceful international relations. But I do mean that without prosperous trade among nations any foundation for enduring peace becomes precarious

---

[17] Ridgeway, *Merchants of Peace*, 384–385. Tooze explains how Nazi ideology and aims affected trade policy. For example, autarchy involved disengagement from Britain and the United States, replaced by suppliers in Latin America and southeastern Europe. The struggle for scarce resources shaped Hitler's ideas about economic policies and practices. Some Nazi officials believed that free trade was 'a Jewish doctrine' that upheld Britain's position of global dominance. Rather than seeing free trade as a policy for the future, the Nazis dismissed it as 'the outdated relic of a bygone era'. A. Tooze, *The Wages of Destruction: The Making and Breaking of the Nazi Economy* (New York: Viking, 2007), 8, 33, 89, 174–175.

[18] *Newsweek* (22 November 1937), 5.

[19] According to Barbieri and Schneider, by 1945 the belief that trade was conducive to peace had become 'so deeply entrenched in mainstream economics that only heretics from the radical fringes of the discipline dared to question it'. K. Barbieri and G. Schneider, 'Globalization and Peace: Assessing New Directions in the Study of Trade and Conflict', *Journal of Peace Research* 36 (4) (July 1999), 389.

[20] Quoted in J. H. Jackson, *World Trade and the Law of GATT: A Legal Analysis of the General Agreement on Tariffs and Trade* (Indianapolis: Bobbs Merrill, 1969), 38.

and is ultimately destroyed.'[21] Simon Reisman joined Canada's Department of Finance after the war and he attended the first GATT meeting in 1947 (and went on to a long and distinguished career as one of Canada's pre-eminent trade negotiators); he also reflected the confident assumption that a liberal trade system was essential to postwar security: 'an open, liberal, competitive, multilateral trading system would contribute to the growth and prosperity of nations as well as to their peace and security'.[22] In the minds of the planners of the postwar trade system, a liberal trade order would contribute to global peace in two ways. First, trade would alleviate poverty and deprivation, conditions that many believed had directly contributed to the start of the war. Second, GATT would help to prevent as well as resolve conflicts that arose over trade. While the architects of postwar economic institutions held up open markets as their ideal, in fact they envisioned a planned liberalism in which market forces were both sustained and offset by government intervention and priorities. This would be a liberal trade regime minus the laissez-faire.[23]

Making trade work for peace and prosperity, and containing its ability to ignite conflict, was one of the many challenges that international organizations confronted in order to encourage international cooperation and support global stability. These organizations – including the IMF, the World Health Organization (WHO), and the Food and Agriculture Organization (FAO) – were international meeting spaces where national delegates discussed policies and practices that promoted an internationalist agenda based on universalistic assumptions. Within these organizations, members had to agree to adhere to rules and norms that entailed some concession of national sovereignty. The belief that institutions could only work if nation-states ceded a piece of sovereignty – which internationalist thinkers thought of as a pooling of sovereignty in service to a common cause – reflected a far-reaching belief that nation-states were a root cause of international conflict. These international institutions modified the structure and operation of international affairs to try to contain the narrow nationalistic outlooks that many believed caused

---

[21] Quoted in D. A. Irwin, P. C. Mavroidis, and A. O. Sykes, *The Genesis of the GATT* (Cambridge: Cambridge University Press, 2008), 11.

[22] S. Reisman, 'The Birth of a World Trading System: ITO and GATT' in O. Kirshner (ed.), *The Bretton Woods–GATT System: Retrospect and Prospect After Fifty Years* (Armonk, NY: M. E. Sharpe, 1996), 82.

[23] Ikenberry makes a similar point about the essential compromise that defined Bretton Woods, such that it appealed to people with diametrically opposed approaches, from laissez-faire to planners. 'A World Economy Restored: Expert Consensus and the Anglo-American Postwar Settlement', *International Organization* 46 (1) (Winter 1992), 307–308, 315–316, 318.

wars. This idea was more openly discussed outside of government, among private citizens, internationally engaged elites, and non-governmental organizations, proposing alternative routes to peace and understanding through such mechanisms as world federation, a universal language, and the denationalization of education.[24] In practice, however, there was an uneasy balance between national and collective interests and priorities because nation-states remained primary and essential actors in world affairs and there was little support within governments to reduce their importance. As one British official wrote in 1942, one of the main aims of British foreign policy was to ensure that 'the sovereign national state is the unit of international society', and that Britain would be paramount within that society.[25]

Internationalist ideas about the future – big picture, long term, common purpose – prevailed when the disastrous consequences of not embracing such ideas were plain to see. Richard Law, the minister of state at the British Foreign Office, led a delegation to Washington in 1943 to discuss the postwar trade system. He understood the importance of timing for an agreement on trade: 'People were capable, at this moment, of sacrificing immediate advantage for the long-term gain, but when the moment of danger was removed they would be in a different mood.'[26] John Winant, US ambassador to Britain, agreed that the window of opportunity opened by the war would not stay open long. 'The fact that the world economy is in a state of flux gives us the opportunity to create a new and better pattern. But it is an opportunity which we will have only for a relatively brief time.'[27]

Wartime and Postwar Planning for a Liberal Trade Order

Early direction about the postwar order came from US president Franklin D. Roosevelt.[28] He wanted senior members of the grand alliance – the United States, Britain, and the Soviet Union, along with China (by which

---

[24] Many people expressed mistrust of nations as the main actors and authorities in the postwar world. One example is E. Reves, *The Anatomy of Peace* (New York and London: Harper & Brothers Publishers, 1945), 125. For a fascinating discussion of debates about postwar order in which the role of the nation was prominent, see O. Rosenboim, *The Emergence of Globalism: Visions of World Order in Britain and the United States, 1939–1950* (Princeton: Princeton University Press, 2017).

[25] Letter to Cadogan, 31 May 1942, FO371/31538, TNA.

[26] Informal Economic Discussions, Plenary, 1st meeting, 20 September 1943, CAB78/14, TNA.

[27] Memorandum on Article VII, Prepared by Winant with the assistance of Hawkins and Penrose, Morgenthau Diary, Book 827, n.d., p 169-E, FDRL.

[28] E. Borgwardt, *A New Deal For the World: America's Vision of Human Rights* (Cambridge: Belknap Press of Harvard University Press, 2005). See also W. F. Kimball, *The Juggler:*

he meant Nationalist China under the leadership of Chiang Kai-shek) – to maintain a collective leadership after the war, although each would be dominant in its own region. These were his so-called four policemen. Roosevelt also articulated four overarching conditions, framed as freedoms, for the postwar world: freedom from fear and want, freedom of religion and association. Freedom from want conveyed Roosevelt's basic economic goal. As he explained, it 'means economic understandings which will secure to every nation a healthy peacetime life for its inhabitants – everywhere in the world'.[29]

The construction of a liberal trade order was one way to attain freedom from want. US officials solicited British support for a postwar liberal commercial order. When Roosevelt and Winston Churchill, prime minister of Britain, met in August 1941 off the coast of Newfoundland, they agreed about the importance of trade to the overall health of international relations, but disagreed sharply about specific commercial practices and policies. The imperial preference tariff system of the British Empire and Commonwealth was a main point of contention. At the Ottawa Imperial Economic Conference of 1932, British and dominion officials had exchanged preferential access to their markets for select items. At the height of the Depression, when there was little evidence of international cooperation, the imperial preference system was taken as proof of Commonwealth solidarity.[30] As a pillar of the British Empire and Commonwealth, imperial preference was anathema to the USA's anti-imperial sensibilities and commitment to democratic political values.[31] But to British officials it symbolized a bond within the Commonwealth which had a psychological and strategic value that they were loath to give up. British predictions about their own dire postwar commercial and

Franklin Roosevelt as Wartime Statesman (Princeton: Princeton University Press, 1991), chapters v, vi, viii.

[29] Roosevelt's 'Four Freedoms' Speech, https://fdrlibrary.org/four-freedoms, accessed 5 May 2018.

[30] In fact, the negotiations in Ottawa had been acrimonious, concessions were made grudgingly, and the results of the negotiations did little to encourage intra-Commonwealth trade. Nonetheless, the extension of tariff preferences selectively among members of the Commonwealth was doubly offensive to American officials: it was discriminatory and it reinforced imperial associations. F. McKenzie, 'Imperial Solutions to International Crises: Alliances, Trade, and the Ottawa Imperial Economic Conference of 1932' in J. Fisher, E. Pedaliu, and R. Smith (eds.), *The Foreign Office, Commerce and British Foreign Policy in the Twentieth Century* (London: Palgrave Macmillan, 2017), 175–180.

[31] F. McKenzie, *Redefining the Bonds of Commonwealth 1939–1948: The Politics of Preference* (Basingstoke: Palgrave Macmillan, 2002), chapter 2. Zeiler refers to the imperial preference system as 'an emblem of empire unity, independence, and strength'. See T. W. Zeiler, *Free Trade, Free World: The Advent of GATT* (Chapel Hill: University of North Carolina Press, 1999), 22.

financial circumstances also prevented them from endorsing liberal international trade without reservations. The British government foresaw a potential need to make use of quantitative restrictions, exchange controls, bulk purchasing, and imperial preferences to stave off national bankruptcy once the war was over: they had to keep these options open. Nonetheless, Sumner Welles, under-secretary of state for the US State Department (soon to be forced out of public life because of sexual indiscretions), drafted a trade clause (of what would become the Atlantic Charter) that would abolish preferential tariffs after the war. The British resisted what seemed to them to be 'the Boston Tea Party in reverse'.[32] In the end, Roosevelt broke the impasse by permitting a loophole for 'existing obligations'.[33] This was an early indication that political intervention at the highest level was necessary to resolve disputes over trade. In the end, the Atlantic Charter declared British and US support for liberal postwar trade practices, with important exceptions.

Preferential tariffs continued to be an irritant in Anglo-American discussions about postwar trade. Their negotiations over Mutual Aid, the formal agreement that laid out the terms and conditions of wartime aid from the USA, included debate on Article VII, which called for a freer and expanding postwar economy and stipulated that 'all forms of discriminatory treatment in international commerce' would be proscribed and eliminated. Although Churchill believed in the benefits of free trade,[34] he saw Article VII as a veiled attack on preferential tariffs and by extension on the Commonwealth and Empire, which were more than proving their worth during the war. Roosevelt intervened again by promising that preferential tariffs could be exempt but added that discussions would be comprehensive and nothing was excluded. His deft, if ambiguous, direction overcame the impasse, but did not remove confusion about the future of preferences. But some things were clear. Britain and the United States were jointly engaged in reshaping the international economy 'when power, but not reputation, had shifted across the Atlantic'.[35] As a result, rivalry and competition underlay their work, in particular

[32] Author interview with Meade, 1993; Lord Croft made the same comment, quoted in R. Gardner, 'The Bretton Woods–GATT System After Fifty Years: A Balance Sheet of Success and Failure' in Kirshner (ed.) *The Bretton Woods–GATT System*, 183.
[33] R. Gardner, *Sterling–Dollar Diplomacy in Current Perspective: The Origins and Prospects of Our International Economic Order* (New York: Columbia University Press, 1980), 40–49.
[34] Toye discerns Churchill's views on free trade through a close study of his political rhetoric in 'Trade and Conflict in the Rhetoric of Winston Churchill' in L. Coppolaro and F. McKenzie (eds.), *A Global History of Trade and Conflict* (Basingstoke: Palgrave Macmillan, 2013), 124–141.
[35] Skidelsky, *Keynes Vol. Three*, 110.

about their respective positions in the postwar world. Nonetheless, they shared broadly similar positions on the need for a liberal trade system.[36]

In fact, British officials were the first to sketch out the postwar trade system. The principal drafters of Britain's postwar trade policy were James Meade, a young economist who had returned from the Economic Section of the League of Nations in 1940 and a future Nobel Laureate in economics, along with Lionel Robbins, an economics professor from the London School of Economics who directed the economic section of the cabinet war offices. They favoured an open and integrated international trade system. Meade drafted his plan for an International Commercial Union (ICU), with only a few caveats in the event of economic downturns or crises. For instance, a state would be able to introduce quantitative restrictions to correct balance-of-payments problems. Meade also envisioned the retrenchment, but not the complete elimination, of imperial preferences. Many of the characteristics of the ICU had earlier been bandied about by the Economic and Financial Organization of the League of Nations, with which Meade had been involved.[37] But it was not only Meade's internationalism that shaped his ideas about postwar trade. As a major trading nation, he believed, Britain had no option: 'If ever there was a community which had an interest in the general removal of restrictions to trade, it is the United Kingdom.'[38] His support for liberal trade was further sustained by his belief that economic factors affected global politics. As he explained in *The Economic Basis of a Durable Peace,* published in 1940,[39] the causal link between economic and political dimensions of international relations was indirect. Economic interactions and policies shaped attitudes and beliefs, sometimes out of proportion to economic costs and benefits. For example, the removal of a tariff might have almost no effect on the standard of living but could still provoke 'widespread national resentment', or conditions of economic uncertainty could spark 'sullen resentment that finds expression – for purely national reasons – against the national enemies'.[40]

[36] F. McKenzie, 'Where was Trade at Bretton Woods?' in G. Scott Smith and S. Rofe (eds.), *Global Perspectives on the Bretton Woods Conference and the Post-War World Order* (Basingstoke: Palgrave Macmillan, 2017), 163–180.

[37] Clavin, *Securing the World Economy,* 281–282.

[38] J. Meade, 'A Proposal for an International Commercial Union' in S. Howson (ed.) *The Collected Papers of James Meade, Vol. III* (London and Boston: Unwin Hyman, 1988), 27–32. This and earlier drafts of the proposal are in T230/125, TNA. S. Howson, *Lionel Robbins* (Cambridge: Cambridge University Press, 2011), chapters 12, 13, 15.

[39] Irwin et al., *The Genesis of the GATT,* 25.

[40] J. E. Meade, *The Economic Basis of a Durable Peace* (London: George Allen & Unwin Ltd, 1940), 14–15.

But not everyone thought as Meade did. John Maynard Keynes, the towering British economist who defined Britain's postwar financial policies, objected to the liberal logic underpinning Meade's proposals. Hubert Henderson and Richard Clarke of Britain's treasury also preferred bilateral trade arrangements on the basis that they would make the most of Britain's leverage as an importing nation. They favoured sterling bloc trade which would preserve convertible dollars, then and later in short supply.[41] Their foremost concern was to address Britain's chronic balance-of-payments problems. People who believed in preserving imperial trade and protecting British agriculture also looked askance at the ICU. Meade was appalled that Britain's financial difficulties would force Britain to behave 'more nationalistically . . . than even Germany had behaved under Schacht and Hitler' in the trade sphere.[42] Despite the backlash, as the British wartime government moved towards a decision on trade policy, the ideas of Meade and Robbins set the course for British postwar trade policy. The ICU was largely compatible with the principal characteristics that informed the RTAA: reciprocity, unobstructed trade, non-discrimination, and internationalism.

The extent of British and US agreement on the future of trade became evident at a secret meeting in Washington in the autumn of 1943.[43] Before the meeting, British officials had decided that if there was sufficient agreement, they would circulate an aide-mémoire that summarized the British position on postwar trade. US and British officials disagreed over particular issues, such as whether subsidies should be used for agricultural exports, how tariff negotiations would be organized, and, once again, whether to abolish or preserve imperial preferences. There were also different ways to understand the workings of international trade. The British stressed high rates of employment as a precondition to the growth of world trade, whereas US officials believed that higher employment would follow from the removal of barriers to trade. But these points of disagreement did not undermine fundamental agreement about the desirability of a liberal trade order. As a result, at the second meeting, British officials disclosed their aide-mémoire.[44] The meetings went on

---

[41] L. S. Pressnell, *External Economic Policy Since the War Vol. I: The Post-War Financial Settlement* (London: Her Majesty's Stationery Office, 1986), 53.

[42] Author interview with Meade, 1993. Keynes believed that there was much to praise in Schachtian economics. See Skidelsky for a discussion of the evolution of Keynes's wartime thoughts on commerce and finance. Skidelsky, *Keynes Vol. Three*, 194–199.

[43] This meeting has been discussed by several scholars. See McKenzie, *Redefining the Bonds of Commonwealth*, 102–106; Pressnell, *External Economic Policy*, chapter 5; Irwin et al., *The Genesis of the GATT*, 37–41; Zeiler, *Free Trade, Free World*, 33–37.

[44] Pressnell, *External Economic Policy*, 118.

until October, beginning the complicated task of mapping out postwar trade.

Progress subsequently stalled because of a backlash in the British cabinet. Ministers including Beaverbrook and Amery, who were close to Prime Minister Churchill, objected on the grounds that imperial preferences, and all that they meant for the solidarity of the British Empire and the Commonwealth, were being sacrificed. Agricultural interests in Britain were also perturbed by the proposals to liberalize international trade. The proposed policy changes were politically explosive and elicited loud opposition and more muted support.

US persistence prevented the derailment of Anglo-American cooperation on postwar trade. But by the time their talks resumed in December 1944, the effects of war that had facilitated agreement were beginning to lessen. Thoughts of dire postwar conditions, with possible loss of markets, sterling indebtedness, depleted gold and dollar reserves, and war debts accrued under Mutual Aid, weakened British support for a liberal trade order. A grim postwar economic scenario was made even more worrying because the British public confidently expected the onset of a New Jerusalem after the war. Basic conditions of life including health care, educational reforms, and affordable housing should benefit all after the war: if not, what were they fighting for?[45]

Changes in personnel did not bode well for future trade negotiations. Roosevelt's death in April 1945 brought Harry Truman to the White House: a no-nonsense politician who had been shut out of most foreign policy matters by his predecessor. Winston Churchill was voted out of office in July 1945, replaced by the able, if understated, Clement Attlee at the head of a Labour government. While one might have expected a Labour regime to be more willing to cede imperial preferences, Stafford Cripps and Ernest Bevin, the two cabinet ministers most involved in international trade negotiations, dug in their heels when confronted with US pressure to cut back the system. Cordell Hull resigned at the end of 1944 because of ill health, but the State Department's commitment to liberalization did not lessen. Will Clayton, a wealthy US businessman who had entered government service in 1940, was appointed assistant secretary of state for economic affairs in the autumn of 1944. As he explained in testimony before the Senate Foreign Relations Committee, he had long been 'an ardent, outspoken and consistent advocate of Cordell Hull's philosophy regarding international economic

---

[45] For a discussion of postwar conditions and expectations in Britain see K. O. Morgan, *Labour in Power 1945–1951* (New York: Oxford University Press, 1984), 285–329 or P. Hennessy, *Never Again: Britain 1945–51* (London: Jonathan Cape, 1992).

matters'.[46] He spearheaded US efforts to liberalize world trade after the war, but he made the task more difficult by fixating on the abolition of imperial preferences without fully appreciating the interests and realities confronting postwar Britain.

At the same time, domestic political complications prevented the USA from pushing liberalization too far. In July 1945, when the RTAA legislation had been up for renewal, Congress was uneasy about delegating powers to the executive. According to Susan Aaronson, more people spoke against its renewal than in favour of it,[47] suggesting limited support for the internationalist logic that informed the RTAA. President Truman responded by promising that all future trade negotiations would be conducted on an item-by-item basis and in a bilateral setting. Canadian officials complained that a bilateral and piecemeal approach was 'hopelessly inadequate'.[48] Many US officials agreed that this approach was a setback. In wartime, the architects of a new postwar trade order had thought boldly, but in peacetime they were more restrained. The only consolation the USA could offer was that bilateral, item-by-item negotiations would take place among a small group of participants (referred to as the nuclear group, which had nothing to do with nuclear weapons) in as many combinations as possible. The subsequent application of the MFN principle would then generalize the benefits. US officials believed that the awkwardly named 'selective nuclear-multilateral approach' came closest to the spirit and scope of multilateral negotiations.[49] But there was no disguising that this was a retreat from earlier discussions about reducing tariff barriers.

Despite setbacks and complications, there was progress. The US government published a draft charter for a postwar trade organization, called *Proposal for the Expansion of World Trade and Employment*. Even though this document was a result of Anglo-American discussions, British officials wanted it to be seen as a US initiative. This would be more likely to secure US support and preserve harmonious Commonwealth relations, which depended on Britain not making claims on behalf of the dominion governments. The president of the Board of Trade advised that British

---

[46] 'Statement of W.L. Clayton Before the Committee on Foreign Relations of the United States Senate – Dec 12, 1944', Clayton Papers, Box 2: folder: Statements, Senate Foreign Relations Committee, 1944, December 12, Hoover Institution.

[47] S. A. Aaronson, *Trade and the American Dream: A Social History of Postwar Trade Policy* (Lexington: University of Kentucky Press, 1996), 45.

[48] Memo by John Leddy of the Informal Talks between Canadian and American Officials on Commercial Policy and Financial Policy, 9 July 1945, *Foreign Relations of the United States*, Vol. 6, 1945, 63–64.

[49] 'Views of the Executive Committee Regarding Draft Tariff Proposals for Proposed Multilateral Agreement on Commercial Policy', 21 July 1945, WHCF/CF/Box 37, TL.

officials could reassure their US colleagues that the government intended 'to express fully their support of the American initiative and to make clear their welcome for the proposals as a basis for international discussion' in parliament.[50] But the British parliamentary debate on the *Proposal* was heated. There were accusations of betrayal and weakness, a view that was reinforced by the simultaneous presentation of the Bretton Woods agreements and the terms of a US$3.75 billion loan from the USA. It looked as though a weakened British government was being forced to give up imperial preferences in exchange for financial aid. Nonetheless, the new Labour government remained committed to the substance of the trade and employment proposals as the way forward.

The USA sent invitations to fifteen countries to participate in trade negotiations in the spring of 1946, but then slowed the pace of discussions about the ITO. US officials did not want Congress to ratify the terms of the loan and the results of tariff negotiations at the same time. The US presidential election in the autumn further delayed tariff negotiations. Because officials feared that enthusiasm for the ITO would wane, they focused their efforts on revising a draft charter.[51] US diplomats made 'missionary visits' to Canada, Cuba, Chile, Czechoslovakia, Belgium, Norway, France, the Netherlands, Australia, New Zealand, South Africa, and India to shore up support for the draft trade charter. The US State Department subsequently published a revised version of the trade charter – *Suggested Charter for World Trade* – in September 1946. Because it was produced by the United States, it provoked criticism. But there was also broad and deep support for the rationale behind the reform of world trade and the *Suggested Charter* became the basis for the next stage of international discussions.[52]

The USA next proposed a conference on trade and employment to map out the principles of a trade charter and organization. The two strands of what would become GATT – bilateral tariff negotiations combined with trade principles and rules – were now in play.[53] Trygve Lie, secretary general of the United Nations, appointed Eric Wyndham White, a thirty-three-year-old British lawyer and international civil servant, to chair the trade and employment meetings.

In October 1946, representatives from all the nuclear group countries except the Soviet Union gathered in London to discuss the future of trade on the basis of the US draft. Delegates divided into groups to consider commercial policy, restrictive practices, commodity policy, and the

---

[50] C.P. (45) 297, 'Commercial Policy', Memo by President Board of Trade, 24 November 1945 CAB 129/4, TNA.
[51] Tel 40 Askew, 26 February 1946, BT11/2828, TNA.
[52] Irwin et al., *The Genesis of the GATT*, 104–110.   [53] Ibid., 92, 107.

organization of the International Trade Organization. The meeting confirmed that there was far-reaching support for a rules-based approach to postwar trade, as well as considerable agreement on basic features such as non-discrimination, but there were concerns about the emphasis on lowering tariffs. H. C. Coombs, head of the Australian delegation, challenged the logic that eliminating impediments and prohibiting restrictive practices would lead to an expansion of world trade from which all would benefit. In Australia, officials believed that the way to increase trade was to raise standards of living and employment rates, thereby increasing demand and purchasing power. Indeed, in their minds, global economic growth was as important to preserving peace as was the prevention of nuclear war. While admitting that the 'behaviour was less dramatic than that of the Atom Bomb', the return of another global economic collapse like the Depression would be 'scarcely less dangerous to civilization than uncontrolled radio-activity'.[54] New Zealand officials also doubted that trade liberalization alone would lead to economic stability.[55] They linked full employment to economic development; they wanted a diversified economy with people employed across industrial and agricultural sectors. As their representatives explained, New Zealand 'would rather be a poorer country with a diversity of employment opportunities than be richer and have employment concentrated in the production of a few agricultural items'.[56]

British officials also wanted a return to full employment, which could only be achieved by a revival of global trade because so many British jobs were linked to exports. While they agreed that lowering tariffs would stimulate job creation in export industries, it would also open the market to imports, which could increase unemployment in affected sectors. A policy that placed all of its full employment eggs in a tariff liberalization basket 'would be little short of calamitous'. But British doubts that lower tariffs would spark job creation did not dent their support for trade liberalization, which they believed would cause widespread economic activity and growth. They also endorsed the aim of full employment in trade talks, which put them in line with key Commonwealth partners such as Australia and New Zealand and which encouraged dominion governments to endorse the commercial proposals.[57] As they later explained, the

---

[54] Memo by J. B. Bridgen from Australian Embassy, Washington, Australian International Economic Policy, March 1947, A1068/ER47/70/1, AA.

[55] Digests of 1946 Working Party Papers, n.d., NASH6/Bundle 113/0149, NZNA.

[56] Summary of Foreign Reactions to the Suggested Charter for an International Trade Organization, 2 October 1946, Edminster Papers, TL.

[57] C. P. (46) 364, 'International Employment Policy', Note prepared by Treasury, Board of Trade and Economic Section, 30 September 1946, CAB 129/13, TNA.

British position on this issue was between those who focused on the decrease of tariffs as the means to full employment and those who emphasized full employment as the engine of trade expansion.[58] But British officials did not press strongly for a full employment provision in the ITO, believing that it was a matter best addressed in multiple forums.[59]

Indian officials discussed the development of its industrial base as a postwar priority. That did not mean that India rejected the liberal objectives of the ITO. The government endorsed the end of preferential tariffs and strongly supported the principle of non-discrimination. But officials questioned whether lower tariffs would promote widespread prosperity. Before their departure to the conference, India's delegates were reminded that 'Free competition is not an unmixed blessing, if it is competition between countries of unequal strength, nor are tariffs an unmixed evil, if they serve as an instrument for raising the standard of living in poor and undeveloped countries.'[60] Hence R. K. Nehru made a case for the right to use protective devices to stimulate the growth of an industrial sector, noting that these were the means that had 'brought wealth and industrial strength to other countries'.[61]

The draft charter was duly amended to ensure that the ITO would be broadly relevant to the various economic priorities and conditions of participating countries. The participants decided that quantitative restrictions could be used to promote economic development and correct balance-of-payments problems. They included a provision to stabilize the price of primary commodities, without which other participants might lose interest in the ITO and opt to pursue their objectives in organizations such as the FAO. On some issues the original wording was adjusted, but not always meaningfully. For example, an employment provision was added, but according to US officials the principles laid down were 'completely innocuous and quite acceptable from our point of view'.[62] Other proposed changes caused real vexation. For example, calls for industrial development policies that would permit some form of protection provoked US frustration with 'crazy people, with India the wildest of the lot,

[58] Outline of Opening Statement, early 1947, BT11/3258, TNA.
[59] Draft brief on International Employment Policy, prepared by Board of Trade, Treasury and Economic Section, September 1946, FO371/52986, TNA.
[60] Brief for the Delegates to the First Meeting of the Preparatory Committee on International Trade and Employment to Commence in London on 15 October 1946, 53 (4) – TB/52: Brief to the Government's Representative to 6th GATT session, NAI.
[61] McKenzie, *Redefining the Bonds of Commonwealth*, 172.
[62] Wilcox to Clayton, 9 November 1946, RG43: Records of International Conferences, Commissions and Expositions, Box 118: preparatory Committee – October 15 Meeting, NARA.

Brazil and Chile utterly irresponsible, China and Lebanon tagging along'. Even though US officials did not welcome all changes, they recognized their political necessity: 'If we will not do this, I am afraid that our whole program is lost.'[63] US officials were reassured that the revised document was more broadly relevant while still leaving most of the charter intact. Of the eighty-nine articles in the current version of the draft trade charter, seventy-four were unchanged and 'the essential principles of the American position' had been preserved.[64] According to Wilcox, a flexible style of leadership had paid off: 'We have displayed no disposition to force our views on others and have shown ourselves willing to join in reasonable compromise.'[65] Yet there was a strong sense of US ownership and leadership of the ITO. Wilcox had put it starkly at the start of the meeting.

The United States has set the program. It has written the document. It has planned the organization. It has outlined the procedure. The rest of the world is now moving in step with us, in confidence that we are acting in good faith and that we shall do those things that we have urged them to do, and that we ourselves have promised to do. This places a heavy responsibility upon us.[66]

A sense of ownership was important to the US commitment to the ITO, but the process of consultation and negotiation was increasingly and meaningfully multilateral. The inclusion of more participants and revisions to the draft elicited far-reaching buy-in for the ITO. For example, in India, officials decided that they would seek a seat on the permanent board, if one was set up. Even if India did not yet count among the economically strong nations of the world, its potential, the size of its population, early demonstrations of its willingness and ability to act as a global leader, and the importance of Asian representation on international organizations made this a plausible bid: 'No international organization can function properly which fails to accord a rightful position to Asian countries.'[67] They clearly intended to be active participants in the ITO.

The momentum behind a liberal trade order seemed to be strengthening in the spring of 1947. Thousands of officials from 23 countries arrived

---

[63] Ibid.
[64] Memo by the Deputy Director of the Office of International Trade Policy (Nitze) to the Under Secretary of State for Economic Affairs (Clayton), 5 December 1946, see annex 2, 'Results of the London Conference', *FRUS 1946, Vol. 1*, 1359.
[65] Wilcox to Clayton, 16 November 1946, RG43: Box 111, NARA.
[66] Wilcox to Clayton, 26 October 1946, RG43: Box 111, NARA.
[67] Brief for the Delegates to the First Meeting of the Preparatory Committee on International Trade and Employment to Commence in London on 15 October 1946, 53 (4) – TB/52: Brief to the Govt's Representative to 6th GATT Session, NAI.

in Geneva to conduct bilateral tariff negotiations: this would be the first practical step towards trade liberalization. The most important negotiations were those conducted by the United States with Britain, Canada, and Australia. They were test cases of the degree to which liberalization could be achieved. But Anglo-American and Australian–American negotiations went badly from the start and threatened to derail the ITO.

Australian officials hoped for a 50 per cent reduction in US tariffs on wool. Instead, the USA offered to bind the current rate. That was disappointing. Even worse, Australian officials confronted the possibility that the USA would increase tariffs on imported wool. This was the result of legislation making its way through Congress – the Robertson bill – which authorized the government to charge a 50 per cent *ad valorem* duty on imported wool if imports threatened the well-being of US wool producers. The Australian delegation threatened to walk out of Geneva and asked other members of the Commonwealth to put their negotiations with the USA on hold until the wool question was resolved. President Truman ended up vetoing the wool bill to ensure that negotiations could move forward and prevent the collapse of the conference. He went further and authorized the delegation to make an offer to reduce the domestic tariff on wool by 25 per cent. Although this was far less than the 50 per cent reduction they had hoped for, Australia's delegates took it.[68]

Bigger obstacles loomed as Britain and the USA clashed over imperial preferences. Clayton was aghast that Britain, as well as Canada, Australia, New Zealand, and South Africa, had made so few concessions to reduce or remove preferential tariffs. He believed that the British had already promised to end imperial preference and been compensated for this on several occasions. Clayton left Geneva and advised President Truman and Secretary of State Marshall to abandon the negotiations.[69]

Given the esteem in which Clayton was held, it did not seem possible to endorse the Geneva negotiations without his support. But world politics changed the stakes associated with the Geneva conference. As the United States and the Soviet Union squared off in an increasingly antagonistic conflict, the Anglo-American relationship assumed new importance. With Clayton away from Geneva, more far-seeing US officials worked towards an agreement. To conclude the negotiations meant giving larger tariff cuts than they had hoped to make and receiving less in return. As Thomas Zeiler explains, these compromises were accepted because

---

[68] McKenzie, *Redefining the Bonds of Commonwealth*, 187–199.
[69] UK High Commissioner in Canada to CRO, tel. 934, 4 October 1947, DO114/110, TNA.

economic gain was not the bottom line; GATT was 'designed to ensure US values and security, not just profits'.[70]

In all, there were 123 bilateral negotiations in Geneva and 45,000 tariffs were reduced. Wyndham White fairly described the process as 'a vast negotiation of exceptional complexity'.[71] Rather than delay the introduction of new commercial practices by waiting for the finalization of the trade charter – which was the main agenda item for the Havana conference, scheduled to begin immediately after the Geneva conference had ended – the chapter of the draft agreement dealing with commercial practices was bundled with the results of the tariff negotiations and presented to participating governments for ratification under the name General Agreement on Tariffs and Trade. The agreement and the schedules of concessions were printed in four volumes, available for purchase for US$5.[72] No one expected GATT to be long-lived. It was an interim agreement, soon to be replaced by the ITO as the final piece in a new postwar economic order alongside the IMF and the World Bank.

At the end of the Geneva meeting, Dana Wilgress, a senior Canadian trade official who had been the chair of the contracting parties, expressed the internationalist thinking that underpinned GATT. He explained that members had chosen the path of multilateralism, collective welfare, laws and rules, and ultimately order and peace. The alternative was unthinkable, 'chaos and the law of the economic jungle. Nations will continue to drift in the direction of economic blocs and bilateral barter trade. Inevitably this would mean lowered standards of living and continuous economic warfare.'[73] Others also saw GATT in this way, believing in an internationalist ethos which upheld the importance of a rules-based international order that promoted cooperation and stability and countered aggression and conflict.

Reaction: Better to Have GATT than Not

Officials participating in the Geneva Conference understood that the success or failure of their efforts had implications for global peace and prosperity. The stakes were high. Given this belief, one might have expected that the results of their efforts would be widely celebrated and well known. That was not the case. There had been sporadic media

---

[70] Zeiler, *Free Trade, Free World*, 2, 195.

[71] Wyndham White, 'The International Trade Organisation: Blueprint for a World Trading System', speech at the Centre d'Études Industrielles, Geneva, 16 February 1950, WTO.

[72] 'Texts Placed on Sale', *New York Times*, 18 November 1947, 16.

[73] Speech of Canadian Delegate, Dana L. Wilgress, for Delivery before Plenary Meeting, Friday, 28 November 1947, RG20: Vol. 358/24581-C (part 1), LAC.

coverage of the Geneva conference in leading publications such as the *New York Times* and *The Economist*. But news of the meeting rarely appeared on front pages because negotiations were conducted in secret and dragged on for six months. When the terms of the General Agreement were released in mid-November 1947, there was extensive coverage for a few days before attention turned to the final drafting meeting of the ITO in Havana from late November 1947 until March 1948. The start of the Cold War, along with the many challenges of recovery from the Second World War, also deflected attention elsewhere. US officials were not surprised that trade had become a low priority. US analysts realized that growing public concern about the Soviet Union and the incipient Cold War diminished interest in trade liberalization: 'Compared with food shortages, relations with Russia, inflation and the atomic bomb, interest in foreign trade ranks last by a considerable margin.'[74] Despite lack of sustained attention and discussion, government debates, newspaper commentary, and government tracking and analysis of public reaction make it possible to gauge early attitudes towards global trade, trade liberalization and GATT. While the agreement needed the support of many participants to come into effect, US ratification was crucial. Therefore, this discussion begins with the reaction in the United States.

The General Agreement had important backers in the United States, including President Truman, who described it as a 'landmark in the history of international economic relations'.[75] Because of its provisional nature and because tariff negotiations were conducted under the auspices of the RTAA (meaning no tariff reductions were larger than 50 per cent), the Truman administration did not require Congressional approval of GATT. Officials thought this was a lucky thing, believing that otherwise the agreement 'would have been torpedoed'.[76] Indeed, many elected officials criticized the tariff changes that had been negotiated in Geneva. Senator Millikin described the reductions as drastic and suggested that 'In anything resembling normal times, some of the cuts would be catastrophic'. Other critics suggested that US officials had been out-negotiated and that the agreements reached in Geneva were bad deals for the USA. Representative Harold Knutson, also chair of the Ways and Means Committee, decried 'do-gooders who have traded us off for very dubious and nebulous trade concessions that can never be realized'.[77] The reaction might seem exaggerated or extreme. But for people who stood to lose, the worst consequences – losing a job or closing a business – were

---

[74] Current Popular Opinion on Foreign Trade Issues, 21 October 1946, RG59/Box 2/ Foreign Trade Issues, Opinions on, Papers of Clayton-Thorp, TL.
[75] Zeiler, *Free Trade, Free World*, 121.   [76] Ibid., 122.
[77] 'Threaten to Curb Reciprocal Pacts', 20 November 1947, *New York Times*, 3.

nothing less than catastrophic. Not all objected to the agreements or agreed with this dire outlook. Some commentators noted that the tariff reductions would have no immediate effect. The *Los Angeles Times* said the tariff reductions would have 'little more immediate effect on international trade than the issuance of a series of memorial postage stamps'.[78] Some thought it would take a few years for tariff cuts to be felt. Others suggested that even when they did begin to have an impact, there would be few adverse effects in the USA because it was not a trade-dependent country. Because trade liberalization causes disruptive change, from which some will benefit while others suffer, both sides of the debate were right to some extent. What is more important is that trade and trade liberalization elicited strong and divided responses.

Emotional and ideological currents also shaped the reaction and made clear that people had preconceived ideas about trade and tariffs, ideas to which they clung regardless of the presence or absence of objective evidence. As a result, people's reasoning about trade was not always logical or consistent. For example, a 1946 US study found that 66 per cent of respondents agreed that 'high tariffs decrease trade' and 75 per cent understood that the USA must import in order to export. But from these two premises, it did not follow in respondents' thinking that tariffs should be lowered: 35 per cent said tariffs should be lowered and 35 per cent that lowering tariffs would be bad.[79]

Reactions to trade liberalization were largely determined by whether individuals or groups believed they would benefit or suffer from the results. Producers wanting to increase export opportunities mostly welcomed the tariff cuts negotiated at Geneva; producers supplying the domestic market mostly disliked competition. For example, in the northeastern USA, wool importers welcomed the agreement whereas, wool and cotton textile producers objected to the terms of the negotiations.[80] Other industries critical of the agreement included alloy steel, cement, fancy leather, and firearms. Opinion varied within industries and across the whole economy.

There were pockets of enthusiastic support for GATT and for a liberal trade order steeped in internationalist thinking about world affairs. Some of the people who supported GATT likened it to the Marshall Plan, 'the most promising step yet taken to end the kind of tariff frictions and

[78] 'The New Tariff Agreement', *Los Angeles Times* (23 November 1947), A4.
[79] Current Popular Opinion on Foreign Trade, 21 October 1946, RG59/Box 2/Foreign Trade Issues, Opinions on, Papers of Clayton-Thorp, TL.
[80] Letter C. 124/973 from the Chancery in Washington to North American Department at the Foreign Office, 12 December 1947, FO371/62328, TNA.

cut-throat competition that can help to breed war'.[81] But the connection between trade and war was not universally accepted. In 1946, 57 per cent of Americans saw 'no connection between high tariffs and wars'. Nonetheless, there was considerable support for an international organization 'to help nations cooperate in expanding their trade': 83 per cent of those included in the poll believed such an organization was either 'very important' (60 per cent) or 'fairly important' (23 per cent), although many were nonetheless 'generally puzzled' and 'wondered what it could do'.[82] The government made some effort to promote awareness of GATT and to elicit support for the thinking behind it. Even so, a Gallup poll in the USA at the end of 1947 found that only 35 per cent of Americans had heard of GATT or the Geneva conference.[83]

Scholars disagree on the scope of support for trade liberalization in the United States. Aaronson describes extensive opposition to the renewal of the RTAA in 1945.[84] She concludes elsewhere that protectionism was 'the American way for much of U.S. history'.[85] But Destler suggests that liberalism became part of the postwar consensus among elites, policy-makers, and internationalists in the USA, a consensus that he claims lasted until the 1960s.[86] The response to GATT suggests divided reaction. Based on economic calculations alone, one's position could be to either support or oppose GATT and trade liberalization. After the war, the geopolitical argument tipped the balance in favour of GATT. The liberal trading order was important because of the worldview that informed it and the kind of world it was supposed to create. In the minds of GATT's strongest advocates, that should be a world of stability, cooperation, and plenty. The alternative was unthinkable: a world marked by insecurity, chauvinism, unilateralism, hardship, and zero-sum attitudes. This internationalist outlook was strong enough in 1947 that the US government ratified the General Agreement, but its endorsement was far from whole-hearted.

[81] US Public Reaction to the General Agreement on Tariffs and Trade, 5 December 1947, RG43: Records of International Conferences, Commissions and Expositions, Second Preparatory Committee Meeting, 1946–1947, Box 136, file: Trade (Geneva) – Domestic Reaction to GATT, NARA.

[82] Current Popular Opinion on Foreign Trade, 21 October 1946, RG59: Box 2/Foreign Trade Issues, Opinions on, Papers of Clayton-Thorp, TL.

[83] Gallup Poll, 11/28–12/3, 1947, in G. H. Gallup (ed.) The Gallup Poll: Public Opinion 1935–1972, Vol. One, 1935–1948 (New York: Random House, 1972), 695.

[84] Aaronson, Trade and the American Dream, 45–47.

[85] S. A. Aaronson, Taking Trade to the Streets: The Lost History of Public Efforts to Shape Globalization (Ann Arbor: University of Michigan Press, 2001), 57.

[86] I. M. Destler, American Trade Politics, 4th edition (Washington, DC: Institute for International Economics, 2005), 6.

In Britain, the reaction to GATT was bound up in attitudes about empire, status, and economic insecurity. One focus of opposition was the effect of the Geneva negotiations on the imperial preference tariff system. British negotiators had made grudging concessions affecting preferential tariffs, and in the end only a small percentage had been touched. Subsequently, British officials accurately explained that the preferential system was largely intact. Nonetheless, there were angry denunciations in the House of Commons as members of parliament believed that Britain was confronting a historic fork in the road: either to integrate within a global trade system or to stick with an imperial trade order. There were also concerns raised about Britain's uncertain economic future, unknown global economic conditions, and the ability of governments to use trade policy to protect or promote economic developments, for example by raising tariffs or by pursuing closer trade ties with western European countries. Others believed that the future of imperial and Commonwealth trade was limited and argued that it was delusional to assume that older patterns of exchange would persist, especially as the dominions were undergoing rapid industrialization. Still others tried to disentangle attachment to the empire and Commonwealth from trade and tariffs.[87] Harold Wilson, the president of the board of trade, insisted that the bonds that united the Commonwealth were more substantial than tariffs. His rejoinder was compelling, but it overlooked the fact that the dominions valued their Commonwealth association because of tangible benefits, even if they talked about them in loaded emotional terms.[88]

Britain's exporters were divided about the importance of preferential tariffs and imperial and Commonwealth markets. Prior to the Geneva conference, groups that were particularly interested in Commonwealth markets or that benefited from the protective effect of preferential tariffs lobbied the government to retain them. But a study by the National Union of Manufacturers reported that barriers to British exports took many forms, the most common complaint being the inability to obtain an import licence. These problems were experienced across the Commonwealth and the report noted that tariffs were a greater barrier in the dominions than outside the empire.[89] Commonwealth markets were not accessible to many British exports.

As one would expect, *The Economist* followed developments in Geneva. Although it had been a champion of free trade for Britain and the world

---

[87] Hansard, 466 H.C., Deb 5s, 29 January 1948. See, in particular, speeches by Lyttleton, Mackay, Boothby, Thorneycroft, and Reid.
[88] McKenzie, *Redefining the Bonds of Commonwealth*, 240–250.
[89] National Union of Manufacturers – Questionnaire on Export Trade, December 1947, T230/134, TNA. There were 1,146 replies received to the questionnaire.

for over a century, its reports acknowledged widespread apprehension about freer trade and the possibility that trade could be destabilizing. Nonetheless, it endorsed the creation of a multilateral trade system as the best option for Britain, even though that option was not without problems.[90] As the Geneva meeting advanced, *The Economist* offered periodic commentary on the proceedings, making insightful observations about the irrelevance of economic orthodoxy to the negotiations. Trade liberalization would be supported if it was relevant and realistic, or if it aligned with 'the earthly facts of real life'. It also observed that the ITO did not explain how trade would benefit people in inspirational terms; there was a public relations problem from the outset.[91] In the end, the magazine was underwhelmed by what had been achieved, likening the General Agreement to a 'mousy agreement', welcome but not impressive, and certainly not the 'black rat' that some detractors claimed.[92]

The British attachment to the imperial preference system and the imperial trade network that it facilitated was informed by questions of identity, status, influence, and well-being. These associations were also implicated in political debates in other parts of the Commonwealth. In Australia, primary producers, including fruit growers, dairy farmers, and sugar producers, had lobbied the government to preserve imperial preferences.[93] When H. C. Coombs, who led the Australian delegation to Geneva, suggested that there was a limited future for imperial preferences, some called for him to be replaced as leader of the delegation.[94] Despite vocal support for Australia's connection to Britain, the Labor government of Australia was less tied to the imperial connection than the Liberal party. John Dedman, the minister for reconstruction who had flown to Geneva to take charge when Australian–American negotiations had been at a perilous point, was more blunt about rejecting pro-Empire trade arguments when he told his colleagues that they would be foolish 'to allow old habits of thought to hide all signposts to the future'.[95] Government analyses reinforced the view that Australian economic security lay in global prosperity and access to world markets. Moreover, Australian officials believed they had done well in the negotiations,

[90] 'Prelude to Geneva', *The Economist* (29 March 1947), 444.
[91] 'Paris and Geneva', *The Economist* (27 September 1947), 505–506.
[92] 'Tariffs and Trade', *The Economist* (22 November 1947), 828.
[93] The following message from the Representatives of the Fruitgrower and Trade Union organizations was among the shortest, but it captured the gist of other messages: 'This meeting asks the Federal Government to fight to the last ditch to retain Empire Preference.' Letter from D. Kellett to Chifley, 20 June 1947, A461/G323/1/6 Part 1, AA.
[94] For example, letter from E. M. Hanlon, premier of Queensland, to Chifley, 20 February 1947, A461/G323/1/6 Part 1, AA.
[95] *Hansard*, 11 November 1947, 1887.

gaining more than they had given up.[96] Despite the fact that the US offer on wool had been less than hoped for, Australian officials praised the USA for making a 'serious endeavour' at Geneva to open its market to imports and insisted that the negotiations overall would provide access to new markets.[97] Finally, many Australian exporters looked favourably on a global trading system because they were confident about their competitiveness.[98]

In New Zealand there were anxious protests about the damage done to imperial preference. There was an emotional tone to these concerns, stemming from New Zealand's heavy dependence on the British market for its main agricultural exports – butter, meat, and wool – which made up over three-quarters of its total exports after the war. In 1939, 65 per cent of New Zealand's exports had gone to the UK, compared with less than 4 per cent to the USA. Although there was an increase in trade with the USA after the war – exports rose to 6 per cent in 1947 – New Zealand's dependence on the British market also increased to 76.6 per cent. The Labour party in New Zealand also advocated for controls, such as import restrictions, to offset price fluctuations and to limit competition. Walter Nash, the minister of finance, doubted that free trade would deliver on its promises of universal benefits. As he explained to his colleagues in parliament, 'the old free-play-market philosophy cannot bring peace and prosperity',[99] at least not to a country like New Zealand. These concerns were raised even more sharply in relation to the IMF, which New Zealand opted not to join. Despite reservations, New Zealand voted narrowly (40–34) to ratify the General Agreement.[100]

Because Canadian exporters were not nearly as dependent as New Zealand on the British market, there was a more positive reception of the General Agreement in Canada. By the start of the war, US and British markets were roughly of equal importance for Canadian exports; the USA had long eclipsed Britain as a source of imports. Despite long-established trade with the USA, there were still supporters of the British trade connection. For example, the Canadian Manufacturers' Association was confident about imperial preferences and uncertain that the USA, 'which has grown up and prospered under a highly protective tariff psychology', would embrace open markets and

---

[96] *Hansard*, 26 February 1948, 255–256.

[97] General Agreement on Tariffs and Trade, for Cabinet, Agendum No. 1019F, A2700/ XM volume 22, AA; *Hansard*, 26 February 1948, 255–256.

[98] 'Geneva Pact to Prod Australian Trade? Expansion of Markets', *Christian Science Monitor* (20 November 1947), 6.

[99] *Hansard*, 27 June 1947, 50.

[100] This detail included in Letter 254 from Alfred Rive, 8 July 1948, RG19: 3707/ITO Vol. 2, 1948, LAC.

competition.[101] Despite such reservations, Prime Minister Mackenzie King of Canada took to the airwaves to praise the agreements as 'the widest measure of agreement for the freeing of world trade that the nations had ever achieved'. He said its goals were consistent with Canada's 'long-run course' and that together members would support 'peace by prosperity and economic co-operation'.[102] Canada's *Financial Post* was also enthusiastic, insisting that GATT had brought 'epochal changes' to international trade.[103] Behind the public rhetoric, officials including Mackenzie King worried about Canada's close trade relations with the USA. The government had entered into secret continental free trade negotiations with the USA in 1947. Although the negotiations had gone well, Mackenzie King withdrew his support, fearing that a Canadian–American trade agreement would result in US dominance and undermine ties with Britain.[104] The multilateral form of GATT facilitated multiple trade relations and kept more options open; this made it attractive to the Canadian government.

Even for those countries intent on building up their own industries, and who had reason to fear that competition would undermine those plans, the benefits of freer international trade were compelling. In India, the shortcomings of the General Agreement were well known, especially with regard to quantitative restrictions, a particularly useful device that could be used to support infant industries. But India stood to benefit from the overall expansion of trade as well as from a rules-based order. Hence, the Indian government concluded that 'the balance of advantage lies in accepting the Charter rather than in rejecting it'.[105]

The General Agreement also elicited considerable apprehension. These fears took two main forms: first, that smaller or more vulnerable countries would suffer from international competition, and second, that GATT would be an instrument of US economic domination. For example, in Pakistan, an official in the Commerce Department described

---

[101] Letter from J. T. Stirett, General Manager of the Canadian Manufactures Association, to Mackenzie King, 27 November 1947, MG21 J1: Vol. 432/1104/394175–82, LAC.

[102] Text of an address made by the Rt Hon W. L. Mackenzie King, Prime Minister of Canada, over the CBC network, 17 November 1947, A571/1944/1109 pt. 14, AA.

[103] 'Expect Other Pacts Will Follow Geneva', *Financial Post* (22 November 1947), 1.

[104] For an account of these negotiations, see M. Hart, 'Almost but Not Quite: The 1947–1948 Bilateral Canada–U.S. Negotiations', *American Review of Canadian Studies* 19 (1) (Spring 1989), 25–58.

[105] Brief for the Indian delegation to the United Nations Conference on Trade and Employment, 6/11/1947, 53 (4) – TB/52: Brief to the Government's Representative to 6th GATT session, NAI.

GATT as a US creation[106] that, it was presumed, would serve the USA's interests first and foremost. In France, members of the communist party attacked the General Agreement, along with the Marshall Plan, as 'instruments of capitalistic "imperialism"'. They implied that as a result of the agreements, France would be flooded with US imports and would become subordinate to the United States.[107] The underlying threat was not just to French industries and agriculture, but also to French culture and identity. The response to tariff reductions echoed those elsewhere, predicting the ruin of entire sectors of the economy. In France's case, some foresaw total economic demise. The headline of *L'Humanité* read: 'French Industry and Agriculture Ruined by Geneva Agreement'.[108] But rejecting membership was not an option. According to Olivier Wormser, then a young diplomat but who would in time exert great influence over French trade policy, political considerations meant that France had to join GATT.[109] While US officials might disregard such criticisms as communist propaganda, latent anti-Americanism and fear of American dominance was not limited to communists.

Several things stand out about the reaction to the General Agreement. First, GATT elicited relatively little public reaction. This is important to acknowledge even though it seems obvious. Lack of attention would be both a help and a hindrance moving forward. Second, there was never unqualified enthusiasm for GATT or trade liberalization. While protectionism or autarky did not seem to be viable or desirable alternatives, freer trade created problems too. At best there was lukewarm enthusiasm for GATT, and this temperature was determined by blending heated opposition and cool support. Third, trade was divisive rather than unifying. Some people insisted on liberal trade, whereas others demanded protection. Their reasons for or against could have economic, social, political, or foreign policy rationales. Lower tariffs and a liberal trade system were never going to make everyone happy. Fourth, people thought about trade in relation to their role as producers more than as consumers. The main benefits for consumers were likely to be lower prices and increased choice that would improve standards of living, but few seemed to appreciate that. In 1946, 46 per cent of Americans thought exports would make 'no

---

[106] Letter from W. Godfrey, Office of the Senior United Kingdom Trade Commissioner in Pakistan, to J. P. Summerscale, Commercial Relations and Treaties Dept, Board of Trade, 4 June 1948, BT11/3915, TNA.

[107] 'French Communists Aim Attacks on Tariff Pacts', *Christian Science Monitor* (17 November 1947), 15.

[108] Ibid.

[109] Olivier Wormser Papers, NOTE relative à l'Accord Général sur les tarifs douaniers et le commerce, n.d. MAEF 000067, reel 157, Historical Archives of the European Union [HAEU].

difference to them personally', meaning they did not connect lower tariffs with a higher standard of living.[110] The main issue for producers was about the viability of their business, whether it be manufacturing shoes, raising cattle, or making Hollywood films. The stakes for individual producers or businesses threatened by competition were much higher than for individual consumers, who might save a few pennies on daily shopping and more significant amounts on major purchases. The difference in rewards and losses are crucial to understanding why opponents of liberal trade were always more vocal and better organized than supporters.

By the beginning of 1948, Australia, Belgium, Canada, Cuba, France, Great Britain, Luxembourg, the Netherlands, and the United States had become the first contracting parties to the General Agreement. Others soon followed suit. GATT was launched without fanfare or celebration. This was fitting given its long and unanticipated history.

Wyndham White and the Secretariat, 1948–1952

The final trade and employment conference was held in Havana from November 1947 to March 1948, with fifty-three countries participating. The result was a significantly revised charter in which economic development, rather than trade liberalization, was the top priority. Because the story of the Havana conference is part of a longer tale of GATT's relation to development, I leave a full discussion of it to Chapter 5. For now, the point to keep in mind is that even though GATT was supposed to be a temporary measure, it began to function right away.

GATT existed under the auspices of the Interim Commission for the International Trade Organization (ICITO).[111] The ICITO pulled together a small secretariat, listed in Table 1.1. Eric Wyndham White was appointed executive secretary, a logical choice given his role as chair of the trade and employment conferences since 1946. Julio Lacarte, a Uruguayan diplomat, was his deputy. (Lacarte later served as the chair of various committees and working parties, and was a representative of Uruguay for over sixty years.) Jean Royer, who had been a member of the French delegation to the Geneva and Havana conferences, became the special assistant. He played similar roles to Wyndham White, shaping policy and resolving disputes, and according to Michael Hart was 'a

[110] Current Popular Opinion on Foreign Trade, 21 October 1946, RG59/Box 2/Foreign Trade Issues, Opinions on, Papers of Clayton-Thorp, TL.
[111] The ICITO had a legal existence that shadowed the GATT until both were absorbed into the WTO on 1 January 1995.

Table 1.1   *ICITO Secretariat, 1948*

Executive Secretary	Eric Wyndham White (UK)
Deputy Executive Secretary	Julio Lacarte (Uruguay)
Special Assistant	Jean Royer (France)
Commercial Policy Advisor	F. A. Haight (South Africa)
Information Officer	Richard Ford (UK)
Research Assistant	Constant Shih (China)
Research Assistant	G. Maggio (Italy)
Administrative Assistant	Dorothy Peaslee (USA)
Legal Advisor (on loan from UN)	Alan Renouf (Australia)
Research Assistant (on loan from UN)	Hugh Gosschalk (UK)

master of the GATT's rules'.[112] The UN propped up the ICITO by lending it officials. For instance, Alan Renouf of Australia was sent as a legal advisor. He stayed for a year and then returned to the Australian diplomatic corps. His position was not immediately refilled. The UN also supplied other personnel and shared its expertise to boost the resources and capabilities of the tiny secretariat. In general, the selection criteria for the secretariat were to be inclusive, representative, and effective. But the underlying goal, as Amy Sayward has shown for the World Bank, was to create 'a denationalized professional staff'.[113] As Wyndham White explained, appointments to the secretariat should be based on 'the highest standards of efficiency, competence, impartiality and integrity'.[114] Although some members would soon return to positions in their national bureaucracies, they transcended national perspectives and interests while part of the secretariat.

The secretariat was rudimentary by any standard and by comparison with other international organizations. In 1947, the World Bank had a staff of over sixty people, a permanent home, and ample space; its employees had a health plan, along with a health office, and a pension plan was set up in 1948. The bank also opened field offices and made its first reconstruction loans in 1947.[115] In striking contrast, GATT had no

---

[112] M. A. Hart, *A Trading Nation: Canadian Trade Policy from Colonialism to Globalization* (Vancouver: University of British Columbia Press, 2002), 169.

[113] A. L. Sayward, *The Birth of Development: How the World Bank, Food and Agriculture Organization, and the World Health Organization Changed the World, 1945–1965* (Kent, OH: Kent State University Press, 2006), 24.

[114] Wyndham White to Leddy, 7 May 1951, RG43: 285/file GATT, NARA.

[115] See one of the first telephone directories for the bank at http://web.worldbank.org/WB SITE/EXTERNAL/EXTABOUTUS/EXTARCHIVES/0,contentMDK:20080726~p agePK:36726~piPK:36092~theSitePK:29506,00.html, accessed 3 March 2016. The World Bank site notes that by the end of 1948, 'the Bank was a functioning institution

permanent home, no human resources apparatus, insecure funding, and a miniscule staff, much of it on loan, and its officials were less well paid than their counterparts at other organizations. Salaries and benefits would be ongoing sources of discontent. Wyndham White threatened to resign in 1963, allegedly because his salary and pension were lower than those of the heads of other international organizations.[116] Officials nonetheless remember the first secretariat for its excellence and effectiveness.[117] According to Jake Warren, a Canadian official and diplomat who led the Canadian delegation to the Tokyo round, the secretariat was 'frugally managed but intellectually strong'. And Rodney Grey, a Canadian trade official who was very close to Wyndham White, observed that that was the way Wyndham White wanted to keep it. He had no interest in building an empire.[118]

Wyndham White was clearly in charge of the secretariat. Renouf observed that he was 'a master of administration and of tactics at a conference'. Lacarte agreed that it was 'very much run by Wyndham White'. Reisman described him as 'exceedingly intelligent' and 'the leader'. Warren also described Wyndham White as 'exceptional' and claimed that he ran a tight ship. While a few scholars have commented on the importance of Wyndham White to the successes of GATT, he is largely unremembered. As de Souza Farias observes, this is surprising because he was the 'face and soul' of GATT for twenty years, he was well regarded by world leaders and trade experts, and he received much media attention at the time.[119]

What do we know about him? He had studied law at the London School of Economics (LSE) and seemed to have had progressive political instincts, having joined the Reform Club. Shortly before the war, he began to practise law and taught law at the LSE. When the war began, he joined the Ministry of Economic Warfare. He moved into the international civil service after the war; he was appointed to UNRRA and the

at last'. That gulf separating the resources has persisted. In 2008, the World Bank had a staff of 10,000 compared to 621 for the WTO. See R. Blackhurst, 'The Role of the Director-General and Secretariat' in A. Narlikar, M. Daunton, and R. M. Stern (eds.), *The Oxford Handbook on the World Trade Organization* (Oxford: Oxford University Press, 2012), 146.

[116] GATT secretariat, nd, RG25: 5648/283/14050–3-40 pt. 3, LAC.
[117] Alan Renouf said the calibre of the secretariat was high and Lacarte described it as efficient. Author interviews with Renouf, 8 May 2008 and Lacarte, 20 May 2005.
[118] Author interview with Warren, 18 May 2005 and Grey, 12 January 2005.
[119] F. McKenzie, 'Eric Wyndham White' in B. Reinalda and K. Kille (eds.), *The Biographical Dictionary of Secretaries-General of International Organizations* (2012, online, also known as *IO Bio*), www.ru.nl/fm/iobio; R. de Souza Farias, 'Mr. GATT: Eric Wyndham White and the Quest for Trade Liberalization', *World Trade Review* 12 (3) (July 2013), 464.

Emergency Economic Committee for Europe. In 1946, Trygve Lie, the head of the UN, seconded him to chair meetings of the International Conference on Trade and Employment. At subsequent meetings in Geneva and Havana, Wyndham White stayed on as chair. No one could foresee that this would lead to a twenty-year career as the head of GATT, but he was well suited to this role for several reasons. He believed in the liberal internationalist view of trade. He had a strong personality, which he impressed on delegations and the rest of the secretariat. According to Renouf, he was also determined and fearless. Blind in one eye, he taught himself to ski and then skied down Mont Blanc alone.[120] He was similarly determined as the head of GATT to sustain the momentum of trade liberalization. He frequently threatened to resign as a ploy to reach agreement. The threat became a little stale in time and he did not follow up on it until 1967. He thrived in an atmosphere of crisis and was forceful and inventive in bringing deadlocked delegates together – in the green room – in all-night sessions in which he wore down opposition. He also seems to have benefited by looking older than his years, which gave him a gravitas that made his strong-arm tactics and bold leadership widely acceptable.

The ICITO secretariat translated the Havana charter into Chinese, Spanish, and Russian, in anticipation of the first meeting of the ITO.[121] But according to Wyndham White, the secretariat needed 'a definite program ... rather than a series of tasks'.[122] As Renouf recalled, Wyndham White thought of the secretariat as an 'honest broker' that would help delegates reach agreement.[123] Wyndham White himself explained that they were 'breaking new ground', and at the 1946 Church House meeting, he used his administrative authority – on such matters as determining how long meetings would last and accepting silence as acquiescence – to cajole participants into agreement.[124] As he subsequently explained, he did not see GATT as the instrument of its members: the secretariat 'shall not seek or receive instructions from any government'. Rather the responsibility of the executive secretary 'shall be exclusively international in character'.[125]

---

[120] Author interview with Renouf.
[121] Report by the executive secretary of the ICITO on the work of the secretariat, 13 July 1948, ICITO/EC.2/5, GDL.
[122] Summary Record of Informal Meeting of Representatives of Executive Committee of ICITO present in Annecy, 24 June 1949, ICITO/1/14, GDL.
[123] Author correspondence with Renouf, 3 March 2008.
[124] Souza Farias, 'Mr. GATT', 468–470, 476.
[125] Wyndham White to Leddy, 7 May 1951, RG43: Box 285/file GATT Administration, NARA.

The immediate future of GATT was uncertain. Until the end of 1950, when it became clear that the USA would not ratify the ITO, there were discussions about doing away with the secretariat and having its various functions performed by UN officials or using national trade experts to oversee the GATT sessions, then held twice a year for about six weeks each.[126] A few members quit: Lebanon, Syria, and China. Others were contemplating it: Brazil was apparently reassessing its membership because GATT seemed only to benefit 'economically developed countries'.[127] As the British official R. J. Shackle remarked during the Annecy round of negotiations in 1949, the initial enthusiasm for GATT (not very significant) seemed to be fading and the quality of delegations had decreased. GATT's 'hand-to-mouth' resources were hopelessly inadequate. Overall, there was 'a general feeling of listlessness and lack of leadership'. Shackle doubted GATT could go on in its present fashion.[128]

Wyndham White was proactive about developing and protecting GATT. Once he had concluded that the ITO was defunct, he called on members to elaborate the 'GATT machinery'.[129] He encouraged more rounds of negotiations, for instance at Torquay in 1950, to add new members. Before the Torquay round, Canadian officials had been pessimistic about GATT; they were more optimistic afterwards. Despite GATT's limitations, they were confident that it could 'survive in its present form' and they valued the organization as 'a code of ethics for international trade'.[130] Wyndham White also fought to preserve GATT's independence. He, and many members, objected to the USA's suggestion to attach GATT to the UN and run it under the umbrella of the UN's Economic and Social Council (ECOSOC). According to British officials, these objections showed that 'the GATT is jealous of its independence and strong enough to resist railroading by the United States'.[131]

The presence of a proactive and independent secretariat raises questions about its relations with member countries, especially the United States. No one could deny the importance of the USA, but not all early GATT participants saw the United States as the leader. While Warren acknowledged that there was 'a germ of truth' in the supposition of US

---

[126] Note on the future organization and structure of the GATT, 7 July 1950, RG43: Box 290, file GATT, NARA.

[127] Brazil threatened to quit in 1951, Rio to State, 2 March 1951, RG43: Box 285, file 6, NARA.

[128] UK del to Annecy, n.d. but 1949, Shackle to Holmes.

[129] Record of conversation, 4 August 1950, FO371/82970, TNA.

[130] 'Position and Prospects of GATT', 18 April 1950, RG25: 6511/9100-X-40 pt. 2.1, LAC.

[131] Sixth Session and Future of GATT 1951, 25 October 1951, FO371/91962, TNA.

leadership, the reality was more complicated. Others, including members of the first secretariat, confirmed that the USA was a powerful presence, but they insisted that it did not run GATT or the secretariat. As Renouf put it, tongue in cheek, Wyndham White ran GATT, 'ably assisted by the US'. Secretariat members describe the early operation of GATT as informal, easy-going and without a hierarchy. Lacarte likened the larger group of officials who supported GATT to a 'friendly mafia' or a 'closed club' and explained that they had a 'feeling of fellowship, of joint endeavour'.[132] Wyndham White certainly cultivated close personal ties with national trade officials. The Canadians who knew him well – Grey, Warren, and Reisman – remembered him with warm affection. When Wyndham White fell on hard times after his retirement from GATT, they hired him as an advisor to the Canadian delegation during the Tokyo round. Wyndham White corresponded directly with national officials. His letters pop up in archives of many contracting parties. He shared confidences, explained trouble spots, and built coalitions to overcome obstacles and intransigence. According to one US trade official, he made use of personal ties to allow him to lead through proxies, such as Canadian and Indian officials, thereby obscuring his own direction.[133] Wyndham White and the GATT secretariat had to be careful not to appear to be too independent or to threaten the sovereignty of its members. If the secretariat pushed too hard, it might alienate members or force an explicit clarification of GATT's reach. This had happened in the World Health Organization, led by the Canadian Brock Chisholm, when he pressed the organization to take up the question of population control. This was a complex issue that provoked strong opposition. Chisholm's attempt to exert institutional independence backfired. Instead of taking the lead, he was forced to acknowledge that the role of the secretariat was 'to carry out the wishes of the national delegations'. According to Matthew Connelly, the situation in the WHO 'had a chilling effect on other UN agencies'.[134] Wyndham White avoided situations that would result in a similar admission of GATT's subordination to its membership.

The informal organization was reinforced by the precedent of not making decisions by vote. This was very different from the weighted voting system of the IMF and World Bank which reinforced a hierarchical

---

[132] Author interviews with Warren, 18 May 2005, Renouf, 8 May 2008, and Lacarte, 20 May 2005.

[133] Eckes, A. E. Jr. (ed.), *Revisiting U.S. Trade Policy: Decisions in Perspective* (Athens, OH: Ohio University Press, 2000), 31–32.

[134] M. Connelly, *Fatal Misconception: The Struggle to Control World Population* (Cambridge: Belknap Press of Harvard University Press, 2008), 150, 151.

system. Instead it functioned through consensus. Although this made GATT seem more inclusive, a consensus could not be reached without the tacit acceptance of key GATT members. Early on those were the USA and Britain, but the leadership structure evolved to include the EEC, India, Brazil, and Japan. Any GATT member could add issues to the agenda and force the pace of, or obstruct, discussions on any matter.

The GATT secretariat anticipated that as more international meetings were held in Geneva, it would have to find new quarters. The secretariat considered renting office space in buildings under construction where rents were lower. In the end, the Palais des Nations provided space until 1952. GATT also had acute budget concerns. Revenue was raised through annual subscriptions of the membership, with six categories of weighted contributions. At the top end of the scale, the United States and Britain each contributed US$11,000; at the bottom end were Burma, Ceylon, Cuba, Lebanon, Luxembourg, Southern Rhodesia, and Syria, which paid US$900 each.[135] Even with the graded scale of dues, many members paid late and the secretariat faced chronic financial pressures. The ICITO had to borrow US$86,490 from the UN Working Capital Fund, to be repaid within two years, but this offered only a brief financial reprieve.[136] By 1950, Wyndham White insisted that the 'pay as you go' budgeting system must end. GATT needed regular and additional revenue to finance its ever-expanding operations, but it would continue to depend on annual subscriptions.[137]

By the early 1950s, GATT had established itself, but remained insecure. The Federation of Indian Chambers of Commerce and Industry described its precarious state: 'GATT in a way has become at once a more permanent arrangement instead of being the forerunner of the I.T.O. and also a more shaky arrangement, for no country seems to fully favour, for one reason or another, its general objectives.'[138] While some members, including New Zealand, had preferred the ITO to GATT, others, such as South Africa and the USA, clearly preferred GATT to the ITO. Australia drew up a long list of benefits that stemmed from GATT, including forcing other nations to curb their use of import controls and ensuring that the basis for international economic cooperation in the IMF and the

---

[135] Financing of Secretariat Services, 13 September 1948, GATT/CP.2/41, GDL.

[136] GATT/ICITO repaid the UN all outstanding loans (US$216,773.87) in 1953.

[137] Budget Estimates for 1951, Note by the Executive Secretary, 24 October 1950, GATT/CP.5/10, GDL.

[138] Letter from the Federation of Indian Chambers of Commerce and Industry to the Secretary of the Government of India, Ministry of Commerce and Industry, 23 June 1953, 52 (50)/TB/52: Examination of Note Circulated by GATT Secretariat Regarding the Value of the General Agreement to the Under-Developed Countries; Government's Comments on the Note, Commerce and Industry, NAI.

World Bank continued. Moreover, membership in GATT had not pre-vented Australia from introducing measures it deemed necessary and did not undermine trade relations with other Commonwealth members. Indeed, Commonwealth trade seemed to improve as a result of GATT. Leaving GATT would also have been likely to damage relations with the USA.[139] Others agreed that there were important political benefits to membership. As an Indian official explained, as long as big powers remain in the GATT club 'it would . . . be extremely impolitic to break away'.[140] There were more positive reasons to support GATT. GATT established a standard to which all countries, strong and weak, would be held. As a result, many valued it as part of a rule- and norm-based system that could restrain US unilateralism. There were also real benefits to be enjoyed from lowering tariffs. Pursuing trade liberalization within GATT offset the unequal distribution of economic power and negotiating authority. Finally, the world probably could not do any better.[141] Others agreed that a world without GATT would soon 'revert to the unrestricted anarchy of the 1930s'.[142]

[139] Confidential 'Notes on Australia's Position in Relation to the GATT and Havana Charter for an International Trade Organisation', n.d., between Annecy and Torquay rounds, AA1976/34/Bundle 1, AA.

[140] Extract from Annex II of Document No. GATT/CP.4/1/Rev.3, 28 February 1950, 52 (58) TB/50: Third Round of Tariff Negotiations Scheduled for September, 50 at Torquay – Proposals for, NAI.

[141] Notes on GATT, n.d., MG31 – E6: LePan Papers, Vol. 9/file 97, LAC.

[142] The Sixth Session and the Future of the General Agreement on Tariffs and Trade (G.A.T.T.) Geneva 1951, 25 October 1951, FO371/91962, TNA.

2   'An Arrow in the Western World's Quiver'
The Cold War Challenge to GATT

The central purpose of GATT was to prevent and, if necessary, defuse, conflicts caused by trade.[1] But the Cold War turned GATT into a partisan body that worked to defeat communism as an economic doctrine and break apart the communist bloc. And yet most histories of the Cold War, even those that focus on its economic dimensions, do not discuss GATT aside from a few studies of embargoes.[2] This is surprising given the centrality of capitalism in the Cold War standoff and the use of commodities to win hearts and minds. As Charles Maier has observed, 'Peaceful competition meant primarily economic competition; the rivalry between capitalism and state socialism.'[3] Histories of GATT reinforce this disconnect by paying little attention to the Cold War, for several reasons. According to some scholars, GATT depoliticized trade; for others, the like-mindedness of GATT members allowed them to set politics side.[4] Karin Kock agrees that, in general, political matters had

---

[1] Some of the material in this chapter appeared in F. McKenzie, 'GATT in the Cold War: Accession Debates, Institutional Development, and the Western Alliance, 1947–1959', *Journal of Cold War Studies* 10 (3) (Summer 2008), 78–109. The quotation is from A. E. Eckes, Jr. (ed.), *Revisiting U.S. Trade Policy: Decisions in Perspective* (Athens, OH: Ohio University Press, 2000), 22.

[2] I. Jackson, *The Economic Cold War: America, Britain and East–West Trade, 1948–63* (Basingstoke: Palgrave Macmillan, 2001), focuses on CoCom, but still only makes one passing reference to GATT. S. G. Zhang, *Economic Cold War: America's Embargo against China and the Sino-Soviet Alliance, 1949–1963* (Washington, DC: Woodrow Wilson Centre Press; Stanford, CA: Stanford University Press, 2001), makes no mention of GATT. R. A. Pollard, *Economic Security and the Origins of the Cold War, 1945–1950* (New York: Columbia University Press, 1985), discusses the ITO, precursor to the GATT, on only a handful of occasions.

[3] C. S. Maier, 'The World Economy and the Cold War in the Middle of the Twentieth Century' in M. P. Leffler and O. A. Westad (eds.), *The Cambridge History of the Cold War, Vol. I: Origins* (Cambridge: Cambridge University Press, 2010), 44.

[4] J. A. Finlayson and M. W. Zacher, 'The GATT and the Regulation of Trade Barriers: Regime Dynamics and Functions' in S. D. Krasner (ed.), *International Regimes* (Ithaca, NY: Cornell University Press, 1983), 314. G. Curzon and V. Curzon, 'GATT: A Trader's Club' in R. W. Cox and H. K. Jacobson (eds.), *The Anatomy of Influence: Decision Making in International Organizations* (New Haven, CT, and London: Yale University Press, 1974), 325, 328.

been 'carefully avoided in GATT', although she acknowledges that the Cold War 'could not altogether be avoided'.[5] Historical works also focus on rounds of negotiations, examining tariff negotiations and technical questions in an approach that obscures the geopolitical context, overlooks the connection between trade and ideology, and understates the diplomatic significance of the process and outcome. The only well-developed connection with the Cold War relates to the establishment of GATT and the demise of the International Trade Organization. As Richard Toye and Thomas Zeiler show, Cold War considerations prompted the United States to make concessions to developing countries at the Havana conference in order to build up a broad-based multilateral alliance. But the Havana charter came to be seen as an ineffective way to combat communism.[6] Beyond this early phase, few historians of GATT have taken Cold War considerations into account. The result is that the Cold War is usually seen as marginal to the workings of GATT, and the pursuit of trade liberalization has been disconnected from the bipolar conflict whose beginning and end mirrored those of GATT. This needs to be corrected.

The Cold War changed the context in which international institutions operated. As John Ikenberry explains, the containment order 'overshadowed' the western order, which revolved around institutions.[7] GATT was redefined as a forum of the western alliance. Czechoslovakia was the only communist signatory, having joined GATT prior to the communist coup there in February 1948. Most of the other founding members associated themselves with the western alliance, albeit awkwardly in some cases – France – and a few positioned themselves as non-aligned – India. The Cold War also imparted a new meaning to trade liberalization, emphasizing security and survival rather than peace and stability in the minds and policies of western governments, especially the United States. Liberal trade and the economic growth that it begat were seen as ways to defend the values and institutions of the capitalist and democratic world, as George Kennan had advised in his long telegram.[8] A British official noted, 'The GATT

---

[5] Kock, *International Trade Policy and the GATT, 1947–1967*, 73.

[6] R. Toye, 'Developing Multilateralism: The Havana Charter and the Fight for the International Trade Organization, 1947–1948', *International History Review* 25 (2) (June 2003), 284, 294. Zeiler claims the Havana charter came to be seen as a global planning exercise that was incompatible with capitalism. T. W. Zeiler, *Free Trade, Free World: The Advent of GATT* (Chapel Hill: University of North Carolina Press, 1999), 137–138, 148–151.

[7] G. J. Ikenberry, *After Victory: Institutions, Strategic Restraint, and the Rebuilding of Order After Major Wars* (Princeton and Oxford: Princeton University Press, 2001), 163–164, 170–172.

[8] The Chargé in the Soviet Union to Secretary of State, 22 February 1946, www.gwu.edu /~nsarchiv/coldwar/documents/episode-1/kennan.htm.

is written in the language of the free world.'[9] Or so the provisions of the General Agreement were reinterpreted in the context of the Cold War.

This chapter explains how GATT was repositioned geopolitically and how its trade-liberalizing mission came to be associated with the security and ideology of the west. It examines relations between members – early on between ideological rivals, Czechoslovakia and the United States – but mostly relations among countries that belonged to the western bloc. The narrative turns on the question of the accession of communist countries (Poland, Hungary, Romania, Bulgaria, Yugoslavia, the Soviet Union, and China) as well as strategic allies (West Germany and Japan). James Mayall describes the western democratic members of GATT as 'gate-keepers' who ensured that it remained a western institution.[10] But the question of accession was more complicated than admitting democratic allies and excluding communist foes. Ideological compatibility did not determine admissibility. The consequences of closer association or ongoing disassociation in relation to Cold War objectives were crucial considerations about who was let into, allowed to associate with, or shut out of GATT. GATT played a tactical role in fortifying the west and in weakening the east.

The political scientist Leah Haus has written the most thorough account of the applications of communist countries to join GATT, focusing on Poland, Hungary, Rumania, Bulgaria, and the Soviet Union. She argues that political and security considerations were most important in deciding whether or not to admit communist countries. She has mapped the trajectory of the Soviet–American conflict onto the GATT story of accession, presenting the western alliance as largely unified about how to use trade to achieve Cold War goals.[11] In fact, the western bloc was not unified. The picture of the western alliance that emerges from the extended debates about membership includes diverse views, priorities, and attitudes and different strategic conceptions of the Cold War, and whether or not it was appropriate or necessary to make GATT serve an ideological-security function. Moreover, the views of members, including the USA, were not static, a point that Haus also makes.

[9] 'Poland and Yugoslavia: Proposed Association with the GATT', Draft EPC Paper, October 1958, BT11/5704, TNA.
[10] J. Mayall, 'The Western Alliance, GATT and East–West Trade' in D. A. Baldwin and H. V. Milner (eds.), *East–West Trade and the Atlantic Alliance* (New York: St. Martin's Press, 1990), 22.
[11] L. H. Haus, *Globalizing the GATT: The Soviet Union's Successor States, Eastern Europe, and the International Trading System* (Washington, DC: Brookings Institution, 1992), 6–8, 80–81, 98–99. Haus writes that 'the West strongly supported' the accession of Poland, Romania, and Hungary in the 1960s and 1970s and the 'West' blocked the accession of the Soviet Union and Bulgaria in the 1980s.

Decisions about who to let in, exclude, and keep on the margins affected GATT's institutional identity, capabilities, and legitimacy. GATT was frequently criticized because its membership was skewed to the west. This exacerbated its institutional insecurity. There was pressure from the secretariat to expand membership in response to the first requests of communist countries to become observers in the 1950s. Peremptory refusal was not politically possible. Some countries stayed out (the Soviet Union and the People's Republic of China, PRC) or were kept out (Bulgaria) and others were partially admitted (Poland, Hungary, Romania, and Yugoslavia), but in general GATT remained a western forum and an economic instrument of the capitalist democracies. With the end of the Cold War, Bulgaria, the Soviet Union/Russia, and the PRC once again sought membership, but the doors were not flung open. Because the institution was no longer susceptible to the charge of having a restricted or self-selecting membership (by the end of the Uruguay round there were more than 100 members), some feared that the admission of major countries would disrupt global trade and the institution. As GATT officials looked forward to a new future, revolving around the establishment of the World Trade Organization, they also harkened back to 1945. The rhetoric of peace and prosperity was once more ascendant, replacing the rhetoric of security and survival.

The Start of the Cold War and the Establishment of GATT, 1946–1947

Soviet officials did not attend the preparatory meetings that led to the establishment of GATT/ITO. Their absence did not mean they were not interested in global trade. Nor did it foreshadow Cold War divisions. Even though relations among the former wartime leaders were strained by 1946 – Churchill had made his 'iron curtain' speech in March of that year – the hope was that the Soviet Union would join the ITO.[12] Soviet officials encouraged this hope by explaining their absence from the first major international meeting on trade – held in London in October and November 1946 – as a result of personnel shortages rather than ideological antipathy. But evidence of mistrust cannot be ignored. Nor was it one-sided. An American official noted that even though the Soviets would not be present, 'their stooges in the Czech delegation' would be.[13] Still, the Americans made sure that nothing was done to preclude Soviet

[12] Haus also contends that the USA wanted the Soviet Union to join. *Globalizing the GATT*, 89–90.
[13] Office Memorandum from Ben Moore to Winthrop Brown, 16 October 1946, RG43: Box 118, Preparatory Committee – October 15 Meeting, NARA.

involvement down the road. For example, state trading provisions were included in the charter.[14] Despite their absence, Soviet officials were generally pleased with the progress that had been made. In a meeting with American trade officials, a Soviet official alluded to hidden provisions of the draft charter, but overall he described the terms as reasonable and promised to consult with his government.[15] There was reason for the Soviet Union to support the establishment of a global trade order. According to Oscar Sanchez-Sibony, the recovery of foreign trade was central to Soviet plans for economic recovery and long-term growth. Moreover, Stalin feared the onset of another global depression.[16]

Although the goal of GATT/ITO was to have universal membership, Soviet inclusion posed many challenges. As a Canadian analysis noted, the problem stemmed from the Soviet Union's 'totalitarian nature', meaning the state controlled 'production, distribution, consumption, and the allocation of materials and labour'. How could the Soviet system be reconciled with the ITO, which assumed there were standard measures and a willingness to disclose economic information? Uncritically, Canadian officials asked how the ITO could include a country that used trade for political purposes. There was also concern that the Soviet Union did not really want 'the outside world' to prosper and that it would attempt to disrupt the economies of other states. Given these doubts, Canadian officials recommended 'firm and realistic' terms for the trade charter. If the Soviet Union participated, then it would be held to such terms. But Soviet membership in the ITO was also valued because it would preserve a unified global community: it would be 'a step toward a gradual coordination of the Soviet and democratic worlds'.[17] That hope soon faded. Dana Wilgress was a senior Canadian trade official in the 1940s who had started his career in Russia as a junior trade official during the First World War. He feared the Soviet Union might try to sabotage the ITO. 'Russia might conceivably someday ... come in, with a view to wrecking or dominating.'[18] By early 1947, Canadian analysts hoped that countries they described as 'completely under Soviet domination'

---

[14] Dam helpfully reminds us that it was not just communist societies that used state trading practices. K. W. Dam, *The GATT: Law and International Economic Organization* (Chicago: University of Chicago Press, 1970), 317.

[15] Memorandum of Conversation between Klentsov (chief of Soviet Trade Delegation, London), Wilcox and Armstrong, 5 November 1946, RG43: Box 118, file London – Foreign Reactions, NARA.

[16] O. Sanchez-Sibony, *Red Globalization: The Political Economy of the Soviet Union from Stalin to Khrushchev* (New York: Cambridge University Press, 2014), 58–59.

[17] International Trade Organization Project: The Position of the U.S.S.R., n.d., RG25: F-6/1035/8-H, LAC.

[18] Telegram No. 79 from Canadian Consulate General, New York to SSEA, Ottawa, 21 January 1947, RG20: vol. 456/0–7/1947, LAC.

(Bulgaria and Rumania) and on the 'margins of the Soviet zone' (Austria, Czechoslovakia, Finland, Hungary, and Poland) would be admitted. The benefits would be both economic and political; trade with them would 'to some extent lessen the rigidity of the blocs into which the world is likely to be divided'.[19] Trade and GATT might break down Cold War divisions.

When the Geneva conference began in April 1947, Soviet observers openly interpreted the trade negotiations according to Marxist-Leninist logic. The Hungarian economist Evgenii Varga said that the USA was using the Geneva conference to solve its own economic problems, such as high prices, chronic unemployment, and a productive capacity that outstripped domestic demand. He portrayed American trade policy as exploitatively self-interested: to enrich the United States while keeping 'industrially backward, agrarian countries' in a perpetual state of impoverishment.[20] An article in TRUD, the official publication of the Soviet trade unions, characterized American conduct at Havana as imperialist, with the aim of opening the world's markets to American monopolies and thereby establishing American global dominance, 'enslav[ing] not only Europe, but the whole world'.[21] Sanchez-Sibony has differentiated between the oppositional rhetoric of Soviet officials and the pragmatic pursuit of integration into the global economy: 'the Soviets sought to buy into the very system of financial and commercial exchange that could guarantee the quick recovery of fortress Soviet Union'.[22] Nonetheless, the Soviet critique of the negotiations in Geneva shaped the views of western officials about the nature and intentions of Soviet policy.

Soviet attacks on the GATT/ITO had an unintended salutary effect. At the Geneva conference in 1947, when Anglo-American negotiations were deadlocked over imperial preferences, as I describe in Chapter 1, Cold War considerations helped resolve their dispute. President Truman did not believe that a disagreement over a tariff could be allowed to jeopardize relations with a key ally just as the superpower standoff intensified. The Cold War was a midwife at the birth of GATT.

Although Zeiler writes that the onset of the Cold War compromised 'free trade universalism',[23] GATT's legitimacy remained tied to as

---

[19] International Trade Organization Project: Membership, Relations with Non-Members, and Sanctions, n.d., RG25: F-6/1035/8-H, LAC.

[20] E. Varga, 'The Geneva Trade Talks', *Novoe vremja* (*New Times*, Soviet Union) No. 20 (16 May 1947). Ford sent a copy of Varga's article to Ottawa in his despatch of 28 May 1947.

[21] 'Blackmail at Havana', translation, TRUD, 28 December 1947, RG43: Records of International Conferences, Commissions and Expositions, subject file 1947–48, Habana Conference – General to Interim Commission – ITO Post Habana, NARA.

[22] Sanchez-Sibony, *Red Globalization*, 59.   [23] Zeiler, *Free Trade Free World*, 137.

inclusive a membership as possible. As a Canadian analysis explained, membership should be 'as wide as possible' and '[a]ny nation willing to assume the obligations of membership should be welcomed'. Political considerations ought to be 'irrelevant to the question of membership in the I.T.O.'. Membership in the UN was not a prior condition, and neither was the position of countries during the war (as enemies, neutrals, or pariah states such as Spain and the Argentine).[24] The commitment to universal representation remained a baseline expectation against which GATT was subsequently judged.

GATT, Containment, and the Western Alliance

When GATT made its debut in 1948, the Soviet Union denounced it as a tool of the United States and noted that it did not meet its own standard of universal membership. There was, however, one newly established and one imminent communist member of GATT: Czechoslovakia and the PRC. The United States took the lead in containing Czechoslovakia within GATT, whereas Britain and others sympathetic to American opposition to the PRC helped to orchestrate its exclusion.

At the end of the Chinese civil war in 1949, the communist forces, led by Mao Zedong, had prevailed on the mainland and the Kuomintang, led by Chiang Kai-shek, had fled to Taiwan, or as it was called the Republic of China (ROC) to distinguish it from the People's Republic of China on the mainland. The United States had invested money and resources in China during the Second World War and hoped it would remain a close ally after the war. When it became clear that American hopes for China would not be fulfilled, Washington set out to isolate the PRC. One way to do so was to deny the government standing in international organizations such as the UN and GATT.

The American goal looked easy to achieve in GATT. China had participated in the 1947 Geneva conference and signed the General Agreement, but the ROC withdrew from GATT on 7 March 1950. While the GATT secretariat and most members were willing to accept the ROC decision, Britain was in a bind. Two months earlier, the Attlee government had recognized the PRC as the government of China. It could not therefore accept the ROC decision. The PRC also contested the validity of Taiwanese withdrawal, insisting that Beijing spoke for the Chinese people. Discussion of Chinese membership in GATT was 'tiresome', according to British officials. But it was not a question they

---

[24] International Trade Organization Project: Membership, Relations with Non-Members, and Sanctions, n.d., RG25: F-6/1035/8-H, LAC.

could ignore. While they hoped the issue might resolve itself through inaction, they could not count on this. Some were concerned that Czechoslovakia would raise the question of PRC membership. It had earlier requested that GATT invite Albania, Transjordan, Mongolia, and Yemen to the Havana conference.[25] Indian officials also suspected that if the ROC sent representatives to GATT, Czechoslovakia would make a formal motion to expel them.[26] The British believed that the only way to avoid an awkward diplomatic fallout was to prevent China from participating in GATT. But China would have to decide for itself to stay away, with encouragement from other GATT members. Because British officials were not hopeful that the Chinese government would make an explicit statement of its withdrawal, they suggested that evidence of de facto disengagement – such as not implementing tariff concessions negotiated in 1947 or extending trade advantages to other communist countries – could support the claim that 'China's conduct amounts to a repudiation of her G.A.T.T. obligations'.[27] India, which had also recognized the PRC as the legitimate government of China, welcomed the British suggestion. They did not support membership for the PRC and they did not want a debate in GATT over who was the legitimate representative of the Chinese people.[28]

GATT and its members were able to side-step divisive questions about who represented the people of China and whether or not GATT distinguished between different kinds of political systems because neither the ROC nor the PRC sent representatives to GATT meetings.[29] The PRC retained its seat on the ICITO, the temporary body that had been set up in 1948 to bridge the transition from GATT to the ITO. The lapse of the ITO left the ICITO in place as a link to the UN. In practice, it did nothing, but it had a residual standing. The PRC's decision to stand aloof from the ICITO and GATT was consistent with its general rejection

[25] Telegram G.4, L. D. Wilgress, Head of Canadian Delegation, Geneva to SSEA, 10 July 1947, RG20: Vol.456/0–6/1947, LAC.

[26] Extract of letter from M. J. Desai, leader of the Indian delegation to GATT, to C.C. Desai, Secretary to the Government of India, 16 February 1950, 52(5) – TB/49: Fourth Session of the Contracting Parties to the General Agreement on Tariffs and Trade – China's Withdrawal from the GATT, Commerce and Industry, NAI.

[27] 'The Position of China in the G.A.T.T.', September 1951, FO371/91999, TNA. The British had no desire to highlight this difference of opinion with the USA and therefore opted 'to take as inconspicuous a part in the discussions as possible'. UE166/3. Minute sheet, Tench's minute, 29 August 1951, FO371/91999, TNA.

[28] Letter from B. N. Bannerjee to M. J. Desai, 15 March 1950, and Telegram from Externsec, Colombo, to Foreign, New Delhi, 15/3/1950, 52(5) – TB/49: Fourth Session of the Contracting Parties to the General Agreement on Tariffs and Trade – China's Withdrawal from the GATT, NAI.

[29] Report of the United Kingdom Delegation, Torquay Conference 1950/1, January 1952, BT11/4520, TNA.

of the post-1945 international order. With respect to trade and its overall economic development, the goal was self-sufficiency. So it stayed out of GATT as well as the Council for Mutual Economic Assistance (CMEA) set up by the Soviet Union.[30] But China's membership status remained unclear. They were absent rather than excluded. Nonetheless, with the Soviet Union and the PRC on the outside, GATT's members were overwhelmingly capitalist and democratic.

GATT was further shielded from communist attacks by keeping out of the United Nations. The United States had proposed attaching GATT to ECOSOC as a way to support it after it was clear that the ITO would fail. This made sense, as GATT belonged to the cohort of specialist organizations established during and after the war to promote peace and manage conflict. The UN could absorb the costs of GATT, whose resources were scarce. US officials also wanted to attach GATT to the United Nations to protect it from Congress, which jealously guarded its authority over trade policy, upheld sovereignty as a cardinal principle, and looked on GATT with suspicion. But British authorities advised against such a move. Within the UN, GATT would be vulnerable to Soviet criticisms.[31] Given the polarization and paralysis of many UN functions as a result of the Cold War, the British view prevailed. This decision positioned GATT squarely in the western alliance and allowed members to use GATT for the ideological and strategic purposes of its members. As Mayall observes, although GATT was not an official organ of the western alliance, trade liberalization was 'consistent with the broad objectives of NATO'.[32]

The relevance of GATT to the welfare, strength, and security of the western alliance was made explicit in response to the fear of an impending depression in the United States which would undermine US leadership, weaken links among allies, and boost Communist propaganda. Fear of another depression had informed the postwar global governance architecture, in particular the importance attached to economic stability, full employment, and open markets. Although the 1950s and 1960s were in fact decades of rapid economic growth, in 1949 US officials feared that an economic downturn in the United States would spark a global depression and give rise to nationalistic economic policies. The effects would seep into the political realm: belief in international cooperation would weaken, the USA's leadership would be undermined, and its ties with other countries would be strained. This scenario took on heightened meaning

---

[30] H. K. Jacobsen and M. Oksenberg, *China's Participation in the IMF, the World Bank, and GATT: Toward a Global Economic Order* (Ann Arbor: University of Michigan Press, 1990), 45.

[31] 'Future of the G.A.T.T.', memo by J. A. Turpin, 21 August 1951, FO371/91962, TNA.

[32] Mayall, 'The Western Alliance, GATT and East–West Trade', 21.

in light of the Cold War. 'No development could play more into the hands of the Soviet Union than a U.S. depression.' Soviet propaganda that attributed economic suffering to capitalist practices would be vindicated. The Soviet Union would be in prime position to 'woo' vulnerable countries.[33] The analysis reflected the politicized conception of economic policies and practices. The flip side of the forecast was the belief that raising standards of living, especially in poor countries, would weaken the appeal of communism. Clayton explained the logic: 'If people everywhere are employed, have enough to eat and wear and decent houses in which to live, they are not likely to turn to dangerous totalitarian philosophies and leaders.'[34] Or as Kennan put it more graphically in his telegram: 'World communism is like malignant parasite which feeds only on diseased tissue.'[35] Prosperity would also permit members of the western alliance to afford the large defence budgets needed to deter communist expansion.[36] US foreign economic policy did not separate economic and diplomatic consequences: 'economic action must go hand in hand with political and military measures for mutual defense against Communist aggression'.[37] As a result, the USA wanted a new round of tariff negotiations – subsequently held in Torquay from 1950 to 1951 – as a non-military measure to fight against communism. It would strengthen free nations individually and jointly so they could withstand economic aggression. Successful negotiations would also be a victory for the west, particularly important after the start of the Korean War in June 1950.[38] As it happens, the interim secretariat of GATT also wanted to hold another round of negotiations as a way to move forward after the failure of the ITO. Following the Torquay round, four more countries joined: Austria, Peru, Turkey, and West Germany .

The accession of West Germany to GATT was the result of the USA's aim to strengthen critical and vulnerable allies. In 1948, the USA had begun to press for the accession of three occupied territories: West Germany, southern Korea, and Japan. The US government did so even though Britain, France, and other members were far from

---

[33] Foreign Effects of a U.S. Depression, 1 July 1949, RG43: Box 278, Anti-Depression Policies, NARA.

[34] UN Radio Interview with William L. Clayton, Chief of U.S. Delegation, 26 November 1947 (Press Release ITO/41), RG20: Vol. 358/24581-C, pt. 1, LAC.

[35] The Chargé in the Soviet Union to Secretary of State, 22 February 1946, www.gwu.edu /~nsarchiv/coldwar/documents/episode-1/kennan.htm.

[36] Memo by the Secretary of State to the President, 20 November 1950, *FRUS 1950, Vol. I*, 782.

[37] Foreign Effects of a U.S. Depression, 1 July 1949, RG43: Box 278, Anti-Depression Policies, NARA.

[38] US Department of State Press Release, No. 895, 1 September 1950, RG25: 6511/9100-X-40 pt 2.2, LAC.

enthusiastic.[39] The possibility of West Germany's accession was especially controversial because the fate of Germany, then occupied by the
United States, Britain, the Soviet Union, and France, was actively
contested. British and French officials discouraged their US colleagues
from 'starting a debate ... as to who should represent Germany'.[40] But
US officials believed that trade would help Germany's economic recovery, a foreign policy priority by 1948. No longer regarded as ex-enemy
states, these territories were rather seen as vulnerable partners and Cold
War battlefields, and their economic strength was also needed to withstand the appeal of communism and to drive regional economic
activity.[41]

Czechoslovakia was a founding member of GATT. The United States
had to accept this. To try and expel Czechoslovakia would have involved
the exercise of brute power, which was neither possible nor politic. There
was self-awareness in the US government that it must be scrupulous
about working within international obligations and must stand for law
and order in international relations.[42] As a result, Czechoslovakia was
'the lonely outpost of Iron Curtain countries among the Contracting
Parties'.[43] Concerns that Czechoslovakia would promote Soviet interests
within GATT were realized when it protested the accession of West
Germany.

The Czech representative to GATT, Dr. Zdenek Augenthaler,
objected to West German membership on the grounds that it was not
a fully sovereign state.[44] West Germany did not have 'autonomy in the
conduct of its foreign relations which would give it the necessary capacity
to become eligible for accession to the G.A.T.T.'.[45] International agreements stipulated that Germany was to be treated as a single economic
unit. Therefore, West Germany's admission to GATT would be 'contrary
to the existing international agreements and might create a situation

[39] Secretary of State to Embassy in UK, 24 June 1948, *FRUS 1948, Vol. I, pt. 2: General; The United Nations* (Washington, DC: United States Government Printing Office 1976), 919.

[40] Wilgress, Head of Canadian Delegation, Geneva, to Secretary of State for External Affairs, tel. G.4, 10 July 1947, RG20: Vol. 456/0–6/1947, LAC.

[41] H. B. Schonberger, *Aftermath of War: Americans and the Remaking of Japan, 1945–1952* (Kent, OH, and London: Kent State University Press, 1989), 163–164; S. Yoneyuki, *Pitfall or Panacea: The Irony of U.S. Power in Occupied Japan, 1945–1952* (New York: Routledge, 2003), chapter 1; R. J. McMahon, *Dean Acheson and the Creation of an American World Order* (Washington, DC: Potomac Books, 2009), 96.

[42] Czechoslovak Adherence to GATT, memorandum for Brown, Wood, and Thorp, 7 April 1948, RG43: Box 282, NARA.

[43] Letter from R. J. Shackle to O. C. Morland, 14 September 1949, BT11/4344, TNA.

[44] Summary Record of the Tenth Meeting, 23 August 1948, GATT/CP.2/SR.10, GDL.

[45] General Agreement on Tariffs and Trade Working Party 10 Future Tariff Negotiations: Draft Report of Working Party, GATT/CP3/WP10/2/9, GDL.

prejudicial to the final solution of the problem of Germany and specially [*sic*] to its unity'.[46] Czech protests continued throughout the period of the Berlin blockade and the establishment of the Federal Republic of Germany in 1949.

Czechoslovakia's objections were taken seriously in part because of the esteem in which Augenthaler was held. In 1919, he had earned a doctorate in law and economics from Charles University. Afterwards he joined the Czechoslovak Ministry of Foreign Trade and subsequently moved to the economics division of the Ministry of Foreign Affairs. In 1939, he joined the resistance. Later in the war, he became the deputy chief of the economics division of the Ministry of Foreign Affairs for the Czechoslovak government-in-exile. He became head of division in 1945. He was well known within GATT circles, having been a delegate to the ITO preparatory conferences in 1946 and 1947.

Still, most members backed the US position, although not immediately. Canada and the Netherlands did so early on, but Britain, France, and Belgium took more time before deciding that West Germany's membership was 'desirable on grounds of general foreign policy'.[47] West Germany's accession to GATT also made sense in light of developments in European and transatlantic relations in coming to terms with a persistent fear of Germany alongside the necessity of 'linking Western Germany more firmly to the Western World'.[48] Membership in GATT was consistent with the Brussels Treaty of 1948, the creation of NATO in 1949, and the launch of the European coal and steel community in 1950.

The matter came to a head in 1950 when the Czech representative moved to reject West Germany's accession. Czechoslovakia's was the only vote in favour of rejection.[49] In 1951, West Germany became a contracting party even though it was still recovering from the devastation of the Second World War and could not implement all GATT rules.

US–Czechoslovak ideological clashes then shifted to the question of whether or not the USA could refuse to grant export licences on goods of strategic significance. Czechoslovakia insisted that such action violated GATT rules. Many GATT members agreed. But voting followed political lines. Seventeen countries voted to support US action as compatible with GATT; three abstained (India, Lebanon, and Syria) and two were

[46] Summary Record of the Nineteenth Meeting, 6 September 1948, GATT/CP.2/SR.10, GDL.

[47] Trade Negotiating Committee, Proposed Third Round of Tariff Negotiations, Note by the Board of Trade, 19 September 1949, BT11/4344, TNA.

[48] US Department of State, Press Release no. 895, 1 September 1950, RG25: 6511/9100-X-4 pt. 2.2, LAC.

[49] Summary Record of the Eleventh Meeting, 2 March 1950, GATT/CP.4/SR.11, GDL.

absent (Burma and Luxembourg). Only Czechoslovakia voted to censure the USA.[50] Because the USA was 'under attack', members knew that 'no other decision was possible' even though they regarded the US position as weak 'in certain respects'.[51]

Czechoslovak–US sparring continued when the USA announced it would revoke all tariff benefits that it extended to Czechoslovakia, an act permissible under Article XXV of the General Agreement[52] and made necessary by a US law that prevented the United States from extending commercial concessions to the Soviet Union or any Soviet bloc country.[53] Willard Thorp, US assistant secretary of state for economic affairs, admitted that the USA's decision was based on mutually hostile relations: since the Geneva conference of 1947, 'relations between the two Governments had steadily deteriorated and had by now fallen below the minimum degree of tolerance and respect which was essential to the effective discharge of the obligations of the Agreement'.[54] The Czechoslovak spokesman denounced the termination of benefits and privileges as 'illegal and contrary to all the principles of international law and to the letter and spirit of the Agreement'. The USA's action was characterized as 'brutally pursuing its own selfish aims, which it places above the law and above the international co-operation it pledged itself not only under the General Agreement but also under the United Nations Charter'. Czechoslovakia responded to the USA's decision by revoking all tariff benefits that it extended to US exports. The Czech representative drew an explicit connection between Czech–US disputes in GATT and 'the policy of violence and the so-called "cold war" pursued by the United States'. He claimed that GATT members endorsed the US decision as a 'result of pressure exercised by the United States', an allegation that GATT members denied.[55]

---

[50] Summary Record of the Twenty-Second Meeting, 8 June 1949, GATT/CP.3/SR.22, GDL.

[51] Letter from Louis Couillard, Acting Head Canadian Delegation, to Secretary of State for External Affairs, Ottawa, 14 June 1949, RG25: F-6/Vol. 1065/3-0-0, LAC.

[52] Article XXV stipulated that 'In exceptional circumstances not elsewhere provided for in this Agreement, the Contracting Parties may waive an obligation imposed upon a contracting party by this Agreement; Provided that any such decision shall be approved by a two-thirds majority of the votes cast and that such majority shall comprise more than half of the contracting parties.'

[53] The law was the Trade Agreements Extension Act of 1951. 'Termination of Obligations between the United States and Czechoslovakia under the Agreement: Statement by the United States', 10 August 1951, GATT/CP.6/5, GATT/CP.6/1–56/DR.1–27, GDL.

[54] Summary Record of the Twelfth Meeting, 26 September 1951, GATT/CP.6/SR.12, GDL.

[55] Memorandum by the Delegation of Czechoslovakia concerning the Declaration of the Contracting Parties on the suspension of the obligations of the United States under the Agreement with respect to Czechoslovakia, 24 October 1951, GATT/CP.6/49, WTO;

Voting in GATT was not typical at this early stage or later on. Members strove for consensus, although unavoidably some were more satisfied than others. But on questions linked to Cold War rivalry, US officials counted votes and interpreted results in terms of a geopolitical score sheet. Hence the USA had to have the necessary support (a two-thirds majority or sixteen votes) to abrogate its commercial relationship with Czechoslovakia,[56] or it 'would be a sharp victory for the Soviet bloc'.[57] Washington lobbied members for support. Britain and Luxembourg were unenthusiastic about US intentions, and France, Italy, and the Netherlands wavered until the last minute. Unilateral action was an option. But GATT approval lent legitimacy to US actions, whereas action outside of GATT 'presupposes US entirely in wrong on this question'.[58] When the vote was taken, twenty-four members backed the US position, four abstained (Burma, Denmark, Finland, and Indonesia), and only Czechoslovakia voted against.[59] The USA had isolated Czechoslovakia in GATT.

Although early Czech–US skirmishes in GATT brought Cold War tensions to the surface, GATT was not incapacitated by ideological deadlock. After its initial protests, Czechoslovakia rarely acted as the spokesperson for the communist world within GATT councils, aside from its intervention about the waiver for the European Coal and Steel Community (ECSC; see Chapter 3). Trade negotiators recall Czechoslovakia as either quietly committed to GATT or a nominal member.[60]

The communist revolution in China, the Sino-Soviet alliance, and the Korean War shifted US thinking about Japan: rather than focusing on economic restructuring to make it democratic, competitive, productive and peaceful, the US now needed Japan to be a bastion against communism in Asia.[61] But immediately after the war, Japan was occupied and

Summary Record of the Twenty-Sixth Meeting, 26 October 1951, GATT/CP.6/SR.26, WTO; Summary Record of the Fourteenth Meeting, 27 September 1951, GATT/CP.6/SR.14, GDL.

[56] For more details of American lobbying, see *FRUS 1951 Vol. I*, section IV: Termination of Obligations between the United States and Czechoslovakia Under GATT, 1381–1424.

[57] Memorandum by the Assistant Secretary of State for Economic Affairs (Thorp) to the Secretary of State, 11 September 1951, *FRUS 1951 Vol. I*, 1405.

[58] The Acting Secretary of State to the Embassy in the Netherlands, 31 August 1951, *FRUS 1951, Vol. I*, 1394.

[59] The United States (GATT) Delegation to the Secretary of State, 28 September 1951, *FRUS 1951 Vol. I*, 1421.

[60] Author interviews with Warren and Lacarte. Lacarte suggested that Czechoslovakia was under some pressure from Moscow, but he did not know how that worked. Wyndham White subsequently said that Czechoslovakia was 'not really an effective participant' in GATT. Memo from Warren to Bryce, re Proposed Ministerial Trade Conference, 25 September 1962, RG25: 5688/283/14050-3-40 pt. 3, LAC.

[61] M. Schaller, *The American Occupation of Japan: The Origins of the Cold War in Asia* (New York and Toronto: Oxford University Press, 1985), 122–140.

suspect. From an economic perspective, the application of Most Favoured Nation (MFN) treatment to Japan's exports would be likely to accelerate its economic recovery, without which US policy-makers feared Japan might not stay on a democratic path.[62] Japan's economic recovery was even more urgent because ten GATT members discriminated against Japanese exports. US State Department officials feared that ongoing discrimination would 'create the basis for highly dangerous economic and political frictions in the future', possibly alienating Japan as an ally of the west.[63] It was hoped that if Japan joined GATT, such discrimination would cease.

Japan was eager to join GATT. Soon after the final peace treaty with the USA was signed in 1951, the new government in Tokyo requested observer status in GATT, a preliminary step to full membership. Although Washington initially advised the Japanese government to postpone its application until after the 1952 US presidential election,[64] it came out 'openly and strongly in favour of Japanese application'.[65] US officials still feared that unless Japan was admitted into GATT and had access to global markets, Tokyo might be compelled to 're-orient their trade toward Communist China and the Soviet bloc'.[66] Because trade contact was seen as a slippery slope to political alignment, Japanese trade with communist countries could make it susceptible to communist control.

US officials insisted that continued Japanese exclusion was 'no longer fair, practical or wise'.[67] But other GATT members believed that Japan competed unfairly in world trade. Britain was particularly anxious about Japanese competition, especially with their textile producers, and cited price-cutting and low labour costs as two unfair practices. British officials understood that excluding Japan from GATT could have detrimental political consequences such as the possible collapse of the first post-occupation government in Japan, which might result in 'a return to the former evils of cut-throat competition and other malpractices'.[68] France

---

[62] Secretary of State to Certain Diplomatic Missions, 11 February 1949, *FRUS 1949, Vol. I*, 657; A. Forsberg, 'The Politics of GATT Expansion: Japanese Accession and the Domestic Political Context in Japan and the United States, 1948–1955', *Business and Economic History*, 27 (1) (Fall 1998), 185.

[63] The Department of State to the British Embassy, attachment, The Acting Secretary of State to the Embassy in the United Kingdom, 16 June 1949, *FRUS 1949 Vol. I*, 694.

[64] Tokyo to Foreign Office, Tel. No. 1079, 26 February 1952, FO371/98985, TNA.

[65] Washington to Foreign Office, tel. 1491, 6 August 1952, FO371/98985, TNA; Draft memo, 'Japan and the G.A.T.T.', January 1953, FO371/105031, TNA.

[66] Memorandum by the Chairman of the Interdepartmental Committee on Trade Agreements (Corse) to the President, 20 August 1952, *FRUS 1952–1954, Vol. I*, 116.

[67] Summary Record of the Sixth Meeting, 23 September 1953, S.R.8/6, GDL.

[68] Tokyo to Foreign Office, tel. 89, 27 January 1953, FO371/105031, TNA.

also worried about competing with Japanese-manufactured products at home and in its overseas territories. They attributed Japan's high competitiveness to the low standard of living and low wages of Japanese workers: 'elle repose sur des bases malsaines, elle résulte de la misère d'un peuple et non d'une meilleure productivité'. This was a conveniently one-sided logic. The possible disastrous implications of Japanese admission were laid out. France would impose restrictions on Japanese imports, and these would have to apply to all members to fulfil the GATT rule on non-discrimination. Members would then retaliate.[69] Countries such as Belgium and the Netherlands also had concerns about Japanese export competition and commercial practices, but they supported Japan's application. As Belgian policy-makers saw it, 'Continued exclusion of Japan would be bad propaganda and contrary to policy of her reintegration in free world.'[70]

Win Brown, US assistant secretary for economic affairs, appealed to the British in 1953. Excluding Japan from GATT and discriminating against its exports contradicted 'our general political aims of welcoming Japan into this general comity of nations'.[71] This had some effect on British policy-makers. When a group of Conservative members of parliament from Lancashire constituencies lobbied Peter Thorneycroft, the president of the board of trade, to enforce British discrimination against Japan, Thorneycroft advised them to take into account international factors 'such as the desirability of keeping Japan out of the Soviet orbit'.[72] Rab Butler, chancellor of the exchequer, agreed that 'it is essential that Japan should remain in the Western camp. We can hardly therefore seek to delay her accession to G.A.T.T. indefinitely, and there seems no point in trying to put it off for another year'.[73] Consideration of the health of the Anglo-American relationship helped to shift the British position.[74]

[69] Note: Accession du Japon au Gatt, 22 octobre 1954, MAEF000068, reel 158, Papers of Olivier Wormser, HAEU.

[70] Canadian Ambassador, Brussels, to Secretary of State for External Affairs, tel. 222, 11 September 1953, RG25: Vol. 6511/9100-P-10–40, pt. 2.1, LAC; Canadian chargé d'affaires A.I., The Hague, Netherlands, to Secretary of State for External Affairs, 'Dutch Views on Japan's Admission to G.A.T.T.', 31 August 1953, RG25: Vol. 6511/9100-P-10–40 pt. 2.1, LAC.

[71] Record of Conversation between J. E. Coulson and Winthrop Brown, 14 January 1953, FO371/105031, TNA.

[72] 'The Cotton Industry and Japan and India', Note of a meeting, 29 July 1954, BT64/4929, TNA.

[73] 'Review of the General Agreement on Tariffs and Trade', Memorandum by the Chancellor of the Exchequer, July 1954, CAB21/3850, TNA.

[74] 'Japan and the G.A.T.T.', letter from Frank Lee, Board of Trade, to Sir Edward Bridges, Treasury, 16 December 1954, CAB21/3850, TNA.

In 1955, Japan joined GATT with unanimous support. However, Britain, France, and twelve other members invoked Article XXXV, the non-application provision, which permitted them to withhold MFN treatment.[75] As a result, Japan did not receive the full array of commercial benefits that usually went along with GATT membership. This was seen as a disappointment in Japan, where it was more important to sell their goods in foreign markets than to be reintegrated into the so-called family of nations.[76] Japan's representative expressed astonishment at the number of reservations.[77] But from a US point of view, Japan was now more securely anchored to the western alliance.

Institutional Insecurity: Overtures to Poland, Romania, and Hungary, 1953–1959

In the first phase of the Cold War, the United States had accepted that the satellites of the Soviet Union were 'lost to west'. According to the US chargé in Moscow, trying to wrest them free was 'wishful thinking'.[78] This was consistent with the US doctrine of containment, famously articulated by George Kennan. But the Eisenhower administration, elected in 1952, reconsidered Cold War tactics. International trade was implicated in this reassessment. US strategists remained convinced that global trade could fortify the economic health of the free world and reinforce the political and military pillars of the western alliance.[79] Establishing commercial contact with Soviet bloc members might help 'break their economic dependency on Moscow'.[80] The possible geopolitical reorientation of Soviet bloc members seemed much less far-fetched following the ascendancy of Nikita Khrushchev in the Soviet Union. In 1956, Khrushchev denounced Stalin's brutal leadership. Khrushchev's

---

[75] Article XXXV read: 'This Agreement . . . shall not apply as between any contracting party and any other contracting party if: a) the two contracting parties have not entered into tariff negotiations with each other, and b) either of the contracting parties, at the time either becomes a contracting party, does not consent to such application.'

[76] H. Takeda, author of Part III', *Attainment of Economic Self-Support* in M. Sumiya (ed.), *A History of Japanese Trade and Industry Policy* (Oxford: Oxford University Press, 2000), 345. As Takeda explains: 'Japan viewed GATT membership more as a necessary step towards realizing the goal of export promotion than as the fulfillment of the admittedly important goal of being recognized as a formal member of the international economic community.'

[77] Note: Accession du Japon, Point 21 de l'ordre du jour, 5 octobre 1955, MEAF000068, Papers of Olivier Wormser, reel 158, HAEU.

[78] The chargé in the Soviet Union (Kohler) to Secretary of State, 27 January 1949, *FRUS Vol. V*, 3.

[79] 'Foreign Economic Policy and the Trade Agreements Program', September 1957, *FRUS 1955–1957, Vol. IX*, 61.

[80] Jackson, *Economic Cold War*, 115.

proposal to relax Soviet control was meant to strengthen the connections between Moscow and the satellites by making such connections voluntary and mutually beneficial. But it sparked restiveness; the eastern alliance seemed suddenly looser.[81] Khrushchev also shifted the aims of Soviet production from heavy to light industry and to economic competition with other states. As Sanchez-Sibony explains, Khrushchev saw integration in the global economy and access to foreign markets as ways to strengthen the Soviet Union.[82]

The Soviet pursuit of economic integration was diverted by ongoing Soviet criticism of GATT. In 1956, after the era of peaceful co-existence had been announced, the Soviet Union denounced GATT in ECOSOC as an elite club of rich, industrialized nations who selfishly pursued their commercial interests without regard for less well-off countries. Soviet representatives called for the creation of a new international trade organization open to all members of the United Nations.[83] The Soviet charge struck at GATT's Achilles heel. Its membership was nowhere near universal or representative of all forms of government. In the ensuing debate, it became clear that GATT had many detractors and few champions. Typical of the discussion was the Yugoslavian remark that although GATT was not 'worthless', it was certainly 'inadequate'.[84] The debate ended with a widely endorsed resolution calling for further study of international trade cooperation. Argentina, Brazil, Czechoslovakia, France, the USSR, and Yugoslavia all sponsored the resolution – representatives from east and west, north and south – revealing a far-reaching dissatisfaction with, and in some cases hostility to, GATT.[85]

Wyndham White, always worried about GATT's well-being, took note of the criticism in ECOSOC. In an evaluation written the same day as the Soviet proposal for a universal trade organization, he noted that problems in east–west trade 'could hardly be ignored by an organization with any serious claim to be considered as responsible for initiating consultations on international trade problems and international negotiations on trade matters'.[86] Because members of GATT maintained that accession was

---

[81] D. S. Painter, *The Cold War: An International History* (London and New York: Routledge, 1999), 37.

[82] Sanchez-Sibony, *Red Glogalization*, 82–85.

[83] 'Measure for the Development of Trade Co-operation', Agenda item 2(a) (XXII), draft resolution by USSR, 18 July 1956, E/C. 734, United Nations [UN].

[84] Summary Record of 206th Meeting of the Economic Committee, ECOSOC, 30 July 1956, E/AC.6/SR. 206, UN.

[85] World Economic Situation: Measures for the Development of Trade Co-operation, 28 July 1956, 22nd session, E/AC.6/L.160, UN.

[86] Letter from the Executive Secretary of the General Agreement on Tariffs and Trade (White) to John M. Leddy, 18 July 1956, *FRUS 1955–1957, Vol. IX*, 201.

possible for all countries,[87] the onus was on them to come to terms with centrally planned economies. In 1957, Wyndham White forced GATT members to confront the challenge when the secretariat granted Poland and Romania observer status, a preliminary step to full membership.[88] The next year, Hungary applied for observer status and Yugoslavia, which had been an observer since the early 1950s, applied for associate membership.

Members reassessed the de facto practice of keeping communist countries out of GATT. A decision about their admissibility based on GATT rules and economic objectives should have led to a refusal, even with GATT provisions for state trading countries. How could nations without a tariff structure or a free market join? How could they participate in trade negotiations to lower tariffs? But economic considerations were not the only factors shaping reactions, especially that of the United States. Cold War advantage was also taken into account.[89] For example, NATO assessments of peaceful co-existence suggested that even if the military threat had receded, the economic dimension of the Cold War rivalry 'has become more outspoken and more manifest'.[90] NATO examined economic forms of cooperation as a way to strengthen the western alliance. GATT was identified as one of the international organizations that was carrying out this work. Tariff liberalization enhanced the collective economic strength of the west.[91]

The possible accession of Poland, Hungary, and Romania was especially significant because all were members of the CMEA, established in 1949 to tighten Soviet control over eastern Europe. Although the CMEA had been idle under Stalin, the trade of Soviet bloc countries was overwhelmingly with the Soviet Union and other bloc markets.[92] Under

[87] Committee of Political Advisors, Meeting of the Committee held on 5 August 1958, Action Sheet, AC/119- R (58) 24, NATO digital archives. http://archives.nato.int/

[88] T.N. (57) 23, Trade Negotiations Committee, Request for Association with the G.A.T.T.: Poland, 2 October 1957, BT11/5628, TNA.

[89] Haus, *Globalizing the GATT*, 6.

[90] Long-Term Planning: Report by the Council in Permanent Session: Part II: The Competence and Objectives of NATO in the Economic Field, 28 April 1961, C-M (61) 30, Part II, NATO digital archives.

[91] Survey of Article 2 Activities. Prepared by the International Staff, 12 April 1956, C-M (56)45, NATO Archives Online, accessed 8 May 2018, http://archives.nato.int/survey-of-article-2-activities. See also Committee of Three, Preliminary Working Paper, Political Cooperation, 6 September 1956, CT-WP/4.

[92] In the 1950s, approximately 60 per cent of Hungary's exports flowed to five main communist bloc trading partners: Czechoslovakia, East Germany, Poland, Romania, and the Soviet Union. Of the five, exports to the Soviet Union far outweighed the others. Hungary had a small trade with some western countries like West Germany and Austria. Poland had a more diversified trade, consistently selling approximately 10 per cent of its exports to Britain and the United States. However, these western markets did not

Khrushchev, Soviet interest in the CMEA revived in the hope that stronger and mutually beneficial economic links would reinforce the socialist world. At a plenary meeting of the CMEA in 1957, long-term coordinated plans were laid out to increase specialization and technological expertise while deepening economic dependence on the Soviet Union.[93] This use of trade to strengthen the Soviet alliance met with some resistance. Joining GATT appealed to many Soviet bloc countries.

Poland's application to GATT was a crucial test case. At this time, Poland was pressing Moscow to develop a national form of socialism which would strengthen local authority and state autonomy. The Soviet Union agreed in exchange for Polish membership in the Warsaw Pact. Still, Poland's eastern alignment seemed fluid. As a US report noted, membership in GATT might 'provide a bridge to facilitate the western orientation of iron-curtain countries'.[94] Polish officials encouraged this line of thinking, explaining that 'The main significance of her joining was political as would be the significance of her being refused admission.'[95] Canadian officials agreed that there were 'political advantages in encouraging the association of Poland with Western oriented institutions such as GATT'.[96] But British and French officials were worried that Polish membership might set a precedent for the admission of other Soviet bloc countries, even the Soviet Union.[97] More communist members might transform GATT's 'relatively practical discussions about the administration of the provisions of an international treaty' into 'polemical debates'.[98] Wyndham White consulted the NATO secretariat about Polish accession. NATO was also concerned that Poland and

---

improve their relative importance over the course of the decade. B. R. Mitchell, *International Historical Statistics, Europe 1750–1988* (Basingstoke: Palgrave; New York: Stockton, 1992).

[93] Z. Brzezinski, *The Soviet Bloc: Unity and Conflict* (New York: Praeger, 1961, 1965), 286–288; Z. M. Fallenbuchl, 'The Council for Mutual Economic Assistance and Eastern Europe', *International Journal* 43 (Winter 1987/8), 108.

[94] 'Significance of the GATT Intersessional Committee Meeting, April 14 – May 2, 1958', RG59: Records of Component Offices of the Bureau of Economic Affairs, 1941–1963/ Box 4, file 4.3: Common Market-GATT Intersessional (Incoming Telegrams) (1958), NARA.

[95] Minute sheet, R.B. Tippets, 21 May 1958, BT11/5628, TNA.

[96] Instructions for the Canadian delegation to the 13th session of GATT, 16 September 1958, RG20: vol. 1922/20–28 pt. 7, LAC.

[97] Minute sheet, minute by C.W. Jardine, 11 June 1958, BT11/5628, TNA. Note introductive: Admission de la Pologne au GATT – Attitude coordonnée des Six, 25 juillet 1959, BAC26/1969–510/2, HAEU.

[98] 'Proposal for the Accession of Poland to the G.A.T.T.', draft brief, 14 April 1958, T.N. (58) 10, BT11/5628, TNA.

Czechoslovakia might constitute a communist critical mass in GATT and 'take a different attitude in the future'.[99]

Wyndham White believed that the US stand on Poland would be decisive. But according to Canadian officials, US leadership in GATT was at a low point and the Congressional stance on Polish accession to GATT was 'chilly'.[100] As a Canadian official put it in a discussion with Wyndham White, 'The virtue of U.S. influence seemed to have gone out of the field of trade.'[101] The British also complained of not being able to count on US leadership 'either in excluding the Poles or insisting on some form of second-class membership'. Although one might have expected Czechoslovakia to support Poland's application, in fact, like the majority of GATT members, it wanted to move slowly and keep discussions 'private and informal until minds are made up'.[102]

Poland enjoyed the support and advice of Wyndham White. He cautioned Polish officials that full membership was unlikely 'because of the fundamental differences between the economic system of Poland and that of other GATT members'.[103] He advised against a formal application for membership until Poland could be sure of a positive outcome. He also lobbied other GATT members, emphasizing Cold War considerations, such as 'greater independence of the Soviet Union and ... new ties with the West'.[104] Although Wyndham White did not envision GATT as a NATO-type organization, a Canadian official explained that he 'hopes that NATO countries would look at the GATT programme against a broader background of East–West relations'.[105] Wyndham White used the Cold War environment to strengthen GATT's institutional legitimacy.

But commercial considerations in relation to accession were problematic. The GATT practice was for new members to make tariff

[99] Committee of Political Advisers Approach by Poland to Become Member of GATT, 4 August 1958, NATO Confidential W.P., AC/119-WP (58) 64, RG20: vol. 1922/20–28 pt. 7, LAC.

[100] Brussels to External, 11 April 1958, RG25: Vol. 7976/14051–1-40 pt. 1.1, LAC.

[101] Meeting of the Interdepartmental Committee on External Trade Policy, 21 March 1958, RG25: vol. 7978/248/14051–1-40 pt. 1.1, LAC.

[102] 'Attitudes of Other Governments to Polish Accession', August 1958, BT11/5628, TNA. Some speculated that Czechoslovakia was jealous of its special status as the only communist contracting party and did not want 'other Iron Curtain countries to come in on easy terms'. T.N. (G)(57), 15th meeting, 12th Session, 9 November 1957, Extract, BT11/5628, TNA.

[103] Gatdel Geneva to External, 26 November 1958, RG25: vol. 7978/248/14051–4-40 pt. 1.1, LAC.

[104] Note of a meeting with Eric Wyndham White, Executive Secretary of the G.A.T.T., n.d. [1958], BT11/5628, TNA.

[105] Geneva to Department of External Affairs, 12 February 1959, RG25: Vol. 7978/14051–4-40 pt. 1.1, LAC.

concessions as an entrance fee in exchange for the commercial benefits that would flow to them through the MFN principle. Poland could only guarantee import quotas for western products. This was not a significant concession. Moreover, Poland had no intention of reforming its economy to better cohere with GATT.[106]

Britain strongly resisted full membership for Poland even though it extended MFN treatment to Poland at the time. Its officials pointed out that Poland could not uphold the rules of GATT and it could not make tariff concessions because it had no tariffs. Admission with a lower standard of expectation was unfair to other members 'who have accepted fairly precise commitments under an international treaty'.[107] Polish promises to buy more imports from GATT members, and to be guided by liberal economic principles such as the cheapest source of supply, were wishful at best, delusional at worst. As Muriel Seaman, a British Board of Trade official, astutely pointed out, GATT existed precisely because there was no trust where trade was concerned: 'That is the whole point about tariff bindings and rules about discriminatory import charges, etc. The Poles can hardly expect GATT members to be willing to take a new member on trust in matters on which they don't have to trust each other already.'[108]

British officials at the Board of Trade also rejected geopolitical arguments in relation to Polish admission. First, they denied that association with GATT would bring about a diplomatic realignment, particularly because Khrushchev's intention to use the CMEA to create 'an integrated economic empire' was moving forward and Poland's 'freedom of manoeuvre' seemed restricted as it now required the permission of the CMEA to import western products.[109] Second, Poland's admission could be detrimental to GATT, setting a precedent for the admission of other communist countries and transforming GATT from a practical organization into a political one, an assessment that upheld the fiction of GATT being a technical organization.

The British Foreign Office agreed with the Board of Trade's assessment. Its officials doubted that accession would weaken ties with the Soviet Union, whereas GATT would almost certainly suffer if communist countries became members.[110] The Foreign Office did not want Britain

[106] Haus, *Globalizing the GATT*, 27.
[107] Minute by C. W. Jardine, 11 June 1958, BT11/5628, TNA.
[108] Minute by Muriel Seaman, 'Poland and the G.A.T.T.', 16 May 1958, BT11/5628, TNA.
[109] 'Proposal for Polish accession to G.A.T.T.', 26 June 1958, BT11/5628, TNA.
[110] D. N. Royce to P. C. Petrie, UK delegation to NATO, Paris, 8 September 1958, FO371/133210, TNA.

to stand out as the main obstacle to Polish accession, but Britain's position had already attracted criticism. Indian officials thought they were being 'unduly negative' about Polish accession.[111] Christopher Jardine of the Board of Trade admitted that Britain was 'much distrusted on this issue' and Wyndham White was fuming.[112] Instead of calling for rejection, the British proposed a second-class category of membership, 'a half-way house', neither in nor out, and certainly not prejudicial to British commercial interests.[113]

Not wanting to stand alone, Britain brought together GATT members opposing accession for Poland, including the Netherlands, Norway, South Africa, and West Germany. London hoped to win more allies from the Commonwealth and Scandinavia, in which case 'the U.S. will be pretty isolated and one may yet hope for a sensible outcome'.[114] At an informal meeting of representatives from fifteen countries organized by the British delegation in May 1959, a consensus emerged around association short of full membership, supported by officials from Austria, Denmark, Italy, Malaya, New Zealand, South Africa, Sweden, and Switzerland. The Canadian representative alone expressed doubt. He noted that Canada effectively treated Polish trade according to GATT terms 'and had not found that this gave rise to any special problems'.[115]

W. T. Beale, the US representative, admitted that the USA 'favoured the development of closer trading relations with Poland and had been moving in this direction for the last 2 or 3 years' (see Figure 2.1). He deferred to the majority opinion in favour of limited association, although he wanted a decision that would be acceptable to Poland and would strengthen GATT.[116] In effect, the USA's stance was non-committal on Poland. Because GATT members' positions ranged from opposition to accommodation, the British compromise found favour, neither shutting Poland out nor letting it in. When Poland forced the issue by applying for membership in 1959, members created a new category of 'associate state' with partial access to GATT forums but without commercial privileges; this came into effect in 1960.

[111] Note from F. G. Lee to Mr. Sanders, 'Poland and the GATT', n.d., FO371/133210, TNA.

[112] Letter, C. W. Jardine, UK delegation, Geneva, to C.W. Sanders, CRE department, Board of Trade, 8 November 1958, FO371/133212, TNA.

[113] Draft paper: Proposal for the Accession of Poland to G.A.T.T., July 1958, FO371/133210, TNA; see also letter from David Ormsby-Gore to Sir David Eccles, President, Board of Trade, 27 October 1958, FO371/133211, TNA.

[114] Letter from C.W. Sanders, Board of Trade, to D. Royce, Foreign Office, 4 March 1959, FO371/141146, TNA.

[115] Polish application for accession to the G.A.T.T. Note of a meeting held in the Hotel Beau Rivage, 21 May 1959, FO371/141145, TNA.

[116] Polish application for accession to the G.A.T.T.

Exports

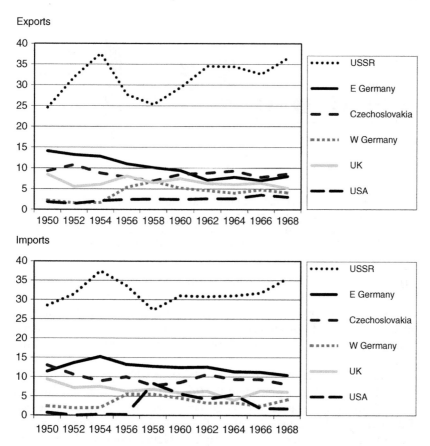

Figure 2.1 Poland's trade with principal partners, 1950–1968: exports
and imports (per cent of total)
Source: B. R. Mitchell, *International Historical Statistics, Europe
1750–1988* (Basingstoke: Palgrave; New York: Stockton, 1992).

At the same time that members were debating Poland's admission, they
were also considering Yugoslavia's request to become an associate member. Because Yugoslavia was a non-aligned communist state, its case was
different from Poland's. The USA was eager to establish ties with
Belgrade and had earlier sent it money for aid and weapons. Yugoslavia
also had significant trade relationships with several contracting parties,
including Britain, Italy, the United States, and West Germany (see
Figure 2.2). Yugoslavia's accession would go some way to refuting Soviet

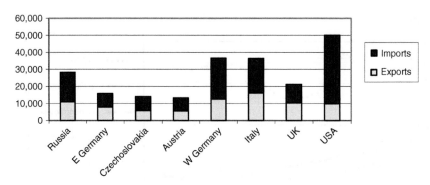

Figure 2.2 Yugoslavia's imports and exports with principal trading partners, 1958 (in million dinars)
Source: B. R. Mitchell, *International Historical Statistics: Europe, 1750–1988* (Basingstoke: Palgrave; New York: Stockton, 1992).

criticism about GATT's exclusive membership. Its accession was therefore 'consistent with our policy of endeavouring to increase the scope and prestige of the GATT as the principal forum for international trade problems'.[117] Washington was not alone in backing Yugoslavia's accession; Austria, France, Greece, and India did too.

Britain was less enthusiastic, in part because whatever was decided for Yugoslavia would set a precedent for Poland. Because they did not want Poland in, their stance on Yugoslavia had to be more reserved. Furthermore, the British Board of Trade doubted that Yugoslavia was becoming 'a free enterprise economy'.[118] Nenad Popovic, Yugoslavia's undersecretary of trade, lambasted British diplomats. According to Popovic, Britain's stand was 'a depressing demonstration of the ineptitude of British "Economic Diplomacy", which was, as usual, making hay of Britain's political interests'.[119] British officials attached greater weight to economic considerations than the USA did. The difference in emphasis arose because Britain was much more of a trading nation than the

---

[117] Request for Approval of Proposed Position on Yugoslav Request for Association Participation in the GATT, 16 February 1959; Draft Position Paper for United States Delegation to Meeting of Working Party on Relations with Yugoslavia, March 16–20, 1959, 11 February 1959: RG59: Office of the Asst. Legal Adviser for Economic Affairs: Records relating to GATT 1947–1966, Box 23, file Yugoslavia – GATT, NARA.

[118] S. D. Wilks, CRE, Board of Trade, 'The Accession of Yugoslavia and Poland to the G.A.T.T.', 6 February 1959, BT11/4527, TNA.

[119] Letter, T. W. Garvey, British embassy, Belgrade, to D. A. H. Wright, Foreign Office, 22 November 1958, FO371/133212, TNA.

United States.[120] Trade policy was more readily instrumentalized in the service of grand strategy in the USA. In the end, Britain proposed an intermediate position on Yugoslavia,[121] a decision, they insisted, that had 'nothing whatever to do with our political like or dislike of the country'.[122] Yugoslavia was granted provisional associate status in 1959 along slightly more promising lines than Poland. A British commentator explained the difference: Poland enjoyed 'glorified observer status not looking forward to ultimate accession', whereas Yugoslavia enjoyed 'glorified observer status looking forward to accession as a possibility'.[123]

Creating a new category of membership for Poland and Yugoslavia reflected western indecision about whether isolation and containment or contact and engagement was the best way to bring about the defeat of communism. It also revealed diverse and evolving views among members about how to live with the Cold War. France and India were prepared to accept communist states on their own economic terms; Britain, Australia, New Zealand, Germany, and the Scandinavian countries were not willing to make a lopsided agreement that sacrificed their economic interests for the sake of political considerations. As for the USA, it distinguished between different kinds of communist countries and saw the Soviet bloc as less fixed than in the early days of the Cold War. US commercial diplomacy was consistent, however, in seeing trade as a useful tool to achieve desirable diplomatic outcomes.

The diversity of views among members of the western alliance was also apparent when Hungary applied for observer status in 1958. Only two years after the Hungarian revolution had been crushed, the Eisenhower administration was not willing to extend any benefits or recognition to the communist regime in Budapest. Hungary's application nonetheless required delicate handling because GATT had never before declined a request for observer status. Moreover, Yemen had made a similar request which it was expected would be granted even though Yemen was not in an economic position to implement all GATT principles.[124] Turning Hungary away would confirm that GATT discriminated against

---

[120] The value of British international trade ranged from 35 per cent to 40 per cent of GDP in the 1950s compared to roughly 7 per cent for the United States.

[121] Letter, H. B. C. Keeble, Foreign Office, to C. S. Sanders, Board of Trade, 30 April 1959, FO371/141147, TNA.

[122] Minute by C. W. Sanders, 11 February 1959, BT11/5704, TNA.

[123] Letter from Sanders to Wilkes, 16 March 1959. Unlike the Polish agreement, the Yugoslavian agreement stipulated that there would be annual meetings at which the possibility of full membership would be considered. Haus, *Globalizing the GATT*, 104–105.

[124] UK delegation, Geneva to Foreign Office, tel. 514, 16 October 1958, FO371/133207, TNA.

communist countries and this would undermine the organization's ability to counter Soviet calls for a new and inclusive world trade organization. As British and French officials observed, the UN had recently rejected the Soviet proposal on the grounds that 'the G.A.T.T. was open to all prepared to accept the obligations of membership. This needs living up to.'[125] Unless Soviet bloc countries were admitted, the GATT could not deny that it was 'un club fermé'.[126] The British Foreign Office suggested that Hungary should be granted observer status through a diplomatic sleight of hand: set up a credentials committee to review the Hungarian request. While it deliberated, Hungary would sit in on GATT sessions as a de facto observer; once the session was over, the credentials committee would announce its decision to reject Hungary's request. But the United States was not interested in softening the blow. As one Foreign Office memo explained, 'The Americans ... wish to continue to express their disapproval of the Hungarian Government in every way possible.'[127] Confronted with determined US opposition, Hungary withdrew its application and denied publicly that 'GATT is an organization open to all'.[128]

Universal Membership: Accession of Communist Countries to GATT, 1960–1968

The challenge of accommodating communist countries with centrally planned economies in GATT did not go away: Poland and Yugoslavia continued to press for full accession. Throughout the 1960s, their requests continued to be entangled in Cold War considerations, made more complex by the emergence of a non-aligned movement, some of whose leading members – such as Egypt – also sought entry into GATT. Their applications were linked. There was no justification for denying Egypt provisional accession to GATT. But according to Wyndham White, if Egypt was admitted, then it would not be possible to continue to hold Yugoslavia back. Many GATT members agreed with him. Further strengthening Yugoslavia's bid was Belgrade's recent introduction of economic reforms, such as a single exchange rate and a provisional

---

[125] 'Application by Hungary for Observer Status at G.A.T.T.', brief prepared by the Northern Department, 20 October 1958, FO371/133207, TNA. Note Introductive: Admission de la Pologne au GATT – Attitude coordonnée des Six, 25 juillet 1959, BAC26/1969–510/2, HAEU.

[126] Note d'information: Problèmes concernant l'admission de la Pologne au GATT, 6 avril 1959, BAC026/1969–510, no. 1, HAEU.

[127] Application by Hungary for Observer Status at G.A.T.T.

[128] Memo from the Executive Secretary, GATT, to Leaders of Delegation to the Thirteenth Session of the Contracting Parties, 24 October 1958, FO371/133207, TNA.

tariff. Such measures demonstrated that it embraced GATT norms and practices. As George Ball, the US undersecretary of state, saw it, Yugoslavia was already moving away from 'the Soviet bloc model' towards 'an intermediate stage in the process of trade liberalization'. US officials interpreted these economic changes as confirmation of a changing political and geopolitical outlook.[129]

British officials were less convinced.[130] However, the political consequences of British opposition were unappealing. As one official explained, opposition to Yugoslavia's accession would 'only attract opprobrium', injure Britain's relations with Yugoslavia, and undermine GATT's efforts 'to represent itself as an organisation which welcomes the non-aligned States'.[131] The value of expanding economic links between Yugoslavia and the west was heightened in light of growing Yugoslavian trade with Soviet bloc countries. Yugoslavia had also begun to send observers to the CMEA in 1962.[132] These developments made GATT more receptive and Yugoslavia moved towards provisional accession. All that was left was to participate in a round of tariff negotiations, and its membership would be complete. This final step occurred during the Kennedy round and Yugoslavia fully acceded in 1966. US diplomatic analyses celebrated Yugoslavian accession because it weakened the hold of the Soviet Union over the communist bloc and tied Yugoslavia 'to the Free World economic system'.[133]

US officials still had high hopes that increased trade contacts would lessen the economic dependence of Soviet bloc countries on the Soviet Union, possibly leading to a '"mellowing" of communism' in the belief that '"fat Russians" would lose their revolutionary fervor'.[134] The changed perspective extended to Poland. At the 1963 GATT ministerial gathering, the Polish vice-minister of foreign trade announced that his country wanted to participate in the upcoming Kennedy round. US

[129] Letter, G. Ball to John W. Byrnes, 28 August 1963, RG59: Records of Undersecretary of State George W. Ball 1961–66, Box 22, file: Yugoslavia, NARA.
[130] Memo, Yugoslavia and G.A.T.T., n.d.; Letter, A. C. McCarthy to S. D. Wilks, Board of Trade, 16 August 1962, both in FO371/164436, TNA.
[131] Geneva, UK delegation to EFTA, to FO, tel. 127, 25 October 1962, BT241/678, TNA.
[132] Foreign Office, no. 116 Intel, 'Yugoslavia and the C.M.E.A.', 9 October 1964, BT241/679, TNA.
[133] Memo from Anthony M. Solomon to Secretary, n.d., RG59: Office of the Assistant Legal Adviser for Economic Affairs, Records re Trade and GATT, 1947–66, Box 24, file: GATT – Underdeveloped Countries re Com III, NARA.
[134] Thomas L. Hughes to the Secretary, 16 July 1963, Memo: Trade Expansion as a Potential Lever in US Relations with the USSR and Eastern Europe, RG59: Bureau of European Affairs, Office of Soviet Union Affairs, Economic Affairs Section, US–Soviet Trade Relations, Economic Subject files, Box 2, file A12, Trade Policy 1961–63, NARA.

officials reasoned that closer association between Poland and GATT would align Poland more closely with the west. Gradual adherence to GATT rules and standards would prompt internal reforms that would corrode communist structures and practices.[135] Joining GATT repositioned Cold War blocs by 'building bridges of increased trade, ideas etc. to Eastern Europe'.[136] The time was ripe to seize opportunities with respect to the Soviet bloc countries 'to increase US influence, to erode the Communist system by exposure to Western ideas and institutions and to break down the strength and unity of international communism'.[137] The US press also proclaimed the geopolitical advantages of Polish membership in GATT. It would expose Polish consumers to foreign advertising, free-world products, and the values they represented. As Bernard Nossiter of the *Washington Post* explained it, '"Drink Coca-Cola" signs may some day blossom along Warsaw's Cracow Boulevard.' Such commercial opportunities, he hoped, would 'open up the Polish economy, and presumably Polish life, to much stronger Western influences'.[138] Coca-Cola was a powerful Cold War symbol of entrepreneurship, democracy, and prosperity: it embodied American values and the American way of life. Consuming Coca-Cola would spread American ideas and values.[139] The geopolitical benefits of such a strategy would be gradual, but in the Cold War it was the long run that mattered.

Wyndham White also wanted Poland to join. Even with the onset of détente, there was no sense that the Cold War would end any time soon. To be credible as *the* international body regulating trade, GATT had to make room for communist countries. Wyndham White also pressed the geopolitical argument that Polish ties to the Soviet Union would weaken if Poland joined GATT, an argument he believed was even more urgent

---

[135] US Relations with Eastern Europe: 5. Problems of Multilateral Association: The General Agreement on Tariffs and Trade, 16 July 1964, RG59: Bureau of European Affairs, Records re Poland 1957–66, Box 1, file FT (Free World), NARA.

[136] Telegram, Washington to US Mission Geneva GATT, 26 June 1964, RG59: Bureau of European Affairs, Records re Poland 1957–66, Box 1, file FT (Free World), NARA.

[137] US Policy Towards Poland and Yugoslavia, 5 April 1963, RG59: Bureau of European Affairs, Records re Poland 1957–66, Box 1, file FT (Free World), NARA.

[138] B. D. Nossiter, 'Poles Make Western Trade Bid', *Washington Post*, 19 June 1964, A21.

[139] There are many works that examine the spread of American commercial influence. They are not simply accounts of cultural capitulation, but also of resistance, adaptation and appropriation. V. de Grazia, *Irresistible Empire: America's Advance Through 20th-Century Europe* (Cambridge, MA: Belknap Press of Harvard University Press, 2005); R. Wagnleitner, *Coca-Colonization and the Cold War: The Cultural Mission of the United States in Austria after the Second World War*, translated by D. M. Wolf (Chapel Hill and London: University of North Carolina Press, 1994); J. R. Schutts, 'Born Again in the Gospel of Refreshment? Coca-Colonization and the Re-making of Postwar German Identity' in D. F. Crew (ed.), *Consuming Germany in the Cold War* (Oxford and New York: Berg, 2003), 121–150.

now because it was known that the Soviet Union and other CMEA countries had not responded favourably to Poland's request to participate in the Kennedy round. Poland's initiative was 'inconsistent with the attitude of the Soviet Union to GATT as a perverse institution marked down for destruction'.[140]

Canada, Australia, and Sweden were persuaded by geopolitical arguments to support Poland's bid for accession. British trade officials still needed convincing. Their main objection was that Polish accession would be 'embarrassing to us in the commercial field'. Britain already extended MFN benefits to many Polish goods, but they also wanted to preserve the ability to impose quotas against Polish products 'should we consider this necessary at any time'.[141] They justified their opposition in terms of upholding GATT norms and standards. New members such as Poland should be 'Gattworthy'. The British Board of Trade recognized that its position was at odds with the views of most members: 'The overwhelming feeling is ... that the Contracting parties have a fleeting chance to make a dent in relations with COMECON [CMEA] countries.'[142] M. J. Lackey, a British official with extensive experience at GATT, reported drily from Geneva that national representatives were 'dazzled by the political advantages prophesied by Eric Wyndham White'.[143] British assessments dismissed this argument as 'possibly somewhat melodramatic'.[144]

A split now arose between the British Board of Trade and the Foreign Office. The Foreign Office set out to 'reverse' British policy on Poland's accession.[145] Foreign Office pressure, in conjunction with fear of standing out as singularly obstructionist, brought the Board of Trade round. As William Hughes wrote, 'We should drop our doctrinaire opposition to admitting Communist countries to the G.A.T.T. and should welcome in principle the accession of Poland.'[146]

Now the challenge was to determine Poland's admission price. In the end, Poland agreed to increase its imports from GATT members by 7 per cent. British members of the Board of Trade were not impressed.

[140] Geneva, UK delegation to GATT, to FO, tel 18 saving, 7 February 1964, FO371/178098, TNA.
[141] FO to Geneva, tel. 152, 17 April 1964, FO371/178098, TNA.
[142] Geneva, UK delegation to GATT, to FO, tel. 81 saving, 26 March 1964, FO371/178098, TNA.
[143] M. J. Lackey, UK Delegation, Geneva, to R. Goldsmith, Board of Trade, 'Poland and the GATT', 8 September 1964, FO371/178098, TNA.
[144] Draft saving telegram to Geneva, 'Poland and the GATT', FO371/178098, TNA. This line was cut from the final version sent out as tel. 80 on 26 March 1964.
[145] Meeting in the Board of Trade, 2 April 1964, 'Poland and the G.A.T.T.', FO371/178098, TNA.
[146] Minute, W. Hughes to C. Jardine, 12 May 1964, BT241/425, TNA.

Nonetheless, Poland made a formal application to join in December 1966 and the process was finalized in 1967.

Hungary, Romania, and Bulgaria were sufficiently encouraged by Polish accession to seek closer association with GATT. Romania entered into secret discussions with Wyndham White in 1964. The Romanian pitch was that membership in GATT was a form of 'revolt' against Soviet efforts to tighten the CMEA.[147] US analysts concluded that it was in their interests to foster Romania's desire for 'national independence and internal liberalization'. If successful, there could be a spillover effect.[148]

Members accepted Romanian accession in principle. But negotiations over Romania's admission price were troubled. Romania offered to balance its imports from and exports to GATT members, an offer that was disappointing (only 5 per cent of its trade was with GATT members) and that raised reasonable doubts about the extent to which Romania would open to international trade.[149] As a British report noted, 'G.A.T.T. was a commercial treaty, not a charitable organisation.'[150] Romania also wanted the EEC to remove the quantitative restrictions that it applied to their products. EEC members were reluctant to do so, fearing market disruption as a result of low-cost imports.[151] Support for Romania's accession had also waned slightly as GATT members realized that the communist countries were more interested in receiving benefits than in extending concessions – though this was true of all GATT members.[152] Over the next three years, they wrestled with Romania's admission price. Romania was prepared to promise to use all of its convertible reserves to purchase goods from GATT members; in return it wanted MFN treatment and the gradual lifting of discriminatory quotas against its exports.[153] Romanian accession was finalized in 1971.[154]

Hungary and Bulgaria were up next. They were granted observer status in 1966 and 1967 respectively and began to move towards full accession. The USA now welcomed the Hungarian request for membership, even

[147] Note of conversation with Mr. Wyndham White, 26 June 1964, BT241/426, TNA.
[148] Memorandum for Mr. McGeorge Bundy, The White House, re NSAM 333: Follow-up on the Miller Report, draft, 6/2/65, RG59: Office of the Assistant Legal Adviser for Economic Affairs, Records relating to GATT 1947–66, Box 28, file: Trade – East-West Statute, NARA.
[149] Accession of Romania to GATT, n.d., RG19: F-2/5654/8714–24-12 pt. 1, LAC.
[150] Draft letter to Mr. Buxton, Geneva, n.d., BT241/1495, TNA.
[151] Accession of Romania to GATT.
[152] K. E. Boyes to H. R. Marshall, UK Mission, 'Rumania: Accession to GATT', 11 March 1969, BT241/1114, TNA.
[153] Letter, Jane D. Russell to M. G. Potter, 'Rumania: Accession to GATT', 30 August 1968, FCO59/296, TNA.
[154] Letter, R. G. Britten, Trade Policy Department, to Mr. Bottomley, 20 April 1971, FCO 69/252, TNA.

though the USA was still prohibited from extending MFN benefits to Hungary.[155] The British attitude was mixed. The Hungarians waved aside British questions about the Soviet attitude towards closer association with GATT. Hungarian officials had informed the Soviet Union of their intention and the Soviet Union had not objected, although it did not see any benefit for itself in GATT. Given its status as a great power, its officials would perceive that membership in international organizations would only serve to 'restrict their freedom of action'.[156] In 1973, Hungary acceded. Bulgaria's case was more complicated as it was bound up with concern about Soviet admission; as a result, it was kept at arm's length for another twenty years.

The Exclusion of Great Communist Powers: the Soviet Union, China, and the End of the Cold War

Although the 1970s was a period of détente in the Cold War, it marked the beginning of a period of crisis for GATT. In the twenty-five years following the end of the Second World War, global trade had grown quickly. In this expansive environment trade liberalization had moved steadily forward, particularly in the Kennedy round. But by 1970, the global economy was marked by volatility, inflation, rising unemployment, and slower growth. The jump in the price of oil was at the centre of global economic upheaval. As production costs rose, people lost their jobs. The oil crisis exacerbated inflation, pushing up prices for basic commodities. The interconnected challenges of unemployment, slow growth, and inflation prompted industry, special interest groups, and governments to call for protection. William Roth, the US special trade representative, warned of the danger of protectionism: 'Protectionism is endemic in all countries . . . like many sicknesses [it] is highly contagious.'[157] Some feared that its spread would be 'a profoundly disruptive force in international relations'.[158] It also threatened GATT. Increasing protection could undo the achievements of earlier rounds of trade negotiations and would make it harder to conclude new agreements. The appeals for protection also challenged the legitimacy of liberal trade and undermined the internationalist ethos that sustained support for GATT's mission.

---

[155] Minutes of Council Meeting, 23 July 1969, C/M/56, GDL.

[156] G. E. Millard to C. S. R. Giffard, FCO, 'Hungary, the E.E.C., E.F.T.A. and G.A.T.T.', 14 May 1969, BT241/1495, TNA.

[157] Review of the work of the contracting parties and future programme, Statement by Roth, 23 November 1967, W.24/40, GDL.

[158] H. B. Malmgren, 'Coming Trade Wars? (Neo-Mercantilism and Foreign Policy)', *Foreign Policy* 1 (Winter 1970/71), 120.

The other shock to the global economy was the end of the Bretton Woods system of fixed exchange rates. There had long been strain on the system and some countries had previously devalued their currencies. But the US departure from Bretton Woods in 1971 was the *coup de grâce*. Nixon's sudden announcement that the US dollar was no longer convertible into gold, and that it would float, dismantled pillars of the postwar financial order. Nixon also imposed an across-the-board 10 per cent import surcharge which would reduce imports, correct the US balance of payments, and keep dollars at home. GATT objected to the surcharge, arguing that it was the wrong remedy for the USA's economic difficulties and harmed other countries. As one working party put it, the import surcharge was 'counter-productive in relation to the objective of fostering price stability and increasing export and industrial competitiveness, apart from damaging to the interest of other contracting parties and undermining the world trade system'. The organization would accept the measure as long as it was temporary, but warned that its continued use 'could not but have far-reaching effects on the world economy and international trade'.[159] US foreign economic policy aggravated GATT's institutional insecurity.

As for the Cold War, a period of détente began and inter-bloc rivalry relaxed somewhat. This relaxation informed the terms for the Tokyo round of trade negotiations by making Soviet and Chinese participation possible. The PRC sent observers; the Soviet Union did not. However, this opening did not last. When the Soviet Union requested observer status in 1983 and 1984, they were turned away. This was a difficult stand to take as observer status had been granted automatically to other countries, including Algeria, El Salvador, and Costa Rica. The USA requested a thorough review of the process by which observer status was granted, noting that no criteria existed. The US representative suggested that there should be time limits for observers and that governments of observer countries should be clearer about their intentions in relation to GATT.[160] The EEC also objected to permanent observers or, as they called them, 'voyeurs'.[161]

The Cold War dynamic had also been jolted by the ascendency of Mikhail Gorbachev to the Soviet leadership. He redirected Soviet foreign economic policy, emphasizing global interdependence.[162] As Jonathan

---

[159] Report of the Working Party on United States Temporary Import Surcharge, L/3573, 13 September 1971, GDL.

[160] Council Minutes, 11 July 1984, C/M/180, GDL.

[161] Mayall, 'The Western Alliance, GATT and East-West Trade', 25.

[162] Haslam points out that this new direction did not preclude class struggle. 'The UN and the Soviet Union: New Thinking?' *International Affairs* 65 (4) (Autumn 1989), 678–679.

Haslam explains, the Soviet goal was to become thoroughly enmeshed in 'the available structures of the international system'.[163] That included participation in GATT. At the Soviet party congress in 1986, 'radical economic reform' was endorsed. The goal, according to the Politburo, was 'greater integration of the USSR in the multilateral trade system'. This paved the way for 'a complete turnaround' in relation to GATT. While the Soviet Union had earlier denounced GATT as 'the reincarnation of capitalism', N. V. Checkin, the head of department for International Economic Organizations in the Soviet Ministry of Foreign Trade, now expressed support for its fundamental principles and practices: MFN, non-discrimination, reduction of barriers to trade, and the transparency of trade policies.[164] *The Economist* confessed its surprise at the Soviet request to participate in GATT and called it an 'unlikely would-be participant'. But the move made sense given the Soviet Union's reliance on oil (and other fuel sources) as its main earner of hard currency. The Soviets wanted to diversify their exports, but to do so they needed better terms of access to foreign markets. Hence the appeal of GATT.[165] It asked to participate in the Uruguay round. But in the west, the reaction to Soviet reforms was marked by caution and mistrust and the Soviet request was denied.

Although Bulgaria had participated in the Tokyo round as an observer, there was considerable opposition to its more extensive involvement in GATT because it was 'viewed as a stalking horse for the Soviet Union'.[166] In 1986, when Bulgaria asked to accede to GATT as a developing country, the EEC and USA objected for several reasons: they doubted that Bulgaria would fulfil its obligations and disagreed that Bulgaria should be considered a developing country, which would mean that its burden of obligations would be significantly reduced. More surprisingly, an EEC official denied that membership was open to all: 'the time had passed for the GATT to be a completely open institution'. Other members suggested that a working party should be set up, which was the usual practice. But another GATT practice was to make decisions by consensus. The result was that Bulgaria's application was set aside.[167] It approached the organization again in 1988, noting that its previous policy of 'economic and social development through accelerated industrialization' had failed and it accepted the need for 'radical economic reforms'. It now spoke as

---

[163] Haslam, 'The UN and the Soviet Union', 682–683.
[164] A. Aslund, 'The New Soviet Policy Towards International Economic Organisations', *World Today* 44 (February 1988), 28–30; Haus, *Globalizing the GATT*, 90.
[165] 'Clubland', *The Economist* (29 March 1986), 58.
[166] Haus, *Globalizing the GATT*, 77.
[167] Council Minutes, 27 October 1986, C/M/202, GDL.

a convert to liberal trade, noting the importance of 'efficiency criteria and market instruments' in its economic future.[168] This was consistent with the reforms advocated by the Soviet Union and did not signal rupture with the Soviet bloc. But these overtures also confirmed that Bulgaria had serious economic problems and that access to global markets – even more than access to global supplies – was essential to its economic growth.

With the sudden break-up of the communist bloc and the end of the Cold War in 1989, requests of former communist states to join GATT openly acknowledged the failure of central planning and the triumph of 'the liberal trade ideal'.[169] Latvia and Estonia affirmed the recovery of their independence and repudiated a centrally planned approach to trade. They pledged themselves to reforms, but to do so they required a receptive and supportive international environment.[170] They were not immediately allowed to join GATT. There were studies of their economies and of the extent of their reform, and courses were organized to better acquaint their officials with market economics, suggesting that compliance with GATT's liberal philosophy remained the basic condition. Nonetheless, the end of the Cold War strengthened GATT. Not only was GATT's relevance affirmed 'to every quarter' of the world, as the Brazilian representative noted, but it was central to global reconstruction. He added that post–Cold War global economic adjustment had begun not in the IMF or the World Bank, but in GATT and 'the more matter-of-fact domain of trade'. He praised GATT's long-standing ability to 'face up to new challenges'.[171]

Following the fall of the Berlin Wall and the disintegration of the communist bloc, the Soviet Union again requested observer status. This time it was granted without delay. The Soviet Union's approach was interpreted as a vindication for GATT and liberal trade. As a US official put it, 'The USSR was now taking steps to part with its economic past.' The prosperity that the west had enjoyed since the end of the Second World War was credited with 'the trade liberalization brought about under GATT'. The original conception of GATT was restored and the universal relevance of liberal trade was affirmed. As the EEC

[168] Accession of Bulgaria, Memorandum on Bulgaria's Foreign Trade Regime, 22 June 1988, L/6364, GDL.
[169] S. Dryden, *Trade Warriors: USTR and the American Crusade for Free Trade* (New York: Oxford University Press, 1995), 7.
[170] Accession of Estonia: Memorandum on the Foreign Trade Regime, 28 March 1994, L/7423; Accession of Latvia: Memorandum on the Foreign Trade Regime, 29 August 1994, L/7526. Lithuania's request in 1994 used the same language: it had 'recovered its independence'. Accession of Lithuania: Memorandum on the Foreign Trade Regime, 14 December 1994, L/7551, all in GDL.
[171] Minutes of Meeting, Council, 16 May 1990, C/M/241, GDL.

representative explained, the Soviet Union as an observer had 'brought further support to the universal vocation of the multilateral trading system'. It allowed GATT to finally live up to its commitment to universalism. This in turn revived rhetoric that equated trade with peace and prosperity rather than with security and survival. According to the EEC representative: 'From now on a world of concord, peace and prosperity could be built by all, jointly, through the multilateral trading system. Trade had henceforth acquired the nobility it deserved.'[172] But as with other former communist states, the Soviet request was not fast-tracked. While the political significance of Soviet membership, soon to be Russia, was acknowledged, there were grave concerns about how it would affect the workings of GATT and the global trade system. The response to the Soviet Union's application was cautious, involving close scrutiny of its economic structures and practices, all of which prolonged the process of accession.

At the same time that the Soviet Union and former bloc members were requesting membership in GATT, the PRC also resumed contact with the organization. Since the late 1940s, China had had little contact with GATT, other than to protest the possible granting of observer status to Taiwan.[173] This changed in the early 1980s, following the Sino-American rapprochement, the end of the Cultural Revolution, and the ascendency of Deng Xiaoping. In 1980, China resumed its seat on the ICITO and began to send officials on commercial policy courses at GATT. It also sent representatives to GATT council meetings and meetings of the contracting parties, and it became an official observer in 1982. China's accession seemed a real possibility because it had implemented domestic reforms that introduced elements of a market economy. Its Ministry of Foreign Economic Relations and Trade was established in 1982 and it relaxed control over China's trade, giving importers and exporters more choice. China's trade pattern had been shifting over a long time so that by the mid-1980s, 85 per cent of its exports went to and 90 per cent of its imports came from GATT members.[174] China signaled its support for and de facto compliance with the GATT system when it began to participate in sidebar trade negotiations that fell under GATT's authority. It became

---

[172] Council Minutes, 8 June 1990, C/M/241, GDL.
[173] S. Chan, 'Taiwan's Application to the GATT: A New Urgency with the Conclusion of the Uruguay Round', *Indiana Journal of Global Legal Studies, Symposium: Global Migration and the Future of the Nation-State* 2 (1) (Fall 1994), 278–279. Taiwan had lost its observer status in GATT in 1971.
[174] Jacobson and Oksenberg, *China's Participation in the IMF, the World Bank, and GATT*, 85–86.

a signatory to the Multifibre Arrangement in 1984.[175] Shortly there-
after, the Chinese government officially requested observer status.[176]
GATT members overwhelmingly supported this move in the hope it
would lead to full membership.[177]

In 1986, China applied to resume its membership. There had been
significant preparatory work between Chinese and GATT officials to
facilitate the process of accession. Ake Linden, GATT's legal advisor,
went to China in 1984 and 1985 to explain how the system worked.
In 1986, China's premier Zhao Ziyang invited Arthur Dunkel, director-general of GATT, to China and told him about China's imminent application. Zhao assured Dunkel that China's planned
commodity economy would be compatible with GATT's free market
criteria.[178] In a speech to GATT, China's representative outlined the
many ways in which China conformed to the ideals of the organization. He also expressed concern about the rise of protectionism and
the implications for a liberal trade system, and he endorsed the
Uruguay round.[179]

GATT members were enthusiastic about the possibility of China
becoming a full-fledged member. They believed it would be good for
GATT and for the liberalization of global trade. At a meeting of the
GATT Council in August 1986, officials from Bangladesh, Australia,
and Hungary suggested it would increase GATT's 'authority', 'effectiveness', and 'vitality' and would extend the reach of trade liberalization.
The geopolitical significance of such a development was evident. An EEC
official described it as a 'major political event'. A US official also welcomed the possibility of Chinese membership.[180]

But China's request to join GATT was unusual. Because it had been an
original signatory to the General Agreement, the Chinese government
insisted that GATT members acknowledge that it was resuming its
original seat, rather than acceding anew. This would communicate the

[175] D. Shangming and W. Lei, 'China and GATT' in P. Zhang and R. Huenemann (eds),
China's Foreign Trade (Lantzville, BC, and Halifax, NS: Oolichan Books and Institute
for Research on Public Policy, 1987), 68. Jacobsen and Oksenberg are helpful for the
details of re-engagement, 83–85.

[176] China – Request for Observer Status, 26 October 1984, L/5712, GDL.

[177] Council meetings, 6–8 and 20 November 1984, C/M/183, GDL.

[178] W. Liang, 'China's WTO Negotiating Process and Its Implications', Journal of
Contemporary China 11 (33) (2002), 686.

[179] China – Statement by H. E. Mr. Qian Jiadong, 17 December 1986, SR.42/ST/15, GDL.
This speech conveys the Chinese government's desire for a stable international community. By joining GATT and adhering to GATT norms, it would signal that it would
be 'a "cooperative" member of the international community'. Liang, 'China's WTO
Negotiating Process and Its Implications', 685.

[180] Council Minutes, 4 August 1986, C/M/201, GDL.

illegality of Taiwan's decision to withdraw in 1950.[181] The ongoing
geopolitical tensions of East Asia were playing out in GATT, as they
had in other international organizations. The Chinese government
insisted that China be treated as a developing country, which meant
that it would be allowed to make use of various trade practices to promote
economic development and it would receive more trade concessions than
it gave. Noting the many reforms that had been made in the previous
decade, and the positive effect this was having, Chinese officials nonetheless insisted that China was 'a low-income developing country . . . and
its per capita GDP was still among the lowest in the world'.[182] Despite
general support for China's accession, there were concerns that Chinese
membership would change GATT and global trade, possibly to the disadvantage of current GATT members. As an EEC representative put it,
'Nothing would be the same' once China resumed its seat.[183]

Although political considerations meant that China's request was
viewed positively, by the mid-1980s, economic considerations made
China's accession problematic. Could a 'planned commodity economy'
fit into the GATT system? A working party was set up and over 3,000
questions submitted to the Chinese government. Some questions were
specific, such as whether or not user fees would be levied on planes and
ships arriving in China or whether or not China would adhere to codes on
import licensing, anti-dumping, and subsidies. Others were more structural or administrative, such as wanting to know the percentage of private
and public ownership and the distribution of decision-making authority
at the central and municipal levels of government.[184] The purpose of
these questions was to understand how China's economy worked in order
to ensure that it could comply with GATT practices and rules and that
there would be genuine benefits to all members and to the trade system.
Membership involved rights and obligations, and established members
wanted to be sure that new members would not become free riders or
undermine the mission of GATT. Once the working party set to work,
mistrust of China emerged. As one member of the working party said,
they had to have confidence that Chinese concessions would not be
revoked or undermined by other practices, such as subsidies or pricing.
Members wanted to be sure that they could defend themselves against

[181] Y. Qin, 'China and GATT: Accession Instead of Resumption', *Journal of World Trade* 27
(2) (Spring 1993), 77.
[182] Working Party on China's Status as a Contracting Party. Introduction and General
Statements. Note by the Secretariat. 29 March 1988. Spec (88) 13, GDL.
[183] Council Minutes, 4 March 1987, C/M/207, GDL.
[184] Working Party on China's Status as a Contracting Party: Questions and Replies
Concerning the Memorandum on China's Foreign Trade, L/6270,
27 November 1987, GDL.

any injuries that might result from China's membership. Whether China was resuming its seat or acceding anew was not the main issue for GATT members. China would have to negotiate its way into GATT, as all other members had.[185]

A study of this scale took a long time to complete, and the underlying, and sometimes explicit, anxiety of GATT members dragged out the process over many years. Before they were finished, the Tiananmen Square massacre occurred. This shattered the confidence of many contracting parties about the significance of domestic reforms in China. Significantly, the USA's stance on China's accession reversed. Rather than supporting and facilitating accession, the USA took steps to isolate China. Working-party meetings were either cancelled or ineffectual. Progress came to an abrupt halt.[186] But the reversal was not permanent. By the early 1990s, Chinese officials were once again working hard to find a way in. Membership was important to the Chinese government as 'a tool to break the isolation and a barometer to test its status'.[187] But even though China was determined to become a member, the end of the Cold War removed the earlier political advantage that Chinese membership in GATT would have brought to the USA and the western alliance. Although some GATT members had held out the hope that negotiations over China's accession could be based solely on economic considerations, implying that political considerations would impede progress, in fact geopolitical conditions and priorities had facilitated membership for communist countries as much as it had blocked them. Given that China was 'the last important holdout of the Communist ideology',[188] the potential geopolitical benefits of its accession were no longer overriding. China never acceded to GATT; it finally became a member of the WTO in 2002.

Conclusions

The end of the Cold War occurred at the mid-point of the Uruguay round, the longest, most complex, and most acrimonious of all GATT rounds of negotiations. During the Uruguay round, GATT's weaknesses were exposed, along with growing scepticism about the merits of liberal trade, increasing reluctance of members to fulfil their obligations to the organization, and vocal and well-organized protests about the destructive consequences of globalization. This was not a high point for GATT. And

---

[185] Working Party on China's Status as a Contracting Party.
[186] Liang, 'China's WTO Negotiation Process and Its Implications', 693.
[187] Ibid., 699.   [188] Ibid., 693.

yet the end of the Cold War seemed to vindicate its ideological precepts: that liberal trade was universally relevant and beneficial and that it deepened interdependence that engendered cooperation among states and stabilized the world community. Briefly, GATT and liberal trade were swept up in triumphalist accolades. In fact, the Cold War had transformed and challenged GATT for forty years, raising doubts about its claims of inclusivity and universality. It had become a western-dominated forum and an instrument of the democratic-capitalist cause. By admitting western allies, shutting out communist countries such as China and the Soviet Union, drawing neutral countries closer, and subsequently admitting Soviet bloc allies in an effort to undercut communist solidarity, GATT became a pillar and instrument of the 'free world'.[189] From an institutional perspective, the association of GATT with the western alliance was not unwelcome: it strengthened its purpose and rationale, which was constantly being questioned if not denounced, and the ideological sympathy between members made it easier for them to work together.

The instrumentalization of GATT membership to achieve Cold War objectives revealed how trade could be politicized in service to foreign policy. Of all GATT members, US attitudes towards trade and GATT were most visibly shaped by geopolitical interests. Washington used GATT to fortify the western alliance. The values embedded in liberal trade policies and practices were bedrock principles of capitalism. Freer trade, by making national economies more specialized and efficient through access to resources and markets, would make capitalism, in its many variations, stronger globally. This thinking persisted throughout the Cold War. As Michael Smith, deputy United States trade representative from 1979 to 1988, saw it, GATT was 'an arrow in the Western world's quiver, much like the Marshall Plan became'.[190] But the USA's use of trade policy was only one way to think about foreign economic policy. The British government weighed economic and security considerations more equally and was more inclined to treat them as distinct lines of policy. Even after the British Foreign Office had begun to criticize the narrow or 'academic' approach of the Board of Trade, commercial considerations remained a priority. The clash of priorities and conceptions over trade resulted from different weightings of geopolitical and economic goals, as the British and US cases make clear. Political factors other than those related to the Cold War were also in evidence. In the case of France, priorities focused on European integration and independence from the USA. For other states, such as Japan, the USA's desire to tie

[189] Toye, 'Developing Multilateralism', 284.
[190] Eckes, Jr., *Revisiting U.S. Trade Policy*, 22.

them to the western bloc could be exploited in order to achieve their main aim: access to markets. The relationship between the economic and political content of trade policy varied across GATT members, and it was not only the USA that added international political aims to the trade policy mix.

Discussions about admitting new members to GATT revolved around questions of the compatibility of trade practices with GATT rules and norms. Despite the apparent fidelity to liberal trade, rules were reinterpreted, applied differently, or ignored, in order to ensure that decisions about applications strengthened the security of western bloc countries. On the surface, compliance with rules upheld the liberal internationalist project, but there were ulterior, often unacknowledged, motives that reinforced western centrality and leadership and privileged the interests of some members over others. As a result, the liberal trade order fell short of its promise to work for the good of all. These motives were further obscured because there had to be a commercial justification for any policy or decision in GATT. GATT-speak was coded, and, if taken at face value, it conceals underlying motivations and overarching goals.[191]

The GATT secretariat encouraged communist countries to join in the 1950s and 1960s. Wyndham White needed an answer to the charge that GATT was exclusive, and he used the Cold War to bring more countries into GATT. He prompted and advised communist countries and played up Cold War advantages and disadvantages to offset concerns about their economic suitability. Similarly, Arthur Dunkel made repeated trips to China to encourage China's leadership to request membership. But the secretariat could not impose its will on members, who brought their own interests and concerns to GATT. The secretariat tried to reconcile the competing goals of its members. Sometimes that meant seeking out like-minded countries to support a position. At other times, they sought compromise. But members clearly had multiple positions and interests. Japanese and West German membership was a high priority for US officials; other cases such as Poland, Hungary, or Romania allowed for more give-and-take among members; whether or not to admit China also hinged on the USA's views. Some GATT members followed the USA's lead. Others objected. The USA got its way on some issues, such as West German accession, but faced stiff resistance on others, such as Japan, Poland, and Yugoslavia. All members had the chance to voice their views and did so. They were not silenced, even if they did not prevail. The

---

[191] Haus made this same point about EEC objections to Bulgarian accession. They feared it would establish a precedent for the Soviet Union, but they never said so, instead basing their position 'exclusively on trade policy issues'. Haus, *Globalizing the GATT*, 75.

accession debates show that GATT was an organization with multiple and shifting centres of power.[192]

The Cold War was inescapable in the accession of communist countries to GATT. Subsequent chapters of this book will show that Cold War concerns and priorities seeped into other issues such as the establishment of the EEC and the promotion of development, but also that there were limits to its reach and influence, as the chapters on agriculture and regionalism reveal. Global trade was not simply a tool picked up at will to serve a Cold War initiative or goal. The growth of world trade and the expansion of market opportunities were not sacrificed on the altar of ideology all the time. This was evident when the accession of communist countries was under consideration as well as in the rigorous review that was carried out when former communist countries applied to join. There was no rush to open the doors to GATT if this might destabilize the global trade system. It would be foolish to deny the importance of the Cold War to GATT; it would be wrong to make sense of the entire history of GATT, and other international organizations, only in relation to the Cold War.

[192] Capling contends that American literature exaggerates US involvement and minimizes that of smaller powers. A. Capling, *Australia and the Global Trade System: From Havana to Seattle* (Cambridge: Cambridge University Press, 2001), 3–4. J. L. Gaddis makes a similar point about NATO. Gaddis notes that despite American preponderance of power, it did not impose its will on the organization, but rather worked tirelessly to convince its allies to support American positions. In practice that meant that the USA frequently accommodated and privileged the interests and views of other members, allowing all members to influence the work and development of NATO. *We Now Know: Rethinking Cold War History* (Oxford: Clarendon Press; New York: Oxford University Press, 1997), 200–201.

3   'Take It or Leave It'
The EEC Challenge to GATT

Although the European Economic Community (EEC) became a dominant player in GATT, it was both a constructive and a divisive force, at times strengthening, at other times threatening the authority, even the survival, of the organization.[1] Many historians of European integration have shown how experience within GATT supported the EEC's development as a unified actor and contributed to its rise as a global leader. Pascaline Winand examines how the six founding members of the EEC – 'the Six' – were able to function as a bloc during the Kennedy round negotiations of the 1960s; this was a diplomatic triumph for Europe.[2] Taking this argument further, Piers Ludlow claims that the EEC emerged from the Kennedy round as a 'commercial heavyweight'. His study reflects primarily on the history of European integration, although he makes important contributions to the history of GATT and the question of leadership.[3] Lucia Coppolaro also studies the EEC in the Kennedy round and she concludes that it emerged from the round as a 'world trading power' and 'an equal partner with the United States', and that to this day trade remains 'one of the few fields where the EU is able to speak with a united and powerful voice'.[4] Not everyone agrees that the

---

[1] Some of this material appeared in F. McKenzie, 'The GATT–EEC Collision: The Challenge of Regional Trade Blocs to the General Agreement on Tariffs and Trade, 1950–1967', *International History Review* 32 (2) (June 2010), 229–252, www .tandfonline.com/

[2] P. Winand, *Eisenhower, Kennedy, and the United States of Europe* (Basingstoke: Macmillan, 1993), 359. G. La Barca also examines US–EC relations over twenty years. He focuses on the formulation of national trade policies: *The US, the EC and World Trade From the Kennedy Round to the Start of the Uruguay Round* (London: Bloomsbury Academic, 2016).

[3] N. P. Ludlow, 'The Emergence of a Commercial Heavy-Weight: The Kennedy Round Negotiations and the European Community of the 1960s', *Diplomacy & Statecraft* 18 (2) (July 2007), 351–368.

[4] L. Coppolaro, *The Making of a World Trade Power: The European Economic Community (EEC) in the GATT Kennedy Round Negotiations (1963–1967)* (Farnham: Ashgate, 2013), 1–2. In a more recent study of EEC leadership in GATT, Coppolaro helpfully distinguishes between being a powerful and influential actor and a leader; she describes the EC as a 'reluctant partner' in GATT and emphatically not a leader until the Uruguay Round when it began to act more proactively. L. Coppolaro, 'A Power without Leadership: The

EEC spoke with a single voice on trade. P. H. L. Van den Bossche argues that determining a common trade policy within GATT was a challenge for EEC members, such that 'Controversy and confusion reign with regard to the competence and conduct of the European community in the field of international economic relations.'[5] All of these studies add to our understanding of GATT, but their main contribution is to the study of the EEC.

Histories of GATT pay a lot of attention to the EEC. Five of the Six were original members of GATT (West Germany joined in 1951). Their initial impress on the organization was light, mostly because they were preoccupied with the urgent challenge of postwar recovery. They sent representatives to the Geneva and Havana meetings where they pressed for greater acceptance of regional trade arrangements. Jean Royer, a French delegate who subsequently joined the original GATT secretariat as a special assistant, argued that European 'economic integration' was consistent with and advanced the goals of global trade.[6] Thierry Grosbois and Diane de Bellefroide agree that these early advocates of a European trade bloc saw it as compatible with, rather than an alternative to, a global trade system.[7] The drafters of the General Agreement agreed, and customs unions and free trade areas were permissible under Article XXIV, although GATT was to have oversight to ensure that regional agreements 'do not deteriorate into new discriminatory preferential regimes'.[8]

The EEC rightly figures centrally in studies of the Dillon, Kennedy, Tokyo, and Uruguay rounds of negotiations in relation to agriculture, development, subsidies, regional trade blocs, and the leadership and governance of GATT. US–EEC negotiations are generally regarded as the key negotiations in these rounds and it was the resolution of their differences – such as over steel and chemicals in the Kennedy round or

EC in the GATT Trade Regime', in U. Krotz, K. K. Patel, and F. Romero (eds.), *Europe's Cold War Relations: The EC Towards a Global Role* (Cambridge: Bloomsbury Academic, 2019), 127–144.

[5] P. H. L. Van den Bossche, 'The European Community and the Uruguay Round Agreements' in J. H. Jackson and A. O. Sykes (eds.), *Implementing the Uruguay Round* (Oxford: Clarendon; New York: Oxford University Press, 1997), 23.

[6] Third Committee: Commercial Policy. Summary Record of the 44th Meeting, Havana, Cuba, 11 March 1948. E/Conf.2/SR.44, 13 March 1948, GDL.

[7] T. Grosbois, 'La Belgique et le Benelux: De l'universalisme au régionalisme' in M. Dumoulin, G. Duchenne and A. Van Laer (eds.), *La Belgique, les petits états et la construction européenne* (Bern: Peter Land, 2004), 91; D. de Bellefroide, 'The Commission pour l'étude des problèmes d'après-guerre (CEPAG), 1941–1944' in M. Conway and J. Gotovitch, eds, *Europe in Exile: European Exile Communities in Britain, 1940–1945* (New York and Oxford: Berghan Books, 2001), 130.

[8] Report of the Canadian Delegation to the UN Conference on Trade and Employment at Havana, published in M. Hart, *Also Present at the Creation: Dana Wilgress and the United Nations Conference on Trade and Employment at Havana* (Ottawa: Centre for Trade Policy and Law, 1995), 118.

agricultural subsidies in the Uruguay round – that determined the success of the rounds. Like scholars of European integration, GATT scholars ask when and with what effect the EEC emerged as a leader in the organization.[9] Scholars also assess the EEC's contribution to trade liberalization. The EEC was a magnet for critics, who claimed it was protectionist, obstructionist, and narrowly committed to its interests, especially in relation to agriculture and development. But other historians have judged the EEC role to be more constructive and credit it with pushing liberalization forward by encouraging across-the-board tariff reductions in the Kennedy round, taking up the mantle of leadership during the Uruguay round, and supporting the creation of the WTO.

This chapter examines the ways in which the EEC emerged and acted as a leader in GATT and assesses the EEC's contribution to trade liberalization and the overall mission and function of the organization. Several questions emerge from studies of the EEC's involvement in GATT. First, did regional trade blocs complement or undermine GATT? Second, was GATT the creature of national members or could it act independently to fulfil its mission? Third, how did members reconcile individual interests and national sovereignty with their obligations to the organization and global well-being? The answers reveal why members valued GATT, their understanding of what membership involved, and the extent of their support for a liberal trade system.

Most of the chapters in this book follow a theme from the establishment of GATT following the Second World War to its absorption into the WTO in 1995. This chapter ends in the late 1960s, by which time the EEC had established itself as a unified actor and powerful force within GATT. However, the story of the EEC does not end here. As an influential member of GATT, it figures prominently in every chapter and on all major issues. The theme of regionalism does not end here either. It continues into Chapter 4, picking up the story in the 1970s and carrying through to the 1990s. The EEC story continues too in Chapter 4, because it was actively involved in negotiating regional trade agreements. Chapters 3 and 4 together present my discussion of regional trade agreements in GATT.

---

[9] Zeiler opts for the 1960s, whereas Winham claims the EEC was 'an economic superpower with considerable negotiating experience' by the start of the Tokyo Round in 1974. T. W. Zeiler, *American Trade and Power in the 1960s* (New York: Columbia University Press, 1992), chapters 6 and 8; G. R. Winham, *International Trade and the Tokyo Round Negotiation* (Princeton: Princeton University Press, 1986), 70. Deese agrees that it was only in the Tokyo Round that the EEC acted as a leader and worked jointly with the USA in a 'leadership duopoly'. D. Deese, *World Trade Politics: Power, Principles and Leadership* (London and New York: Routledge, 2008), 13, 58, 92–93.

First Step towards European Integration: the ECSC and GATT

During the Second World War, people wondered how they could prevent a third world war. In Europe, members of the governments-in-exile and people in the resistance identified regional economic integration as a way towards a peaceful future.[10] The advocates of integration hoped it would blur international divisions and inculcate identification with and attachment to a larger group. Not everyone believed in a reimagined Europe for these reasons. Some thought it would expedite recovery from the war and that it would strengthen their countries individually and help them withstand the threat of communism. For many reasons, six western European countries – France, West Germany, Italy, Belgium, Luxembourg, and the Netherlands – pooled their resources soon after the war ended. The first step on the road to integration occurred in 1950 when French foreign minister Robert Schuman proposed a common market for coal and steel products: this would become the European Coal and Steel Community (ECSC).[11]

But to the GATT secretariat in Geneva, regional economic integration was problematic even though it was likely to promote stability, security, and prosperity, also central aims of GATT. The problem with the ECSC was that it contravened the Most Favoured Nation clause, the heart of the General Agreement. Nor did it conform to GATT's criteria for free trade areas because it dealt with only one sector of trade. As Wyndham White observed, the ECSC was 'an important test of the attitude of the GATT to European integration and of the possibility of harmonizing the universal and regional approaches to trade liberalization'.[12]

Members of the ECSC applied to GATT for a waiver; in other words, they sought permission to deviate from the rules. The justification for the waiver was twofold. First, it was argued that the reason GATT rules did not cover sectoral free trade initiatives such as the ECSC was because the original drafters had not anticipated such a scenario. Second, it was suggested that the ECSC would not raise barriers to trade with the rest of the world; rather, it would remove barriers to trade in coal and steel

---

[10] See the reports of the Commission pour l'étude des problèmes d'après-guerre, especially the first report, July 1941, and the fifth report, August 1943, published in W. Lipgens (ed.), *Documents on the History of European Integration*, *Vol. 4* (Berlin and New York: De Gruyter, 1985), 420–421 and 441–443.

[11] See, for example, J. Gillingham, *Coal, Steel and the Rebirth of Europe, 1945–1955: The Germans and French from Ruhr Conflict to Economic Community* (Cambridge and New York: Cambridge University Press, 1991).

[12] 'Europe in the GATT', an Address by Wyndham White at Europe House, London, May 1960, WTO.

products among the six participating states. In time, as the six participating countries became more competitive, they would be able 'to trade even more freely with the rest of the world than hitherto was the case'.[13] The ECSC was therefore held to be consistent with the spirit and ultimate aims of GATT.

Waivers in GATT were fairly common. They were granted in the hope of balancing observance of GATT rules with national economic well-being. But this request provoked opposition, led by Czechoslovakia. Karel Svec, the Czech representative, stated that the ECSC created additional barriers to trade and was discriminatory in practice. Furthermore, he held that the ECSC was not compatible with GATT's promotion of 'peaceful co-operation among nations with different economic systems' because coal and steel were the basis of western Europe's war economy. He concluded that 'the Schuman Plan does not aim at the peaceful reconstruction of Europe, but at the preparation for a new war'.[14] There was a thinly disguised Cold War logic behind his remarks. But it was also a compelling defence of GATT. Svec's objections identified a fundamental tension between complying with rules and upholding members' rights. He also drew attention to the implications of the waiver: 'What would then remain of our General Agreement if all the contracting parties approached the problem of their international obligations in the same manner?'

Willard Thorp, the US assistant secretary of state for economic affairs, did not dispute the Czech interpretation of GATT rules, but he insisted that the ECSC was liberal in intent and would benefit the overall state of international relations.[15] This was a weak defence of the ECSC in relation to GATT. In fact, the US government had reservations about the coal and steel agreement, especially if a cartel were to be set up which would counteract freer world trade.[16] But the prospect of geopolitical benefits overrode economic concerns. Washington hoped that the proposal would resolve mistrust in Europe.[17] Furthermore, a strong Europe would be a better partner in a Cold War world. The United States therefore

[13] European Coal and Steel Community: Statement by the Netherlands Government, 8 September 1952, L/17, GDL.
[14] Working party 4 on the European Coal and Steel Community: Statement by the Czechoslovak Delegation at the Tenth Meeting of the Seventh Session, 29 October 1952, W.7/47, GDL.
[15] Summary Record of the third meeting, 6 October 1952, 3 pm, re European Coal and Steel Community, 9 October 1952, SR.7/3, GDL.
[16] See, for example, The Chargé in France (Bohlen) to the Secretary of State, 25 October 1950, FRUS 1950, Vol. III, 761–765. Winand, Eisenhower, Kennedy, and the United States of Europe, 22.
[17] The Acting Secretary of State to the Secretary of State, 10 May 1950, FRUS 1950, Vol. III, 695.

supported the ECSC 'for reasons of broad political and military policy'.[18] In so doing, the USA put commercial interests behind geopolitical goals and privileged the integration of western Europe over support for GATT.

Other GATT members, and the secretariat, remained apprehensive about the ECSC. Their doubts provoked a stiff clarification from ECSC members that they did not expect meaningful debate or need GATT approval. As Max Suetens, Belgium's ambassador to GATT, explained, the request for a waiver was a formality:

There is no question of discussing the merits of the Schuman Plan. It is simply a matter of first listing the conflicts between the two international instruments ... and secondly of defining the waivers necessary to reconcile these conflicts.[19]

Win Brown, acting head of the US delegation to GATT, described the European attitude as 'very stand-offish', a stance that persisted into the next session when the ECSC reported on the implementation of the terms of the treaty. Brown was also struck by the burden of US leadership in international economic relations: 'I am more impressed than ever by the weight of responsibility which rests upon us in making the decisions as to our future foreign economic policy and the magnitude of the opportunity which we have to influence the course of what actually happens.'[20] US influence was wielded without fanfare, but it was effective. The ECSC received its waiver, with twenty-seven members voting for and only Czechoslovakia voting against, while Cuba and Indonesia abstained.

Although waivers compromised GATT's principles and undermined its mandate, this waiver was cast as a triumph. It was formally announced at a special ceremony in the Palais des Nations at the end of 1952. While Svec wondered why 'a breach of the General Agreement' should prompt a celebration,[21] others believed a celebration was warranted. The French praised GATT for its flexibility and pragmatism. The organization was not dogmatic and could accommodate initiatives in the organization of trade that stemmed from real-world conditions. GATT was stronger because it had found a way forward: 'Il apparaît qu'il s'agit ainsi d'un

---

[18] Memorandum by the Assistant Legal Adviser for Economic Affairs (Metzger) to the Deputy Legal Adviser (Tate), 25 February 1953, re Renewal of the Reciprocal Trade Agreements Act and Related Problems – A Current Appraisal, 150. The Ambassador in France (Bruce) to the Secretary of State, 23 May 1950, *FRUS 1950, Vol. III*, 705. J. Evans, *The Kennedy Round in American Trade Policy: The Twilight of the GATT?* (Cambridge, MA: Harvard University Press, 1971), 54.

[19] Summary Record of the third meeting, 6 October 1952.

[20] The Acting Chairman of the United States Delegation to the 8th Session of the GATT (Brown) to the Chairman (Waugh), 24 October 1953, *FRUS 1952–1954, Vol. I*, 167.

[21] Summary Record of the 17th Meeting, 10 November 1952, 10 am, SR.17/7, GDL

succès pour le GATT qui sort renforcé d'une épreuve assez périleuse pour lui.'[22]

In fact, this was not a victory for GATT, which was not stronger because of its accommodation. GATT members had been presented with a *fait accompli*, not for the last time where European integration was concerned. They did, however, decide to accept the ECSC with good grace. The French opinion also hinted at potential problems for GATT down the road because the episode condoned the violation of GATT rules. Without acknowledging it, the USA had played an important part in subverting GATT for the sake of a more united Europe, a position it would stick to as integration gathered momentum.

The GATT Review of 1954–1955, or ITO Redux

The ECSC waiver was not a devastating blow to GATT's authority, but Wyndham White anticipated that further integration would challenge GATT's role and effectiveness. He was determined to uphold GATT's relevance and legitimacy against all threats, of which European integration appeared to be one. His concerns were compounded by a suggestion emanating from western Europe that responsibility for trade among industrial countries should be transferred to the Organization for European Economic Cooperation (OEEC) in Paris, thereby gutting the GATT of members who were responsible for a large portion of world trade. The secretary general of the United Nations, Dag Hammerskjold, also proposed that GATT should be brought under UN auspices, a move Wyndham White resisted.[23] Both of these suggestions highlighted the limitations and vulnerability of GATT. The precariousness of its existence was unintentionally aggravated by the attempt to once again turn it into a proper organization (whose working name was the Organization for Trade Cooperation, OTC) during a sweeping review held in 1954 and 1955. Below is a short explanation of that review and the failure of the OTC. It draws out some of the challenges that determined what GATT could and could not do, what it could and could not become. It also exacerbated the anxious climate surrounding the organization. This was the background against which the next step in European integration – concluding the Treaty of Rome – must be set.

Several factors prompted the review. By the mid-1950s, the world was already different from the war-devastated one in which GATT had been

[22] Note: 7ième session des parties contractantes à l'Accord générale sur les tariffs douanières et le commerce, 1 décembre 1952, MAEF 000067 (Papers of Olivier Wormser), reel 157, HAEU.
[23] Stevenson to Wakefield, letter, 14 December 1954, FO371/110158, TNA.

established. Its terms needed to keep pace with change. Although thirteen new contracting parties had joined since 1949 (Syria and Lebanon withdrew, and Liberia joined in 1950 but withdrew in 1953), raising the total membership to thirty-one, the two most recent tariff rounds – at Annecy and Torquay – had not yielded significant results. The momentum of trade liberalization was slowing, and this raised questions about the organization's effectiveness. The United States also supported a review. In 1954, President Eisenhower asked Clarence B. Randall, the chairman of Inland Steel Company, to examine US foreign economic policy. Randall cautiously endorsed a liberal and multilateral approach to international economic questions. He believed GATT's role was to offer advice about trade policy, oversee multilateral trade negotiations, and facilitate the resolution of trade disputes. He recommended that GATT should be given a proper institutional home so that it could fulfil its responsibilities more effectively.[24]

Wyndham White was hopeful that the review would strengthen GATT as well as the USA's commitment to liberal trade practices. He was also aware of the risk involved. It could become an opportunity for anti-liberal elements in the USA to call for a retreat from freer trade and a multilateral system.[25] Dana Wilgress, who chaired the review, was also worried about the risks of failure: 'If we cannot succeed in our main objective of reinforcing GATT the result might very well be anarchy in trade.'[26]

The review was predictable and surprising, scripted and ad hoc. There were proposals to bolster GATT's authority. Denmark, Norway, Sweden, and West Germany wanted tighter enforcement on business practices that restricted trade. West Germany and Chile called for measures to deal with double taxation. West Germany and Sweden proposed provisions to deal with transportation insurance. Old battles were waged anew. Representatives from developing countries wanted to ease restrictions on the use of quantitative restrictions. (This is discussed at length in Chapter 5.) The British revived the question of imperial preferences. The French representative suggested that regional trade blocs were superior to a multilateral trade organization. He warned, 'Countries should beware of rushing into a factitious [sic] universal system which would lead again to nationalist autarchy ... It was effective regional action which gave the basis for a more universal programme.'[27] The review also became an

---

[24] *Report to the President and the Congress*, Commission on Foreign Economic Policy (Washington, DC: US Government Printing Office, 1954), 44, 45.

[25] Memorandum by the Executive Secretary, 13 April 1954, sent to C. M. Isbister, 15 April 1954, RG19: F-2/4203/8710–1 pt. 1, LAC.

[26] M. Hoffman, 'Tariff Body Opens Key Geneva Talks', *New York Times* (29 October 1954), 2.

[27] Summary record of the 21st Meeting, 6 December 1954, SR.9/21, GDL.

occasion to express dissatisfaction with the General Agreement and freer world trade generally. In his opening remarks, Edgar Faure, the French Minister of Finance, suggested that there should not be a rush towards liberal trade and that freer trade brought dangers with it.[28]

Members agreed on terms for a new organization. Its main task would be to implement the General Agreement, study world trade with an eye to its promotion and expansion, and initiate rounds of tariff negotiations. It would have an assembly which would meet annually, an elected and broadly representative executive of seventeen members, and a secretariat that would appoint a director-general. Members would each have one vote in the assembly; the secretariat would submit the budget to the assembly; and the executive would discharge duties delegated to it by the assembly.

It was not immediately clear whether or not the review was a success. According to Win Brown, the results were limited partly because US leadership had been restrained. More optimistically, he suggested that the review had revealed that the General Agreement was basically sound and needed little modification.[29] John McEwan, Australia's minister of commerce, was more enthusiastic about the proposed 'dramatic' changes. They had turned him from 'a severe critic of the General Agreement on Tariffs and Trade ... to a warm supporter'.[30] Alexandre Kojève of France placed the review midway between success and failure. GATT had not become 'la grande charte du commerce libéral', remaining instead a looser and more flexible arrangement. As such, it had preserved both its strengths and its weaknesses. That was welcome since Paris wanted GATT to be 'modeste et limitée'.[31]

US support was essential for the creation of the OTC. President Eisenhower submitted the OTC to Congress for approval in the spring of 1955.[32] He appealed to US self-interest, explaining that over the preceding eight years, GATT had achieved impressive tariff reductions, to the benefit of US exporters. But mostly he sold the OTC along Cold War lines. Failure to consolidate GATT and entrench cooperation in

---

[28] M. L. Hoffman, 'Britain Proposes World Trade Plan', New York Times (9 November 1954), 1, 10. Hoffman noted that the other delegates were shocked by Faure's remarks.
[29] Draft Report by the Acting Chairman of the Delegation to the Ninth Session of the General Agreement on Tariffs and Trade (Brown), 9 March 1955, FRUS 1955–57, Vol. IX, 94–95.
[30] Editorial, Sydney Morning Herald (4 June 1955), republished in J. Crawford, N. Anderson, and M. G. N. Morris (eds.), Australian Trade Policy 1942–1966: A Documentary History (Canberra: Australian National University Press; Toronto: University of Toronto Press, 1968), doc 5:5, 162.
[31] Note: 9ème session du GATT, 28 mars 1955, MAEF000068, reel 158, HAEU.
[32] As H.R. 5550.

trade would incite restrictions, a reduction of world trade, and a loss of market share for US exports, all of which 'would play directly into the hands of the Communists'.[33] He went further, claiming that the OTC was the commercial equivalent of NATO. By ratifying the OTC, 'We would ... cooperate further with the free world, in this struggle against Communist domination, to the greater security and the greater prosperity of all.' He tried to pre-empt opposition to the OTC by emphasizing that it was not a supranational entity and that it had not expanded GATT's scope beyond trade. Echoing the French view, Eisenhower noted that it was 'limited in its functions'.[34]

Critics were not persuaded. Some objected that the OTC was contrary to US interests. Still others claimed that it was unconstitutional and would hoodwink the USA into supporting the ITO – the OTC was often referred to as a 'little ITO'. Some of the criticism emanated from the usual suspects, such as the protectionist American Tariff League. But much of the opposition was rooted in the belief that US independent decision-making should not be compromised. As the British embassy in Washington pointed out, it was the 'instinct for untrammeled sovereignty' that motivated many of GATT's detractors.[35] To the postwar architects, giving up a piece of sovereignty was essential for an institutional and rules-based international order to work. But the commitment to nation-states as the main actors and centres of decision-making ran deep. GATT was tolerable to its powerful members because of its institutional weakness.

To come into effect, the OTC needed the support of members whose trade made up 85 per cent of the total external trade of all GATT members. Because US trade accounted for 20 per cent of the total, it effectively had a veto. Two years later, US representatives to GATT were reassuring the collective membership that the executive would push for formal approval.[36] But that never transpired. It was ITO redux.

Brown had predicted that if the USA did not ratify the OTC, then GATT would also perish.[37] But GATT carried on. Wyndham White

[33] Washington to Foreign Office, No. 218 Saving telegram, 15 April 1955, FO371/14934, TNA.
[34] Letter from the President to the Congress requesting approval of United States membership in the Organization for Trade Cooperation, draft, 30 March 1955, RG59: Office of the Assistant Legal Advisor for Economic Affairs, Records re Trade and GATT 1947–66, Box 16, file Trade Agreement Authority OTC I, NARA.
[35] J. H. A. Watson to D. S. Laskey, FO, 17 May 1954, FO371/114935, TNA.
[36] Note: Travaux de la 12ème session du G.A.T.T., 2ème rapport, de Monsieur André Philip à Monsieur Christian Pineau, Ministre des affaires étrangères, 24 janvier 1958, MAEF000068, reel. 158, HAEU.
[37] Draft report by the Acting Chairman of the Delegation to the Ninth Session of GATT, 103.

believed that it had been weakened by the review. Membership had not been made more attractive, compelling, or inclusive. The scope of the General Agreement remained narrow, leaving it unable to answer its many critics. Even if GATT enjoyed strong support from Britain, Australia, and Canada, US leadership was sorely lacking. Wyndham White feared that GATT would be 'a frail instrument indeed'.[38] The absence of US support for GATT, however, was not the only reason to worry about the future. French mistrust of the organization began to inform its policies towards and behaviour in GATT. Because negotiations over the Treaty of Rome were in progress, French views of GATT assumed an even greater importance.

Gaullist Trade Policy: A Critique of Liberal Trade

French views of GATT were influenced by the overall postwar liberal international project. The various elements of the peace – from the creation of the United Nations to the division of Germany – had profound implications for France, but France had had little say in how those decisions had been reached. From the French point of view, an Anglo-American cabal, or more broadly an Anglo-Saxon group, dominated the postwar order.[39] This was especially true in economic organizations. French officials believed the British enjoyed 'un champ de manoeuvres favorable' in GATT, whereas the United States dominated the International Monetary Fund.[40]

Even though France had retained the honorific of a great power, its influence in world affairs was sharply curbed after the war. This was a condition to which French leaders were not resigned and they set out to restore France to a leading international position.[41] This goal also informed French foreign economic policy. No one explained this more clearly than Alexandre Kojève, a Russian émigré and nephew of Vassily Kandinsky. An eminent Hegelian philosopher who pronounced that the end of history had arrived (an observation brought into the mainstream by

[38] E. Wyndham White, 'An Appraisal of the Present Situation in the General Agreement on Tariffs and Trade', sent by Wyndham White to John Leddy, 18 July 1956, *FRUS 1955–57, Vol. IX*, 199–203.

[39] T. Judt, *Postwar: A History of Europe Since 1945* (New York: Penguin Press, 2005), 112–117. Also see C. Nuenlist, A. Locher, and G. Martin (eds.), *Globalizing de Gaulle: International Perspectives on French Foreign Policy 1958–1969*(Lanham, MD: Lexington Books, 2010), especially Part II.

[40] Travaux du GATT, 2 mars 1955, MAEF000068, reel. 158, HAEU.

[41] See, for example, P. Mélandri, 'The Troubled Friendship: France and the United States 1945–1989' in G. Lundestad (ed.), *No End to Alliance: The United States and Western Europe: Past, Present and Future* (Basingstoke: MacMillan, 1998), 112–133.

Francis Fukayama), Kojève was an influential intellectual with access to leading French minds and political leaders. He became a civil servant after the war, with a particular interest in economics. Kojève believed that liberalism did not serve France's interests: 'l'idéologie néo-libérale anglo-saxonne va à l'encontre de tout ce qui s'est fait en France depuis la guerre (et même avant) dans le domaine économique et commercial'.[42] He endorsed the logic of regional trade forums, such as the OEEC, and regional trade agreements as a way to put France in a stronger international position.[43] To GATT, the OEEC alternative was a threat.

Kojève's memos went to Olivier Wormser, director of the Direction des relations économiques extérieures (DREE), and Bernard Clappier, the head of external affairs in the Ministry of Finance. They were the dominant figures in French foreign economic policy from 1954 to 1964. As Kojève's biographer put it, together they could decide 'la pluie et le beau temps'.[44] Kojève acknowledged the power concentrated in the hands of Wormser and Clappier. As he once explained to Sir Edgar Cohen, a senior British trade official, France under de Gaulle was 'now a monarchy', and only two ministers mattered (Couve and Baumgartner), but as they were not interested in trade, they 'could be relied upon to accept agreed advice from Wormser and Clappier'.[45] He did not expand on his own influence, although Clappier later explained that Kojève's role was to be 'l'inspirateur', whereas he and Wormser simply carried out policies.[46] British officials believed that Kojève's influence reached the president's office: he was 'the man whom de Gaulle refused to receive but to whose opinion he deferred'.[47] Without a doubt, Kojève and de Gaulle were both committed to France's restoration as a great power. At the end of the Second World War, Kojève had presented de Gaulle with a memorandum that outlined a Latin Empire as the basis of French world influence.[48] 'C'est l'idée-idéal de l'Empire latin, où le peuple français aurait pour but et pour devoir le maintien de son rang de primus inter pares'.[49] Kojève's memos revealed his preoccupation with issues of power, status, and influence, and these in turn influenced his recommendations with respect to GATT.

[42] Note pour Monsieur Clappier, 'Le nouveau GATT et l'Union française', 25 mars 1955, MAEF000067, reel 158, HAEU.

[43] Note: Travaux du GATT.

[44] D. Auffret, *Alexandre Kojève: La Philosophie, l'état, la fin de l'histoire* (Paris: Grasset, 1990), 442.

[45] Geneva, UK del, to FO, tel. 549, 29 May 1960, FO371/150284, TNA.

[46] Auffret, *Kojève*, 458–459.

[47] C. G. Harris, British embassy, Vienna, to L. G. Holliday, Foreign Office, 2 February 1960, FO371/150258, TNA.

[48] See R. Howse, 'Kojève's Latin Empire', *Policy Review* 126 (August/September 2004), 41–48.

[49] Quoted in Auffret, *Kojève*, 398.

Kojève did not believe that GATT served France well. He associated liberalism with Anglo-American values and ideology. Starting from this assumption, GATT obstructed France's recovery and diminished its influence. GATT was even more uncongenial to France because the USA and Britain deviated from GATT norms and rules whenever liberalism proved inconvenient. Furthermore, Kojève argued that French membership in GATT would compromise its international standing and influence because France would have to request exemptions and waivers, in so doing opening itself to criticism. 'En se trouvant ainsi dans un état d'accusée permanente devant un forum dit "internationale", où elle plaidera d'ailleurs coupable, la France sera amoindrie du point de vue psychologique et politique, en perdant de plus en plus ses chances d'exercer un leadership international ou même régional (européen).' Kojève also noted that within GATT, France would be subject to pressure to sever its special economic connections with its overseas territories. According to Kojève, French trade policy had to be '[d]'un régime très souple et diversifié d'aide à l'exportation qui sera nécessairement critiqué par le GATT'. Although Kojève maintained that it was possible to contemplate quitting GATT, especially as so many countries still remained outside, it was also possible to work from within to make it better suit French interests, even to aspire to leadership within the organization. As he observed, 'la situation peut changer radicalement au sein du GATT en faveur de la France'. He advised working within GATT in association with other western European members, all the while casting doubt on the legitimacy of the dominant liberal logic and proposing the OEEC as a more congenial option.[50]

The Presentation of the Treaty of Rome to GATT Members

As the next successful stage in western European integration unfolded, Wyndham White tried to put GATT in a position of strength. In a speech in Geneva in December 1956, he explained that a European regional trade bloc would have to conform to GATT guidelines and practices.[51] Privately he complained that GATT did not weigh in the minds of officials drafting the common market arrangement: 'there is little disposition to associate GATT with the preparatory discussions of this project

[50] Note pour Monsieur Clappier: 'Le nouveau GATT et l'Union française', 25 mars 1955, and Note: Travaux du GATT, 2 mars 1955, both in MAEF000067, reel 158, HAEU.
[51] 'The Achievements of the GATT', an address by Wyndham White at the Graduate Institute of International Studies Geneva, December 1956, WTO.

even though its realization would clearly have profound implications for the Contracting Parties'.[52]

There was no GATT discussion of the European common market prior to the finalization of the Treaty of Rome in March 1957. French officials had insisted that because there was nothing definite to discuss, GATT consideration would be 'premature and possibly dangerous'.[53] But once the terms of the treaty were finalized, three elements clashed with GATT rules. First, the EEC proposed to phase in the reduction of all tariffs in 10 per cent increments over a ten-year period. Lower duties would not be generalized to other GATT members and were therefore discriminatory. Second, the EEC envisaged, without laying out all of the details, the creation of a common agricultural policy (CAP). This would involve protection and would be likely to have a restrictive, possibly distorting, effect on the flow of international trade and to raise prices by subsidizing European agricultural production. Third, the EEC would extend tariff privileges to associated overseas territories (AOTs), in other words former and present colonies, which was also discriminatory. It was a measure that principally affected French colonies and was important to France for political reasons.[54]

Wyndham White believed the Treaty of Rome threatened GATT's survival.[55] He urged members to meet in a special session to scrutinize the treaty before its ratification.[56] Representatives from the Six objected to any GATT discussion of the substance of the Treaty of Rome, insisting that GATT must only discuss the procedure by which subsequent discussions would be held. Wyndham White was known to lose his temper on occasion and he did so now. He told P. A. Forthomme, a Belgian official, that GATT was acting in a 'moderate and reasonable' fashion. He advised the Six to 'drop their suspicions of GATT and come to this meeting in a spirit of cooperation'.[57]

At a GATT meeting in the autumn of 1957, concerns about the implications of the EEC were revisited. Representatives from Brazil, Burma, Ceylon, Chile, Cuba, India, Peru, Turkey, and Uruguay were highly critical of the provisions for AOTs. The proposed CAP provoked

---

[52] Letter from the Executive Secretary of GATT (Wyndham White) to John Leddy, 18 July 1956, *FRUS 1955–57*, Vol. IX, 201–202.
[53] NATO PARIS to External, 5 October 1956, RG20: A-4/3088/885–15 pt. 1, LAC.
[54] Note of a meeting with Mr. Eric Wyndham White, Executive Secretary of the G.A.T.T., n.d., BT11/5628, TNA.
[55] Geneva to External, GATT – Attitude of the Executive Secretary (Wyndham White) Towards the Common Market, 13 May 1957, RG19: 4205/8714–24-9 pt. 1, LAC.
[56] Geneva to External, 13 May 1957, RG19: 4205/8714–24-9 pt. 1, LAC.
[57] Geneva to External, 9 April 1957, RG19: 4206/8718–08, LAC.

concern about the creation of an 'agricultural iron curtain'.[58] The spokesperson for Ghana noted the grave impact the common market would have on cocoa and timber exports and pointed out that Ghana openly admitted exports from the Six. The Indian representative was concerned about the 'possible conflict between regionalism and multilateralism'. There was debate about whether or not the proposed common market satisfied GATT criteria. Australia, Canada, Japan, and New Zealand, backed by a group of developing nations, insisted that GATT members must scrutinize the Treaty of Rome before its ratification.[59]

The Six insisted that the treaty had to be considered as a whole; it could not be assessed in a piecemeal fashion.[60] In effect, this approach meant that the treaty could not be revised. The possibility that the Six might quit GATT hovered over the discussions, although this was not a card the Europeans could play because West Germany and the Benelux members were loath to take such a step.[61] A US official observed that the EEC position tended to be that of the lowest common denominator,[62] and that was usually the French position As a Canadian official observed, the Six did not want to 'lose sight of GATT', but there was little they could do without 'upsetting French sensibilities'.[63]

The intractable stance of the Six 'shocked' Wyndham White. He was 'disappointed by the defiant attitude which had been displayed by the Six', but more generally he was alarmed by 'a tendency in Europe recently for continental countries to pay lip service to the broader institutions while, in actual fact, they preferred regional action which would enable them to practice discrimination'.[64] He told Claude Isbister, a senior

[58] T. E. Josling, S. Tangermann, and T. K. Warley, *Agriculture in the GATT* (Basingstoke: Macmillan, 1996), 43.
[59] Summary of Speeches made by Ministers or Representatives of Ministers during Ministerial Meeting, 12th session, CAB21 / 4720, TNA.
[60] Note: GATT et Traité de Rome, 12 décembre 1957, MAEF000068, reel 158, HAEU.
[61] Note: Gatt et restrictions quantitative allemandes, 20 décembre 1957, MAEF000068, reel 158. As an official (possibly Kojève) remarked earlier in the year, the threat to quit the GATT 'risque de mettre à une rude épreuve la solidarité des six, encore assez précaire si l'on en juge d'après les expériences de la XIIème session.' Note pour Monsieur Clappier, La communauté européenne à la XIIème session du GATT, 10 décembre 1957, MAEF000068, reel. 158, HAEU.
[62] Washington to External, 21 May 1958, RG25: G-2/Vol. 7976/14051–1-40 pt. 1.1, LAC.
[63] Brussels to External, 15 May 1957, RG19: F-2/4205/8714–24-9 pt. 1, LAC. Another Canadian report one year later repeated the observation that the EEC was only capable of acting according to the lowest common denominator, 'and that is pretty low'. Clarke to Plumptre, 26 May 1958, RG19: F-2/4208/8718–04, LAC.
[64] Meeting of the Interdepartmental Committee on External Trade Policy, 21 March 1958, RG25: vol. 7976/248/14051–1-40 pt. 1.1, LAC. For instance, Wyndham White had received reports that Denmark was considering 'dropping its multilateral commercial policy and pursuing regional and bilateral arrangements'. Geneva to External, 27 March 1957, RG19: F-2/4205/8714–24-9 pt. 1, LAC.

member of the Department of Trade and Commerce in Canada, that the common market had 'created genuine fears and apprehension in many quarters'. His own fear was that it would give 'an impetus to the search for regional arrangements with a strong bias towards discrimination and autarchy', trade practices that both repudiated and undermined the goals of GATT and the internationalist outlook on which it rested.[65] The entire postwar architecture could collapse under the strain of rival regional trade agreements: 'He fears that the multilateral system will be replaced by a series of regional arrangements that will use restrictions against each other. Once this process to discriminate begins, the use of discriminatory restrictions would "spread like the plague".'[66]

Wyndham White did not believe GATT could control or influence the Six without US support.[67] But the United States could do little because French officials had threatened not to ratify the EEC if US officials criticized the terms of the treaty. According to one US official, 'This was a pistol at their head'.[68] Therefore, the United States endorsed GATT examination after the treaty had been ratified. Other members agreed to hold over the question of the compatibility of the Treaty of Rome and GATT. French officials saw this as a triumph. Not only would the common market come into effect without scrutiny, but also the Treaty of Rome could not subsequently be challenged in a piecemeal fashion.[69] The USA's intention had been to support both the EEC and GATT: 'They must both continue to exist without any lessening of the integrity of each.'[70] But the effect of US actions favoured the EEC: Washington had given 'rather more comfort to the common market countries than to its other partners in the GATT'.[71]

Although members of GATT had accepted the EEC on European terms, they continued to try to influence the nature and workings of the

[65] Wyndham White to Isbister, 15 March 1958, RG25: 7976/248/14051–1-40 pt. 1.1, LAC.

[66] Canadian Permanent Mission, Geneva to External, 3 March 1958, RG25: G-2/Vol. 7976/14051–1-40 pt. 1.1, LAC.

[67] Interdepartmental Committee on External Trade Policy, 21 March 1958, RG25: vol. 7976/248/14051–1-40 pt. 1.1, LAC.

[68] Geneva to External, 19 May 1958, RG19: F-2/4208/8718–04, LAC. Winand, *Eisenhower, Kennedy, and the United States of Europe*, 114.

[69] Note pour Monsieur Clappier, "La communauté européenne à la XIIième session du GATT", 10 mars 1957, MAEF000068, reel 158, HAEU. Direction générale des affaires économiques et financières, Service de cooperation économique, Note a.s. GATT et restrictions quantitatives allemandes, 20 décembre 1957, MAEF000068, reel 158, HAEU.

[70] Summary of Talks with British on October 9, 1957, RG59: Records of the Assistant Legal Advisor for Economic Affairs, Records relating to Trade and GATT 1947–1966, Box 7, file: GATT-Common Market. NARA.

[71] NATO Paris to External, 7 March 1958, GATT and the EEC, RG20: A-3/2524/4–581-20 pt. 2, LAC.

common market to make it compatible with GATT norms of openness and non-discrimination and to ensure it contributed to the growth of world trade in ways that were widely beneficial. The United States in particular wanted the Six to be more accommodating, flexible, and internationalist. The conduct of the Six in GATT would be a test of their good faith. As Canadian officials pointed out, it was 'the only world-wide forum where concerted pressure can be brought to bear on the Common Market with a view to influencing the development of its commercial policies in an outward-looking and non-restrictive direction'.[72] Although members of the EEC sought to justify their behaviour, they clearly resented being painted as a transgressor of rules. As a British official observed, 'countries do not like blatantly to break the G.A.T.T. rules, and this is a genuine and continuing restraint upon them'.[73] GATT attempts to show that the EEC acted contrary to the rules were not likely to be well received. Nevertheless, members tried to more closely align the EEC with GATT, in the hope that this would uphold the primacy of liberal trade and strengthen GATT's authority as the arbiter of the trade practices of its members. Their efforts revolved around three issues: restrictive trade practices in West Germany, oversight of the CAP, and recognition that the common external tariff (CET) of the EEC had injured third parties. But first it needed a justification to do so.

The Haberler Report: Trying to Influence the EEC

In 1958, GATT commissioned a study on the patterns of world trade. Gottfried Haberler, Jan Tinbergen, Roberto de Oliveiro, and James Meade, four eminent economists, considered the impact of the EEC on world trade patterns. Their report – *Trends in International Trade*, usually referred to as the Haberler report – challenged the EEC's claim that it was compatible with GATT. It underscored the problems of agricultural protection, an issue that Wyndham White admitted 'has hung like a cloud over the GATT for many years'.[74] For many reasons, including domestic electoral concerns and the link between self-sufficiency and security, industrialized countries protected domestic agricultural production, even when it was inefficient. This was the case in Europe and the United States. The prospect of the CAP threatened to take agricultural protectionism to new heights. But there was still a chance of influencing

---

[72] Memorandum to the Cabinet, 'Instructions for the Canadian Delegation to the Fourteenth Session of GATT', 30 April 1959, RG20: vol. 1922/20–28 pt. 7, LAC.

[73] Memo for the Prime Minister, 'The G.A.T.T.', 27 October 1958, BT11/5771, TNA.

[74] 'Europe in the GATT', Address by Eric Wyndham White to Europe House, London, May 1960, WTO.

the EEC. As Jean Royer, the deputy executive secretary of GATT, explained: 'The time to do this is now, particularly before the signatories of the Rome Treaty come to final conclusions about the common agricultural policy.'[75]

GATT now had seemingly impartial and expert authorization to try to influence the development of the CAP. They followed standard bureaucratic practices and struck a committee – called Committee II – to investigate the use of non-tariff barriers (NTBs) to protect domestic agriculture and then study the impact of such policies on international trade. Even though agricultural protectionism was a global practice, GATT's eyes were fixed on Europe. As Finn Gundelach of the GATT secretariat explained, the main task of Committee II was 'to exercise a moderating influence on the EEC in the formation of its common agricultural policy'.[76] We will return to the CAP in Chapter 6, which examines agricultural protectionism, but GATT efforts to influence the CAP during its implementation phase belong in this chapter because they show how GATT responded to and was affected by regional trade blocs.

GATT attempts to influence the CAP hit a road block immediately: the EEC refused to allow it to scrutinize its agricultural policies on the grounds that the policies were not yet finalized and therefore examination was premature.[77] The USA promised to keep the emerging CAP off the GATT agenda in 1960. In return, they expected the Europeans to be more flexible in Geneva.[78] The USA was stepping up, but US credibility was strained because of its own agricultural waiver in 1955.[79] Gundelach nonetheless encouraged US officials to see the committee as a way 'to get some leverage on the EEC', and not to be dissuaded by criticism of US agricultural practices.[80]

Committee II busied itself for two years with general studies of agricultural protectionism, to the consternation of many members. Only in November 1962 did the EEC's agricultural practices come before the committee. The EEC representative insisted that the emerging CAP had been designed with GATT obligations in mind and, in his opinion, 'the system ... was compatible with the General Agreement'. The committee

[75] Royer to Meade, 29 January 1958, Meade papers, 17/21, LSE Archives.
[76] Memorandum of Conversation re Future Activities of GATT Committee II, 29 March 1960, RG59: GATT394.41/1960–63/Box172, file 392.41/3–1860, NARA.
[77] Memorandum of Conversation re Future Activities of GATT Committee II, 29 March 1960.
[78] Washington to External, 29 August 1960, RG19: F-2/4208/8718–04, LAC.
[79] Draft Report by the Acting Chairman of the Delegation to the Ninth Session of the GATT (Brown), 9 March 1955, *FRUS 1955–1957*, *Vol. IX*, 96, 97, 100.
[80] Memorandum of Conversation re Future Activities of GATT Committee II, 29 March 1960.

could not respond since their terms of reference did not include investigating the extent to which the CAP did or did not conform with GATT. However, several GATT members let it be known that their silence 'should not be taken to mean that they concurred in this view'. The community representative was then questioned about how CAP practices affected cereals, pig meat, eggs, poultry, fruits, and vegetables. There was no denying that the CAP was protectionist, although at this early juncture the committee could not show how European agricultural protection affected world trade. Some committee members did make the point that the CAP displaced traditional third-party suppliers, in particular developing countries that exported to Europe. The community representative's response combined admission, contrition, and pugnacity. First, he insisted that the EEC was doing exactly what all other countries did to enable domestic suppliers to act as 'residual suppliers'. Second, the EEC did think about third-party suppliers with sympathy, although he denied that an increase in intra-European trade had injured the trade of third parties.[81] It was evident that this committee could not curb agricultural protectionism in western Europe. As US officials reported, the Six would make no commitment that might hinder 'their freedom of action'. The fact that the Six sent low-level functionaries to these meetings reinforced the point that they would not subject themselves to GATT oversight.[82]

In 1965, Committee II conducted another round of consultations with the EEC. The EEC representative made no apologies for the CAP and insisted that it conformed with GATT. Despite the questions and criticisms of Committee II, GATT could not change the workings of the CAP. This was another defeat for GATT in its confrontation with the EEC.[83]

German Import Restrictions and Upholding GATT Rules

Washington's handling of the European common market elicited considerable criticism. The US representative on Committee II rarely intervened in discussion. The other committee members resolved to write 'a hard hitting report which would alert the USA to the dangers that

---

[81] Report of Committee II on the Consultation with the European Economic Community, 13 November 1962, L/1910, GDL.
[82] Official Report of the United States Delegation to GATT Committee II on Expansion of Trade (6–20 October 1960), 21 November 1960, RG59: GATT 394.41, 1960–63/Box 716, file 394.41/11–1560, NARA.
[83] Report of Committee II on Consultations with the European Economic Community, 13 March 1965, L/2389, GDL.

exist'. Wyndham White complained of 'a complete lack of any constructive role on the part of the United States'.[84] But officials in the US State Department were convinced that they should avoid heated political debates in GATT which 'could well get out of hand and end in an open rift or stalemate'. They wanted to bypass entirely the question of the compatibility of the EEC and GATT, instead focusing on quiet diplomatic overtures to the Six to consider possible adverse effects on third-party countries, including developing countries. Nonetheless the United States was not pleased with the way the Six had handled themselves in GATT. Isaiah Frank, deputy director of the Office of International Trade, came to the 'reluctant conclusion that it was easier to deal with the Russians'.[85] A US official remained hopeful that 'as working relationships between the Six tightened, their common positions would become less extreme'.[86]

Although the USA was restrained during these early GATT discussions of the common market, it more forcefully objected to Germany's use of import restrictions on industrial items, agricultural goods, and primary products from dollar countries. When West Germany first joined GATT in 1951, its precarious economic circumstances had made import restrictions appropriate. Ten years later, Germany was no longer economically weak. The West German economy grew by 7 to 8 per cent per annum in the 1950s, when the global average was 5 per cent. Unemployment was low at 3.5 per cent in 1958, dropping to less than 1 per cent by 1961. The trade balance had shifted from a US$1 billion deficit in 1949 to a US$200 million surplus in 1953. There was no compelling economic reason to continue to use quantitative restrictions. But as with so many trade issues, the reasoning was not exclusively economic. Some GATT members feared that if West Germany were allowed to discriminate, then the EEC's violation of GATT rules would be legitimized. An alarmed Canadian official explained the high stakes involved: 'if the CP's [contracting parties] accepted either the German restrictions or EEC without modification the rule of law in international trade would break down and the free world would risk returning to the economic anarchy of the 1930s'.[87] The US State Department agreed. As a *Time* magazine correspondent noted, 'State points out that if one member, Germany, can flout the fundamental principles of GATT, ... it will have a damaging effect on the whole posture of

---

[84] Note of a meeting with Mr. Eric Wyndham White, Executive Secretary of G.A.T.T., nd 1958, BT11 / 5628, TNA.

[85] Geneva to External, 19 May 1958, RG19: F-2/4208/8718-04, LAC.

[86] Washington to External, 21 May 1958, RG25: G-2/Vol. 7976/14051-1-40 pt. 1.1, LAC.

[87] Geneva to External, 19 May 1958, RG19: F-2/4208/8718-04, LAC.

GATT.'[88] Having capitulated on the Treaty of Rome, some GATT members saw it as imperative to take a stand on German import restrictions.

The Six also saw meaning beyond the practice of import restrictions. For them, what was at stake was the integrity and development of the EEC.[89] They linked the right to use import restrictions to the anticipated agricultural provisions of the CAP, still in gestation. French officials believed there was an English-speaking clique consisting of Australia, Canada, and the United States behind the move to stop Germany from using quantitative restrictions and that what this clique really wanted was to strike 'un coup décisif' against the EEC itself.[90]

At a meeting in April 1958, German import restrictions were at the top of the agenda. Wyndham White wanted to prevent an open clash. He advised members to use a waiver to give Germany the opportunity to save face.[91] The USA took a more confrontational line. Douglas Dillon, US deputy under-secretary of state for economic affairs, encouraged Germany to seek a waiver, but also pointed out that GATT members could invoke another GATT article (XXIII) that would allow them to suspend their trade concessions because they believed they had been wronged by Germany. A *Time* magazine correspondent praised Dillon for his tough diplomatic talk and noted that the Article XXIII option was 'very strong medicine, and Dillon took a very firm position when he suggested its possible use'.[92] The United States introduced a resolution which denounced Germany for not fulfilling its international obligations and strongly urged Germany to either lift the restrictions or seek a waiver. This was strong stuff in GATT meetings.

German officials lobbied members to oppose the resolution. They promised US officials that they would press the Council of Ministers to moderate the association between the Six and AOTs if Washington withdrew its support for the resolution. Washington refused.[93] They also resorted to threats, such as reducing imports of agricultural goods from Denmark and sugar from the Dominican Republic.

[88] Rappleye to Gruin, 24 October 1958, *Time* Magazine Dispatches, second series, MS 2090.1, box 13, file 226, Houghton Library, Harvard.

[89] Direction des affaires économiques et financières, Service de coopération économique, Note, 6 janvier 1958, MAEF000068, reel 158, HAEU.

[90] Direction générale des affaires économiques et financières, Service de coopération économique, Note a.s. GATT et restrictions quantitatives allemandes, 20 décembre 1957, MAEF000068, reel 158, HAEU.

[91] Geneva to External, 9 April 1958, RG25: vol.7976/248/14051–1-40 pt.1.1, LAC.

[92] Rappleye to Gruin, 24 October 1958.

[93] Geneva to External, 6 May 1958, RG20: A-3, 2526, 4–581-25 pt. 1.1, LAC.

The resolution passed by a vote of twenty-one in favour, six – the Six – opposed. This vote took place despite the opposition of Wyndham White, who insisted that GATT 'could not condemn an important C.P. like Germany in such a brutal manner'.[94] Canadians credited the passage of the resolution to US backing and credited the resolution with restoring the confidence of the contracting parties that 'the GATT could still serve their interests'.[95]

But the larger EEC challenge remained. The difficulty in dealing with the EEC in GATT was compounded by the internal workings of the EEC. Although the Commission had its own representative, Baron Snoy, national representatives were also present at GATT. A Canadian official described them as 'narrow regionalists with a propensity for Machiavellian tactics which makes it difficult to find common ground'.[96] He had Kojève in mind. Kojève was vividly, but not warmly, remembered by the representatives of other countries.[97] US officials in Geneva agreed that the Six were unreasonable. US sympathy for the 'sensitivity of the six' gave way to firmer support for GATT rules and norms. There were several reasons for this change in position. Now that the EEC had come into being, the United States could not be silenced with the threat of refusing to ratify the Treaty of Rome. The inflexibility of the Six was wearing on US officials, who believed the EEC could be more accommodating.[98] Moreover, the USA had recalculated the balance between economic disadvantages and political advantages. There was a growing sense in Washington that the EEC might be politically disadvantageous for the USA as it emerged as a leading power bloc in world affairs and as a rival.[99]

European officials complained that 'everybody was now against them even their old friends the USA'.[100] Olivier Wormser described the USA as being 'la tête de l'opposition au Traité de Rome'.[101]

---

[94] GATT Intersessional Committee, April 1958, RG25: 7976/248/14051–1-40 pt. 1, LAC. M. G. Clarke to Wynne Plumptre, 26 May 1958, RG19: F-2/4208/8718–04, LAC.
[95] Geneva to External, 19 May 1958, RG19: F-2/4208/8718–04, LAC.
[96] M. G. Clarke to Wynne Plumptre, 26 May 1958, RG19: F-2/4208/8718–04, LAC.
[97] Canadian officials paint vivid but largely unflattering pictures of him. For example, Jake Warren described him as 'a student of Nietzsche, a great nihilist and a shadowy figure' and as 'a smoky character'. With respect to his intellectual abilities, which were formidable, Warren characterized him as Jesuitical, 'but more so'. 'He could twist things so black was white and white was black.' Author interview with Warren.
[98] GATT Intersessional Committee – April 1958, RG25: 7976/248/14051–1-40 pt. 1.1. 9, LAC.
[99] Geneva to External, 19 May 1958, RG19: F-2/4208/8718–04, LAC.   [100] Ibid.
[101] Télégramme, Direction des affaires économiques et financières à l'Ambassade Washington, 16 mai 1958, MAEF000068, reel 158, HAEU.

Carl Corse, a Europeanist in the US State Department, summed up US frustration with the EEC outlook and attitude.

> I don't know what they expected to gain. It could be that, having gotten away with what some people might describe as "blackmail" in connection with the Common Market negotiations, they (you know who) may feel they can get away with anything.[102]

Apprehension about the EEC and its implications for other trading countries did not go away. Australia tried to curb the protectionist and discriminatory aspects of the EEC. Australian officials asked for a vote on a resolution that the EEC was in violation of the General Agreement. The EEC threatened to quit GATT if such a vote were held. By 1959, many members had contemplated quitting GATT but few used this threat as effectively as the EEC. Without its support, GATT would not be credible. The vote was called off.

The Common External Tariff of the EEC in the Dillon Round, 1961–1963

In 1958, GATT set up a consultation process for any members who believed that the establishment of the CET of the EEC disadvantaged their exports. US officials welcomed this development as 'a real beginning in establishing a healthy GATT/Common Market relationship'. The apparent accommodation also eased the strain on US foreign policy, which held out seemingly incompatible goals as 'a staunch supporter of both European integration and the GATT'.[103] But accommodation would not be achieved easily. The Six would not make amends for any incidental injury to third parties as a result of the establishment of the common market. A German official explained that the Six felt no obligation to maintain or honour current patterns of trade. Some disadvantage to Europe's trading partners was to be expected. The Six 'should not be … asked to agree to maintain imports from third countries as though no Common market existed'.[104]

Nonetheless, working parties were set up to study injuries to third parties. The British pressed for consideration of particular commodities

[102] Corse to Tuthill, 22 May 1958, RG59: Box 4, file 4.3 – Common Market – GATT Intersessional (Incoming Telegrams) (1958), NARA.
[103] Significance of the GATT Intersessional Committee Meeting, April 14 – May 2, 1958, RG59: Box 4/file 4.3 – Common Market – GATT Intersessional (Incoming Telegrams) (1958), NARA.
[104] Bernard Norwood to Isaiah Frank, 7 May 1958, RG59: Box 4, file 4.3 – Common Market – GATT Intersessional (Incoming Telegrams) (1958), NARA.

that were of interest to their colonies, such as cocoa, coffee, sugar, and bananas. Although the Six had agreed to the working parties, they had not agreed to comply with their findings. For instance, the working party on tropical commodities found that if the AOTs were included under the auspices of the common market, trade would be diverted from current primary producers, including developing countries. The Six denied these claims and retreated behind the reasoning that some price had to be paid (putting up with loss of markets) in order to enjoy the indirect benefits of the EEC. Furthermore, the Six would only consider cases where real damage had occurred, not hypothetical or anticipated damage.

The next attempt to address the harm done to third parties by the CET occurred during the Dillon round of tariff negotiations, 1960–1961. The Dillon round had two stages. In the first stage, parties injured by the establishment of a common external tariff – which in some cases raised duties that had been bound in earlier GATT negotiations – would negotiate with the Six for compensation. The second stage would be a full round of tariff negotiations. Although the stages were separate, the secretariat used the prospect of improved access to global markets as leverage to decrease tariffs.

Negotiations went badly from the outset. The EEC refused to make concessions to countries whose exports were disadvantaged by the CET. The rationale was that while some previously bound rates would rise, others would fall and it would all even out. The Europeans also objected to the idea that they should make concessions for nothing in return. As a German diplomat put it, the 'negotiations must not be mistaken for Santa Claus'.[105] The real problem was that making concessions would acknowledge that they had acted badly. This situation dragged on into 1961 with little sign of movement.

Characterizing the negotiations as anti-EEC put the USA on the defensive. As a result, the USA quietly accepted the EEC's refusal to offer compensation for introducing a common external tariff, a decision that other GATT members saw as 'unfortunately weak and rather equivocal'.[106] When negotiations stalled, the USA remained supportive of the EEC. At a full GATT meeting in February 1961, the US representative gently prodded the EEC to be more forthcoming on agricultural and industrial items. But he emphasized that additional offers from the Six were an improvement; he praised 'their excellent relations with the

[105] Brussels to External, 28 April 1961 re Article XXIV:6 Renegotiations, RG20: A-3/2525/4–581-20 pt. 10, LAC.
[106] TarifDel to Geneva, 12 January 1960, re Tariff Conference – Recent Developments, RG20: A-3/2525/4–581-20 pt. 8.2, LAC. The date is 1960 on the document but it clearly refers to 1961 events and is in a file with other documents all from early 1961.

delegation of the Commission' and stated his optimism that a satisfactory conclusion could be reached. This view was in stark contrast to that of Austria ('they regarded the list of offers of the Community as being entirely inadequate'), New Zealand ('very little' progress had been made and 'on the key items the position remained completely unsatisfactory'), Sweden ('the new offers covered only relatively peripheral marginal export interests'), Australia ('for a major part of agricultural items the Community's offers were either unsatisfactory or non-existent'), Uruguay ('their negotiations with the Community were developing in a totally unsatisfactory manner'), and Denmark ('for nearly all agricultural items of significance to Denmark either no offers or clearly unsatisfactory offers have been put forward').[107]

EEC officials were not moved. They refused to negotiate with any country in the second stage if they turned down offers made in the first. They also announced that their offers were final: it was a 'take it or leave it' position.[108] Wyndham White knew how to exploit crises to break deadlocks. He now proposed that GATT members break off the first part of negotiations and cancel the rest of the round. 'This might bring the Six to their senses.' Washington disagreed with such tactics, making a case for the two stages to proceed in tandem.[109] The Six then agreed to negotiate in the second stage with any country with whom the first attempt at negotiations had not succeeded. But they also announced that 'they had exhausted all their possibilities of negotiation', and they ended negotiations to compensate for the CET. Other GATT members did not want to drop out of the round. As US Under-Secretary of State George Ball explained, the failure of the round could wreck GATT and bring about 'a return to anarchy in our commercial relations'.[110]

The GATT secretariat could create opportunities for the EEC to demonstrate its acceptance of GATT norms and rules, but it depended on its most powerful members exerting pressure on the EEC to bring this about. The United States was the only country with the clout to attempt this, but it was restrained by its long-standing support for the EEC and by its own imperfect record in support of opening world markets. Other GATT members complained about the absence or ineffectiveness of US leadership. Although the USA's stance vis-à-vis the EEC was less pliable than before, and this made an impression on the Dutch and the

[107] The representative for Indonesia was the only one as upbeat as the US representatives. TN 60/S.R. 8, 17 February 1961, GDL.
[108] Brussels to External, 1 February 1961, re ArtXXIV:6 Renegotiations – New Offers of EEC, RG20: A-3/2525/4–581-20 pt. 9; TarifDel to External, 9 May 1961, re Art XXIV:6 Renegotiations: Donne's Statement, RG20: A-3/2525/4–581-20 pt. 10, LAC.
[109] Tarif Del to External, 1 May 1961, re Tariff Negotiations – Negotiations with the Six and Beginning of Dillon Round, RG 20: A-3/2525/4–581-20 pt. 10, LAC.
[110] Letter from Ball to Freeman, 11 December 1961, FRUS 1961–1963, Vol. IX, 506.

Germans according to British observers, they doubted it would be sufficient to move the EEC as a whole. This was because the French, who 'have the whip-hand in the Community', were not deterred by the possibility of falling out with the USA. As a seasoned British diplomat observed: 'they regard the United States with a certain arrogant contempt'.[111]

The refusal of the Six to compensate parties injured by the CET tells only one side of their involvement in the round. They also galvanized the tariff negotiations when they offered to extend the first two phased reductions of the CET (a 20 per cent reduction in total) to all GATT members. This offer was unprecedented in GATT negotiations, which until now had been locked into item-by-item negotiations on a bilateral basis. The problem with the offer was that it exceeded the negotiating latitude of most GATT members, including the USA, which was legally bound to item-by-item negotiations.[112] US negotiators were hamstrung by additional domestic restraints known as peril points, the lowest possible tariff beyond which US domestic producers would be injured. Their offers could not go past the peril points. US officials were well aware of the 'meagerness' of their offers as a result.[113] US Secretary of State Dean Rusk advised President John F. Kennedy to risk Congressional ire and disregard peril points in order to sweeten the USA's list of offers.[114] It was not the Six who were holding back liberalization. Nonetheless, the EEC's offer did not dispel fears among other GATT members. As M. van Oorshot reported following the round, the tariff negotiations 'n'ont également pas crée ni la confiance ni même une attitude favorable des Parties contractantes envers le CEE'.[115]

The EEC Steps Forward in the Kennedy Round, 1963–1967

US President Kennedy introduced the Trade Expansion Act (TEA) in 1962 for economic and foreign policy reasons.[116] Kennedy hoped the

---

[111] UK delegation GATT (Cohen) to Lord Home, 5 March 1962, FO371/164425, TNA.

[112] Y. Alkema, 'European-American Trade Policies, 1961–1963' in D. Brinkley and R. T. Griffiths (eds.), *John F. Kennedy and Europe* (Baton Rouge: Louisiana State University Press, 1999), 222.

[113] Telegram from Embassy in Japan to Consulate General in Geneva, 12 July 1961, *FRUS 1961–1963, Vol. IX*, 472.

[114] Memo from Secretary of State Rusk to President Kennedy, 11 September 1961, *FRUS 1961–1963, Vol. IX*, 474–478. Reference slip attached to memo in RG 59: Office of the Assistant Legal Advisor for Economic Affairs, Records re Trade and GATT, 1947–1966, Box 24, file Trade – GATT – 5th Round 1959–61, NARA.

[115] Conclusions de la XXIème réunion du Comité de directeurs de la politique commerciale, Bruxelles, 26 avril 1962, BAC001/1967–84, HAEU.

[116] S. Dryden, *Trade Warriors: USTR and the American Crusade for Free Trade* (Oxford and New York: Oxford University Press 1995), 33.

TEA would facilitate the sale of US exports and restore a positive balance of payments, as well as revitalizing the relationship between the USA and western Europe. He projected a vision of international relations, dubbed his grand design, in which an Atlantic condominium of like-minded and cooperative allies would fortify the western world economically, politically, and militarily. As the president explained: 'This work goes to the very heart of the many policies and programs, domestic and foreign, which will help to shape the world environment in which the United States must maintain initiative, command respect, and provide leadership.'[117] In other words, the TEA was instrumental to US global politics. It was also a departure in US trade policy. It called for across-the-board tariff cuts to a maximum of 50 per cent.

Growing protectionist forces in the USA objected to the TEA. But the initiative also had powerful backers in the USA, such as Christian Herter, secretary of state from 1959 to 1961 and former governor of Massachusetts, and Will Clayton, former under-secretary of state for economic affairs, who had led the US delegation at the founding conferences of GATT (Geneva, 1947) and the ITO (Havana, 1947–1948). These two elder statesmen emphasized the importance of trade in fortifying the western alliance, especially the links between the USA and western Europe, which were out of sync, as GATT deliberations had revealed. If trade were not used to build that relationship, it might instead undermine it. They explained this to a Congressional subcommittee: 'In our experience we have found no international issues more divisive than economic issues.' They insisted that international political goals should take priority over 'the short-term, special interest of its politically powerful minority groups'.[118]

Despite the advice of Herter and Clayton, the passage of the TEA showed the power of domestic economic interests. When the TEA became law, the office of the United States trade representative (USTR) was created so the State Department would not be able to use trade policy to serve international goals at the expense of domestic economic interests. Kennedy countered by appointing Christian Herter as the first USTR. Herter had already enjoyed a long and distinguished political career. At 67 and in failing health, he accepted the demanding

---

[117] Norwood was paraphrasing Kennedy from November 1962, cited in A. E. Eckes, Jr. (ed.), *Revisiting US Trade Policy: Decisions in Perspective* (Athens, OH: Ohio University Press, 2000), 49.

[118] 'A New Look at Foreign Economic Policy in Light of the Cold War and the Extension of the Common Market in Europe' by Christian A. Herter and William L. Clayton, presented to Sub-committee on Foreign Economic Policy of the Joint Economic Committee, Congress of the United States, 1961, Herter Papers, File 106, MS AM 1829, Houghton Library, Harvard University.

position because he understood that there was 'more international politics wrapped up in these trade matters than most people realize'.[119]

The importance of the Kennedy round was a source of vulnerability for
the USA. As Pierson Dixon, the British ambassador in Paris, noted, the
fact that Washington and London kept saying how important the round
was made its failure attractive to Paris: 'the French in general have no
great enthusiasm for the Kennedy Round and ... General de Gaulle
would be only too pleased if it ended in failure'. He went on to predict
that the French would refuse to cooperate in the round in order to bend
the other five to their views on the CAP, then a source of intense intra-
EEC tension. Paris would subsequently claim that the CAP was carved in
stone and therefore Kennedy round negotiations could only apply to
industrial goods. The round would fail and blame would be shared
between the Six and the USA, 'in consequence probably embittering
relations between Europe and the USA, which de Gaulle would regard
as desirable in itself'. Such an outcome would also facilitate the development of an autonomous European bloc, by which the French meant free
of US influence. Dixon called this the 'Wormser plan'.[120] Given the
recent French veto of the British application to join the EEC, Dixon's
cynicism about French motives is understandable. Meetings with the
architects of French trade policy – Wormser, Clappier, and Kojève –
strengthened his opinion. Although Wormser and Clappier denied that
France would block the round, the British were not reassured.[121] 'Having
been led up the garden path by the French on previous occasions, we are
bound to treat even the statements of their best officials with caution.'[122]
British officials were not alone in believing the French capable, if not
desirous, of wrecking the Kennedy round. Dutch officials also feared 'the
French will kill the Kennedy Round'.[123]

---

[119] Blumenthal, quoted in Eckes, *Revisiting US Trade Policy*, 71.
[120] Pierson Dixon to Patrick Reilly, Foreign Office, 29 March 1963, FO371/172328, TNA.
Reilly was less certain that the French would participate in the Kennedy Round 'only to
destroy it'. See Reilly to Rumbold, 6 August 1963, FO371/172328. Pierson Dixon to Sir
Patrick Reilly, 8 May 1963, FO371/172328, TNA.
[121] Record of Conversation, 5 April 1963, FO371/172328, TNA.
[122] Letter from Harpham to Hughes, Board of Trade, 3 May 1963, FO371/172328, TNA.
[123] Letter and briefing papers from William R. Tyler to Mr. Johnson, 'Your appointment
with the Netherlands State Secretary for Economic Affairs', 28 January 1964, RG59:
Lot File: Records of the Component Offices of the Bureau of Economic Affairs,
1941–1963, Box 3, file: Economic Affairs (Gen), E7 Visits, July–December 1963,
NARA. Ludlow contends that France did not want the Kennedy round to fail although
French officials appreciated that they had great leverage vis-à-vis their EEC partners, as
well as the other GATT members, by being perceived as hostile to the round. He
acknowledges that France was more supportive of the round's success once its grand
design features had been diluted. Ludlow, 'The Emergence of a Commercial Heavy-
Weight', 362–363.

In the lead-up to the negotiations, the French did several things that suggested that they would not be disappointed if the round failed. They supported the German proposal to negotiate lower tariffs on the basis of écrêtement, meaning tariff cuts would be unequal so that high tariffs, of which the USA had many, would be reduced by a greater proportion than moderate tariffs (European tariffs were mostly in this range) and low tariffs. This proposal was not well received in Washington, where it appeared to be a way for the EEC to avoid making significant inroads into the common external tariff.[124] John Tuthill, the USA's representative to the European Community, confronted Walter Hallstein, the EC president, about the écrêtement proposal. Tuthill insisted that it was 'a smoke screen put up by the French in order to avoid serious tariff cuts'. He also took issue with a speech in which Hallstein talked about the importance of resisting efforts to dilute the EEC, 'comme le sucre dans le thé'; Hallstein insisted he had been quoted out of context. Finally, he made the point that the Europeans could not hide behind technical arguments. What was at stake was political and 'involve[ed] the entire Atlantic Alliance'.[125] Tuthill next confronted Sicco Mansholt, the EC commissioner for agriculture, and pointed out the charade of écrêtement. He believed Mansholt had been 'sincerely shocked'. He recommended that George Ball, the under-secretary of state, follow up with Mansholt, 'to give him another injection of spine stiffener'.[126] Although Tuthill believed such confrontations were effective, it is doubtful that they swayed the Commission or isolated France. The EEC dynamic was not one in which a protectionist France was pitted against five more liberal-minded members. The other five members of the EEC shared the French commitment to economic integration and regional trade. Despite differences and disagreements, they were 'driven to negotiate with a single voice' and so were able to compromise and work together in GATT.[127]

The USA more effectively countered the écrêtement proposal at a ministerial meeting of GATT in May 1963. Herter pushed for meaningful liberalization of trade according to an equal linear formula. Confronted with European resistance, Herter held firm. European unity weakened in the face of US resolve, in particular along French–West German lines. Chancellor Erhard of West Germany favoured a looser

---

[124] E. H. Preeg, *Traders and Diplomats: An Analysis of the Kennedy Round of Negotiations under the General Agreement on Tariffs and Trade* (Washington, DC: Brookings Institute, 1970), 4.

[125] Memo of Conversation, Hallstein and Tuthill, 20 May 1963, JMAS/95 (Jean Monnet Series), HAEU.

[126] Tuthill to Ball, 20 May 1963, JMAS/95, HAEU.

[127] Coppolaro, *The Making of a World Trade Power*, 201–202, 205–206, and passim.

and more open association among the Six and cherished a strong Atlantic association.[128] As a member of the US State Department reported, 'Erhard became hysterical when he thought we might walk out.'[129] President Kennedy then yielded slightly by agreeing that the highest US tariffs could be reduced by a disproportionate amount. There would be an economic cost to the USA once the actual bargaining began: it would have to cut more deeply into its highest tariffs, on items such as chemicals. There was a diplomatic cost in refusing. As Ball put it, 'if the U.S. refused to yield some ground it would be playing into de Gaulle's hands, proving the General's point that the U.S. planned to run the world its way'.[130] The inclusion of agriculture remained undecided, although the final resolution stated that 'agriculture and primary products' fell within the scope of the negotiations.[131] *Time* magazine reported this as a French diplomatic loss which the French had not taken well.

The French subsequently turned to underhanded politics to regain their lost advantage. Kojève spread a rumour that Wyndham White, the soul and spine of GATT, anticipated the end of the organization and was contemplating retirement.[132] French officials also called for a new, and global, international trade forum. British officials observed that what had begun as an idea that Kojève 'peddl[ed] ... in corridors' had since been endorsed by Wormser and pitched to US diplomats in Paris.[133] Kojève admitted to US officials that he was working towards the dissolution of GATT as part of the 'general shake-up of the international trade machinery'. He boldly claimed that his personal view would be French policy within six months and would represent the Commission's position within a year.[134] Wyndham White was understandably demoralized and did contemplate giving up, a move that the

[128] Visit of Chancellor Erhard of Germany, 28–29 December 1963, Talking Points for the President on Trade Negotiations, 20 December 1963, RG59: Box 3, file: Economic Affairs (Gen), E7 Visits, July–December 1963, NARA.

[129] GATT Negotiations (world), Zim to Bermingham, 23 May 1963, *Time* Magazine Dispatches, second series, Box 32, file 612, MS 2090.1, Houghton Library, Harvard University.

[130] GATT Negotiations ADD (world), Bermingham to Zim, 24 May 1963, *Time* Magazine Dispatches, second series, Box 32, file 612, MS Am 2090.1, Houghton Library, Harvard University.

[131] Arrangements for the Reduction or Elimination of Tariffs and other Barriers To Trade and Related Matters And Measures for Access to Markets for Agricultural and Other Primary Products, MIN (63) 9, 22 May 1963, GDL.

[132] Burgh to Jardine (BT), 12 June 1963, FO371/172328, TNA.

[133] Geneva to Foreign Office, 14 June 1963, FO371/172328, TNA.

[134] Central Intelligence Bulletin, 1 June 1963, Freedom of Information Act Electronic Reading Room, www.foia.cia.gov/sites/default/files/document_conversions/5829/CIA-RDP79T00975A007000320001-8.pdf

British believed would stop the Kennedy round before it had even begun and would destroy GATT.[135]

Pierson Dixon feared that his counterparts in the US embassy in Paris had not properly understood 'the real French position'.[136] US officials were concerned about French intentions with respect to the Kennedy round, but they did not articulate their concerns as forcefully or in the same way as the British did. Moreover, they had a tendency to place too much faith in their 'friends' in the Quai d'Orsay and not enough in well-known figures such as Wormser, Clappier, and Kojève, although their influence was beginning to wane as time went on. (Clappier became a deputy governor of the Bank of France in 1964; Wormser was appointed ambassador to Moscow in 1966; Kojève died in 1968.)[137] Washington also placed too much faith in the European Commission, which could not alone determine trade policy. As Coppolaro explains, the Council of Ministers was a bastion of national interest and it kept close watch over trade policy.[138]

US diplomats in Paris prepared a report asking the apposite, if belated, question: 'What are the French really up to in the GATT?' The report noted that the French stance towards GATT had been entirely self-serving: they stood up for GATT when it was in their interests to do so; they criticized GATT when it suited them. Overall, the French had never been keen on GATT because the organization seemed to be 'tailored to fit the United States interests and the organization has grown up in Geneva as anti-EEC and dominated by the Anglo-Saxons'. While the report's general characterization of French self-interest applied to all GATT members, the analysis identified the deep political forces that shaped French trade policy, especially French determination to maintain their independence vis-à-vis the United States. The report's conclusion was to downplay the grand design and Atlanticist aims of the Kennedy round. Better to adopt a more technical economic approach which, if successful, would serve 'the objectives of our Atlantic policy'.[139] Despite this sound advice, US policy-makers continued to talk about the Kennedy round in loaded terms. As an internal memo saw it, 'the negotiations are a test of

---

[135] 'The French and G.A.T.T.', 21 June 1963, FO371/172328, TNA.
[136] Pierson Dixon to Sir Patrick Reilly, 8 May 1963, FO371/172328, TNA.
[137] Bohlen to Herter, 15 April 1964, Herter Papers, file 52, MS Am 1829, Houghton Library, Harvard University.
[138] Coppolaro, *The Making of a World Trade Power*, 63. It had earlier created the 111 committee which advised the commission on trade policy. Membership on the 111 committee explicitly served and safeguarded the individual national interests of the Six.
[139] Memorandum, J. M. Myerson to the Ambassador, 'The Future of the GATT', 17 June 1963 in U.S. Mission to the European Communities to Brussels, 21 January 1963, JMAS/95, HAEU.

whether the EEC will be an outward looking community ready to share with the U.S. the responsibilities of free world leadership or whether the EEC will turn inward on itself'.[140] Herter repeated that the aim of the Kennedy round was 'to achieve a partnership in prosperity embracing all the nations of the Free World'. Within this broadly cast partnership, the US–EEC tie was crucial. As Herter put it, 'it offers this generation of mankind ... its best hope for establishing freedom on so broad and strong a foundation that it will prevail over all the dangers that beset it'.[141]

When the Kennedy round officially opened in May 1964, there was not much reason for optimism.[142] Intra-EC struggles, such as the empty chair crisis of 1965, a second failed bid by the UK to accede to the EEC, and the finalization of the CAP all obstructed and prolonged the negotiations.[143] While the US–EEC negotiations were not the only set of negotiations of importance, the success of the round was contingent on agreement between them. Their negotiations did not always go well, especially over chemicals. At times, the round, like others before and after, seemed likely to collapse. Wyndham White made use of his formidable mediating skills to bring about agreement between the USA and the EEC.[144] After extended and frustrating discussions, and a number of blocked pairs of negotiations, a final agreement was reached.[145]

The Kennedy round achieved more significant liberalization than any round since 1947, especially for manufactured goods. The USA made tariff cuts affecting US$6.4 billion worth of goods; it received tariff cuts affecting US$6.7 billion, of which US$2.7 billion came from the EEC.[146] Tariffs on manufactured goods were lowered on average by 35 per cent. Liberalizing agricultural trade did not make much progress,

[140] EEC and Trade Negotiations, Background Paper re Vice President's Visit to the Benelux Countries, 3–10 November 1963, RG59: Box 3. file: Economic Affairs (Gen), E7 Visits, July–December 1963, NARA.

[141] C. A. Herter, 'U.S. Aims in the Kennedy Round', *Atlantic Community Quarterly* 2 (2) (Summer 1964), 240, 246.

[142] Many historians have written about the Kennedy round. See, for instance, J. Evans, *The Kennedy Round in American Trade Policy: The Twilight of the GATT?* (Cambridge, MA: Harvard University Press, 1971); E. H. Preeg, *Traders and Diplomats: An Analysis of the Kennedy Round of Negotiations under the General Agreement on Tariffs and Trade* (Washington, DC: Brookings Institute, 1970); and T. W. Zeiler, *American Trade and Power in the 1960s* (New York: Columbia University Press, 1992).

[143] N. Piers Ludlow, *The European Community and the Crises of the 1960s: Negotiating the Gaullist Challenge* (London and New York: Routledge, 2006).

[144] Coppolaro, *The Making of a World Trading Power*, 192–197. Evans suggests three factors pushed the participants to agreement: the prospect of tangible economic benefits; concern about the psychological backlash if the round failed; fear of being blamed for the failure of the round. Evans, *The Kennedy Round*, 279.

[145] For details, see Evans, *The Kennedy Round*, chapter 14.

[146] Zeiler, *American Trade and Power in the 1960s*, 237.

a disappointment to many GATT members, though not to the EEC. US officials had considered making the liberalization of trade in agriculture a deal-breaker for the round. In the end, they decided against this. The overriding aim of the round was defined by the US State Department and it was to support the EEC 'at any price'.[147] They hoped that the damage could be redressed later on.[148] US officials persuaded President Lyndon Johnson to accept the US–EEC settlement. To turn away would fuel protectionism and isolationism in Europe.[149]

Although the political significance of the Kennedy round had been diluted over many months of bargaining, the international backdrop – 'the depths of the Cold War' – gave meaning to the outcome.[150] US officials recalled that they had kept 'their eye on the big picture',[151] and that was international and political. As Mike Blumenthal, who took over the US negotiations after Herter's death, recollected, the importance of a united and prosperous Europe was never challenged.

You have to remember that while canned hams or backs and necks may be critical, they are not really that important. Europe flourished and that was important. The fact that our chickens could no longer be exported to Europe was tough for Arkansas but it didn't change the course of history. But, if the Common Market had broken apart, it would have changed the course of history. And so we must always remember the connection between the economic and the political.[152]

Blumenthal's assessment rested on the belief that the EEC was vulnerable. Certainly it was strained by its own internal pressures, as the empty chair crisis revealed. But the Kennedy round had not threatened the EEC. Indeed, as several scholars have pointed out, the EEC showed that it was the equal of the USA and a 'commercial heavyweight' in its own right. But US–EEC relations had been strained by the round: their negotiations fuelled competition, engendered mistrust, and highlighted differences in foreign policy priorities.[153]

---

[147] Memo by Courtenay P. Worthington for Ambassador Blumenthal Per Your Request: An 'Essay' on Agriculture, 3 May 1965, RG59: Bureau of European Affairs: Office of the OECD, European Community and Atlantic Political-Economic Affairs, Records relating to the Kennedy Round Trade Negotiations 1963–1970, box 1, file K.2 Kennedy Round, NARA.

[148] Interview with Raymond Andrew Ioanes, Association for Diplomatic Studies and Training, Foreign Affairs Oral History Project Agriculture Series, interviewed by James O'Brien Howard, 12 July 1994, www.loc.gov/item/mfdipbib000551

[149] Evans, *The Kennedy Round*, 279   [150] Eckes, *Revisiting US Trade Policy*, 5.

[151] Ibid., 98.   [152] Ibid., 83.

[153] Dryden, *Trade Warriors*, 113. Mahan agrees that the Kennedy Round became 'a wedge that divided the Atlantic alliance'. E. R. Mahan, *Kennedy, de Gaulle, and Western Europe* (Basingstoke: Palgrave Macmillan, 2002), 106.

For other US observers, the main issues concerned US leadership, credibility, and influence in world affairs. As Dean Acheson saw it, 'The Kennedy Round is a political struggle for power; it is one of the forces that will shape the future of European unification and of our Atlantic relations. What we do will bear on whether de Gaulle and nationalism are to prevail.'[154] For those who continued to believe that European unity and strength was the primary aim of US foreign policy, the Kennedy round confirmed Europe's recovery as a leader in world affairs. For those intent on renewing the Atlantic bond, the negotiations were sobering. As Thomas Zeiler explains, the Kennedy round was not 'a grand cooperative effort, but a quibbling, tough discussion between business rivals'.[155]

Conclusions

Although the establishment of the EEC was regarded as a progressive, even enlightened, development in European history that might bring peace, or at least stability, to the continent and that strengthened the western alliance in relation to the Cold War, its reception in GATT was mixed. Sir Edgar Cohen of Britain listed some of the reasons why the EEC was 'generally disliked and distrusted': community officials were 'overbearing in manner and . . . unyielding in debate'; their overall stance was 'protectionist and their philosophy reactionary'.[156] The perception of the EEC as a narrowly self-interested bloc persisted even though the EEC had contributed to the liberalization of global trade: it had generated momentum in liberalizing trade in industrial goods during the Kennedy round. As an EEC representative explained with some insight, even though the economic community was a catalyst to the growth of trade for its own members and for trading partners beyond, the presence of the EEC elicited 'anxieties and apprehensions which are not based on facts and figures'.[157] But the EEC also prevented liberalization in other areas such as agriculture.[158] Inconsistent support for liberalization did not set the EEC apart or explain the wariness which it elicited in GATT. Trade negotiations are an inherently competitive process and the aim of all participants is to get the most possible for the least in return. All members pressed for liberalization in those areas in which they were most

---

[154] Dryden, *Trade Warriors*, 86.

[155] Zeiler, *American Trade and Power in the 1960s*, 181.

[156] Sir Edgar Cohen to Lord Home, 'General Agreement on Tariffs and Trade', UEE 1024/24, 6 March 1962, CAB134/1957, TNA.

[157] Statement by the Representative of the Community on the Implementation of the Rome Treaty, 15 March 1965, L/2394, GDL.

[158] Coppolaro reaches the same conclusion in *The Making of a World Trade Power*, 7.

competitive and invoked a variety of reasons to justify protectionism where they were less competitive.

Mistrust of the EEC was an understandable response for smaller powers having to deal with a much stronger entity. By the early 1960s, the EEC was undoubtedly a formidable presence within GATT, although as Coppolaro notes, being an equal partner did not make it a leader.[159] Regardless, a shift in power was recognized at the time. According to Myer Rashish of the US State Department, 'No longer is the U.S. the sole dominant economic power in the advanced world and no longer is the U.S. in a position to direct the course of international economic policy through its own initiatives.'[160] For GATT, the issue was not simply whether there was a new leader, but how that leader acted. The United States was criticized for its inability or unwillingness to act as a leader in GATT and when it used GATT to advance its own interests. The problem with EEC leadership was that it prioritized regional interests unapologetically and accepted that its trade policies would have repercussions for other countries; this was starkly evident with respect to agricultural trade, as will be discussed in Chapter 6. For EEC members the institutions that mattered were internal, especially in working out the parameters of authority of the Council of Ministers and the Commission, the focal point of supranational cooperation. The EEC did not have much regard for GATT as an institution, even though it valued trade negotiations, and it used GATT to serve its interests. In this, the EEC countries were no different from other GATT members, but they were more conspicuous and perhaps more skewed in their commitment to promoting European interests over, possibly even at the expense of, those of an expanding global trade system.

The creation of a European common market reinforced the economic goals and political objectives of GATT. It stabilized European inter-state relations and contributed to economic growth and rising standards of living in western Europe. In wartime and early postwar discussions, the advocates of the regional organization of Europe believed that it complemented plans for global governance, albeit on a smaller scale. Yet, in the eyes of the GATT secretariat and many GATT members, the EEC threatened the organization and the cause of liberalization. Despite being a powerful collective actor within GATT, the EEC was never

---

[159] Coppolaro, *The Making of a World Trading Power*, 206. Deese sees the USA as a structural leader in the GATT during the Kennedy Round. Deese, *World Trade Politics*, 60–67.

[160] Memo by Rashish, 'For Discussion at Meeting of Trade Negotiating Subcommittee, 29 October 1963', Herter Papers: Box 7/file: Committee for Economic Development, 5/63–11/63, JFKL.

a champion of the organization. At times it was an outspoken critic, suggesting that GATT was inadequate, that it served poorly the economic interests of western European nations, that liberal trade was an instrument of US economic and political influence, and that GATT usurped the sovereignty of its members. When the EEC did work in tandem with the organization, it was because its interests were well served. Even so, the Six valued the regional approach as a necessary annexe to the global trade order. This view reflected a narrower commitment to individual interests (in this case, the individual interests of six countries), as well as a belief that states at similar stages of economic development could work together more effectively. When the success of the EEC came at the expense of third parties, it also undermined the liberal promise that all would benefit from trade. The preference for regionalism was also an indictment of the shortcomings of GATT: the inclusive organization did not do enough to support the economic well-being of its members (even those that were privileged within the organization) because of its institutional mandate, design, and operations. While regional and global approaches to trade did not need to be in conflict, the EEC and GATT pitted these options as mutually exclusive.

Nonetheless, Wyndham White believed that GATT had passed the EEC test because of its flexibility.[161] This was a rosy interpretation of events. John Jackson explains that flexibility really meant 'ignoring or bending rules.'[162] GATT had survived its 'head-on collision' with the EEC,[163] but it had also been circumvented and its authority had been diminished. EEC officials evaded GATT processes and oversight, for example by refusing to permit GATT discussion of EEC policies and practices not yet established or by sending low-level functionaries to GATT meetings. In the Dillon round, the EEC refused to compensate for trade lost as a result of the CET and then threatened to withhold any further concessions in the second part of the trade negotiations, showing that GATT had little leverage over them. However, the organization of the Dillon round, and the inclusion of negotiations to compensate for the CET, were also admissions that other countries had the right to expect redress for damage to their trade. GATT members could ask for compensation even if there was no guarantee that they would get anything.

---

[161] 'Europe in the GATT'. Address by Wyndham White, Europe House, London, May 1960, WTO.
[162] Memorandum on the defects of GATT from John H. Jackson, General Counsel to Fred Sanderson, Member, Planning and Coordination Staff, Department of State, 21 February 1973, RG364: Box 63, file GATT Disputes 1973–74, NARA.
[163] 'Europe in the GATT', Address by Wyndham White, Europe House, London, May 1960, WTO.

GATT provided mechanisms to articulate grievances even if it could not resolve conflicts. Moreover, GATT had the ability to scrutinize trade policies and insist that members justify actions that deviated from liberal trade practices. Even if it could not exert pressure to change policies, this process was valued. As a correspondent for *Time* magazine, who was clearly well connected to the US State Department, observed: 'This process of public laundering of policy has been one of the most useful quiet processes through which GATT has been effective for years.'[164] This process was evidence of GATT's normative sway and functional utility and allowed the organization and its secretariat to influence national policies.[165] It helps to explain why the EEC did not simply quit GATT. Repudiating GATT would signal its rejection of cooperation, rules, and interdependence within the global community.

---

[164] Dispatch, 24 October 1958, Notes from *Time* Magazine Dispatches, 2nd series, 1956–1968, MS. 2090.1, Box 13, File 226, Houghton Library, Harvard University.

[165] This is one of the main points that Pedersen develops in her study of the League of Nations Permanent Mandates Commission. The Permanent Mandates Commission became a site of public accountability and galvanized a process of internationalization which transformed global geopolitics. As Pedersen put it, 'Bureaucracy, more than idealism, tamed the demons of power.' S. Pedersen, *The Guardians: The League of Nations and the Crisis of Empire* (Oxford: Oxford University Press, 2015), 46.

4 'Spread Like the Plague'
The Regional Challenge to GATT

The regional challenge to GATT did not end with the establishment of the EEC. The EEC subsequently negotiated numerous agreements with states outside of Europe, many of which had been former colonies. The EEC's membership grew in 1973 when Britain, Ireland, and Denmark joined. The EEC's example sparked other regional agreements: before long almost every GATT member, including some of its most consistent backers such as Canada, Australia, and the United States, had joined at least one regional agreement. Their proliferation (with the potential for trade restrictions to 'spread like the plague',[1] as quoted in the previous chapter) came to be seen as a threat to the organization because they contradicted the commitment to the MFN principle, which was 'the keystone of the GATT trade rules'.[2] The rise of such agreements also suggested that regional trade agreements could advance trade liberalization more effectively than the unwieldly GATT could.[3] As John Evans explains, the most significant question about regional trade agreements was not whether they raised or lowered tariffs, but how they affected 'the future integrity of the GATT as a multilateral contract'.[4] GATT had to respond to the regional challenge. New measures included the creation of more robust infrastructure (such as the GATT Council in 1960) and new

---

[1] Canadian Permanent Mission, Geneva to External, 3 March 1958, RG25: G-2/Vol. 7976/14051-1-40 pt 1.1, LAC.

[2] GATT, *Trade Policies for a Better Future: The 'Leutwiler Report', the GATT and the Uruguay Round*, with an introduction by A. Dunkel (Dordrecht, Boston, and Lancaster: Martinus Nijhoff Publishers, 1987), 25.

[3] Baldwin claims that it was only in the 1990s that regional trade agreements raised systemic considerations about 'whether regionalism was good or bad for the multilateral trading system'. My research suggests that regional trade agreements were associated with a broader range of institutional and systemic questions from the beginning, such as whether or not they supported a rules-based international order. R. Baldwin, 'Preferential Trading Arrangements' in A. Narlikar, M. Daunton, and R. M. Stern (eds.), *The Oxford Handbook on the World Trade Organization* (Oxford: Oxford University Press, 2012), 631–654.

[4] J. W. Evans, *The Kennedy Round in American Trade Policy: The Twilight of the GATT?* (Cambridge, MA: Harvard University Press, 1971), 59.

rounds of negotiations that would demonstrate the organization's relevance and primacy in the regulation and management of global trade. Some believed the threat extended beyond GATT and could affect the entire global governance system, causing conflict – possibly even war – and creating winners and losers. In the 1980s, there were predictions that the world would be divided into embattled regional trade blocs in North America, Europe, and Asia. Regionalism was a challenge to GATT in its own right, but it was also symptomatic of a drift away from the liberal faith that had underpinned the global order since the Second World War.

Debates about Regional Trade: Trade Creating or Trade Diverting?

Writing soon after the Second World War, Jacob Viner was one of the first economists to study regional trade agreements. Half a century later, his ideas remain relevant. For Viner, the essential feature of a regional trade bloc is that members exchange preferential terms of trade that are not extended to third parties. One can call this preferential, which implies positive advantage for members, or discriminatory, because those outside the agreement face disadvantageous terms in those markets.[5] Viner asked whether such blocs were trade creating or trade diverting. If they were trade creating, then they were consistent with an expanding and open global trade system. If they were trade diverting, then they were incompatible with and threatening to liberal trade. Viner recognized that customs unions (one of the most common forms of regional trade agreements, along with free trade agreements) could do both: 'Customs unions are, from the free trade point of view, neither necessarily good nor necessarily bad.'[6]

Other scholars have also made the case that regionalism need not threaten the multilateral liberal effort. Bhalla and Bhalla describe regional trade agreements concluded after 1980 as 'generally outward-looking and ... an engine of growth' and they observe, along the lines that Viner had suggested years earlier, that such arrangements could be

[5] Participants in a regional trade agreement need not be geographically adjacent. As Mansfield and Milner explain, a region can be defined in terms of geographical proximity, norms, political cultures, or shared languages. E. D. Mansfield and H. V. Milner, 'The New Wave of Regionalism', *International Organization* 53 (3) (Summer 1999), 590–591.
[6] J. Viner, *The Customs Union Issue* (New York: Carnegie Endowment for International Peace; London: Stevens & Sons United, 1950), 44, 52. Subsequent scholars have slightly reformulated Viner's original question. Bhalla and Bhalla ask whether regional trade agreements were stumbling blocks or building blocks to global free trade. A. S. Bhalla and P. Bhalla, *Regional Blocs: Building Blocks or Stumbling Blocks?* (Basingstoke: Macmillan Press; New York: St. Martin's Press, 1997). See Mansfield and Milner, 'The New Wave of Regionalism' for a useful summary of the literature on regionalism.

simultaneously trade diverting and trade creating.[7] In a slightly different vein, Paul Volker, the American economist and chair of the Federal Reserve in the 1980s, concludes that even though regional trade blocs are trade diverting, their overall effect has been 'relatively benign'.[8] But others, including Hoekman and Kostecki, argue that the proliferation of regional trade agreements is cause for concern because of their effects on global trade and the global system.[9] Although at one time Jagdish Bhagwati suggested there was some doubt about whether regional agreements 'have been a sanguine and benign development or a malign force that will serve to undermine the widely shared objective of multilateral free trade for all', he subsequently came out strongly against such arrangements.[10] He calls preferential trade agreements a 'pernicious development' that emasculated the General Agreement: 'like termites ... eating away at the multilateral trading system relentlessly and progressively'.[11]

The drafters of the General Agreement had not identified regional trade as a particularly injurious trade practice, unlike cartels and quantitative restrictions. They saw such restrictions as instruments of chauvinistic, autarkic policies and indicative of a conception of economic growth as spoils over which nations fought, creating a toxic environment for international relations generally. But before long, the GATT secretariat saw regional trade blocs as threats. In part this was a result of GATT's success in growing its membership. More members meant that negotiations became cumbersome and protracted. While the original meeting in Geneva in 1947 lasted six months, the Tokyo round of the 1970s took seven years to complete. A large membership was good for GATT, showing that it lived up to its own standard of universal representation, but the effect on trade negotiations undercut that gain. As Steve Dryden observes about the Uruguay round, GATT could only take 'tiny steps' in moving trade liberalization forward.[12] GATT had become 'the General

---

[7] Bhalla and Bhalla, *Regional Blocs*, 18, 25.

[8] Quoted in J. Bhagwati and M. Hirsch (eds.), *The Uruguay Round and Beyond: Essays in Honor of Arthur Dunkel* (Ann Arbor: University of Michigan Press, 1998), 217.

[9] B. M. Hoekman and M. M. Kostecki, *The Political Economy of the World Trading System: From GATT to WTO* (Oxford and New York: Oxford University Press, 1995), 223–224.

[10] J. Bhagwati, 'Regionalism and Multilateralism: An Overview' in J. Bhagwati, P. Khrishna, and A. Panagariya (eds.), *Trading Blocs: Alternative Approaches to Analyzing Preferential Trade Agreements* (Cambridge, MA, and London: MIT Press, 1999), 26.

[11] J. Bhagwati, *Termites in the Trading System: How Preferential Agreements Undermine Free Trade* (Oxford: Oxford University Press, 2008), xii, xvii–xviii, 28.

[12] Quoted in E. H. Preeg, *Traders in a Brave New World: The Uruguay Round and the Future of the International Trading System* (Chicago and London: University of Chicago Press, 1995), 89.

Agreement to Talk and Talk'.[13] In contrast, regional agreements seem more dynamic and move at a faster pace.

Although scholars have identified several stages in the expansion of regional trade agreements, many flag the period from the 1980s as the time of real challenge to GATT and multilateral trade.[14] Bhagwati claims that the first wave of regionalism involving African and Latin American countries in the 1950s and 1960s was a fairly minor challenge to the multilateral trade order because the agreements were not long-lasting and did not involve significant amounts of trade. He suggests that regionalism had 'virtually died' by the end of the 1960s. He acknowledges the importance of the EEC, which he says 'started the pandemic', but the critical moment was when the USA concluded regional agreements in the 1980s – first with Israel and then with Canada. This decision 'grossly aggravated' the regional trend.[15] This periodization emphasizes the importance and agency of the largest powers and reinforces the idea of US hegemony as central to GATT and the liberal trade order.

In fact, regional trade agreements were continuously concluded throughout the period covered in this book, although the number grew especially quickly in the 1990s (see Figure 4.1). Observing the chronology draws attention to the impact of small members on GATT and the way the legitimacy of international rules was both upheld and subverted by all GATT members. The GATT secretariat affirmed the organization's right to oversee regional agreements and to ensure that the terms were compatible with GATT standards. The process whereby such agreements were presented to the secretariat and membership, and the attempt to make GATT scrutiny more than a pro forma inspection, confirmed the commitment of members to national economic interests first and

---

[13] Bhagwati, *Termites in the Trading System*, 22.

[14] Mansfield and Milner identify four waves of preferential trade agreements (PTAs): the first in the mid- to late nineteenth century, when PTAs were mostly trade creating and resulted in an interdependent international economic system revolving around Europe; then 1919–1939, when PTAs were instruments of and reflected acrimonious political rivalry; next from 1950 to the late 1970s; and the most recent wave from 1980 to1995. 'The New Wave of Regionalism', 596–601. Bhalla and Bhalla identify a first stage in the 1960s, mostly among developing countries, and then another phase in the 1990s as a response to global protectionism. Bhalla and Bhalla, *Regional Blocs*, 1–2. VanGrasstek's periodization emphasizes the WTO era. For the GATT period, he identifies two phases: 1948 to the early 1980s (when he says regional trade agreements were 'scarce'), followed by the Uruguay Round, 1986–1994. C. VanGrasstek, *The History and Future of the World Trade Organization* (Geneva: World Trade Organization, 2013), 468, 471–472.

[15] Bhagwati, 'Regionalism and Multilateralism: An Overview', 10. Bhagwati, *Termites in the Trading System*, 14, 29. Also see A. Panagariya and T. N. Srinivasan, 'The New Regionalism: A Benign or Malign Growth?' in Bhagwati and Hirsch (eds.), *The Uruguay Round and Beyond*, 222–223.

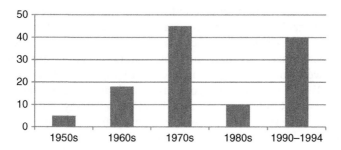

Figure 4.1 Number of regional trade agreements concluded, by date of notification to GATT
Source: WTO, Regional Trade Agreements Information System (RTAIS), extracted on 13 June 2019 at 20:01, http://rtais.wto.org/UI/Charts.aspx

foremost. They asserted their rights and minimized their responsibilities. But the story is not one of complete defeat for GATT. By going through the motions of submitting their agreements to GATT, members upheld the ideal of multilateralism and entrenched the practice of accountability.

The Proliferation of Regional Trade Agreements, 1960–1972

Although Bhagwati claims that the authors of the General Agreement had not expected that there would be many regional agreements, they had in fact prepared for that possibility. Article XXIV of the General Agreement laid out criteria for regional free trade agreements and customs unions, such as those covering most of the trade among the signatories. But the Article was hazy about the duration of regional agreements and about timetables and plans by which to make them more compliant with inclusive liberal practices.[16] GATT members and the secretariat had to determine whether each regional agreement conformed to Article XXIV, even though there was considerable ambiguity about what made an agreement compatible.

The default GATT position was that regional and global free trade arrangements were compatible. However, this 'positive view' masked underlying apprehension. Wyndham White believed that the GATT secretariat should take action to prevent the proliferation of regional trade agreements. He had little faith in the leading members of GATT,

[16] Article XXIV of the General Agreement: A Note by the Secretariat, 11 August 1987, MTN.GNG/NG7/W/13, GDL.

who he believed were 'preoccupied with internal political problems' and were, as a result, 'neglecting international commercial matters'. Recent experience with the EEC justified his scepticism. The six European states were '"mesmerized" by their "new toy"', and other continental European nations were intent on 'gaining access' to the EEC. Britain was also 'obsessed' with the EEC. Opposition to such agreements was tepid. He described the USA as 'weak and inept' and largely oblivious to the challenge of the EEC. Canada was 'retreating' from liberal trade policies, focusing on relations with the USA and the Commonwealth. Latin America was 'a mess'. He sweepingly described all of Asia as 'weak'.[17]

The establishment of the EEC prompted the creation of the European Free Trade Area (EFTA), an agreement that brought together Austria, Britain, Denmark, Norway, Portugal, Sweden, and Switzerland. EFTA was a consolation prize for the British, who had opted to stay out of the EEC but who did not want to be shut out of European trade. Some officials hoped that EFTA could be the basis for a free trade link with the EEC. In the end, nothing came of this.[18] But for GATT, EFTA was more proof of the appeal of the regional alternative to trade organization. It also tested GATT's ability to oversee regional agreements involving its members. In several ways, EFTA fell short of GATT criteria for a trade-creating agreement. EFTA's coverage extended only to industrial goods. The omission of agriculture meant it did not include 'substantially all trade'. Regardless, EFTA members insisted that the agreement was trade creating and liberalizing. Not all GATT members were convinced, even though 'The virtues of "free trade" are sung in all keys.'[19] The United States and France wanted EFTA members to request a waiver from GATT under Article XXV, indicating that they regarded EFTA as a derogation of GATT rules and aims. The agreement would then be accountable to GATT in a more meaningful way.[20] But EFTA countries wanted the EFTA Convention to be treated just as the Treaty of Rome had been, meaning there would be no vetting or oversight by GATT.[21] They succeeded and registered the agreement under Article XXIV.

[17] The Canadian Permanent Mission, Geneva to USSEA, Tel. 141, 3 March 1958, RG25: 7976/248/14051–1-40 pt. 1.1, LAC.

[18] J. Ellison, *Threatening Europe: Britain and the Creation of the European Community, 1955–1958* (Basingstoke: Macmillan Press; New York: St Martin's Press, 2000), 216–217.

[19] Commentary on the pamphlet entitled 'EFTA, European Free Trade Association', issued by the governments of the seven, 11 January 1960, BAC61/1982–24 pt. 2, HAEU.

[20] Note pour M. le ministre Rey, 30 October 1960, BAC61/1982–24 pt.3, HAEU. Paris to Foreign Office, Tel. 18 Saving, 21 January 1960, FO371/150258, TNA.

[21] External to Washington, 28 October 1960, re Pre-GATT Talks, RG20: A-3/2527/4–581-29 pt. 2.2, LAC.

GATT discussions of the compatibility of EFTA with its rules and norms gave EEC officials an opportunity to argue for the benefits and timeliness of regional economic trade blocs – 'l'intégration régionale est un phénomène d'une grande généralité, caractéristique du monde contemporain' – and to narrow GATT's mandate by denying its ability to reject a trade agreement.[22] But other members were worried about a shift to regional trade. EFTA was soon followed by the creation of the Latin American Free Trade Association (LAFTA) (1960) and the Central American Multilateral Treaty of Freer Trade (1961). Participating countries upheld the agreements as a way to promote economic development and to minimize their dependence on the markets of developed countries. The USA accepted the Central American arrangement on the grounds that 'economic cooperation between two or three countries' could not be considered 'an act hostile to others'.[23] Moreover, US officials worried that if they were rebuffed, Latin American countries might quit GATT.[24] Just as with the EEC and EFTA, there was little meaningful scrutiny of the agreements and there was no attempt to make them more GATT compliant.

Regional trade agreements exposed the limits of GATT's authority while also showing how important it was to have an organization 'whose responsibility it is to foster multilateral trade'.[25] Wyndham White addressed the challenge by creating a permanent council that would give GATT 'a formal organizational character'.[26] The council would attend to all matters arising before GATT on a continuous basis, as opposed to the semi-annual sessions that had been held to deal with GATT business.

Institutional insecurity also lay behind the proposed council. Some feared that the EEC's apparent preference for working through the Organization for Economic Cooperation and Development (OECD) could turn GATT into 'a forum for discussing problems of peripheral

---

[22] Déclaration du porte-parole de la Communauté économique européenne concernant l'Association européenne de libre-échange (point XII de l'ordre du jour de la XVIème sessions des Parties contractantes), 17 mai 1960, BAC61/1982–24 pt. 3, HAEU.

[23] Letter from Thomas C. Mann, Assistant Secretary, to Robert Newbegin, American Ambassador, Tegucigalpa, 28 August 1959, RG59: Box 1/Regional Markets – Latin America, Records of Component Offices of the Bureau of Economic Affairs, 1941–1963, NARA.

[24] External to Washington, 28 October 1960, re Pre-GATT Talks, RG20: A-3/2527/4–581-29 pt. 2.2, LAC.

[25] Establishment of a council of the contracting parties, First report by the special group on GATT Organization, L/1200, 19 May 1960, GDL.

[26] Improving the administration of GATT, 14 January 1960, RG59: Office of the Assistant Legal Advisor on Economic Affairs/Records relating to Trade and GATT 1947–1966, Box 8, file GATT-organization, NARA.

countries such as Australia'.[27] Canadian officials reported that Wyndham White was 'greatly distressed' at developments within the OECD. As its role expanded, the reach and relevance of GATT would shrink.[28] US officials also hoped the council would offset the increasing European preference for the OECD and the 'strong continuing pressures ... for regional orientation in trade policy discussions'.[29] Wynn Plumptre of Canada confirmed that support for the council was strongest among non-European members who wanted to 'reinforce the trade organization of which they themselves are members'.[30] However, the proposal presented problems for the United States, where the most recent attempt to create the OTC had not been approved by Congress. The creation of a permanent council might be seen as 'circumventing Congress'.[31] In the end, the council was established with an open membership and it carried on the work of the intersessional meetings on a regular basis.[32] The case for the council was that it would be better able to deal with GATT business because it met more regularly, not because it had expanded authority. As one US official explained, there could be no 'appearance of creating a new organization or a permanent institution'.[33] The first council meeting was in September 1960.

Wyndham White's attempt to strengthen GATT required a larger staff, and that in turn meant a larger budget to pay for salaries. GATT had always operated on a shoestring, with each contracting party paying annual dues in proportion to its share of global trade. Wyndham White's 1961 budget called for a budget increase of 70 per cent, from US$664,610 in 1960 to US$1,140,788 in 1961.[34] While this was a sizeable jump, the secretariat observed that the budget remained modest 'for an organization charged with world-wide responsibilities in the field

---

[27] External Ottawa to Geneva, Tel. 74, 3 February 1960, Visit of GATT Deputy Executive Secretary to Ottawa, RG25: G-2/7976/14051–1-40 pt. 2.1, LAC.

[28] Geneva to External, Tel. 1291, 19 August 1960, RG20: A-4/3088/885–15 pt. 1, LAC.

[29] Canadian Embassy, Washington, to DEA, 4 May 1960, RG25: 248/7978/14050–3-40 pt. 1.2, LAC.

[30] Memo from Plumptre for the Minister of Finance, 8 June 1960, RG19: F-2/ 4208/8718–04, LAC.

[31] Improving the administration of GATT, 14 January 1960, RG59: Office of the Assistant Legal Advisor on Economic Affairs/Records relating to trade and GATT 1947–1966, Box 8, file GATT-organization, NARA.

[32] Proposals on GATT Organization, Second report by the special group, 31 May 1960, L/ 1216, GDL.

[33] Canadian Embassy, Washington, to DEA, 4 May 1960, RG25: 248/7978/14050–3-40 pt. 1.2, LAC.

[34] Budget Estimates for the Financial Year 1961, Note by the Executive Secretary, 5 August 1960, L/1262. Wyndham White defended the increased budget in Budget Estimates for the Financial Year 1961, Note by the Executive Secretary, 21 October 1960, L/1262 Add. 2, GDL.

of international trade'. The additional revenue was needed to pay the salaries of thirty-seven new posts in the professional and general service categories. The positions included two new assistant executive secretaries for Wyndham White's office, a deputy director and three economic affairs officers for the trade policy division, a deputy director for the trade intelligence division, clerks, stenographers, translators, interpreters, and typists. The staff would still be small, increasing from 71 to 106. Wyndham White wanted to keep it that way. As he explained to US officials, the secretariat could best perform its main functions in facilitating negotiations and consultation between members if it remained 'relatively small in number but high in quality'.[35]

Although most members agreed that GATT's resources were inadequate, some, including the USA, Australia, Germany, and the Netherlands, were apprehensive about its expansion. Wyndham White insisted that the increase was essential. But he depended on members to pay larger annual subscriptions. If members would not support an increased budget, then he had two options: he could delay new appointments, or he could present a plan 'entailing more drastic reductions', which would require cutting back on GATT's programme of work for 1961.[36] This heavy-handed tactic was typical of Wyndham White. He laid out the worst-case scenario – scaling back GATT – in order to elicit agreement for its expansion. In the end, his request for an increase was revised slightly, but members still approved a larger budget for 1961.[37]

The enhanced capabilities of GATT did not weaken the appeal of regional agreements. Australia and New Zealand concluded an agreement in 1965. Anticipating criticism, their governments justified the agreement in terms of geographical proximity, a long history of economic interaction, and complementary economic activities. Because of the relatively small size of their markets, a free trade agreement could contribute to their economies of scale. The agreement was also necessary because of rampant agricultural protectionism, which restricted their access to foreign markets. Although the arrangement applied to only 60 per cent of total trade, this was a preliminary agreement that would eventually have more comprehensive coverage. Finally, they presented the agreement as a way to promote economic development. As a New Zealand official

[35] Improving the administration of GATT, 14 January 1960, RG59: Office of the Assistant Legal Advisor on Economic Affairs/Records relating to Trade and GATT 1947–1966, Box 8, file GATT-organization, NARA.
[36] Permanent Mission of Canada, Geneva, to USSEA, Tel. 79517 October 1960, GATT 1961 Budget, RG25: 7975/248/14050-3-40 pt. 1.2, LAC.
[37] Summary Record of the Second Meeting on 1 November 1960, SR.17/2, and Summary Record of the Tenth Meeting on 18 November 1960, SR.17/10, GDL.

explained, New Zealand and Australia occupied a hybrid position, so that they 'cannot be classified as industrialized or less-developed countries'. But they were happy to work within GATT and to conform – eventually – to the requirements of Article XXIV, whose vagueness they held up as a virtue.[38]

The United States objected to the agreement and wanted no suggestion of 'GATT sanction' or 'GATT cover whatsoever'.[39] Australia and New Zealand dug in their heels. In response to lengthy questionnaires, they insisted that the agreement was compatible with GATT standards. When asked whether 60 per cent trade coverage was 'too small to be considered as a base for a free-trade area in the GATT sense', they insisted that it was a 'substantial base on which to build'. They admitted that some trade would inevitably be diverted but this would be offset by 'an increase in the total demand for imports into the area': it would be trade creating overall. Finally, they defended the terms of the agreement by insisting that the agreement had to be 'tailored to the circumstances of the Member States'.[40] A follow-up working party noted the many ways in which the agreement fell short of GATT's rules for a free trade area: the coverage of trade was partial, and there was no explicit timetable to extend coverage. But the working party could only ask New Zealand and Australia to note its reservations and continue their efforts to expand world trade.[41] Even when challenged by smaller members, GATT could not enforce compliance with the rules.

A pattern was emerging. When a regional trade agreement was registered with GATT, a working party was set up to examine it. It prepared questions about the terms of the agreement. Governments eventually sent back answers. Members insisted that their agreements were compatible with GATT's liberalizing project. As noted in a much later internal GATT analysis, there was no certain way to measure the economic impact of free trade areas and customs unions: 'As a result, this remains an area in which there is an absence of fully reliable quantitative estimates of the effects of change in trade policies.'[42] The views of GATT members

[38] New Zealand–Australia Free Trade Agreement, Statement by New Zealand Representative at the Council Meeting of 9 November (1965), L/2507, GDL.
[39] GenevaDel to External, 278, 26 March 1966, re GATT: NZ/Australia FTA; GATTDel Geneva to External 294, 30 March 1966, re GATT: NZ/Australia FTA, both in RG19: F-2/5654/8714–24-8 pt. 1, LAC.
[40] New Zealand/Australia Free Trade Agreement: Replies to Questions, 15 March 1966, L/2585, GDL.
[41] Report of the Working Party, Working Party on New Zealand/Australia Free Trade Agreement, 4 April 1966, L/2628, GDL.
[42] A Brief Review of the Literature on the Trade Effects of Article XXIV Type Regional Agreements, 12 October 1989, MTG.GNG/NG7/W/54, GDL.

were typically divided, with the parties to the agreement insisting that the terms were compatible with Article XXIV and those outside the agreement insisting that they fell short. The non-participating GATT members tended not to make their case in 'a uniform and coherent way'.[43] As a result, the final reports of working parties were generally inconclusive and made few, if any, recommendations to bring the regional agreement in line with the General Agreement. Adherence to the principle of non-discrimination and complying with the rules of the General Agreement were essential to the functioning of the multilateral trade order. But it proved to be impossible to enforce compliance, regardless of the size and clout of the participants or the merits of their case.

Nonetheless, the practice of submitting notice and responding to questions confirmed that there was an element of accountability and international scrutiny that members accepted and legitimized. As Susan Pedersen observes in relation to the Permanent Mandates Commission of the League of Nations, the 'dynamic of internationalization' led to unintended results that ran counter to the 'aims, claims, and interests of its members'.[44] For GATT, the process of registering and reviewing such agreements was meaningful. As Rittberger and Zangl explain, a supervisory role 'mak[es] it likely that serious and lasting breaches of norms and rules will be duly noted'.[45] The process upheld GATT as the place to acknowledge and justify trade policy, and implicitly validated the liberal-universal approach as the preferred way to participate in world trade.

The ability of GATT to tolerate deviations testified to the importance of its flexibility. Regional trade agreements could overturn the delicate balance between agreed-upon rules and a more narrowly self-interested pursuit of economic advantage: they could displace GATT as the preferred framework for, and approach to, participation in global trade. It was already apparent by the early 1960s that regionalism had broad appeal and that GATT would have to find ways to ensure that they were integrated into 'an effective world system of trade and payments'.[46] As a result, by the mid-1960s GATT members reported a 'growing apprehension' about the 'erosion of GATT principles caused

---

[43] GATTDEL Geneva to External, 284, April 1965, RG20: 1922/20–28 pt. 14, LAC.

[44] S. Pedersen, *The Guardians: The League of Nations and the Crisis of Empire* (New York: Oxford University Press, 2015), 405–406.

[45] V. Rittberger, B. Zangl, and M. Staisch, *International Organization: Polity, Politics and Policies*, translated by A. Groom (Basingstoke: Palgrave Macmillan, 2006), 214.

[46] Memorandum: Reappraisal of Current Economic Relations Between the United States and Europe: A Summary of the Bowle-Vernon Paper, 5 June 1962, RG59: Box 2/ Economic Affairs E 3 Organizations & Conferences (General), Records of Component Offices of the Bureau of Economic Affairs, 1941–1963, NARA.

by abusive recourse to Art XXIV'.[47] This trend also revealed that members were quick to defend their rights, but less forthcoming when it came to honouring their obligations.

Regional Trade Blocs in Europe, Asia, and North America, 1973–1989

In the 1970s, GATT described the surge of regional trade agreements as 'one of the most remarkable trends of recent years'.[48] The EEC led the way in negotiating regional trade agreements with countries outside the community, many with former colonies, and by enlarging membership of the EEC.[49] By 1973, the EEC had concluded a flurry of regional agreements with countries in Europe (Finland, Iceland, Norway, Portugal, Sweden, Switzerland, and Turkey), the Middle East (Israel, Lebanon, Syria, and Turkey), North Africa (Egypt, Morocco, and Tunisia), eighteen former colonies in Africa through the Yaoundé conventions of 1963 and 1969, and the Mediterranean (Cyprus, Greece, and Malta). The objective was to enhance the EEC's international standing and influence. According to Youri Devuyst, the expansion of the EEC into Francophone Africa and the Mediterranean helped to build it up as a global power.[50] All of these agreements were registered with GATT, meaning that the participants affirmed their compatibility with Article XXIV. Working parties were set up to review the workings, scope, and impact of the agreements.

The EEC could alter global trade patterns either by forcing its goods on the world market or by blocking imports from outside countries. Officials from other GATT countries viewed the EEC's agreements with alarm. Canadian officials estimated that the EEC had incorporated half of all GATT members into such arrangements.[51] Amid the many 'trading problems and irritants' that plagued the liberal trade system, US officials identified the 'growing proliferation of special trade arrangements of a discriminatory character' as their top concern. EEC activity was also worrying because it broadened the community's reach and influence, so

---

[47] GATTDEL Geneva to External, 284, April 1965, RG20: 1922/20–28 pt. 14, LAC.

[48] GATT, *The Activities of GATT 1973*, 48.

[49] Finland was also actively concluding such agreements, for the most part with eastern-bloc countries, reflecting its liminal geopolitical position in the Cold War.

[50] Y. Devuyst, 'European Union Trade Policy After the Lisbon Treaty: The Community Method at Work' in N. Witzleb, A. M. Arranz, and P. Winand (eds.), *The European Union and Global Engagement: Institutions, Policies and Challenges* (Cheltenham: Edward Elgar, 2015), 138, 149–151.

[51] Study: Les accords préférentiels de la CEE, September 1970, RG19: F-2/5654/8714–24–12 pt. 1, LAC.

that before long the USA feared there would be 'a vast web covering the bulk of Western Europe, the Near East and Africa'.[52] The USA's stance was also sustained by long-standing ideological opposition to preferences, evident in their earlier objection to the imperial preference system of the British Commonwealth in the 1930s and 1940s as well as their objection to the use of preferences to promote economic development in the 1950s and 1960s. Because EEC arrangements were preferential, they were objectionable to the USA. Finally, US officials were concerned that regional arrangements undermined GATT: 'It was not possible to move towards freer world trade if at the same time the basic provisions of the General Agreement were being undermined or violated.'[53]

Although US officials disliked most of the EEC agreements, they most strongly objected to the arrangements to associate with Tanzania, Kenya, and Uganda (the Arusha agreements). Washington insisted that the terms fell short of free trade and were unlikely ever to become free trading.[54] US officials called out other GATT members for 'fail[ing] to deal adequately with so flagrant a violation of GATT rules'.[55] Canadian officials stepped up and proposed criteria by which such agreements could be justified, including historical ties, which were not fulfilled in this case. In the European press, Canada was portrayed as leading an attack against the EEC. But the GATT secretariat reported with some satisfaction that it had given the EEC pause about using Article XXIV as a 'cover for limited preferential arrangements'.[56] The representatives of the EEC, Kenya, Tanzania, and Uganda decided to withdraw the Arusha agreements until they could negotiate new terms that would be in compliance.[57] This was one of the few instances where the participants in a regional trade agreement backed down to GATT.

There were many other arrangements that moved forward. A GATT working party was set up early in 1970 to examine the second Yaoundé Convention between the EEC and nineteen former African colonies. Officials from the participating states confidently asserted that their agreement conformed to GATT requirements. The participants had

[52] Summary Record of the Fifth Meeting, 26 November 1971, SR.27/5, GDL. The British also noted US alarm. See Four Power Talks in Geneva, 22 July 1970, BT241/2101, TNA.
[53] Summary Record of the Third Meeting, 18 February 1970, SR.26/3, GDL.
[54] Minutes of Meeting, 26 July 1972, C/M/79, GDL.
[55] Summary Record of the Second Meeting, 2 November 1972, SR.28/2, GDL.
[56] Memorandum from General Director, Office of General Relations (M. G. Clark) to J. H. Warren, Deputy Minister, 25 June 1970, RG19: F-2/5654/8714–24-12 pt. 1, LAC.
[57] Summary Record of the Second Meeting, 2 November 1972, SR.28/2, GDL. Council of Representatives: Report on Work since the Twenty Seventh Session, 30 October 1972, L/3761, GDL. Geneva to Exter, 1063, re EEC Limited Preferential Arrangements, 11 June 1970, RG19: F-2/5654/8714–24-12 pt. 1, LAC.

moved closer to free trade since their first agreement in 1963, but there were sceptics who pointed out that even if tariffs and quotas might be lowered, other measures subverted freer trade. As a result, some demanded further study before they could determine whether or not the agreement was consistent with Article XXIV. EEC and African representatives rejected these claims because they introduced new criteria to determine whether or not trade was being liberalized, measures that EEC official insisted had 'never [been] used hitherto'. Paradoxically, some challenged the agreement because it was too liberal: if its aim was to promote economic development among the 'least developed of the developing countries' (as suggested by the Nigerian representative) then those states needed protection.[58] Behind the reservations was fear that EEC countries were gaining an unfair advantage by exploiting their historic ties to former colonies. Some critics outside GATT were more outspoken in denouncing the Yaoundé agreements as a tool to perpetuate neocolonial relations of dependence.[59] GATT and its members could comment on, but could not alter the substance of, any agreement.

The EEC also registered an agreement with Israel. Members of the GATT working party doubted its compatibility with Article XXIV because it was preferential, was not leading to free trade, and contained no schedule or plan to make it more genuinely free trading. They suggested the EEC and Israel should apply for a waiver under Article XXV. The Israeli representative explained at length why the agreement was important politically (given Israel's precarious geopolitical position) and economically (as a small country, its development depended on such agreements). He also explained why it was acceptable because it conformed to the expectations of the original drafters that regional trade blocs would emerge and the GATT precedent was to judge each regional agreement on its own terms. In the end, the working party could only point to differences of opinion and concluded that GATT members could reserve 'their rights under the General Agreement'.[60]

An EEC agreement with Tunisia and Morocco also provoked debate and division. Japan objected on the grounds that it was not consistent with

[58] Report of the working party on Convention of Association between the European Economic Community and the African and Malagasy States, 20 November 1970, L/3465, GDL. Minutes of Meeting, 2 and 3 December 1970, C/M/65, GDL.
[59] S. B. Ajulo, 'Lomé Convention: A Review', *Journal of African Studies* 13 (4) (Winter 1986),147. Apparently, Nigeria stayed out initially because it associated the agreement with neocolonial intentions.
[60] Report of the Working Party on the Agreement between the European Economic Community and Israel, 22 September 1971, L/3581, GDL.

Article XXIV terms.[61] More generally, the Japanese representative cautioned that agreements that did not comply with Article XXIV 'could lead to the compartmentalization of international trade', undoing 'the efforts made so arduously in the past towards liberalization of trade on the principle of non-discrimination'. He added that the 'free flow of world trade' as well as 'the prestige of the GATT' depended on respecting its principles.[62]

Japan was not alone in its concerns. Australia believed the time had come to take a strong stand; its officials pushed for a high-level meeting, possibly at the ministerial level, to examine the agreement with Tunisia and Morocco.[63] The Chilean representative indicated that he would also oppose the agreement and went so far as to accuse the EEC of 'trying to amend the GATT unilaterally'.[64] The secretariat also objected to the agreement: 'to accept EEC contention that they are covered by Article XXIV would make mockery of GATT'.[65] But the secretariat was willing to tolerate the agreement with Tunisia and Morocco if it put a stop to the snowballing effect of EEC preferential agreements.[66]

In fact, there was little option but to accept them. The EEC could push the question to a vote, which the secretariat expected the EEC would win because roughly half of all members now participated in regional agreements of various kinds and many others were lining up to conclude similar agreements with the EEC. The secretariat could only count on Australia, Brazil, Canada, Chile, Peru, the USA, and possibly Japan to vote against the agreement.[67] Moreover, French officials made it perfectly clear that the agreements with Tunisia and Morocco were essential: 'they were among areas coloured red on the French map of the world'. If forced to choose between northern Africa and GATT, Paris would choose northern Africa.[68]

---

[61] Tokyo to Exter, 499, GATT Working Party on EEC Arrangements with Tunisia and Morocco, 24 April 1970, RG19: F-2/5654/8714–24-12 pt. 1, LAC.

[62] Summary Record of the Fifth Meeting, 19 February 1970, SR.26/5, GDL.

[63] CNBRA to Exter, 1363, 25 September 1970, GATT Council – EEC Preferential Arrangements, RG19: F-2/5654/8714–24-12 pt. 1, LAC.

[64] Geneva to Exter, 1715, 25 September 1970, GATT Council Meeting – EEC Preferential Arrangements, 25 September 1970, RG19: F-2/5654/8714–24-12 pt. 1, LAC.

[65] Geneva to Exter, 1063, GATT Council Meeting: EEC Agreements with Morocco and Tunisia, 16 July 1969, RG19: F-2/5654/8714–24-12 pt. 1, LAC.

[66] Study: Les accords préférentials de la CEE, September 1970; Geneva to Exter, 1155, GATT and EEC Preferential Arrangements, 22 June 1970, RG19: F-2/5654/8714–24-12 pt. 1, LAC.

[67] Geneva to Exter, 1254, 7 July 1970, GATT and EEC Limited Preferential Arrangements, RG19: F-2/5654/8714–24-12 pt. 1, LAC.

[68] Geneva to Exter, EEC Ltd Preferential Arrangements, 11 June 1970, RG19: F-2/5654/8714–24-12 pt. 1, LAC.

The working party reports downplayed the alarm that regional agreements provoked. People expressed their concerns more candidly in plenary meetings and at the GATT council, as well as in internal correspondence and analysis. For example, the British government believed the EEC agreements were preferential agreements in disguise. It referred to 'the inflammatory policy of the EEC in setting up a proliferation of satellite preferential agreements in conflict with the MFN principle and the GATT'.[69] Canadian officials were also alarmed at the growth of preferential agreements propped up by Article XXIV. Such arrangements undermined the multilateral liberal trade order and threatened to replace it with zones of influence revolving around the USA, the EEC, and possibly Japan, which could provoke trade wars.[70] A French trade official confirmed this fear. He told his Canadian colleague that 'if CPs [contracting parties] were to tacitly accept these new preferential agreements … it would amount to "the end of the GATT"'.[71] Olivier Long, Wyndham White's successor as director-general of GATT, suggested they would all return to the 'happy thirties' unless the regional option was curtailed.[72]

Gardner Patterson, deputy director-general of GATT, called for working parties to make decisions. They could not agree to disagree 'if we are to avoid the even greater problems with regard to other EEC preferential arrangements awaiting in the wings'.[73] He pressed for as many of the EEC agreements as possible to be put on the same GATT agenda. Doing so would highlight the number and reach of the agreements and force members to think about the underlying principle and its larger implications. The bigger picture was easy to ignore when regional agreements were considered one by one.[74] The GATT Council agenda of November 1971 did this, listing nine separate agreements involving almost thirty countries.[75]

The USA called for a working party to examine the extent to which the agreements had compromised the MFN principle. According to them,

---

[69] Note of a Meeting, 29 July 1970, BT241/2101, TNA.

[70] Study: les accords préférentials de le CEE, September 1970.

[71] Memorandum from Director, General Trade Policy Branch, to M. G. Clark, General Director, Office of General Relations, EEC Preferential Agreements with Israel and Spain, 12 May 1970, RG19: 5393/8714–24-9 pt. 3, LAC.

[72] Geneva to Exter, 1155, GATT and EEC Preferential Arrangements, 22 June 1970, RG19: F-2/5654/8714–24-12 pt. 1, LAC.

[73] Geneva to Exter, 427, GATT Working Party on EEC Association Agreements with Tunisia and Morocco, 13 March 1970, RG19: F-2/5654/8714–24-12 pt. 1, LAC.

[74] Geneva to Exter, 1641, GATT Council – EEC Preferential Arrangements, 17 September 1970, RG 19: F-2/5654/8714–24-12 pt. 1, LAC.

[75] Council of Representatives: Report on Work since the Twenty-Sixth Session, 15 November 1971, L/3624, GDL.

Article I was becoming the exception and Article XXIV the rule. The US representative disparaged the tendency to whitewash the agreements registered under Article XXIV: there was no serious or methodical scrutiny of the terms, primarily for political reasons. He now called for serious study and explained that the erosion of the MFN principle imperiled GATT. And a world without GATT would see a return to 'chaos ... in a short time'.[76] Ghana, India, South Africa, and South Korea agreed that Article XXIV had supplanted the MFN principle.[77] Japan also supported the USA's proposal to examine regional preferential arrangements more closely.[78]

But other GATT members believed Article XXIV ought to be on par with Article I. The representative from Israel called for a more realistic and pragmatic approach that reflected 'GATT reality today' rather than the legal letter of the General Agreement of twenty-two years earlier. An official from Uruguay explained that downgrading the MFN principle did not represent a crisis but was a development that 'had been foreseen in the General Agreement', and he warned against 'retrac[ing] its steps merely to save the prestige of the Most-Favoured-Nation clause'.[79] The representative from Trinidad and Tobago reminded GATT members that MFN was a tool to bring about ever more liberal trade. There should not be an attachment to it as 'an end in itself' and he warned that GATT must adapt to changing circumstances or become 'totally ineffective because of its inflexibility'.[80]

The EEC also objected to the USA's proposal because it implied that regional and global trade liberalization were at odds. The EEC insisted they were parallel and mutually reinforcing processes. The British had often sounded the alarm about the threats that the EEC posed to GATT and a liberal trade order. Now that they were trying to join the EEC, they supported the European position and accused the USA of setting up the study with a predetermined outcome.[81]

In the end, a working party examined the effect of regional trade agreements on global trade. It reported in 1972. Its findings were vague, massaged so that it could incorporate positions that were in fact incompatible. The report noted that the percentage of trade among members affected by preferential rates had increased from 10 per cent

[76] Summary Record of the Fifth Meeting, 19 November 1971, SR27/5, GDL.
[77] Summary Record of the Ninth Meeting, 24 November 1971, SR.27/9, and Summary Record of the Tenth Meeting, 25 November 1971, SR.27/10, GDL.
[78] Summary Record of the Seventh Meeting, 23 November 1971, SR 27/7, and Summary Record of the Eighth Meeting, 24 November 1971, SR.27/8, GDL.
[79] Summary Record of the Eleventh Meeting, 25 November 1971, SR.27/11, GDL.
[80] Summary Record of the Tenth Meeting, 25 November 1971.
[81] Summary Record of the Seventh Meeting, 23 November 1971.

in 1955 to 24 per cent in 1970. The proportion between preferential and MFN trade had shifted most quickly in 1959–1960 as the six European states entered into their common market and had been sustained by 'the continued dynamism exhibited by the mutual trade of the member countries of the European Communities'. However, since the mid-1960s the rate at which preferential trade was increasing had slowed.[82] The USA's reaction to the report emphasized the absolute increase in the volume of trade affected by preferential rates and insisted that the situation warranted ongoing attention. The EEC representative, on the other hand, reclassified intra-EEC trade as 'intra-national' and dismissed the significance of the findings.[83] With the USA and EEC squaring off in this way, GATT was unable to take a decisive stand on regional trade blocs.

Resisting GATT scrutiny and accountability revealed that members thought about GATT from a self-interested point of view, asking what GATT could do for them rather than what they could do for GATT. This is essential to keep in mind when assessing the EEC's impact. The EEC did contribute to trade liberalization in specific areas, especially manufactured goods. But its actions also undermined GATT, a consequence that many EEC officials considered dispassionately. They saw rights as foremost, with obligations a distant second. They were not different from many GATT members in doing this, but because of their impact on global trade and their influence within GATT, the significance of their attitude was magnified.

The enlargement of the EEC in 1973 exacerbated unease about regional trade blocs. Britain was poised to enter the union, along with Denmark, Ireland, and Norway. (In the end, Norway did not join.) Britain had been one of the early founding members of GATT and it continued to play an important leadership role. Although the British government had decided to stay out of the Treaty of Rome, it soon reversed this decision and made its first bid to join the EEC in 1961. De Gaulle famously vetoed British membership, a bitter blow. British governments subsequently decided to wait out de Gaulle's leadership rather than give up on joining. (The UK's doubts and misgivings about its association with Europe never entirely disappeared, flaring up periodically, most recently in the 2016 Brexit referendum and the decision to withdraw from the European Union.) British membership became a much more serious possibility under the leadership of Ted Heath, whom Desmond Dinan describes as 'the most Europhilic of British

---

[82] Main Findings Concerning Trade at Most Favoured Nation and at Other Rates, 21 June 1972, L/3708, GDL.
[83] Minutes of Meeting, 26 July 1972, C/M/79, GDL.

politicians'.[84] Members of the EEC portrayed enlargement as consistent with general GATT goals to promote 'an expansion of trade and to further economic progress on a wide basis'.[85] But if Britain joined, then the EEC would account for one-third of world trade: 'This is unprecedented in history of the GATT and [was] unforeseen by the founding members when Article XXIV was drafted.'[86]

The working party on EEC enlargement was unusually large and the list of questions unusually long. The process stalled almost immediately over a dispute about how to generate data so that the working party could determine whether or not the terms were compatible with Article XXIV. The EEC refused to disclose statistics about variable levies and preferential tariffs.[87] Canada proposed that other countries could generate that information. The EEC refused to accept such data. Members protested that the EEC was obstructing the working party. Olivier Long complained that the EEC position had become 'progressively more absurd'.[88]

Long's frustration with EEC efforts to evade GATT scrutiny echoed that of his predecessor, Eric Wyndham White, whose very big shoes he had to fill. Long was well qualified to succeed Wyndham White, but ill-suited to the role. He had completed doctorates in both law and political science. He had worked for the Red Cross and was later a Swiss diplomat, specializing in trade. But most people agreed that Long was not an effective leader.[89] As Julio Lacarte noted, even though he 'kept the ship going well' he was 'a less forceful personality' than Wyndham White. Jake Warren claimed he lacked Wyndham White's imagination and drive. Although Long believed that the effectiveness of GATT depended on its 'intrinsic flexibility, capacity to adapt and the diplomatic skill of its operators',[90] he himself was not adept at resolving

---

[84] D. Dinan, *Ever Closer Union: An Introduction to European Integration*, 3rd edition (Boulder, CO: Lynne Reiner, 2005), 60.

[85] Minutes of Meeting, 7 March 1972, C/M/76, GDL.

[86] EEC Enlargement – Article XXIV Negotiations: Talking Points, 8 June 1972, RG19: F-2/5654/8714–24-19–1 pt. 1, LAC.

[87] Geneva to ExtOtt, 2375, 1 December 1972, GATT: Working Party on EEC Enlargement, RG19: F-2/5654/8714–24-19 pt. 2, LAC. Council of Representatives, Report on work since the 28th session, 12 November 1973, L/3955, GDL.

[88] Geneva to ExtOtt, 1473, 25 July 1972, GATT Working Party on EEC Enlargement, RG19: F-2/5654/8714–24-19–1 pt. 1, LAC.

[89] J. Tallberg, 'The Power of the Chair: Formal Leadership in International Cooperation', *International Studies Quarterly*, 54 (1) (March 2010), 254. Tallberg also concludes that Long played little part in overcoming the deadlocks that led to a successful end to the Tokyo round.

[90] G. Marceau (ed.), *A History of Law and Lawyers in the GATT/WTO: The Development of the Rule of Law in the Multilateral Trading System* (Cambridge: Cambridge University Press, 2015), 24.

conflicts.[91] As John Weekes explained, 'He had lots of integrity, but he was not a dynamic mover. He didn't bang heads together.'[92] In fairness to Long, his direction of GATT came at a difficult time; in the 1970s, there was a global economic slowdown and doubts about trade liberalization were increasing.

Long worried that the fragmentation of global trade would result in 'a system of regional blocs fighting each other in the unregulated conditions of the 1930s'.[93] During the Tokyo round, he expressed concern about the future of GATT and the liberal multilateral trade order: 'International trade is under threat. No one can any longer have doubts on that score.' Protectionism was largely responsible for subverting liberal trade. He also feared that GATT rules were becoming meaningless. Rules elicited confidence that promises to liberalize trade would be kept and that governments were, to some extent, constrained in setting trade policy. But members were side-stepping and disregarding the rules, of which Article XXIV was one of many examples. In his mind this exposed 'a decline in international morality in trade relations'.[94]

A report from 1978 following the round identified regional trade blocs as a particular concern.[95] This was not surprising as regional trade arrangements continued to be negotiated throughout the Tokyo round, spreading to Asia, which had not been especially active in the earlier wave. In 1975, the Bangkok agreement brought together Bangladesh, India, Korea, Laos, the Philippines, Sri Lanka, and Thailand. In 1977, Indonesia, Malaysia, the Philippines, Singapore, and Thailand negotiated ASEAN. There were strong political pressures behind the agreement, which many hoped would help alleviate regional tensions and put the participants in a stronger position vis-à-vis the expansion of the EEC.[96] These agreements were well received by GATT working parties because they were cast in terms of promoting development.[97] There was also a sense that these agreements were more likely to be genuinely liberalizing: they did not seem to be camouflaging either protectionism

[91] Grey recalled an incident at the end of the Tokyo round that illustrated Long's passive and ineffective leadership. Representatives of developing countries wanted to be compensated for the loss of preferences. Long did not intervene in any way to resolve this standoff. 'This was the most dramatic occasion when Wyndham White's ability to intervene and his experience were missed.' Author interview with Grey, 12 January 2005.
[92] Author interview with Weekes, 21 March 2013.
[93] Meeting between Hughes and Long, 22 January 1970, BT241/2256, TNA.
[94] O. Long, *International Trade Under Threat: A Constructive Response* (London: Trade Policy Research Centre, 1978), 6.
[95] GATT after the Tokyo Round: Trade Policy Problems of the 1980s, Note by the Secretariat, 12–13 October 1978, CC.18/W/27, GDL.
[96] Bhalla and Bhalla, *Regional Blocs*, 75.
[97] *The Activities of GATT 1978*, 80; *The Activities of GATT 1979*, 68.

or discrimination. The contrast with the reaction to EEC arrangements was striking.

These agreements were soon followed by a preferential trade agreement between Israel and the United States. Although this was a significant departure in US trade policy, it should not have been a complete surprise. As early as 1965, US officials had complained that if regional agreements proliferated, it would be difficult for the USA to resist the trend. Thomas Mann, the USA's under-secretary of state for economic affairs, had then explained: 'People must realize that if the rest of the world abandoned MFN it would be very difficult to expect the U.S. alone to follow this principle.'[98]

The US representative noted that the agreement with Israel conformed to Article XXIV in three crucial respects: substantially all trade between them was covered, the agreement did not raise barriers to trade, and there was a timetable to liberalize all trade within ten years. He went so far as to suggest that the agreement was even more liberalizing than the General Agreement. The questions sent to the working party were routine.[99] There were some quibbles with specific terms of the agreement, but GATT passed no judgement, simply noting that the parties should provide regular updates.[100] Despite the relative calm with which members received this agreement, for many it represented a momentous change. According to Bhagwati, the USA's decision altered 'the balance of forces at the margins away from multilateralism to regionalism'.[101] But there is another possible interpretation of the USA's decision, one that emphasizes ongoing US support for trade liberalization and GATT. As Steve Dryden explains, with the strains on GATT in the 1980s, and the desultory results of various meetings and attempts to push liberalization forward, the USA turned to regionalism to compel 'recalcitrant nations to join the GATT effort to make sure they weren't cut out of the action'.[102] Panagariya and Srinivasan reach a similar conclusion, although their interpretation is more pessimistic, seeing the US shift to regional trade as 'the only means left for keeping the process of trade liberalization afloat'.[103]

---

[98] Memorandum of Conversation between UK and US (Mann and Powell), 8 November 1965, RG364/Box 109/ file LDC's (1963–1967), NARA.

[99] Working party on the Free Trade Agreement between Israel and the United States, meeting on 16 October 1986, Spec (86) 57, GDL.

[100] Working party on the Free Trade Area between Israel and the United States, draft report, 5 March 1987, Spec (87) 8, GDL.

[101] Bhagwati, *Trading Blocs*, 10.

[102] S. Dryden, *Trade Warriors: USTR and the American Crusade for Free Trade* (Oxford and New York: Oxford University Press, 1995), 340.

[103] Panagariya and Srinivasan, 'The New Regionalism', 222.

Frustrated by delays in launching another round of trade negotiations in GATT, the USA entered into free trade negotiations with Canada.[104] The extent of trade interdependence between them was already very high. They had long been one another's principal markets, although many US officials did not realize this. Free trade with the United States had a long and acrimonious history in Canada, where there were chronic concerns about Canada's identity and autonomy vis-à-vis its superpower neighbour, sometimes expressed in anti-USA outbursts and policies. But Canadian exporters depended on access to the US market. Canadian policies went back and forth between promoting greater integration and trying to lessen its dependence on the US market.[105] In the mid-1980s, a Liberal government study confirmed that free trade with the United States was the best policy for Canada's future. A Conservative government, elected in 1984, acted on the recommendation, and negotiations began in earnest.

Shortly after the introduction of the Canada–United States Free Trade Agreement on 1 January 1989, the governments of Canada and the United States submitted the terms of the agreement to GATT for consideration under Article XXIV. The agreement covered the largest bilateral trading relationship in the world, valued at roughly US$200 billion per annum. Throughout the negotiations, Canadian and US negotiators had kept GATT rules and norms in mind.[106] Representatives from Canada and the United States backed up their agreement with confident claims about its compatibility with Article XXIV, suggesting that it went farther towards liberalization than anything in GATT because it included agriculture and services. Canada and the USA pitched the agreement as trade creating. The working party was large and the questions were probing. The complexity and scope of the Canada–United States Free Trade Agreement opened it to considerable criticism for the many ways in which it did not fully conform with Article XXIV. Members expressed concern about its potential impact on third parties and on the world trading system. The representative of Japan tactfully praised the agreement, but noted the need for a genuine and thorough review, unlike the pro forma reviews of other Article XXIV agreements. The EEC representative also praised the agreement, although his remarks were both

---

[104] Dryden, *Trade Warriors*, 340.

[105] The back-and-forth of Canadian–US trade relations is explained in M. Hart, *A Trading Nation: Canadian Trade Policy from Colonialism to Globalization* (Vancouver: University of British Columbia Press, 2002).

[106] M. Hart, C. Robertson, and B. Dymond, *Decision at Midnight: Inside the Canada–US Free Trade Negotiations* (Vancouver: University of British Columbia Press, 1994), 297–298, 319 and passim.

condescending and self-serving. He noted with satisfaction that Canada and the United States 'were reaching the age of maturity' and warned them about the difficulties involved in invoking Article XXIV. He offered to arrange for an EEC official to chair the working party, an offer that was probably not well received.[107]

Internal GATT studies concluded that because of the high volume of trade between Canada and the USA, their agreement could not be trade diverting. Japanese and German trade with North America might drop, but these losses would be more than compensated for through 'an expanded economic pie'. GATT analysis also emphasized the non-economic function of the agreement – to alleviate economic and political sources of strain in the Canadian–US relationship.[108] The coverage of substantially all trade, the reduction of tariffs, and a ten-year timeframe in which to realize total free trade conformed to Article XXIV requirements. Following GATT custom, the working party did not deliver a judgement about compatibility with Article XXIV, instead calling for the two countries to report again in two years' time.[109]

Although the Canada–US Free Trade Agreement was probably more compatible with the spirit and letter of Article XXIV than many other agreements, the shift of two major and longtime GATT advocates to the regional option exacerbated the crisis atmosphere that surrounded the organization in the 1980s.

Following the conclusion of the Tokyo round in 1979, the mood in and around GATT was pessimistic: the future of liberalization was in jeopardy, made more serious by the shift towards protectionist practices and attitudes. *The Economist* suggested that at best the Tokyo round was an 'indispensable dyke against the flood of protectionism'.[110] Protectionism was a direct refutation of GATT, open markets, multilateral cooperation, and an internationalist outlook. At the 1982 meeting of GATT ministers, the first in almost a decade, they accepted that their challenge was to renew 'consensus in support of the GATT system, so as to restore and reinforce confidence in its capacity to provide a stable and predictable trading environment and respond to new challenges'.[111] But rather than invigorate their common purpose, the ministerial meeting brought out tensions and animosity and exposed the extent of the erosion of

[107] Minutes of Meeting, 8–9 February 1989, C/M/228, GDL.
[108] A Brief Review of the Literature on the Trade Effects of Art XXIV Type Regional Agreements, 12 October 1989, MTN.GNG/NG7/W/54, GDL.
[109] Working Party on the Free Trade Agreement between Canada and the United States, 31 October 1991, L/6927, GDL.
[110] 'Freeish Trade', *The Economist* (29 December 1979), 44.
[111] Ministerial declaration, 29 November 1982, L/5424, GDL.

a commitment to a liberal trade order. The disagreement between the US and the EC was particularly acrimonious. Michel Jobert, France's foreign trade minister, accused the US of practising protectionism through its dogmatic liberalism – 'the most subtle and most disguised form of protectionism – that of the absolute power of the strong over the weak'.[112] After all-night emergency meetings, ministers were only able to agree to 'refrain from taking or maintaining' measures that contravened core GATT principles of openness and non-discrimination and vowed to 'resist protectionist pressures in the formulation and implementation of national trade policy'.[113] This was a weak pledge. It was also demoralizing that it needed to be said and that it was all that could be said. *The Economist* dismissed it as 'pious twaddle'.[114]

Arthur Dunkel, recently appointed director-general of GATT, confronted the widespread belief that GATT was 'losing its grip on the evolution and conduct of trade relations'.[115] In calling out threats to GATT and the multilateral trade order he was acting as a 'guardian of the system'.[116] He brought together an expert panel to study the urgent problems confronting world trade and to propose solutions.[117] Their 1987 report – *Trade Policies for a Better Future* – warned that GATT and the liberal trade system were in jeopardy. The underlying cause was the collapse of a shared faith in a liberal and global trade order. The authors examined many problem areas of trade including developing countries and protectionism. The proliferation of regional trade agreements under Article XXIV did not escape their attention. Although flexibility was a much-touted GATT virtue, it had been abused and the result was to 'have seriously weakened the trade rules'. They called for immediate

[112] C. Farnsworth, 'Discordant Notes Mar Trade Talks', *New York Times* (25 November 1982), D1.
[113] Ministerial declaration, 29 November 1982, L/5424; C. Farnsworth, 'A Reporter's Notebook: Behind the Scenes at the GATT Trade Talks in Geneva', *New York Times* (5 December 1982), 8.
[114] 'GATT Pulls Back from the Brink', *The Economist* (30 November 1982), 1.
[115] Dunkel, A., 'Introduction' in *Trade Policies for a Better Future: The 'Leutwiler Report', the GATT and the Uruguay Round* (Dordrecht, Boston, and Lancaster: Martinus Nijhoff Publishers, 1987), 2.
[116] R. Blackhurst, 'The Role of the Director-General and the Secretariat' in A. Narlikar, M. Daunton, and R. M. Stern (eds.), *The Oxford Handbook on the World Trade Organization* (Oxford: Oxford University Press, 2012), 155.
[117] Dunkel did so on his own authority, and the report was financed independently. While Blackhurst admits that the director-general and secretariat could have influence, members 'consciously kept the DG and the Secretariat on a leash that is, if not always very short, never very long … The scope for any kind of independent initiative that runs counter to the wishes of member countries … is extremely limited.' Blackhurst, 'The Role of the Director-General and the Secretariat', 143, 150.

action. 'The situation has been ignored for too long ... further mistakes and abuses should be prevented.'[118]

Adversaries or Partners? Regional and Global Trade during the Uruguay Round, 1986–1994

The Uruguay round (1986–1994) was an opportunity to strengthen GATT as an institution through 'renewed multilateral trade liberalization and a broadened institutional mandate'.[119] But reaching agreement was far from assured, for several reasons. The scope and complexity of the round had expanded to include services and intellectual property. Trade negotiations under GATT were no longer limited to tariffs and commodities. The increased number of participants further complicated negotiations: there were ninety-six in 1988 after Lesotho joined. Alongside the multilateral negotiations, regional agreements spread rapidly. Between 1990 and 1994, one-third of all such agreements were registered.[120] These agreements involved major trading nations and many countries. Even when a multilateral round was underway, GATT members were not putting all their trade eggs in the multilateral basket. Indeed, negotiating regional agreements implied that the failure of GATT might not be disastrous. This might have been a consolation, but the regional alternative also acted as a disincentive to support GATT and multilateral negotiations.

Some observers suggested that the regional option triumphed during the round, at the expense of GATT. At the World Economic Forum in 1989, Lester Thurow, dean of the Sloan School of Management, proclaimed that GATT had been slain by the rise of three regional economic power blocs revolving around Europe, North America, and Japan. He interpreted this changing order in organic economic and political terms. But the consequences were worrying. Economic production had become increasingly competitive rather than complementary in a 'head to head export environment'. Within this new order, the discrepancy between the winners and losers in trade was stark. Governments responded by managing trade and protecting markets against outside producers. The result

[118] *Trade Policies for a Better Future*, 25, 48–49.
[119] Preeg, *Traders in a Brave New World*, 11. The two most comprehensive histories of the round are J. Croome, *Reshaping the World Trading System: A History of the Uruguay Round* (Geneva: WTO, 1995) and Preeg, *Traders in a Brave New World*. Also see J. Wiener, *Making Rules in the Uruguay Round of the GATT: A Study of International Leadership* (Aldershot: Dartmouth Publishing Company, 1995). For a critical view of the round, see G. Dunkley, *The Free Trade Adventure: The WTO, the Uruguay Round and Globalism – A Critique* (London and New York: Zed Books, 2000).
[120] 'Regionalism and Trade: The Right Direction?' *The Economist* (16 September 1995), 23.

was a new multipolar economic system in which trade within blocs increased, whereas trade between blocs decreased. While all customs unions, common markets, and free trade areas contributed to this state of affairs, he singled out the EEC – in particular the next stage in its evolution towards creating a single market – as a grave blow to GATT. However, he added that it would be wrong to blame the EEC alone for the demise of GATT: it was 'a precipitating, not a causal event'. Thurow had no time for nostalgia, instead emphasizing the need to adjust to the new reality so that intra-bloc trade could be managed so as to prevent a return to the 1930s.[121] Thurow's pronouncement marked 'a new nadir in GATT's credibility'.[122]

While some scholars identify US participation in regional trade as the main blow to GATT, others see it as a way to strengthen the multilateral process. For example, Carla Hills, the USTR, raised the possibility of regional agreements with Mexico and Chile as a bargaining lever to press for reforms in controversial areas such as agriculture and to win support in new areas such as intellectual property.[123] John Weekes, Canada's ambassador to GATT during the round, believed that this tactic had succeeded in bringing the round to a close.[124] *The Economist*, a longtime booster of free trade, also agreed that if the USA used this tactic to press GATT forward, then regional and multilateral initiatives could be mutually reinforcing.[125] But this was a risky tactic for GATT and global trade. It would only work if the threat of abandoning multilateral negotiations in favour of regional agreements seemed plausible. Moreover, it was not always evident that regionalism was being used to propel GATT negotiations to a successful conclusion. Robert Mosbacher, the US secretary of commerce, revealed how far US faith in multilateralism had drifted when he announced that the USA could take or leave the Uruguay round: 'We could be okay either way. The U.S. always could make regional or other agreements. In truth, we're doing this now.'[126] There was also domestic support in the USA for bilateral and regional agreements, where US economic clout could be used to fuller advantage than in

---

[121] L. C. Thurow, 'GATT is Dead; the World Economy as We Know It is Coming to an End, Taking the General Agreement on Tariffs and Trade With It', *Journal of Accountancy* 170 (3) (September 1990). 'Europe will be blamed for destroying the GATT. It shouldn't be.'

[122] Preeg, *Traders in a Brave New World*, 89.

[123] James Baker, US Secretary of the Treasury, made the same point about quitting the round. See Preeg, *Traders in a Brave New World*, 80.

[124] Author interview with Weekes.

[125] 'Trade-Block Folly', *The Economist* (20 April 1991), 13.

[126] Preeg, *Traders in a Brave New World*, 122.

GATT: 'Almost everyone agrees that regional negotiation is an effective tactic for expanding American influence on trade issues.'[127]

US and Canadian involvement in regional trade agreements also made it more difficult for them to insist that other GATT members comply with Article XXIV or uphold criteria to ensure that such agreements were trade creating. Instead, it fell to Japan – one of the few GATT members not involved in a regional trade agreement – to try to close loopholes and clarify ambiguous language in Article XXIV. Japanese officials argued that regional trade agreements had expanded beyond anyone's expectations and that they constituted a 'derogation from the basic principle of most-favoured-nation treatment'. The result was that 'a large part of world trade' no longer benefited from the MFN principle. Even though the terms of Article XXIV allowed GATT to make recommendations in response to regional agreements, 'not one single recommendation has been made based on this Article'. The goal was to further liberalize world trade and ensure that the trading interests of third parties were not damaged.[128] The Japanese proposal recommended a ten-year timeframe for bringing free trade into effect – regional arrangements could not last indefinitely as 'interim agreements'. The ratification of regional agreements could not be presumed as 'faits accomplis', but must be subject to meaningful approval. Associate agreements must also be subject to meaningful scrutiny. If tariffs were lowered as a result of an agreement, participants should not be rewarded for reducing duties: 'Article XXIV:6 does not envisage in any way "reverse compensatory compensation" for a customs union, in case that general incidence of tariff level would be reduced at the formation of the union.'[129] Indian officials also suggested that the provision regarding 'substantially all trade' should be clarified. While the founders of GATT had believed that customs unions led to 'global free trade', Article XXIV had become 'the route . . . to depart from the norm of non-discriminatory trade'.[130] Australia, Korea, and New Zealand also backed the call to renegotiate Article XXIV.[131]

EEC representatives denied that regional agreements injured global trade.[132] Japanese officials insisted that they were not trying to rewrite Article XXIV or limit the ability of members to enter into regional trade

[127] P. Passell, 'The World: Regional Trade Makes Global Deals Go Round', *New York Times* (19 December 1993).
[128] Article XXIV: Submission by Japan, 22 December 1989, MTN.GNG/NG7/W/66, GDL.
[129] Proposal of Japan on the GATT Article XXIV and XXVIII, 14 September 1987, MTN.GNG/NG7/W/20, GDL.
[130] Proposal for Review of Article XXIV, 20 November 1987, MTN.GNG/NG7/W/38, GDL.
[131] Croome, *Reshaping the World Trading System*, 98–100.   [132] Ibid., 219.

agreements. Rather, their aim was to ensure a higher standard of conformity with the General Agreement and lay out more clearly compensation for members whose trade suffered from such arrangements.[133]

Despite EEC opposition, Article XXIV was redrafted to include a formula to calculate levels of duty before and after an agreement, to clarify obligations and compensation, to set a timeframe of no more than ten years to phase in free trade, and to permit any dispute arising under Article XXIV to be submitted to the dispute resolution process. The meaning of 'substantially all trade' remained ambiguous.[134]

The EEC refused to accept the revisions and put forward amendments of their own that would weaken the ability of third parties to either receive compensation or revoke concessions to offset injury. The EEC justification was that the article was not balanced because it did not take into account the benefits to third parties that flowed from regional trade agreements. The United States objected to the EEC's proposals on the grounds that they would 'destroy the neutrality of the text and make its acceptance impossible'. The US official added that many countries had made many concessions to arrive at this point. It would be regrettable if those efforts were now 'wasted'. John Weekes, the chair of this negotiating group, forwarded the article to the umbrella Trade Negotiating Group, flagging disagreements, but overall endorsing the revised text as 'representing a reasonable balance between the interests which had been brought to bear on this difficult question' and as a 'useful clarification'.[135] The revised article moved forward, subject to one final and telling clarification by the EEC that GATT could not rule on the conformity of regional trade agreements with Article XXIV. As the end of the round approached, this matter was not resolved.[136]

Arthur Dunkel and Peter Sutherland (Sutherland took on the directorship of GATT towards the end of the Uruguay round) defended GATT against the threat of regionalism. Dunkel conjured up the spectre of the 1930s as a cautionary tale and implored political leaders not to forget 'the painful lessons of our recent past'.[137] As Dunkel explained, the key was to ensure that regional trade agreements were not restrictive. The way to ensure that they were open was to hold them up to GATT standards: 'the

---

[133] Negotiating Group on GATT Articles, 17–19 July 1990, MTN.GNG/NG7/20, GDL.

[134] Croome, *Reshaping the World Trading System*, 220.

[135] Negotiating group on GATT articles, Note on Meeting of 1, 15, and 19 October 1990, 6 November 1990, MTN.GNG/NG7/22, GDL.

[136] Trade Negotiating Committee, Thirty-Sixth Meeting, 15 December 1993: Annex 3: Understanding on the Interpretation of Article XXIV of the GATT; Proposal of 12 December 1993 by the European Communities, MTN.TNC/40, GDL.

[137] 'Multilateralism and Regionalism Can Support Each Other, Says Dunkel, But "Managed Trade" is a Threat', 24 May 1993, GATT/1582, GDL.

GATT represents the only available yardstick for ensuring that such arrangements remain outward looking, liberal, and trade creating'.[138] But their basic line of defence was that regional and multilateral agreements were complementary, 'two sides of the same coin'. Regional and multilateral agreements could work together to promote open and fair conditions for trade and could combat the protectionist challenge to the global trade system. Dunkel dismissed the idea that regional agreements were rivals to GATT and the multilateral trade order: 'there is no good reason why globalism and regionalism should be adversaries ... they can and should be partners in the greater cause of improving world trade conditions'.[139] He reprimanded journalists who perpetuated a mutually exclusive choice as 'a rather easy and quotable diversion from the real challenges'.[140] On the basis of past experience, he suggested that regional agreements – such as the formation of the EEC in 1958 and its subsequent enlargement in 1973 – had helped to galvanize GATT negotiations.[141]

Sutherland was more concerned about how regional agreements affected global trade, suggesting that they could undermine freer trade and could be rivals to GATT. He acknowledged that they were not necessarily working at cross-purposes. Regional agreements could be 'a shot in the arm' or 'a shot in the foot' to multilateral trade. Like Dunkel, he believed that openness was the main criteria to ensure that regional arrangements reinforced the multilateral trade order. He also held up the GATT system as essential to sustaining a fair and liberal trade order because the 'rule of law' prevailed, as opposed to the 'law of the jungle' in which the strongest states dominated the weakest.[142] He called on the leaders of world trade – the alleged fortresses of Europe, North America, and East Asia – to sustain the global trade order 'NOW when the system has proven its universal appeal'; to do otherwise would be 'morally and economically reprehensible'.[143] As the Uruguay round dragged on, Sutherland emphasized the importance of the successful

[138] Address by Dunkel to the Conference of the International Herald Tribune in Association with the International Chamber of Commerce, Paris, 3 April 1992, GATT/1540, GDL.
[139] 'Multilateralism and Regionalism Can Support Each Other'.
[140] Uruguay Round Challenges Outlined by Arthur Dunkel, 18 May 1989, GATT/1455, GDL.
[141] Address by Dunkel to the Conference of the International Herald Tribune in Association with the International Chamber of Commerce.
[142] 'Regional Trading Arrangements Should Be Building Blocks, Not Stumbling Blocks, for the Multilateral System, Says Sutherland', 16 September 1993, GATT/1596, GDL.
[143] Later in the speech, he denied that such trade fortresses existed and added that Europe had deliberately turned away from becoming a fortress. 'More Competition – Less Confrontation – Says Peter Sutherland', 4 September 1993, NUR 064, GDL.

conclusion of the negotiations. Such a success would revive confidence in multilateralism, implicitly refuting claims that regional arrangements were more practical than the GATT process. It was the vitality of the multilateral order that gave countries confidence to participate in regional arrangements.[144] As the proposal to create a World Trade Organization (WTO) took shape (discussed in Chapter 6), Sutherland suggested that it would also be better able to uphold rules and laws and its dispute resolution mechanism would ensure 'that regionalism remains open'. More than just a framework that regional agreements had to fit into or a yardstick against which they could be measured, Sutherland likened the multilateral trade system to a tree, organic and growing, on which regional arrangements would presumably be ripe fruit.[145]

The Uruguay round had attempted to tighten the provisions of Article XXIV to ensure that subsequent regional arrangements would contribute to the growth and liberalization of world trade. The establishment of the WTO further strengthened the organization's ability to uphold rules and norms. However, the substantial results of the Uruguay round did not reduce the appeal of regional trade agreements. Bhagwati might criticize the US administration and others for their newfound belief that regionalism and global freer trade went hand in hand, but this was the way that more and more politicians spoke.[146] Harald Sander notes that not only was regionalism a result of deliberate policy-making, but also it emerged from the increasingly competitive global economic environment: globalization and regionalism were compatible and mutually reinforcing.[147] Whether Article XXIV arrangements were building blocks or stumbling blocks to more liberal and expanding world trade was a question that could never be answered definitively. Some people interpreted these agreements as alternatives to GATT, products of mounting frustration with the prolonged Uruguay round and the slow-moving GATT machinery more generally. Others thought they could be agents of liberalization, supplementary to GATT. The point for GATT was to scrutinize such agreements, thereby holding its members to a process that acknowledged its position as the arbiter and standard-bearer for liberal global trade.

[144] 'Regional Trading Arrangements Should Be Building Blocks, Not Stumbling Blocks'.
[145] 'Sutherland Says WTO Set to Play Central Role in Shaping International Trade Environment', 27 September 1994, GW/07, GDL.
[146] 'Regionalism and Trade: The Right Direction?' *The Economist* (16 September 1995), 23.
[147] H. Sander, 'Multilateralism, Regionalism, and Globalisation: The Challenges to the World Trading System' in H. Sander and A. Inotai (eds.), *World Trade After the Uruguay Round: Prospects and Policy Options for the Twenty-First Century* (London and New York: Routledge, 1996), 32–33.

Conclusions

Economists remain undecided about the overall impact of regional agreements on the accessibility of markets and the impetus they give to the growth of global trade.[148] There is no question that regional trade agreements threatened GATT's institutional authority, relevance, and credibility. Every time a GATT member entered into a new regional trade agreement, it tested GATT's supervisory role. Each such development was also an occasion to measure members' commitment to GATT and their faith that the multilateral process remained effective and meaningful. Even though GATT struck working parties to investigate regional agreements, they rarely rendered a verdict about whether an agreement fell short of or satisfied Article XXIV conditions. As Sutherland noted, of over fifty working parties, only six reached any conclusions at all. For him, the erosion of Article XXIV was damaging to the organization: 'A rules-based trading system is only as good as the credibility of its rules and procedures.'[149] As more and more GATT members entered into regional agreements, there were fewer contracting parties that could insist on rigorous compliance with Article XXIV. There was also a double standard at work, with each member insisting on the virtue of any agreement to which they belonged, but calling out the shortcomings of those to which they did not.

At the heart of GATT membership there was a tension between rights and obligations. The social compact of the GATT community rested on its ability to hold members to their obligations while ensuring that rights were respected. That was the key trade-off that made sacrifices worthwhile. Ultimately this depended on continuing to propel liberalization forward in a way that spread benefits as widely as possible. The proliferation of regional trade agreements confirmed that GATT struggled to deliver results, a struggle made harder by other successes, in particular having an ever-larger membership and expanding its scope beyond tariffs. The challenge GATT faced to deliver results was also complicated by the persistent attachment to national interests above the commitment to a collective good. Mark Mazower flagged this tension in his study of global governance: 'Hardwired ... into the new international bodies from the start was an inevitable tension between the narrower national interests that the Great Powers sought to promote through them and the

---

[148] VanGrasstek claims that the debate about whether regional trade agreements promote or undercut multilateralism 'may be the single most important controversy in the WTO age'. VanGrasstek, *The History and Future of the World Trade Organization*, 464.

[149] Sutherland, 'A New Framework for International Economic Relations', Third Annual Hayek Memorial Lecture, 16 June 1994, GATT/1640, GDL.

universal ideals and rhetoric that emanated from them.'[150] Trying to resolve this tension – or at least keeping it in balance – was a constant challenge for GATT.

Although there was a persistent zero-sum and nationalist reckoning with respect to trade, there were signs that internationalist norms and processes continued to function. Registering regional agreements under Article XXIV might be seen as a formality, but the point is that members continued to comply with this requirement. In doing so, they acknowledged their commitments to GATT and the importance of the appearance of compliance with the rules of trade. This was evidence of an ongoing fidelity to the ideal of the internationalization of trade, even as members sought ways to make trade work for them as best they could. Members accepted the legitimacy of the rules which in turn acted as a restraint on them even as they pushed up against them.

Even though almost all GATT members entered into regional trade agreements, no country would admit that regional trade (or protectionism for that matter) had replaced its commitment to multilateral and liberal trade.[151] Denouncing or rejecting multilateralism was seen as a rogue stance, whereas a policy of multilateralism remained the default option for GATT members. But support was often muted. As *The Economist* explained in relation to the United States, there were believers in free trade in the early 1990s, 'but they are an unassuming lot ... Amid all the shouting, they have been ignored.'[152] We will explore more of the shouting against GATT and trade liberalization in the chapters on development and agriculture. For now, it is important to note that GATT retained a normative and symbolic authority and trade liberalization remained the default policy. It might be supplemented or subverted by regional agreements, but it was not forsaken.

Although GATT exercised a normative authority and mobilized bureaucratic means to enforce the General Agreement, members had great latitude. It was not only the greatest powers that acted in a self-interested way. Small states including Australia, Iceland, Israel, Morocco, New Zealand, and Singapore also entered into regional agreements. While small states had a lot at stake in supporting GATT because it could offset imbalances in economic power, they also sought to

---

[150] M. Mazower, *Governing the World: The History of an Idea* (New York: Penguin Press, 2012), xv.

[151] S. Schultz, 'Regionalisation of World Trade: Dead End or Way Out?' in M. P. van Dijk and S. Sideri (eds.), *Multilateralism versus Regionalism: Trade Issues After the Uruguay Round* (London and Portland, OR: Frank Cass in association with European Association of Development Research and Training Institutes, 1996), 36.

[152] 'Trade-Block Folly', 13.

maximize their commercial opportunities and readily used a variety of instruments to do so. The fact that the strongest members of GATT could not deter them forces a rethinking of the importance of a hegemon in holding up the GATT order.

Regional trade agreements communicated general attitudes, policies, and practices about international relations. The appeal of regional trade was worrying because it might foretell a shift away from, possibly even a rejection of, the liberal order created after the Second World War. Although it is possible for multiple orders to exist simultaneously, the argument made in defence of GATT and the liberal order presented options as mutually exclusive. Trade policy also became an increasingly conspicuous part of global geopolitics. By the 1970s, regional trade agreements were becoming more centrally implicated in the substance of world politics, in two ways. First, they moved to the top of the agenda in inter-state relations. Governments were increasingly concerned with questions of commercial cooperation and competition, and these questions were dealt with at the highest political level. Second, as the global economy slowed and countries confronted economic difficulties, including trade imbalances, dollar shortages, rising inflation, and increasing levels of unemployment, the domestic consequences of trade policy came to the fore and became top political priorities. Trying to determine whether and how trade was politicized misses the point that trade and politics were mutually constitutive. As Richard Cooper explains, aside from war and perhaps migration, trade was 'the most important relationship that countries have with one another'. He goes on to say that 'trade is what most of international relations are about'.[153] The next two chapters flesh out the ways in which trade policy was foreign policy, first in the context of development and relations between the global north and the global south, and then in a study of agriculture.

---

[153] R. N. Cooper, 'Trade Policy is Foreign Policy', *Foreign Policy* 9 (1972/73), 32.

5   'Rich-Man's Club'
The Development Challenge to GATT

The role of trade in supporting economic development was known from the time when GATT was first established. And yet the organization charged with liberalizing and expanding global trade to the benefit of all countries has been dismissed as a rich-man's club that privileged industrialized members and disadvantaged developing countries. According to the liberal interpretation, trade is one way to promote economic development because liberal policies are universally applicable and trade benefits all participants.[1] However, there are critics of the liberal approach to development. In 1950, the Argentinian economist Raúl Prebisch noted that the international division of labour locked Latin American countries into the role of producer of primary commodities and supplier of raw materials rather than promoting their development and industrialization. The benefits of growth were not shared equally between peripheral countries and 'great industrial centres'. According to Prebisch, trade was both part of the problem and part of the solution to the underdevelopment of peripheral countries. He believed that controlling imports was essential to industrial development in Latin America. Although regulating imports would limit commercial exchange, the point was to allow developing countries 'to extract, from continually growing foreign trade, the elements that will promote economic development'.[2] Repeated failed attempts at development – which sometimes exacerbated the very conditions they were supposed to

---

[1] A. O. Hirschman, J. Adelman, E. Rothschild, and A. Sen, *The Essential Hirschman* (Princeton: Princeton University Press, 2013), 60, 67.

[2] R. Prebisch, *The Economic Development of Latin America and its Principal Problems* (New York: Economic Commission for Latin America, 1950), 1, 2, 33, 46–47, 53. This argument makes a case for import substitution. The unequal allocation of the benefits of trade is central to the Singer-Prebisch hypothesis, which argues that trade reinforces systemic dynamics that prevent the development of underdeveloped countries and preserve the centrality and wealth of industrial countries. Hirschman et al., *The Essential Hirschman*, 68. This view was also at the heart of the dependency school and world system view that emerged twenty years later. A. G. Frank, *Capitalism and Underdevelopment in Latin America: Historical Studies of Chile and Brazil* (New York: Monthly Review Press, 1967) is a seminal text of dependency theory. According to Hirschman, the dependency

alleviate – gave rise to postcolonial critiques, perhaps most famously that of Arturo Escobar, who condemned development as a neo-imperial project intent on reforming developing societies to conform to a western conception of modernity.[3] The challenge of development has been further complicated by changing views of the end goal: economic growth, eradicating poverty, closing socio-economic disparities, or expanding individual freedoms. Given the complexity of development studies, it is no surprise that GATT is not central to the scholarly literature. However, when GATT is mentioned, it is often identified with systemic problems that have limited people's opportunities and perpetuated conditions of poverty in developing countries.

Although GATT is marginal in histories of development, development is central to the history of GATT. Attempts were made, from beginning to end, to make GATT better serve the goal of development. They invariably fell short. There are several reasons why: insufficient political will, structural disadvantages, the power of domestic special interests, double standards, fragmentation among developing countries, and institutional rigidity. The challenge of promoting development in GATT says much about institutional insecurity as a force for reform; about the secretariat's agency, especially that of Wyndham White; about the dynamics among and ulterior motives of GATT members; and about the priorities of the global community. The development story of GATT involves much failure and disappointment, but it is not a story of indifference.

This chapter begins with the ITO. When the trade charter was finalized in 1948, development was its top priority. But the ITO was never established. Subsequent complaints by developing countries – that they derived fewer benefits than developed countries from trade negotiations in GATT and that the sectors of greatest interest to them, such as textiles or food products, were often excluded from negotiations – reinforced the view that GATT privileged developed countries. Not everyone was convinced that the problem was with GATT. Some scholars and trade officials suggested that developing countries were ill-suited to, and as a result ill-served by, the organization. Some went so far as to describe developing countries as unconstructive members who asked for much but gave little in return.[4] Some US officials described them as

---

school understood the relationship between the developed and developing countries to be 'in the nature of an antagonistic, zero-sum game'; *The Essential Hirschman*, 70.

[3] A. Escobar, *Encountering Development: The Making and Unmaking of the Third World* (Princeton: Princeton University Press, 2011).

[4] Hudec portrays developing countries as seeking 'special status', the results of which created a 'one-sided welfare relationship' between developing and developed countries

troublemakers and free riders.[5] Other scholars have explained the marginalization of developing countries in GATT as a result of their own indifference; they preferred UNCTAD and so were more active there than in GATT.[6] In general, the literature suggests that developing countries contributed little to GATT, and that they possibly even weakened the organization and a liberal trade order.[7] Such studies reinforce the view of developing countries as marginal, disengaged, inconsequential, or unconstructive.

Recent studies have refocused the narrative of developing countries in GATT; it is less a story of opposition between developed and developing countries and more a tale in which developing countries 'created their own momentum' which then 'interacted with the momentum of the GATT/WTO system'.[8] Along these lines, Wilkinson and Scott argue that developing countries were active participants throughout GATT's existence, although involvement did not guarantee that their views prevailed or that their interests were well served. While their influence might not have been as great as that of other members such as the USA, Britain, and the EEC, there were times when they emerged as leaders and staunch advocates of GATT.[9]

that undermined GATT. R. E. Hudec, *Developing Countries in the GATT Legal System* (Cambridge: Cambridge University Press, 2011), 24.

[5] Kelly claimed developing countries were not credible members of GATT; Newkirk said they caused trouble because they had no sense of having any obligations until the Uruguay Round; both quoted in A. E. Eckes, Jr. (ed.), *Revisiting U.S. Trade Policy: Decisions in Perspective* (Athens, OH: Ohio University Press, 2000), 28, 30–31. Hoekman and Kostecki argue that developing countries became more fully engaged during the Uruguay Round and into the WTO, where they are 'demonstrably much more committed to the multilateral trading system'. B. M Hoekman and M. M. Kostecki, *The Political Economy of the World Trading System: From GATT to WTO* (Oxford and New York: Oxford University Press, 1995), 235–242.

[6] Kock believes they were not attracted to GATT because of double standards about rules. K. Kock, *International Trade Policy and the GATT, 1947–1967* (Stockholm: Almqvist and Wiksell, 1969), 235. Srivinasan describes developing country members of GATT as ambivalent about the organization. T. N. Srinivasan, *Developing Countries and the Multilateral Trading System: From the GATT to the Uruguay Round and the Future* (Boulder, CO: Westview Press, 1998), 3, 99.

[7] Slobodian lays out the neoliberal critique of developing countries in GATT and global trade, emphasizing incompatible ideas about a market-led (and anarchic) order and a dirigiste approach to the global economy, which neoliberals feared could topple the entire global economy. Neoliberals such as Harberler believed the NIEO would foster the expansion of totalitarianism. Q. Slobodian, *Globalists: The End of Empire and the Birth of Neoliberalism* (Cambridge, MA: Harvard University Press, 2018), 221–224, 240–251.

[8] J. M. Finger, 'Introduction to the New Edition' in R. E. Hudec, *Developing Countries in the GATT Legal System*, 19.

[9] R. Wilkinson and J. Scott, 'Developing Country Participation in GATT: A Reassessment', *World Trade Review* 7 (3) (July 2008), 473–510.

Close study confirms that from the first round of tariff negotiations in Geneva in 1947 until the Uruguay round from 1986 to 1994, developing countries consistently sought to reform the organization to make it more responsive to their priorities, although often with little or moderate success. Despite calls for special and differential treatment, which peaked in the 1960s and 1970s, many developing countries endorsed a rules-based trade system that held out the promise of realizing a just, fair, and inclusive global trade order. Notwithstanding complaints that GATT did less for them than for other members, developing countries were consistent champions of GATT, at times more so than developed members.

Although developing countries were active across all aspects of GATT activities, this chapter focuses on their efforts to make GATT better serve development goals. Doing so draws attention to the dynamics among developing countries. India and Brazil stand out as consistent leaders of developing countries, although other countries also stepped forward including Mexico, Peru, Bangladesh, and Nigeria, sometimes as a direct challenge to India and Brazil. Developing countries disagreed on priorities and tactics and, as a result, they never formed a cohesive bloc in GATT. So even though they constituted a majority by the late 1960s, and could influence the agenda, they were not able to significantly reform GATT's practices to make the organization work more productively for development. The relationship between developing and developed countries was also a crucial part of the effort to make development a priority. The dynamic was not a simple one of opposition. There was much agreement and support, although there were differences of principle as well as tactics in conceptions of development. A focus on development also challenges some of the dominant ideas about post-1945 international relations. Such a focus displaces the dominant Cold War framework. As Mark Bradley explains, adopting a Cold War point of view obscures 'the significance of transnational postcolonial visions in the global south that imagined a world apart both from the bipolar international system and from the imperial order'.[10] GATT's engagement with development also challenges the idea that the USA was a hegemon. Other members stood against it on key issues, such as its opposition to the use of preferences to promote development. This case study demonstrates the multicentred and fluid nature of GATT leadership.

---

[10] M. Bradley, 'Decolonization, the Global South and the Cold War, 1919–1962', in M. P. Leffler and O. A. Westad (eds.), *The Cambridge History of the Cold War: Vol. I, Origins* (Cambridge: Cambridge University Press, 2010), 465.

The Early Impress of Development and the Failure of the ITO, 1946–1950

Although the concept of development, linking economic growth and social justice, can be traced back to the nineteenth century,[11] Eric Helleiner and Amy Sayward contend that the Second World War was a critical period in the conception of and commitment to economic development as a global priority. Sayward explains the 'birth of development' as a result of the intersection of disillusionment with national approaches, faith in an internationalist ideology, and confidence that solutions to long-standing problems could be found.[12]

In the early planning stages of the ITO, officials connected trade and development. There was not a consensus about how trade might promote development. This was not surprising as the participating states in the planning and establishment of GATT included Australia, Brazil, Burma, Ceylon, Chile, China, Cuba, India, Lebanon, New Zealand, Pakistan, South Africa, Southern Rhodesia, and Syria, states with widely differing economic circumstances.[13] In international meetings in 1946 and 1947, the draft proposal for the ITO was revised to take their interests and needs into account, but the focus remained on opening markets by lowering tariff barriers.

---

[11] Ekbladh claims the concept of development 'has no clear beginning'. D. Ekbladh, *The Great American Mission: Modernization and the Construction of an American World Order* (Princeton: Princeton University Press, 2010), 3.

[12] Sayward traces ideas about development to the emergence of an internationalist ideology and activism that began in the late nineteenth century. A. L. S. Sayward, *The Birth of Development: How the World Bank, Food and Agriculture Organization, and World Health Organization Changed the World, 1945–1965* (Kent, OH: Kent State University Press, 2006), 1–6. Helleiner makes the case that the priorities of developing countries shaped development thinking in the 1940s, in contrast to the portrayal of development as an American 'invention'. E. Helleiner, 'The Development Mandate of International Institutions: Where Did It Come From?', *Studies in Comparative International Development* 44 (3) (September 2009), 190–192; 208–209. Also see E. Helleiner, *Forgotten Foundations of Bretton Woods: International Development and the Making of Postwar Order* (Ithaca, NY: Cornell University Press, 2014). A Euro-American form of modernity further defined ideas about development, embedded within the postwar international order in organizations such as the World Bank, the Food and Agriculture Organization, and UNICEF. N. Cullather, 'Development? It's History', *Diplomatic History* 24 (4) (Fall 2000), 642.

[13] Dosman claims that the twenty-three members who participated in the Geneva meeting were all industrial countries focused on recovery and were not concerned about development. He refers to them as 'Northern' and 'like-minded'. E. J. Dosman, *The Life and Times of Raúl Prebisch, 1901–1986* (Montreal, McGill-Queen's University Press, 2008), 379–380. This is not correct. Srivinasan counts 11 developing countries among the first participants, a tally that rises to 13 if South Africa and Czechoslovakia are included in this category. Srivinasan, *Developing Countries and the Multilateral Trading System*, 20.

The final meeting in Havana, 1947–1948, transformed the ITO into a development project. Although the participants in the earlier Geneva conference had been broadly representative of countries at different stages of economic development, representatives of the developing world arrived en masse in Havana. While the US expectation was that the draft charter would be approved, representatives from developing countries challenged the universalist view of free trade. To them, free trade was not fair and would prolong systemic exploitation and their economic marginalization. The terms and provisions of the draft charter suited states that already had industrialized and diversified economies. The representative of Mexico was especially critical, denouncing the draft charter for its many 'sins' – in particular its emphasis on the removal of barriers to trade, which could wipe out the rudimentary core of industrialization that developing nations had thus far built up. Instead, the trade organization should focus on the underlying problems of economic inequality and should propose positive measures to promote 'the economic development of all nations and the international co-operation required to expedite it'.[14] Over 800 amendments were proposed. For example, representatives from Latin and Central America, the Middle East, and Scandinavia insisted that the charter should permit the establishment of regional preferential trade blocs to stimulate trade and development. The main challenge in Havana was to reconcile differences between the developed and developing world.[15]

US officials resisted the dilution of the liberal purpose of the ITO, but Cold War considerations prevented them from being inflexible: US officials wanted to build the largest possible network of supporters, and failure in Havana might create openings for the Soviet Union, thereby weakening US leadership and threatening the USA's security. As one US official noted, failure to agree on the ITO would put the Soviet Union 'in a better position to bring other countries under their economic and political influence', whereas the so-called free world would be 'without a rudder in the international economic sea'.[16] As a result, the final draft of the ITO charter emphasized development, defined as 'the productive use of the world's human and material

[14] Address by L. J. C. Ramón Betata, President, the Mexican delegation, United Nations Conference on Trade and Employment, Havana, 26 November 1947, ITO/32, GDL.
[15] J. H. Jackson, *World Trade and the Law of GATT: A Legal Analysis of the General Agreement on Tariffs and Trade* (Indianapolis: Bobbs Merrill, 1969), 45–46.
[16] 'Considerations in Deciding Course for Havana', 30 December 1947, Clayton-Thorp Papers/RG59/Box 4/Memoranda – copies of, July – 31 December 1947, Truman Library.

resources' which would promote the 'individual and general economic development of all countries'.[17]

A comparison of the versions of the trade charter that emerged from the Geneva and Havana meetings reveals the extent of the shift in priorities. The pledge in the Havana charter placed development ahead of trade liberalization. Whereas the General Agreement opened with the MFN principle, it was listed as the sixteenth article in the Havana charter. The removal of barriers to trade was relegated to the fourth part of the Havana charter, in contrast to the General Agreement in which it constituted the bulk of the terms and norms. The Havana charter also included a section on commodity agreements, of particular interest to developing countries.

Still, representatives from developing countries were far from satisfied. They listed the many times that they had compromised or rescinded proposed amendments. The representatives from Chile and Colombia lamented that there was no agreement that nations at different stages of economic development should behave according to different standards and expectations.[18] One size did not fit all, but the one-size approach had largely prevailed. Nonetheless, most developing countries praised the Havana charter as a solid beginning and a document that more fully took into account the widely differing economic conditions of the nations of the world. As China's representative, Dr. Jin Wensi, put it at the closing session, the new charter was 'a delicately balanced document'.[19] Developing countries also looked ahead to the actual implementation of the ITO. Mexico's representative noted that the proof of their efforts would be evident in the actual workings of the ITO.[20] They expected nations that were already economically advanced to help developing countries move beyond their current economic circumstances: there was a 'need for the economically stronger countries to co-operate altruistically in the work of speedily improving the standards of living of the weak countries'.[21]

---

[17] The Havana charter for an International Trade Organization is available from the WTO at www.wto.org/english/docs_e/legal_e/havana_e.pdf

[18] Statement to be delivered by Mr. Walter Muller, President of the Delegation of Chile, to the Conference on Trade and Employment in Havana, Cuba, 21 March 1948, ITO/188; Speech delivered at the 17th Plenary Meeting on Behalf of the Delegation of Colombia by H. E. Dr. Fulgencio Lequerica Veles, Minister of Colombia in Cuba, Delegate to the Conference and Minister Plenipotentiary, 20 March 1948, ITO/187, GDL.

[19] Speech to be Delivered by the Chief Delegate of China at the Closing Session of the Havana Conference, 19 March 1948, ITO/179, GDL.

[20] Address by Licenciado Ramón Betata, President of the Mexican Delegation, in the closing plenary session of the United Nations Conference on Trade & Employment, 21 March 1948, ITO/192, GDL.

[21] Statement to be delivered by Mr. Walter Muller, 21 March 1948.

Industrial nations endorsed the Havana charter, despite its focus on development. French officials agreed that the charter was a compromise, which, while not entirely satisfactory to anyone, could not really be improved upon.[22] Canadian representatives agreed that the charter was a compromise with which it was not entirely happy, but which they accepted in its entirety.[23] The British representative said that too many concessions had been made for the sake of economic development. He also reiterated Britain's well-known anxieties about the rules regarding new preferential arrangements lest they undermine the right of the British Commonwealth to maintain its preferential system. Despite these concerns, Britain described the trade agreement as being of great moment for the future of world international relations.[24] The US official Will Clayton presented the results of Havana as a triumph for the USA's efforts to establish a liberal and multilateral trade system and the work of the conference as a triumph for people intent on building a peaceful and just foundation for international relations: participants had sacrificed a measure of sovereignty in favour of international disciplines that offset narrower national interests that sparked conflict. He said confidently: 'This is a day for history ... This may well prove to be the greatest step in history toward order and justice in economic relations among the members of the world community and toward a great expansion in the production, distribution and consumption of goods throughout the world.'[25] Despite many reservations, there was impressive support for the final version of the International Trade Organization. Of the fifty-six participating nations, only Poland, Turkey, and Argentina refused to sign the Havana charter.

Two visions of international trade emerged from the Havana conference. The prevailing view among industrial countries was that the liberalization of global trade would spark universal economic growth and diversification. The alternative conception hinted at more deeply rooted conditions that could entrench existing economic relationships and patterns and perpetuate a world of haves and have-nots.[26] H. C. Coombs,

[22] Speech delivered by Mr. P. Grousset, Minister of France, Head of the French Delegation, at the Final Plenary Session, 22 March 1948, ITO/211, GDL.
[23] Address of Chief Canadian Delegate to the Final Plenary Session of United Nations Conference on Trade and Development, 20 March 1948, ITO/185, GDL.
[24] Statement by Mr. S. L. Holmes for the United Kingdom Delegation Before the Final Plenary Session of the United Nations Conference on Trade and Employment on 23 March 1948, ITO/198, GDL.
[25] Statement by the Honourable William L. Clayton, Chairman, Delegation of the United States of America, 23 March 1948, ITO/194, GDL.
[26] For examples of US officials and economists who believed that free trade would not promote the development of poor countries but rather would entrench their position as

a well-respected Australian economist, explained the fragile relationship between the two conceptions of international trade. He described them as competing ideas of economic freedom: one revolved around the removal of barriers to trade, the other focused on the creation of opportunities. 'To many of us, mere absence of restraint, while an important element in freedom, is, taken by itself, a negative and empty thing. ... We have been made aware that positive opportunity does not automatically come to the under-developed, the under-privileged, the unemployed, and to the poverty-stricken.' He went on to praise the charter for striking a balance between these two, sometimes clashing, conceptions of freedom.[27]

Clair Wilcox, the director of the office of international trade in the USA, confidently predicted that 'the Havana steamroller cannot be stopped'.[28] Wilcox was wrong. Australia and Liberia were the first to complete the ratification process in 1949, although Australia's ratification was contingent on Britain and the United States doing likewise. Denmark, France, Greece, Luxemburg, Norway, India, Italy, and Sweden were preparing to ratify the ITO by the end of 1950.[29] After weighing pros and cons, Britain came down in favour of ratification because rejecting the ITO would be a blow to 'the faith of progressive opinion throughout the world in international co-operation and place[d] a potent weapon in the hands of the forces of isolationism in the United States'.[30]

But the success of the ITO ultimately depended on US support. President Truman submitted the Havana Charter to Congress for approval in 1949, explaining its importance in terms of global prosperity and international cooperation. Observers from other countries remained confident that the USA would ratify the ITO.[31] Indeed, Truman intended to put it forward again in 1950, but in the end he did not.

'economic colonies', see Helleiner, 'The Development Mandate of International Institutions', 197–203.

[27] Speech by Dr. H. C. Coombs, Head of the Australian Delegation Before Final Plenary Session, 22 March 1948, ITO/212, GDL. Coombs's definition of development foreshadows some of the points made by dependency theorists of the 1960s and 1970s. His ideas also resemble those of Amartya Sen who stresses the importance of 'expanding the real freedoms that people enjoy'. Sen goes farther in explaining how interconnecting freedoms are both means and ends which can be realized through values and quality of life rather than measured through 'utilities, incomes and wealth'. A. Sen, *Development as Freedom* (New York: Anchor Books, 2000), 3, 27.

[28] Wilcox to Clayton, 27 February 1948, *Foreign Relations of the United States, 1948 Vol. I*, 879.

[29] Ratification of the Havana Charter, Note by the Executive Secretary, 31 October 1949, BT11/2906, TNA.

[30] Extract from a memorandum by the President of the Board of Trade on the Havana charter for an International Trade Organisation, C. P. (49) 114, n.d., BT11/2906, TNA.

[31] Letter by J. H. Wilson, Board of Trade, 10 May 1949, BT11/2906, TNA.

Susan Aaronson claims that the government did not adequately educate the US public about the importance of the ITO for domestic interests.[32] There were many other factors that converged against ratification. Protectionism had many backers. Because the ITO diluted free trade principles, it lost the support of traditionally pro-trade business groups. Moreover, the Cold War deflected attention away from the ITO. With GATT in place, there was less urgency to establish the ITO.[33] Whatever the reason, without US backing the ITO lapsed, and the USA was blamed for its demise.[34]

Developing countries had seen the Havana version of the trade charter as only partially satisfactory. Reverting to the Geneva version of trade principles – as laid out in the General Agreement – was a step backwards. But not all concluded that GATT was irrelevant or injurious to the economic growth of developing countries. Indian government analysis from 1952 denied that GATT helped only developed countries and hindered the growth of developing countries. Because global economic conditions after the war's end were abnormal, it was not useful to judge GATT on the basis of its early performance.[35] While it had not delivered as much as might be hoped for, GATT was 'a necessary institution and it can be made more useful by widening its scope'.[36] In 1953, the government of Haiti produced an optimistic memorandum about how liberalism and GATT would benefit the least economically developed nations. It decried the clash of interests between north and south that had undermined the International Trade Organization. It upheld the fundamental

[32] S. A. Aaronson, *Trade and the American Dream: A Social History of Postwar Trade Policy* (Lexington: University of Kentucky Press, 1996), 122, 127–129.

[33] T. W. Zeiler, *Free Trade, Free World: The Advent of GATT* (Chapel Hill: University of North Carolina Press, 1999), 148–150, 163–164; D. Deese, *World Trade Politics: Power, Principles and Leadership* (London and New York: Routledge, 2008), 45; R. Toye, 'Developing Multilateralism: the Havana Charter and the Fight for the International Trade Organization, 1947–1948', *International History Review* 25 (2) (June 2003), 282–305; Irwin, *Clashing over Commerce*, 503–506.

[34] See for example Minute by P. Mennell, The Future of the I.T.O. and G.A.T.T., 23 August 1950, FO371/82970, TNA. 'It is entirely the fault of the United States that the I.T.O. is not already in existence.' Clayton also believed the USA was responsible for its demise. Clayton Papers, Box 2, General Interviews with Mrs. Greenwood, 1947–1958, notes entitled Why the ITO Charter Didn't Pass Congress so Failed Elsewhere, Except We Did GATT – Almost as Good, Hoover Institution.

[35] The Under-Developed Countries and the GATT, 4/10/1952, 52 (50)/TB/52: Examination of Note Circulated by GATT Secretariat regarding the value of the General Agreement to the Under-developed Countries; Government's Comments on the Note, NAI.

[36] Department of Finance, Department of Economic Affairs (E.F.V. Branch), no title, n.d. (but from 1952), 52 (50)/TB/52: Examination of Note Circulated by GATT Secretariat regarding the value of the General Agreement to the Under-developed Countries; Government's Comments on the Note, NAI.

premise of liberalism that all would sink or swim together: 'all the nations of the world are adversely affected by a general clogging of the main channels of trade whereas they benefit by their expansion'. The memorandum went on to assert that north–south incompatibility was superficial: 'there is no such thing, within the GATT, as two groups of diametrically opposed interests, let alone two contending parties'.[37] Haiti's conception of international trade was appealing, but in practice the divide between north and south had begun to make a mark on GATT. That impress would deepen over time.

The GATT Review of 1954–1955 and the Chairmanship of the Contracting Parties

The case for linking trade with development was next advanced during the GATT review of 1954–1955. Members had decided that the General Agreement should be reviewed from top to bottom, with the intention of turning it into a properly functioning international institution, to be called the Organization for Trade Cooperation (OTC). The review created an opportunity to insert development more centrally in GATT. Although the OTC failed, as discussed in Chapter 3, the debate about trade and economic growth, the importance of rules and exceptions, and the priorities of the organization exposed the tension between developed members, who continued to believe in the universalist approach, and developing members, who rejected this logic. The connection between the ways in which international trade could promote development came out most clearly in discussions about quantitative restrictions and commodity agreements.

The emergence of the sub-field of development economics gave more reason to doubt the liberal proposition that open trade would promote general economic growth. The point of departure of development economics was that a laissez-faire and liberal approach did not always encourage development. In countries where resources were scarce, infrastructure and social services rudimentary, and educational systems fragmentary, liberalism might not work as its proponents envisioned. Government intervention was required to rationalize resources and institute the necessary support for long-term and broad-based growth and development. There was also an element in 1950s development thinking that stressed large-scale infrastructure projects – inspired by the example of the Tennessee Valley Authority in the USA – as the path to modern

---

[37] Operation of the General Agreement: Note by the Executive Secretary, 18 June 1953, L/96, GDL.

industrialized economies.[38] Development was a complex problem. International trade could help or hinder it. For an organization unsure of its support and fearing irrelevance, trade-related economic development was both challenge and opportunity.

Wyndham White was concerned that developing countries might lose faith in GATT. But if their efforts to reform GATT were successful, he feared that the support of developed countries would weaken. So, before the review session, he visited several developing countries to encourage support for revision that preserved the basic structure of GATT. He asserted that developing countries would be better protected when all members upheld GATT's rules and provisions. But, he added, there was a need for 'residual flexibility for exceptional cases in which, in view of the special circumstances of those countries, they may have to deviate from the strict letter of the law'. For instance, there could be flexibility in the use of quantitative restrictions. As things stood, members did not need to seek approval before introducing quantitative restrictions, but he believed that the member in question should explain why such a step was being taken and that other members could introduce retaliatory measures. Moreover, the use of quantitative restrictions should necessitate an annual review to ensure that the practice was not being abused.[39] Wyndham White was trying to make two factions happy: developing countries that bristled at the prospect of prior GATT approval for such restrictions, and developed countries, especially the US and the UK, that did not want to be in a position of having to accept as a fait accompli the transgression of GATT rules. On balance, Wyndham White's proposed arrangements would maintain the form of GATT control over the use of quantitative restrictions while permitting developing countries to promote their national economic development as they saw fit.

The USA opposed the compromise on the grounds that quantitative restrictions were not justified now that the urgent needs of postwar recovery had been met. They wanted them banned, except for use in exceptional circumstances and under close GATT scrutiny. If a member planned to impose quantitative restrictions, they would need prior GATT approval. There should also be a strict schedule, after which quantitative restrictions would lift. Moreover, the USA proposed that the member in question would have to demonstrate the severity of their financial crisis and suggested that the IMF – where the

[38] Ekbladh, *Great American Mission*, chapters 1 and 2.
[39] Proposed Secretariat Draft of Article XVIII, Resume of the Statement by the Executive Secretary at a Meeting on Wednesday, 24 November 1954, W.9/40, GDL.

USA was dominant – should decide whether or not there was a real crisis.[40]

The USA's opposition to quantitative restrictions was undermined by their simultaneous application for a waiver to restrict agricultural imports and subsidize US farmers. The US request was ill-timed: how could the USA credibly call for a tightening of the rules when at the same time it was requesting an exemption from them? As an irate Canadian official put it, 'In seeking freedom to impose agricultural quantitative restrictions, the U.S. is offering a bad example to overseas countries, who are only too ready to find reasons to retain Q.R.'s.'[41] The US request for a waiver also suggested that there was a double standard and that economically powerful members could ignore GATT rules with impunity. Win Brown, who led the US delegation to the review session, agreed that the waiver made it seem as though the USA was only interested in getting its way, which in turn 'strengthened the feeling of a large and important bloc of countries that the GATT is an unbalanced and inequitable agreement largely tailored to accommodate the needs of the US'. The waiver application 'overshadowed the whole Conference' and undercut the willingness of participants to commit to new rules or even to strengthen existing ones.[42]

The British then stepped forward to support the regulation of the use of quantitative restrictions. Like the USA, the UK wanted prior approval by GATT before members introduced quantitative restrictions and a rule that, once implemented, such restrictions could be used for only one year, with the possibility of renewal for a second year. In general, British representatives emerged as champions of the General Agreement circa 1947.[43] The aim was to tweak GATT rules, not radically alter them. The British commitment to liberal trade earned it praise. For instance, the *Christian Science Monitor* described it as the champion of free trade.[44]

Not everyone welcomed the British proposal. The representative for Indonesia said that it was 'absolutely unacceptable' for a member to have

[40] Review of the General Agreement, Proposals by the Government of the United States, 15 October 1954, L/246, GDL; Balance of Payments Import Restrictions, United States Statement, Resume of Remarks by the United States Representative at the First Meeting on Friday Morning, 19 November 1954, W.9/23, GDL.

[41] Note for Mr. Howe on Position of United Kingdom at this Session, 7 December 1954, RG19: F-2/4203/8710–1 pt. 1, Library and Archives Canada [LAC].

[42] Draft Report by the Acting Chairman of the Delegation to the Ninth Session of the General Agreement on Tariffs and Trade (Brown), *FRUS 1955–57*, Vol. IX, 97.

[43] Balance of Payments Import Restrictions, United Kingdom, statement made by the United Kingdom representative at the first meeting on Friday morning, 19 November 1954, W.9/22, GDL.

[44] P. Lyne, 'Britain Takes Lead for Freer Trade', *Christian Science Monitor* (2 November 1954).

to seek the approval of GATT members prior to imposing quantitative restrictions. Developing countries, like all GATT members, should have recourse to them to meet balance-of-payments problems. He also exposed a double standard.

I might ask with some emphasis why countries, not only having suffered from war damage in many cases, but which underwent, prior to that, all the social and economic inconveniences of being deprived for some centuries of the right to determine their own future, should not be in a position to avail themselves of the same – and exactly the same – facilities that their fellow contracting parties which experienced war damage after a considerable period of free social and economic development were allowed to make use of for their economic restoration and expansion during these past seven years.[45]

Even though the challenge confronting developing countries was compounded by a long history of economic oppression, he asked only that developing countries be allowed to use the same methods to foster economic development that developed countries had used to recover from the war. Put this way, the continued use of quantitative restrictions did not seem to be asking for much.

France backed the developing countries' position. The French representative objected to what he called GATT's 'interdiction' on the implementation of quantitative restrictions because it curbed national sovereignty on matters vital to national prosperity. This was too important an issue on which to empower GATT at the expense of individual members. Moreover, the proposed two-year time limit struck the French official as wholly unrealistic because 'financial crises do not, like some illnesses, respect a time-limit'. The French went so far as to suggest that developing countries should be entitled to negotiate bilateral agreements as long as they served the needs of economic development.[46] The French used the issue of quantitative restrictions to advance their preference for a flexible GATT with limited ability to encroach on national sovereignty.

US and Canadian delegates were alarmed at the French stand, which violated the cardinal GATT principle of non-discrimination. They doubted the sincerity of France's commitment to developing countries. They believed the French delegation was exploiting north–south tension in order to prevent the strengthening of GATT rules. As Brown described it, 'They bid openly and in an almost humiliating manner for the support

[45] Balance of Payments Import Restrictions, Statement by the Indonesian Representative at the Meeting on Saturday, 30 November 1954, W.P./32, GDL.
[46] Report of Sub-Group 1-B (Balance of Payments Restrictions), Declaration by the French Delegation at the meeting of 17 December 1954, W.9/115, GDL.

of the underdeveloped countries on anything that would weaken the provisions of the GATT.'[47]

But France was not alone in objecting to Anglo-American direction in GATT. Australia challenged the USA's proposal that the IMF should decide whether or not a financial crisis existed and whether the use of quantitative restrictions was warranted. The Australian representative agreed with the French view that the decision to impose quantitative restrictions was highly sensitive – it amounted to 'curtail[ing a] ... people's liberties by imposing import restrictions on them'. In such a case, the sovereignty of a government could not be restricted. Finally, he cast his objection to the US proposal for IMF intervention in terms of a defence of the institutional authority of GATT. Why should GATT delegate its decision-making role to another international organization? 'If financial aspects are to be judged by the Fund, why should not agricultural aspects be judged by the Food and Agriculture Organization, European aspects by the Organization for European Economic Cooperation and so on?'[48] This reasoning was one that Wyndham White, ever sensitive to challenges to GATT's authority, would have strongly endorsed.

India intervened to resolve the standoff. L.K. Jha warned that trying to remake GATT was bound to fail. The organization was in need of revision, but the purpose of the review should be to make an amended General Agreement 'flexible, prompt and realistic'.[49] His moderation, combined with the fact that India did not always align itself with developing countries, gave India an impartiality and credibility that engendered far-reaching respect. But where quantitative restrictions were concerned, Jha sided with developing countries. In a succinct but powerful statement, he disavowed the assumption that quantitative restrictions were bad for trade. Conditions in developing countries required more nuanced thinking. Without quantitative restrictions, developing economies would be susceptible to volatility and economic strain, which was also bad for international trade. The problem with quantitative restrictions was not their use to encourage industrial development but their retention once an industry was established. And this, he pointed out, was a problem in the developed world, not the developing one.[50] Brown singled Jha out as one of the two 'outstanding personalities' at the review. He was 'wise in judgment, eloquent in debate, reasonable in approach

---

[47] Draft Report by the Acting Chairman, *FRUS 1955–57*, Vol. IX, 100. M. Hoffman, 'French Irk Allies with Trade Stand', *New York Times* (30 November 1954), 17.

[48] Role of the Fund, Statement by the Australian Representative at a Meeting on 30 November 1954, W.9/60, GDL.

[49] Summary record of the 19th Meeting, 17 November 1954, SR.9/19, GDL.

[50] Summary record of the 15th Meeting, 22 November 1954, SR.9/15, GDL.

and extremely well informed'. He must have intended to be complimentary when he said that Jha 'thought like a Westerner'.[51]

The final outcome was that the specific articles dealing with quantitative restrictions (Articles XI and XII) were preserved with minor modifications. Governments could introduce quantitative restrictions to stave off balance-of-payments problems without requiring GATT approval. There could be consultation with those members affected by such a decision, but no particular recourse was set out. Nor was there a specified time limit for their use, although members should lift them as soon as conditions warranted. British and US efforts to control and monitor the use of quantitative restrictions had failed.

Article XVIII was also amended so that developing countries could use quantitative restrictions for development purposes. The wholly revised article emphasized the value of consultation but stated only that GATT members had to be informed. If the use of such measures seemed unwarranted, members could consult with others and take compensating action. In effect, the new Article XVIII protected those GATT members that might be adversely affected by the protective policies of developing countries without encroaching on the ability of developing countries to take whatever measures they believed necessary to prompt development.[52]

Representatives of developing nations also tried to incorporate articles from the defunct Havana charter into the OTC, including those dealing with employment, investment, balance-of-payments crises, inflation, commodity agreements, and the general recognition of development as a priority.[53] In contrast to the developing countries' view of the Havana charter as a model, the USA looked at the Havana conference as a cautionary tale. According to US officials, the problem was not with the terms of the General Agreement but with faults in administering it. 'It would have been better if we had made it work better.' Therefore, the US representative explained that their aim was to make a 'simpler, stronger and more effective General Agreement' and to establish an international organization with only the basic function of administering the agreement.[54]

---

[51] Draft Report by the Acting Chairman, 101. Jha became the governor of the Reserve Bank of India and was also ambassador to the US.

[52] Review of the General Agreement on Tariffs and Trade, held at Geneva, 8 November 1954 – 7 March 1955, Commonwealth of Australia. This is a useful comparison of the General Agreement before and after the review. A copy is in RG43: General Records of the Department of State – International Trade Files, Box 278, file Australia, NARA.

[53] Review Working Party IV on Organizational and Functional Questions, Scope of the Agreement, 22 November 1954, W.9/27, GDL.

[54] Commodity Arrangements, Statement by the United States Delegation, 16 December 1954, W.9/111, GDL.

The US stand prevented a radical redesign of an international trade organization. But the diversity of members' interests and priorities meant that GATT would not be given a proper institutional foundation. Like the ITO, the OTC lapsed. Its failure was a blow to GATT and a disappointment to developing countries.

The failure of the OTC made clear that development was not a priority for GATT. This was also evident from behind-the-scenes manoeuvring to keep administrative control in the hands of western and industrial countries. By the mid-1950s, officials from developing countries were seeking out opportunities to take on leadership positions in GATT, such as the chairmanship of GATT sessions, then held twice a year. Sessions began with elections of a chair and vice-chair of the contracting parties who would direct meetings over several weeks. In the early years, chairs were nominated through an informal process and subsequently acclaimed by members. The United States deliberately avoided the chair's role so that it would not turn GATT into 'a United States show'[55] and weaken other members' support. But they had confidence in Dana Wilgress, the experienced Canadian trade official, who was widely regarded as steady and effective in this role.

Developing countries challenged what was portrayed as an informal and collegial process that in practice excluded them from positions that could influence the proceedings of GATT. Holding such offices was also linked to status in world affairs. As Indian officials reflected on their position within GATT, they concluded that they should play a more prominent part, such as serving as the chair of the contracting parties.[56] Wilgress's long service as chair made it awkward to replace him. In 1953, Wilgress's chairmanship was extended and Akhtar Hussain of Pakistan was elected vice-chair. Brazil had proposed a rotating chair for the review session, but subsequently recommended that Wilgress stay in the job because an experienced hand was needed.

After the review, the rationale for re-electing Wilgress began to wear thin. Jha, who had many years' experience in GATT, was in the running. Although some US officials thought highly of him, others wanted to find 'an effective alternative to Jha of India'. They wanted the Belgian candidate – P. A. Forthomme – but doubted he could defeat Jha in a vote.

---

[55] Memo from Weiss to Brown re Proposed Intersessional Working Party on Strengthening of GATT, 17 October 1951, RG43: Box 285, General Agreement on Tariffs and Trade (GATT), NARA.

[56] Indian Delegation to the Seventh Session of the Contracting Parties to the G.A.T.T.: Report, 52 (2) TB/53: Report of the Indian Delegation to the Seventh Session of the Contracting Parties to the General Agreement on Tariffs and Trade – Examination of, Commerce & Industry, NAI.

Instead, the USA supported John Crawford of Australia, who had 'outstanding qualifications for the position' and who could 'bridge' the divide between developed and developing countries. But the Australian government could not spare him.[57] So they appealed to Wilgress to stand for the sake of 'GATT's well-being'.[58] Wilgress bowed out, explaining that developing members had made clear their objections to him.[59] John Evans, a trade expert in the US State Department with long experience in GATT, tried to persuade his colleagues that Jha would be an effective and impartial chair, given that he was respected by developing countries but did not automatically side with them: 'Jha was very competent in GATT matters and believed in the Agreement . . . [Evans] thought that Jha would be a fair chairman and that the US had everything to gain and little to lose by supporting his candidacy.'[60] Instead, the position went to Sir Claude Corea of Ceylon, with two vice-chairs elected: Forthomme and Andrés Vargas Gómez (Cuba). Jha would have to wait one more year. In 1957, he was unanimously elected to the post.[61]

The portrayal of GATT as an informal organization that functioned through inclusive discussion, a balancing of interests, compromise, and consensus disguised the ways in which the existing global power structure was rigid and self-perpetuating. The justification for excluding representatives from developing countries from chairmanship roles was that they were inexperienced or that their judgement was suspect – as compared to 'confirmed GATT men'.[62] Such justifications exposed racial assumptions that informed international relations and legitimized practices that upheld the authority of white and western states. This is a conspicuous example of what Hobson has called 'subliminal Eurocentric institutional intolerance'[63] and it meant that seemingly neutral bureaucratic practices

---

[57] Office memo, re GATT Chairmanship from Thibodeaux to Prochnow and Kalijarvi, 23 March 1956, RG43: Box 286, file GATT Chairmanship 1956, NARA.

[58] Memo prepared by Len Weiss, Re GATT Chairmanship, 17 May 1956, RG43: Box 286, file GATT Chairmanship 1956, NARA.

[59] Memorandum of Conversation between Wilgress and Weiss, 23 May 1956, RG43: Box 286, file GATT Chairmanship 1956, NARA.

[60] Memorandum of Conversation, 28 February 1956, between Carl Corse and John Evans, RG43: Box 286, file GATT Chairmanship 1956, NARA.

[61] At the end of the session the US representative Carl Corse thanked Jha for the 'competent and constructive manner' in which he had performed his duties. Summary record of the Twenty-Second Meeting, 30 November 1957, SR.12/22, GDL.

[62] Canadians described Forthomme this way. Brussels to External, 10 May 1957. RG19: F-2/4205/8714–24-9 pt. 1, LAC.

[63] J. M. Hobson, 'Re-embedding the Global Colour Line Within Post-1945 International Theory' in A. Anievas, et al. (eds.), *Race and Racism in International Relations: Confronting the Global Colour Line* (London: Routledge, 2015), 82. Because of the illegitimacy of scientific racism as an ordering principle on global affairs after 1945, 'Eurocentric

and consensual processes in fact perpetuated the dominance and privilege of western nations.

The Haberler Report: The Importance of Trade to Development

Although Wyndham White could not impose a development mandate on GATT, in 1958 he forced members to consider how GATT should promote development when he recruited Haberler, Tinbergen, de Oliveira Campos, and Meade to study trends in world trade (which I also discuss in Chapter 3 in relation to the EEC). One of their main findings was that developing countries were increasingly marginalized in world trade (see Figure 5.1). Their export growth lagged behind developed countries, whereas their import needs increased steadily.[64] According to Curzon and Curzon, the economic experts gave Wyndham White 'the report he wanted'.[65] The secretariat followed up and established three committees to address the consequences of the establishment of the EEC in relation to agriculture and the role of developing countries in global trade. Developing countries focused on Committee III, whose goal was to come up with an 'imaginative picture' of what practical steps might be taken to increase the exports of developing countries.[66]

The committee studied the trade patterns of eleven commodities exported by developing countries (including cocoa, coffee, tea, tobacco, jute, cotton, and lead) and considered how developing country exports might increase. In May 1960, the committee explained that these commodities were impaired in foreign markets through a variety of measures, including high revenue duties (affecting coffee, tea, and cocoa), state monopolies (affecting tobacco), and quantitative restrictions (affecting cotton, cotton textiles, and vegetable oils).[67] India and Brazil, along with Indonesia and Ceylon, pointed out that their future attitude towards GATT would be shaped by the actions of developed

---

institutionalism locates difference purely in terms of culture and institutions – as in the "rational West" versus the "irrational East".'

[64] GATT, *Trends in International Trade: Report by a Panel of Experts* (Geneva: GATT, 1958).

[65] G. Curzon and V. Curzon, 'GATT: A Trader's Club', in R. W. Cox and H. K. Jacobson (eds.), *The Anatomy of Influence: Decision Making in International Organization* (New Haven, CT, and London: Yale University Press, 1974), 320.

[66] Official report of the United States Delegation to GATT Committee III, Expansion of Trade, 14–25 March 1960, RG59: GATT 394.41/1960–63/Box 172, NARA.

[67] Third Progress Report of Committee III on Expansion of Trade, 27 April 1960, L/1162, GDL.

IMPORTS

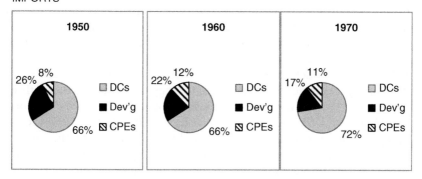

EXPORTS

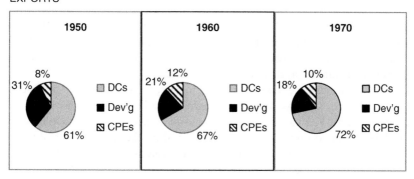

Figure 5.1 Per cent share of world trade (imports and exports), 1950s–
1990s: developed countries (DCs), developing countries (Dev'g), and
centrally planned economies (CPEs)
Source: *UN 1980 Yearbook of International Trade Statistics, Volume
I: Trade by Country* (1981), pp. 1080–1081.

countries in response to the report, in particular by making their markets
more accessible.[68]

But a progress report from the fall of 1960 described a lacklustre range
of responses, including 'no changes' (tea), 'little change' (raw cotton),
and 'very few ... measures' (cotton textiles). Indeed, levels of protection
even seemed to be rising, for instance against tobacco. Where members
had removed quantitative restrictions, developing country officials noted
that this was no more than their GATT obligations required of them. As

---

[68] Hudec argues that following the Haberler report, the focus was on what developed
countries could do for development, rather than trying to make developing countries
conform to GATT rules. Hudec, *Developing Countries in the GATT Legal System*, 46.

for the reduction of tariffs, almost no action had been taken, aside from a few lower tariffs in Denmark and Norway. Although the six members of the EEC had individually removed a few barriers to exports from developing countries, there was a strong current of criticism directed at France, Germany, and Italy, whose use of internal charges on such items as coffee curtailed the export potential of developing countries.[69] One estimate suggested that if these three removed the revenue duties, developing country coffee exports would rise by US$100 million per year.[70] In November 1960, developing countries communicated their dissatisfaction with the lack of progress in making developed markets more open to their exports,[71] suggesting that unless meaningful action were taken soon, they might turn away from the liberal trade system.[72]

Decolonization reinforced the focus on development as a global priority. Membership of GATT swelled in the late 1950s and the 1960s as newly independent countries joined: Ghana and Malaysia (1957), Nigeria (1960), Malaya, Sierra Leone, and Tanzania (1961), Gabon, Senegal, Trinidad and Tobago, and Uganda (1962), Benin, Burkina Faso, Cameroon, Central African Republic, Chad, Republic of Congo, Côte d'Ivoire, Cyprus, Jamaica, Kuwait, Madagascar, Mauritania, and Niger (1963), Kenya, Malawi, Malta, and Togo (1964). The admission of developing countries to GATT bolstered its claims to universal representation. But not all GATT members welcomed mass accession by developing countries, fearing that they would not follow GATT rules and would weaken the organization.[73] The fear was not without justification. For example, Robert Lightbourne, Jamaica's minister of trade and industry, told a Canadian trade official that admission to GATT would not affect the country's extensive use of quantitative restrictions. 'All other countries had violated the GATT almost at will in order to meet

---

[69] Fourth Progress Report of Committee III on Expansion of Trade, 18 October 1960, L/1321; Summary Record of the Fourth Meeting, 20 May 1960, SR.16/4; Summary Record of the Fifth Meeting, 24 May 1960, SR.16/5, GDL.

[70] Expansion of International Trade, Statement by Baron von Platen (Sweden), Chairman of Committee III, at the Plenary Meeting on 14 November, W.17/31, GDL.

[71] Expansion of International Trade, Second Note Submitted by the Less Developed Countries,10 November 1960, W.17/11, GDL.

[72] Official Report of the United States Delegation to GATT Committee III, Expansion of Trade, 26 September – 7 October 1960, RG59: GATT394.41/1960–63/Box 716, file 394.41/11–1560, NARA; Summary Record of the Seventh Meeting, 14 November 1960, SR.17/7, GDL. Canadian officials characterized the attitude and outlook of developing countries as threatening. Geneva to External, re GATT Committee III – March 1–28, 30 March 1961, RG20: A-3/2529/4–581-50 pt. 1, LAC.

[73] Telegram, External to Geneva, 18 February 1963, RG19: F-2/vol. 3953/8720/E96-4, LAC.

their own particular conditions.'[74] To prevent the dilution of GATT rules, the USA proposed a new category of partial membership. This would allow developing countries to participate in GATT meetings, without being committed to its rules and norms or receiving tariff benefits. But this proposal was not popular. Partial membership might encourage criticism without a countervailing sense of responsibility.[75]

So, developing countries joined as full contracting parties. The changed composition of GATT sustained attention on trade as a way to promote economic development. This was reinforced in the United Nations, which declared the 1960s to be the development decade. Cold War competition between the USA and the Soviet Union added to the focus on development as the superpowers vied to prove the superiority of their respective economic systems.[76]

At a GATT ministerial meeting in November 1961, ministers noted the many steps that developed countries could and should take to encourage the growth of trade involving developing countries: reducing barriers to trade, restricting the use of subsidies in areas where developing country exports were competitive, and being mindful of where and how surplus commodities were disposed of. Overall, ministers called for 'a conscious and purposeful effort on the part of all governments to promote an expansion in the export earnings of less-developed countries through the adoption of concrete measures to this end'.[77]

But in practice, GATT did little to advance development. The Dillon round confirmed the marginalization of developing countries. Developing countries could not reduce tariffs with the same latitude as developed members or negotiate on the basis of reciprocity. As a result, they could not participate fully in actual negotiations. Although a new GATT norm was emerging whereby developing countries were not expected to offer equal concessions to those they received, developed countries did not respond well to unequal exchanges. Indeed, many members, including the United States, continued to suggest that the root of the problem was internal to developing countries; therefore, the remedy should also be internal.[78]

---

[74] Office of the Commissioner for Canada, Port of Spain (R. G. C. Smith, Commissioner) to External, 15 June 1962, RG25: G-2/Vol. 7976/14050–5-40 pt. 1, LAC.

[75] Relationship of Less-Developed-Countries to the Work of the G.A.T.T., Brief for UK Delegation to GATT Council, 6 February 1963, CAB134/1958, TNA.

[76] See Ekbladh, *Great American Mission*, chapter 2, on the utility of development in relation to Cold War competition.

[77] Meeting of Ministers, Conclusions Adopted on 30 November 1961, L/1657, GDL.

[78] For example, see Washington to External, 27 February 1959, RG25: G-2/7978/file 14051–5-40 pt. 1.1; Washington to External, 8 March 1960, RG20: A-3/2529/4/581–50 pt. 1, LAC.

Even in sectors where developing countries could compete on a level playing field, they found themselves held back by double standards. This was the case with textiles, a highly protected industry in developed countries. Washington put political pressure on foreign governments to 'voluntarily' restrict textile exports that affected vulnerable (and usually inefficient) US producers. The first such agreement was concluded with Japan in the mid-1950s.[79] Voluntary export restraints (VERs) disguised protectionism, but no one was fooled. From GATT's perspective, such bilateral agreements were objectionable because participants were not accountable and the arrangement allowed 'stronger countries to impose what they want on their weaker trading partners'.[80] They weakened rules, circumvented multilateralism, and thwarted open competition.

These bilateral agreements also held back development where they targeted a sector where developing countries could be competitive. In many developing countries, the clothing and textile industries were central to development initiatives to modernize, diversify, and industrialize their economies.[81] Textiles, long one of the most important areas of global trade, held out the promise of being a take-off industry; according to the development bible of the 1960s, Walt Rostow's *The Stages of Economic Growth: A Non-Communist Manifesto*, this was the key to economic growth and transformation.[82] Despite technological advances, these industries were labour-intensive, and developing countries had a natural advantage: a large and cheap pool of labour. The textile exports of developing countries such as Japan, Egypt, and South Korea made impressive inroads into developed markets around the world (see Figure 5.2).[83] To give an idea of the rapid advances made by developing countries, in 1956 Hong Kong exported US$700,000 worth of cotton textiles to the USA; by 1960 the value had jumped to US$64 million.[84]

[79] Note that Heron identified the first VER as a gentlemen's agreement from 1936 in which Japan agreed to limit cotton exports to the USA. T. Heron, *The Global Political Economy of Trade Protectionism and Liberalization: Trade Reform and Economic Adjustment in Textiles and Clothing* (Abingdon and New York: Routledge, 2012), 18.

[80] Tokyo Round of Multilateral Trade Negotiations, Report by the Director General (Geneva, 1979).

[81] G. H. Perlow, 'The Multilateral Supervision of International Trade: Has the Textiles Experiment Worked?' *American Journal of International Law* 75 (1) (January 1981), 94.

[82] W. W. Rostow, *The Stages of Economic Growth: A Non-Communist Manifesto*, 2nd edition (Cambridge: Cambridge University Press, 1971).

[83] Study on Textiles: Report of the Working Party on Trade in Textiles, 29 December 1972, L/3797, GDL.

[84] Memorandum from the Under Secretary of State (Ball) to President Kennedy, 17 April 1963, *FRUS 1961–63, Vol. IX*, #274, 591.

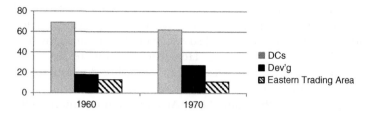

Figure 5.2 Per cent share of world trade (exports) of textiles and clothing, 1950–1970: developed countries (DCs), developing countries (Dev'g), and Eastern Trading Area
Source: Study on Textiles: Report of the Working Party on Trade in Textiles, 29 December 1972, L/3797, p. II-74/75. (Note: these figures exclude intra-EEC trade; Eastern Trading Area includes Eastern European communist countries, plus China, Mongolia, North Korea, and North Vietnam.)

Despite these gains, developed countries still dominated international trade in textiles and clothing. Nonetheless, the advances of developing countries triggered protests and predictions of industrial demise. The problem was serious enough that it landed in senior political laps. President Kennedy had a chart of textile imports in his office, broken down by country of origin and updated daily. The textile industry provided jobs for unskilled and semi-skilled labour, and they were often located in areas for which there were no obvious or easy economic alternatives. The representatives of developing countries were also more outspoken and better organized than US advocates of trade. As President Kennedy explained to the Japanese ambassador: 'the cotton growers in North and South Carolina who did good business with Japan remained mute, while his neighbors in the textile industry were vociferous in their complaints'.[85] Although they did not constitute a clear majority, the opponents of freer trade were vigilant, vocal, and organized, and this gave them disproportionate political influence.

GATT became directly involved in 1961 when the USA asked it to study trade in textiles. Working through GATT would result in multilateral solutions to problems in the textile trade, preferable to the unilateral imposition of quotas which some feared would result in retaliation against the USA and an 'economic war'.[86] The challenge before them was

---

[85] Memorandum of Conversation, 21 April 1961, *FRUS 1961–1963, Vol. IX*, #211, 461.
[86] Editorial note, #213, 464, *FRUS 1961–63*, Vol. IX; Memorandum from the Under Secretary of State (Ball) to President Kennedy, 17 April 1963, *FRUS 1961–63*, Vol. IX, #274, 590.

the same as for all commodities – to find a balance between domestic economic well-being, measured in terms of employment, and ongoing trade liberalization that would sustain global economic growth – but was especially acute in this case. How could cotton textile exports from developing countries increase without injuring domestic producers in developed countries?[87]

The result was the Long-Term Arrangement on International Trade in Cotton Textiles (LTA). Although the agreement encouraged developing countries to export textiles and advised developed countries to relax barriers against cotton textile imports, it privileged domestic market stability above all. That meant that governments could introduce restrictions against cotton textiles if such imports 'cause or threaten to cause disruption in the market of the importing country'.[88] Developed countries continued to impose quotas or other restrictions on imports from developing countries. The USA's under-secretary of state, George Ball, admitted that the agreement was 'a protective device' and explained that it had come about because older industrialized countries were united in their apprehensions about low-wage cotton imports.[89] Ostensibly a measure to liberalize textile trade, the agreement allowed importing countries to restrict the exports of developing countries. Within nine months of coming into force, the USA had introduced 160 actions to restrain cotton textile imports from seventeen countries, affecting both the amount of cotton textile imports and when they were permitted into the US market.[90] Textiles had become an exception in GATT.[91] More seriously, the LTA demonstrated a clear preference for domestic considerations over international ones and for the interests of developed countries over developing ones. It was also an indication that GATT could not mount an effective defence against protectionist forces, which in the early 1960s, a time of impressive global economic growth, were fairly muted. This did not bode well for GATT and the future promotion of trade liberalization. It also vindicated the accusations of many that GATT was a rich-man's club. Not only did it do little for its developing members, it might be making things even harder for them.

---

[87] Agenda, Council 16 June 1961, C/15, GDL.

[88] *The Activities of GATT 1961–62*, 29–30.

[89] Memorandum from the Under Secretary of State (Ball) to Secretary of State Rusk, 25 February 1963, *FRUS 1961–63, Vol. IX*, #262, 562.

[90] Memorandum from the Under Secretary of State (Ball) to President Kennedy, 17 April 1963, *FRUS 1961–63, Vol. IX*, #274, 590.

[91] Heron argues that restrictive measures in the 1950s and 1960s 'delinked' textiles and clothing from the 'wider GATT system'. Heron, *Global Political Economy*, 18, 21.

UNCTAD's Approach: GATT's Chance to Prove its Relevance

Following the 1962 Cairo Conference on the Problems of Economic Development, pressure increased for the holding of a UN-sponsored conference on trade and development, an initiative partly triggered by GATT's shortcomings.[92] This pressure was also a product of decolonization and the emergence of the non-aligned movement, whose members envisioned an 'alternative international order' that rejected the present Cold War and persistent imperial structures that largely defined the international order.[93] Economic justice was a critical component of this alternative order and of the United Nations Conference on Trade and Development (UNCTAD). UNCTAD first met in the spring of 1964, so GATT had almost two years to prepare for what was widely seen as a challenge to and a rebuke of GATT's paltry achievements in the field of development. Developing country members made it clear to Wyndham White that 'they will be judging GATT at UNCTD by progress CPs [contracting parties] make' in the lead-up to the meeting.[94] Wyndham White saw UNCTAD as a challenge and a threat.[95] He tried to pre-empt criticism by increasing the number of developing country members, pushing a development agenda, and aiming to make GATT a permanent international organization. According to the US trade official Margaret Potter Leddy, institutional jealousy prompted him to make GATT more responsive to development.[96] But his motivations were not only defensive or reactive. He had long promoted the membership of developing countries in GATT and tried to make development a higher priority within the organization.

In 1963, Committee III unveiled an eight-point action programme, sponsored by twenty-one developing countries, with specific measures and a timetable to increase developing country exports. For instance, no new barriers, either tariff or non-tariff, could be put in the way of the exports of developing countries. Developed countries should eliminate all quantitative restrictions imposed on exports from developing nations within one year. Tropical products from developing countries would have no tariffs imposed on them in industrialized markets. Tariffs on primary products should be eliminated and tariffs on semi-processed

---

[92] Revised draft intel, GATT and the Less Developed Countries: Entry into Force of Part IV of GATT, n.d., FO371/189603, TNA.
[93] Bradley, 'Decolonization, the global South and the Cold War, 1919–1962', 465, 480.
[94] Telegram, Geneva to External, 19 November 1963, RG19: F-2/vol. 3953/8720/E96-4, LAC.
[95] External to Geneva, 18 December 1963, RG20: Series A-3/vol. 1922/20–28 pt. 12, LAC.
[96] Quoted in Eckes, *Revisiting U.S. Trade Policy*, 29.

and processed products would be reduced by 50 per cent over the next three years. The provisions also dealt with internal taxes, a particular problem in EEC countries, and other internal fees that raised the cost of imports from developing countries. Finally, developed members were expected to look beyond these particular points to find ways in which the export trade of developing countries could grow. These measures were formulated as imperatives, but their implementation depended entirely on the will of developed contracting parties.

At the 1963 ministerial meeting, senior political representatives expressed sympathy for the action programme, and 'declared themselves ready to contribute ... to the fullest extent possible, towards the development of the developing countries'. However, they also said that compliance with the eight points had to square with other GATT obligations. If third parties were adversely affected, their interests would have to be taken into account. None of the action points was therefore easy to implement. Still, they promised to try to eliminate tariffs on primary products, tropical products, and semi-processed and processed items, but acknowledged that this might not be possible. In some cases, these reductions would be pursued through the usual channel of trade negotiations. Given the disadvantages of developing countries in negotiations, this was not very promising.[97]

This was a lukewarm response. The EEC reaction was discouraging. EEC representatives refused to endorse the first seven points on the grounds that they were inadequate. They held that removing barriers to trade was not the most effective method to encourage more exports from developing countries. With respect to tropical products, they insisted that the crux of the problem related to price rather than access to markets. They called for 'more positive measures', without suggesting what these might be, as well as more study to better understand the challenges confronting developing countries.[98] Representatives of developing countries agreed that the terms were inadequate, but had hoped their moderation would make them politically palatable.[99] Phil Tresize, US deputy assistant secretary of state for economic affairs, reported being alarmed at 'how disgruntled the LDCs [less developed countries] are with GATT'.[100]

---

[97] Measures for the Expansion of Trade of Developing Countries as a Means of Furthering Their Economic Development, Meeting of Ministers, 21 May 1963, Min (63) 3, MG32-B41: vol. 12/12–9/G.A.T.T. 1963, LAC.

[98] Measures for the Expansion of Trade of Developing Countries as a Means of Furthering Their Economic Development, Meeting of Ministers, 17 May 1963, Min (63) 2 and 21 May 1963, Min (63) 3, MG32-B41: vol. 12/12–9/G.A.T.T. 1963, LAC.

[99] Measures for the Expansion of Trade of Developing Countries, 21 May 1963.

[100] Interdepartmental Committee of Under Secretaries on Foreign Economic Policy, Summary of Meeting on 23 May 1963, RG59: Records of Component Offices of the

More encouragingly, GATT established a centre to provide technical expertise to assist developing countries in formulating trade policies and participating in trade negotiations, including doing research to help in the development of an export trade, giving advice about marketing, and producing publications of relevant information. Brazil had first advanced this idea in 1962. The creation of such a centre acknowledged that obstacles to the growth of the exports of developing countries were complex and that lowering barriers to exports alone would not solve the export problems of developing countries. The International Trade Centre opened its doors on 1 May 1964.

GATT also established a working group to study the pros and cons of preferential tariffs as a way to boost the exports of developing countries. This was a particularly important initiative because it acknowledged that there were structural advantages and disadvantages in global trade. GATT members first focused on the preferences that developed countries could extend. Early thinking also emphasized the importance of granting preferences as a unilateral gesture, which would satisfy the developing countries' contention that the onus rested on the developed world to do something to support development. But the USA opposed preferences because they were discriminatory and therefore were incompatible with the MFN principle. Moreover, US analyses insisted that preferences would not work. Their view was that the best way to encourage economic growth was to exploit the natural economic advantages of developing countries. By focusing on the production of labour-intensive commodities for export, developing countries would develop in a sustainable way. Developed countries could help by removing the discriminatory barriers that stood in the way of such exports, rather than by introducing a new layer of discrimination.[101] In policy-making circles, there was still a belief in liberal ideas, such as the removal of barriers to trade, as the best way to promote economic growth. But when the natural advantages of developing countries threatened inefficient industries in the developed world, as they did with textiles, they were blocked.

Bureau of Economic Affairs, 1941–1963, Box 2, file: Economic Affairs (Gen), E3 Organizations and Conferences, Interdepartmental Committee of Under Secretaries on Foreign Economic Policy 1963, NARA. Sir Edgar Cohen also believed developing countries were rightly disappointed by the outcome: 'It may have left some of the less developed countries with a sense of having missed a trick; of having lost, despite many strong speeches of support, the unequivocal decision for the Action Programme which their case deserved.' Cohen to Earl of Home, 29 May 1963, CAB134/1959, TNA.
[101] Memorandum from the Under Secretary of State (Ball) to President Kennedy, United Nations Conference on Trade and Development, 12 November 1963, *FRUS 1961–1963, Vol. IX*, 624–625.

US officials admitted that preferences would be less objectionable if they were extended by all developed countries to all developing countries. Britain also endorsed the comprehensive approach. But the Belgians and French favoured individual countries applying preferences to specific industries. This selective and individualized approach would ensure that those countries in most need and those industries with the greatest promise of efficient production would benefit from preferences. Japan and Australia favoured the offering of preferences only to competitive industries and only for a short time. Nigeria and Uganda wanted preferences to be applied to the least developed countries, in contrast to the better off less developed countries. Developing countries already enjoying preferences were reluctant to share their advantages. Israel insisted that preferences should only benefit products with the greatest likelihood of becoming competitive on world markets. But Brazil asserted that preferences should apply to all developing countries, inside and outside of GATT. Developing countries were factionalized and so could not use their numerical advantage to press their point.[102] The result was that there was not effective support for the preference proposal.

There was one tangible step taken to entrench development as a part of GATT's core mission: adding a new chapter on development (it would become Part IV) to the General Agreement. This chapter brought together earlier recommendations, such as a standstill on barriers to the trade activities of developing countries. It also called on developed members to show goodwill and special consideration to help overturn obstacles affecting developing country exports. During the drafting of this chapter, representatives of developing countries were divided between developing and least developed countries. As a French official reported, India and Egypt advanced proposals that did not accord with the interests of the least developed members.[103] Canadian reports described the voices of developing countries as 'loud' but also 'so thin', remarked on an 'almost total absence of African voices from discussion'.[104] The lack of support from developing countries also reflected disappointment with the terms: they were long on good intentions and short on specific actions. US officials therefore thought it likely that developing countries would reject it. But Wyndham White was more confident that they would accept it

---

[102] Report on the first meeting of the G.A.T.T. Working Group on Preferences in Geneva on October 7–11, 1963, Note by the Board of Trade, 22 October 1963, CAB134/1961, TNA.

[103] The author identified African countries as those whose interests were not being taken into account. Note d'information: Project de Chapitre pour le commerce et le développement, élaboré par le Comité du cadre juridique et institutionnel du GATT, 3 novembre 1964, BAC007/1968–3 pt. 2, HAEU.

[104] Geneva to External, 16 October 1964, RG20: Series A-3/vol. 1924/20–28-3 pt. 1, LAC.

because even though it '[fell] short of their aspirations', it did 'present considerable concessions on the part of developed Contracting Parties', at least as long as the 'saner members of the group' – he included Brazil, India, and Nigeria – prevailed.[105]

Forty-five, or two-thirds, of the members had to ratify the new chapter to formally amend the General Agreement. But GATT members did not rush to do so. At a meeting in 1966, one developing country representative after another lamented the slow progress in finalizing Part IV: the representative from Pakistan noted that despite ten years of sustained discussion of development, 'real action had still yet to come'; the representative from Indonesia agreed that Part IV had not been acted upon because 'political will was lacking'; the Brazilian representative said that he had lost faith in Part IV, whereas the Cuban representative suggested that there was little reason to lose faith because Part IV was inadequate from the start.[106] On 27 June 1966, the requisite two-thirds threshold was finally met and Part IV came into effect. This achievement smacked of too little, too late.

Developing countries were not the only members who were disappointed with GATT's attempt to promote development through trade. Despite pronouncements by President de Gaulle about the importance of development, the inclusion of more developing countries made GATT less appealing as a forum in which to advance French interests. Kojève began to advocate for differentiated trade organizations, one for developed countries and another for developing countries. Developing countries could not be forced out of GATT, but Kojève proposed that it should be shut down and a new organization set up exclusively for developed countries. The OECD might also be able to become a new home for the promotion of trade by developed countries. Kojève said this was only a personal proposal, but he also claimed it had the support of Clappier and even Wyndham White. Wormser later echoed Kojève's ideas in meetings with British officials; he complained that developing countries commanded an influence 'out of all proportion to their importance'.[107] They needed 'a forum in which the advanced trading countries could get together in a restricted group' and French officials proposed the OECD as such a forum.[108]

---

[105] Geneva to External, 5 November 1964, RG20: Series A-3/vol. 1924/20–28-3 pt. 1, LAC.

[106] Geneva to Foreign Office, 7 April 1966, G.A.T.T. 23rd Session, Committee on Trade and Development, FO371/189603, TNA.

[107] Letter from W. Harpham, British Embassy Paris, to F. C. Mason, FO, 26 June 1963, FO371/172328, TNA.

[108] Harpham to Mason, 29 June 1963, FO371/172328, TNA.

The French suggestion to disband GATT and create two trade organizations played into the hands of UNCTAD. Members such as France and Brazil 'would like to demonstrate that the G.A.T.T. no longer serves any useful purpose' and should instead support UNCTAD and the creation of a new and inclusive global trade organization.[109] GATT's lack of progress in entrenching development as a priority exacerbated Wyndham White's unease before the UNCTAD meeting. He had hoped 'to have on record ... sufficient evidence of relevant and effective activity'. But other contracting parties were less worried. Washington was satisfied that development had become 'an established policy consideration in the governments of the industrial countries' and looked ahead to the Kennedy round to address the trade concerns of developing countries.[110] This kind of outlook and approach depended on the patience of developing countries. But their patience was running out, and they had another option when UNCTAD convened in the spring of 1964.

UNCTAD's Challenge: Free Trade is Not Fair

Raúl Prebisch, secretary-general of UNCTAD, was a formidable critic of GATT and of economic liberalism. He had been under-secretary of finance in Argentina and later general manager of Argentina's central bank. He was recruited to work for the UN after the Second World War and joined the Economic Commission for Latin America, where he refined his ideas about regional economic development. Early in his career, he concluded that structural dynamics between industrial core countries and peripheral countries stifled economic development, particularly industrialization.[111] By the time he was appointed secretary general of UNCTAD in 1963, overturning the 'trade gap' was central to his thinking about development.[112]

At UNCTAD's inaugural meeting, Prebisch described the virtues of GATT: it supported the rule of law in international trade; the secretariat was talented; its dispute resolution machinery was important; and it was a useful forum for discussion. He also acknowledged that GATT members and the secretariat had been thinking about development since the Haberler report of 1958. Acknowledging these virtues made his criticisms even more hard-hitting. The main problem with GATT was that it

---

[109] Working Party on Preferences, 13 January 1963, CAB134/1963, TNA.

[110] Trade of Less Developed Countries: Report by Action Committee, 23 January 1964, RG59: Office of the Assistant Legal Advisor for Economic Affairs, Records re Trade and GATT 1947–1966, Box 10, file Less Developed Countries, NARA.

[111] Dosman, *Life and Times of Raúl Prebisch*, chapters 12 and 13.   [112] Ibid., 395.

focused almost exclusively on the removal of barriers to trade. This was a passive form of engagement that did not promote development. Also, the assumption that all countries should be treated equally – what he termed 'an abstract notion of economic homogeneity' – was injurious to developing countries. In short, GATT's approach was outdated and as a result the organization was sidelined in the creation of a 'new order which must meet the needs of development'. Prebisch did not hesitate to step on GATT's toes and specified actions that the organization should take in support of developing countries, including better enforcement of rules, particularly with respect to agricultural protectionism. Perhaps most significantly, he endorsed the use of preferences to benefit developing country exports. He criticized GATT for being 'too rigid' by insisting that preferences could only be extended within a full-fledged customs union or free trade area. With respect to preferences among developing countries, he acknowledged that the practice deviated from GATT norms, but the overriding goal of expanding world trade trumped such concerns and made partial preferences between developing countries consistent with the spirit of GATT. As he put it, 'what harm could be done to international trade' if developing countries extended preferences on 'a sizable proportion, even if it were not substantially all, of their trade?'[113]

Wyndham White appeared at the meeting to respond to Prebisch. He outlined a chronology of GATT's activities on development issues. He did not deny that little of substance had resulted, but he deflected attention to the future – in particular the Kennedy round, to begin in a few weeks' time – which he believed was filled with promise for developing country trade. He also insisted that GATT could not simply waive all its rules and obligations. To do so would make it a less effective institution. 'One can of course have an institution where there are no rights, no obligations – just principles, declarations and resolutions ... but they are not of the same character as an organization which rests on an international agreement involving carefully defined legal rights and obligations and machinery for their enforcement.' He also pointed out that developing countries made up two-thirds of GATT's membership and the onus was on them to work within GATT to better pursue their interests and needs. Hence he boldly asserted that GATT was a 'one-time rich-man's club'.

Wyndham White also addressed the question of preferences, a matter that required him to 'take my courage in both hands'. He pointed out that

---

[113] Report by the Secretary-General of the Conference, 'Towards a New Trade Policy for Development', Proceedings UNCTAD I, Vol. II, 5–23.

preferences were currently under discussion in GATT, although nothing had been decided because of the complexity of the issue as well as factions among developed and developing members. To proceed with preferences would engender ill will and divisiveness, the negative consequences of which 'far outweigh the particular advantages which might be derived by the favoured few'. Preferences could also raise the cost of living by making imports more expensive. Developing countries could not afford 'the luxury of discriminating between sources of supply'. He admitted that GATT was acting with 'more prudence than heroism', but the issue remained under consideration rather than shelved.[114] By refusing to allow UNCTAD to be the only credible spokesperson for developing countries, Wyndham White upheld the inclusive and universal ideal of GATT.

The USA also defended GATT at UNCTAD. In part, this reflected US disdain for UNCTAD, which some officials believed was implicated in a Soviet propaganda ploy. As George Ball explained to President Kennedy, UNCTAD had the potential to become a Cold War battleground:

This Conference was originally inspired by the Communist Bloc as a device to demoralize trading relations among the industrialized Western countries and gain a propaganda advantage with the less-developed countries.[115]

But Ball was dubious about UNCTAD not only because of its susceptibility to Cold War manipulation, but also because he believed that the conference was generating unrealistic expectations. He feared that developing countries were being hoodwinked in 'a high-class confidence game conducted in elegant economic jargon'.[116] In his address to the conference, Ball disagreed that the problem of development should be understood in terms of a trade gap. Trade should be considered part of a multifaceted approach to the challenge of development and should be used alongside other economic measures, including promoting full employment, stabilizing prices, removing tariffs and non-tariff barriers, increasing investment and access to foreign capital, improved marketing and competitiveness,

---

[114] Statement by Mr. Eric Wyndham White, Executive Secretary, General Agreement on Tariffs and Trade at the twenty-fourth plenary meeting, held on 8 April 1964, Proceedings of UNCTAD, 23 March – 16 June 1964, Vol. II, 432–439. Dosman writes that his speech was well received from its 'principal presumed opponent'. Dosman, *Life and Times of Raúl Prebisch*, 400.

[115] Memorandum for the President, United Nations Trade and Development Conference, 30 March 1964, RG59: Records of Under Secretary of State George W. Ball 1961–66, Box 31, file UN Trade Conference – Spring 1964, NARA.

[116] Memorandum: UNCTAD, from Ball to McGeorge Bundy, 3 March 1964, RG59: Records of the Under Secretary of State George W. Ball 1961–66, Box 31, file UN Trade Conference – Spring 1964, NARA.

and increased foreign aid.[117] Ball reported to the president that his speech –
'an honest statement of the realities' – had been surprisingly well received.
In contrast to his own honesty, he suggested that others at UNCTAD were
intent on selling false hope to developing countries. According to Ball, no
one was more guilty of this than Prebisch himself.[118] British officials were
also sceptical of Prebisch's interpretation. But they noted that it was
difficult to challenge his ideas because they now 'formed a body of doctrine
accepted by the developing countries as revealed truth which could not be
questioned without an immediate emotional reaction'.[119]

After UNCTAD: Disappointment and Marginalization

Strained personal relations between Wyndham White and Prebisch exacerbated the GATT–UNCTAD rivalry. Prebisch's biographer, Edgar
Dosman, places much of the blame on Wyndham White, who he claims
'personified GATT's narrowness and Atlantic focus'. He repeats
Prebisch's belief that Wyndham White was a recent convert to development and a 'cynical opportunist', who tried to 'destroy UNCTAD's
credibility and bargaining power without a new approach to development' in order to protect his own turf.[120] But many contemporaries
blamed Prebisch more than Wyndham White. Sir Edgar Cohen of the
British Board of Trade described Prebisch as 'ambitious and
disagreeable'.[121] Others likened him to an empire builder. Prebisch himself insisted that UNCTAD must be the 'central organ on all matters of
trade in relation to development. This fact should be fully recognized
within the United Nations family so that GATT may not present itself as
an equal or more competent partner in this field.'[122] To do so, he had to
nudge GATT aside, along with many other international organizations
that worked on development.[123]

---

[117] Address by the Honorable George W. Ball, Under Secretary of State, Before the United
Nations Conference on Trade and Development, Geneva, 25 March 1964, in Records
of Under Secretary George W. Ball 1961–66, Box 4, file Address before UNCTAD,
Geneva, 3/25/64, NARA.

[118] Memorandum for the President, United Nations Trade and Development Conference,
30 March 1964, RG59: Records of Under Secretary of State George W. Ball 1961–66,
Box 31, UN Trade Conference – Spring 1964, NARA.

[119] G.P. (64) 59, GATT Policy Committee, Memorandum by Sir Patrick Reilly: United
Nations Conference on Trade & Development: A Preliminary Report, 30 June 1964,
CAB134/1966, TNA.

[120] Dosman, *Life and Times of Raúl Prebisch*, 380, 417, 421–423.

[121] Cohen, UK Delegation to GATT, to S. Golt, Board of Trade, 23 December 1964,
BT241/1169, TNA.

[122] Dosman, *Life and Times of Raúl Prebisch*, 422–423.

[123] US Strategy for UNCTAD II, A Discussion Paper, 12 October 1966, Records re
Kennedy Round, Box 10, file FT-3, Foreign Trade UN UNCTAD 1966, NARA.

The competition between UNCTAD and GATT resurfaced when UNCTAD contemplated the establishment of a trade office to perform similar functions to GATT's International Trade Centre. The trade centre was one of the only bright spots in GATT as far as developing members were concerned. As a Canadian official reported, most developing countries gave the trade centre 'their warmest support ... as offering an immediate, unique and concrete opportunity to help solve some of their difficulties in the export field'. It was also important for GATT to maintain its presence in this area as UNCTAD had more resources and could displace them.[124] Rather than compete with UNCTAD, Wyndham White proposed a partnership.[125] They established a joint trade centre which added a few elements to the GATT version; it had a shared budget and the director of the centre would be appointed by the director-general of GATT and the secretary general of UNCTAD.[126] Although Wyndham White was satisfied that GATT had not been weakened by working more closely with UNCTAD,[127] others concluded that a shared centre revealed UNCTAD's limited capabilities.[128] Subsequently, Prebisch spoke more favourably about GATT and declared that 'partnership not rivalry' defined their relationship.[129]

The most important measure of GATT's relevance to developing countries was whether their exports rose. Export levels had increased since 1950, but a comparison with western Europe made clear that they did not benefit to the same extent (see Figure 5.3). Immediately after the Second World War, the six members of what would become the EEC were still recovering from the war and exported roughly half of what the almost 100 developing countries exported. Over the next twenty years, the value of developing country exports almost tripled,

C. Robertson, 'The Creation of UNCTAD' in R. Cox (ed.), *International Organisation, World Politics, Studies in Economic and Social Agencies: Papers* (London and Toronto: Macmillan, 1969), 274.

[124] At the time, UNCTAD's staff outnumbered the GATT staff, 1,800 to 300. Eckes, *Revisiting U.S. Trade Policy*, 29.

[125] Geneva to External, 10 February 1966, External to Geneva, 28 February 1966, and TarifDelGva to External, 4 March 1966, all in RG20: A-3/1927/20–28-9 pt. 1, LAC.

[126] Joint GATT/UNCTAD Trade Centre, Note by the Director-General, 6 November 1967, L/2890, GDL.

[127] Geneva to External, 19 July 1967, GATT-UNCTAD Relations: Trade Promotion Centre, RG20: A-3/1927/20–28-9 pt. 1, LAC.

[128] As P. H. R. Marshall wrote about the joint centre: 'it is a sign of weakness on the part of UNCTAD in the sense that they are going for portfolio investment in another firm rather than direct investment in their own subsidiary'. Marshall, UK Mission Geneva, to Golt, Board of Trade, 5 July 1967, BT241/1171, TNA.

[129] Geneva, UK Mission, to Foreign Office, tel 43 saving, 9 April 1966, BT241/1170. TNA.

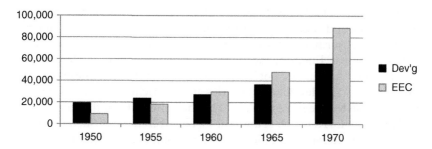

Figure 5.3 Value of exports (millions of US dollars), 1950–1970: developing countries (Dev'g) and EEC countries (France, West Germany, Italy, Belgium, Netherlands, Luxembourg)
Source: *UN Yearbook of International Trade Statistics, Vol. I: Trade by Country*, 1981, pp. 1081, 1083.

whereas that of the six western European states increased almost ten times.

At the UNCTAD meeting in 1964, Wyndham White asked developing countries to put their faith in the Kennedy round. One of the priorities of the Kennedy round was to promote the expansion of exports from developing countries. The form of negotiations was modified to make this possible: concessions could be asymmetrical so that developing countries would receive greater concessions than they themselves made; members were encouraged to reduce tariffs by more than the 50 per cent threshold identified as the general goal; tropical products were supposed to be given special attention.[130]

But the results of the Kennedy round were 'disappointing'.[131] The 50 per cent threshold was surpassed for only a few commodities. The average decrease in tariffs on developing country goods was 29 per cent, lower than the average reduction of 35 per cent. Key sectors had not seen many reductions at all, including tropical products and agricultural commodities. US officials insisted that the Kennedy round brought real benefits and opportunities to developing country trade, but they did not dispute UNCTAD's conclusions, that 'the LDC's got less from the Kennedy Round than did the DC's' and that as a result developing

[130] Meeting of the Committee at Ministerial Level: Resolution Adopted on 6 May 1964, TN.64/27, GDL.
[131] Report of the Ad Hoc Group on Assessment of Kennedy Round Results, 2 November 1967 COM.TD/49, WTO. For a detailed analysis, see Summary of the Results of the Kennedy Round for Developing Countries, 19 October 1967, COM.TD/48, GDL.

countries were 'at a relatively greater disadvantage in world trade after the Kennedy Round than they were before'.[132] Eight developing countries opted out of tariff negotiations and eight more did not sign the final agreement. José Encinas, the representative from Peru, explained that developing countries 'are not in a position to share, to the same extent, the satisfaction of the developed countries at the conclusion and the achievements of the Kennedy Round'.[133] That had always been the case.

Parallel to the Kennedy round, the GATT secretariat pushed members to decide if preferences should be used to promote development. But US officials refused to participate in discussions about preferences.[134] They doubted their effectiveness and continued to believe that the best way to encourage the growth of developing country exports was to remove, in a non-discriminatory way, the barriers that stood in their way. In private discussions, an official explained that the extension of preferences would result in 'a fragmented economic and political structure'.[135] But the US position was not convincing because it had been inconsistent: supporting, or at least tolerating, the establishment of preferences within LAFTA and EFTA, between Italy and Libya, and between Australia and Papua and New Guinea.[136] The UK, in contrast, strongly supported the use of preferences on 'economic, political and humanitarian grounds'. Their thinking was also pragmatic and took long-term results into account. Increasing the exports of developing countries would strengthen their overall economies, raise standards of living, and stabilize existing political conditions, all of which would allow them to become 'useful markets for United Kingdom exports'.[137] They also worried that without progress on preferences, developing countries might push for a reformed international trade system that would displace GATT. And GATT, with its rules of trade, was essential to Britain as a trading nation. But at this

---

[132] Contingency Paper, Kennedy Round Results, 16 January 1968, Records re Kennedy Round, Box 10, file FT3 (UNCTAD II 1968), NARA.

[133] UK Mission Geneva to Foreign Office, tel. 613, 4 July 1967, BT241/1171, TNA. Kim's study confirms that there was a problem with the distribution of benefits from membership in GATT. Developing countries did not benefit to the same extent as a small group of industrial countries. S. Y. Kim, *Power and the Governance of Global Trade: From the GATT to the WTO* (Ithaca, NY: Cornell University Press, 2010), chapter 3.

[134] Geneva, UK Delegation to GATT, to Foreign Office, tel. 193 saving, 24 October 1964, BT241/870, TNA.

[135] Memo of conversation, UK and US, 8 November 1965, RG364: Box 109, file Developing Countries (1963–67), NARA.

[136] U.S. Tactics on Preference Issue, 26 February 1964, memo for under-secretary from E-G Griffith Johnson, RG59: Office of the Assistant Legal Advisor for Economic Affairs, Records re Trade and GATT 1947–1966, Box 10, file: Less Developed Countries, NARA.

[137] Cabinet Economic Policy Committee; Meeting on 3 October at 3 pm [1963], FO371/172320, TNA.

point, US opposition was decisive. The GATT working party on preferences was shelved, apparently without much regret at its failure.[138]

Australia revived the question of preferences when it requested a waiver to apply preferences to approximately sixty categories of semi-manufactured and manufactured goods from developing countries including chewing gum, machine tools, musical instruments, handmade carpets, stationery, washing machines, cricket bats, jute, and hemp woven fabrics. The list of developing countries to receive the preferences was open-ended.[139] The total volume of trade was minimal. The principle – extending preferences to developing countries – was significant.

The USA came out strongly against the waiver. The increase in developing country exports would be 'negligible' because the list included relatively few commodities, the products did not have great export potential and would not encourage investment in these industries, and developing country imports would be likely to displace other developing country suppliers. Any benefits were 'more than outweighed by the disadvantages of the scheme'. Japan, Denmark, Norway, the EEC, Britain, and Sweden agreed that the Australian proposal was inadequate, but most were going to vote for the waiver anyway. Many developing country representatives noted that Australia's proposal did not come close to the global and inclusive ideal, but nonetheless supported it as 'an important first step'. Wyndham White was displeased with this Australian initiative. He favoured the application of preferences for developing countries on an ad hoc basis rather than as a general principle. That would stave off a proliferation of preferential arrangements, which could collectively weaken the MFN principle.[140] US officials tried to persuade Britain to abstain in the vote on Australia's waiver in the hope that other European countries would follow Britain's lead.[141] This did not happen. GATT's inability to decide on preferences at the level of principle meant that an act generally regarded as inadequate now found far-reaching support. The Australian waiver was granted in 1966 by a vote of fifty-one to one.[142]

---

[138] Geneva (UK Del to GATT) to FO, tel 248 saving, 28 November 1964, BT241/870, TNA.

[139] Report of the Working Party on the Australian Request to Grant Tariff Preferences to Less-Developed Countries, 23 December 1965, L/2527, GDL.

[140] Letter from the Special Representative for Trade Negotiations Executive Assistant (Auchincloss) to the Special Representative for Trade Negotiations, 4 May 1965, *FRUS Vol. VIII*, 1964–68, #283.

[141] Albert J. Powers to Ambassador William Roth, Memo: Voting Position of Developed Countries on Australian Preference Waiver, 21 February 1966, RG364: Box 109, file Australia, NARA.

[142] Summary record of the Second Meeting, 28 March 1966, SR. 23/2, GDL.

GATT's dithering allowed others to pre-empt it. In 1968, the OECD and UNCTAD devised a generalized system of preferences (GSP) that was non-discriminatory and non-reciprocal and gave developing country exports preference in developed markets. Although the USA endorsed the GSP because it was a single and coherent system which would stop the piecemeal derogation of the MFN principle, US officials remained convinced that preferences would be of 'relatively minor economic benefit to the LDC's' and would also be a major administrative headache.[143] The new director-general of GATT, Olivier Long, believed that GATT had to catch up.[144] In 1971, GATT members unanimously declared their intention to set aside the MFN provision for ten years to allow developing country exports to enjoy preferences in developed markets.[145]

Frustration at their chronic marginalization in GATT was behind protests from developing countries about the selection of a new director-general after Eric Wyndham White announced his retirement in 1967. Ghana's representative wanted information about how a new director-general would be selected. He pressed for formal discussion, backed by Nigeria, Australia, Norway, and Belgium. Wyndham White's response was a 'blistering attack' against what he saw as unfair insinuations about the arbitrary authority of the director-general. But Ghana's representative did not back down, frustrated by 'the clublike atmosphere of GATT', which obstructed their ability to have influence within the organization. Canadian officials believed Ghana's frustration was indicative of a larger malaise among African members of GATT. This was not an isolated instance; officials from Ghana and Nigeria had criticized Wyndham White on other occasions.[146]

The government of Ghana did not let this matter drop. The Ghanaian representative put the question of the selection of a new director-general on the agenda of the GATT Council. K. B. Lall, chair of the contracting parties, set up an advisory group to consider this question. Its members included the most senior national representatives serving in GATT roles: the chair of the GATT Council, three vice-chairs of the contracting parties, and the chair of the committee on trade and development. He

---

[143] Memo from Mary Jane Wignot to William K. Pearce, Summary Generalized Tariff Preferences Issues, CIEP Review Group, 5 January 1972, RG364: Box 63, file XVII, preferences, NARA.

[144] Record of Conversation between W. Hughes and Olivier Long, 22 January 1970, BT241/2256; Record of Discussion on Generalised Preferences for Developing Countries at Informal Meeting, 26 February 1970, BT241/2256, TNA.

[145] Generalised System of Preferences, 28 June 1971, L/3545, GDL. The vote was forty-eight in favour, none against.

[146] Geneva to External, 30 June 1967 re GATT Council Meeting, June 26 – DirGen and Deputy DirGen, RG19: F-2/4678/8718–04 pt. 3, LAC.

invited all GATT members to submit their suggestions. Minutes from the meeting are frustratingly spare; they record a commitment to discuss this subject at the next council meeting, a discussion that did not take place.[147] According to Canadian reports, there was resentment towards Lall and towards India's presumption of leadership on behalf of developing countries. A new constellation of least developed countries was taking shape, and it targeted not only the institution and developed members but also other developing country pretenders such as India.[148] At the December meeting of contracting parties, Olivier Long was 'approved by unanimous acclamation' as the next director-general. The hope of African members to have one of their representatives in a chair's position was successful: H. E. Mr. Sule Kolo of Nigeria was elected chair of the committee on trade and development.[149]

Why was GATT unable to better serve the commercial interests of developing countries and use trade as a way to promote economic development? Although US records describe developing countries as a 'real factor in world politics' by the mid-1960s, they were not a real force.[150] Because of their numerical majority in international organizations, 'the noise they can create globally is considerable'. But as Mohammed Ayoob explains, noise did not bring about change: 'their actual power to influence events ... is certainly dramatically inferior to their level of visibility and audibility inside and outside international forums'.[151] According to Prebisch and Wyndham White, GATT was the creature of its members. Wyndham White noted that 'international institutions are as effective as the Governments which constitute them' and Prebisch insisted that GATT could only be 'what Governments wanted it to be'.[152] But it was more responsive to some members than others. And among those to whom it was most responsive – especially the USA and the EEC – there was weak political will to support development. There were also structural disadvantages that prevented developing countries from reframing the role of trade within GATT. They could not parlay their numbers or potential into influence and results. Despite the one-member-one-vote system, GATT typically avoided votes in favour of compromise and

---

[147] C/M/41, Minutes of Meeting, Council, 14 July 1967. Note: C/M/42 does not include the selection of the next director general on its agenda.
[148] Geneva to External, 30 June 1967 re GATT Council Meeting Jun26 – DirGen and Deputy DirGen, RG19: F-2/4678/8718–04 pt. 3, LAC.
[149] Summary record of the 19th meeting, 24 November 1967, SR.24/19, GDL.
[150] Report of the President's Task Force on Foreign Economic Policy, 25 November 1964, *FRUS Vol. VIII* 1964–68, #18.
[151] M. Ayoob, 'The Third World in the System of States: Acute Schizophrenia or Growing Pains?' *International Studies Quarterly* 33 (1) (March 1989), 76.
[152] UNCTAD I Proceedings, 23, 437.

consensus. This meant that developing countries could not vote in a new agenda or measures. Nor did developing countries act in unison. Furthermore, as Ayoob observes, when newly independent countries joined existing international institutions, they played the game of world politics by pre-existing rules in order to change those rules. But their participation paradoxically upheld norms, practices, and rules that had not been designed with their aims in mind.[153] As UNCTAD put it, the current "'rules of the game" ... operate in favour of developed countries'.[154] The time had come for new rules, changed power dynamics, and revolutionary tactics.

The New International Economic Order and the Tokyo Round, 1973–1979

Making trade work for development required more than a few policy initiatives. In 1974, the Group of 77 (G77) presented eight demands to the UN General Assembly, including greater control over resources, commodity agreements, diversified exports, more stable prices, and differential treatment with respect to their main exports, which would create a New International Economic Order (NIEO). If the immediate objective was to narrow the gap between rich and poor countries, the underlying political aim was to restructure the global order to bring about equality among all states. That meant ending the dominance of the strongest and most industrialized countries.[155] According to Nils Gilman, the NIEO came at a time when it was possible to imagine a different global order that erased the structures and dynamics of an earlier imperial era.[156] It also emerged when the bargaining position of developing countries had increased following the oil shocks and stagflation of the 1970s.[157] According to some US officials, the success of the NIEO would spell the end of GATT.[158]

The demands of the G77 were neither new nor surprising to GATT members. As Robert Hudec points out, almost every proposal that

---

[153] Ayoob, 'The Third World in the System of States', 67–79.
[154] UNCTAD, 'The Elements of the New International Economic Order' in K. P. Sauvant and H. Hasenpflug (eds.), *The New International Economic Order: Confrontation or Cooperation between North and South?* (Boulder, CO: Westview Press, 1977), 57.
[155] N. Gilman, 'The New International Economic Order: A Reintroduction', *Humanity: An International Journal of Human Rights, Humanitarianism, and Development* 6 (1) (Spring 2015), 6.
[156] Ibid., 1.
[157] R. Jolly, L. Emmerij, D. Ghai, and F. Lapeyre, *UN Contributions to Development Thinking and Practice* (Bloomington: Indiana University Press, 2004), 121.
[158] Eckes, *Revisiting U.S. Trade Policy*, 29–30.

stemmed from the NIEO had been made in Havana in 1947–1948[159] and had continued to be discussed ever since, albeit with little effect. The understanding of structural inequality that informed the NIEO altered the way many GATT members understood the causes of economic inequality and the responsibility of developed countries to remedy this condition. Ministerial declarations at the start of the Tokyo round in 1973 acknowledged that the world trading system had not only privileged economically and politically strong nations, but also hindered the economic growth of developing countries so that there was a glaring and widening gap between rich and poor. This was a fundamentally different admission from previous rounds, which had conceded only that the GATT process did not benefit all equally.

The goals of developing countries in the Tokyo round may be grouped into two categories. First, they wanted to overturn structures that they believed oppressed or disadvantaged them. They called for reform (Mexico), restructuring (Jamaica), reassessing (Sri Lanka), and reordering (Indonesia) of the global trade system.[160] What this meant in practice was non-reciprocity in negotiations and making preferences more extensive and permanent. Differentiation and preferential treatment were needed, not as 'acts of charity' on the part of developed countries, but as the way to reverse 'the inequities of the past'.[161] The second goal was procedural: to more actively and directly participate in negotiations. In previous rounds, developing countries had opted out or, because they were not the principal suppliers of a commodity in question, had not taken part in negotiations. Rather, they benefited as reductions to barriers to trade negotiated by other GATT members were generalized through the MFN process. But Peru's representative explained that they would no longer be satisfied with receiving the 'marginal and residual advantages which the negotiations might provide'.[162] New Zealand's representative, who openly associated with developing countries in terms of their disadvantages in negotiations, put it more starkly: 'we do not wish to participate only as spectators at a gladiatorial context'.[163] At a time of

---

[159] Hudec, *Developing Countries in the GATT Legal System*, 30.
[160] Ministerial Meeting, Statements Delivered at the First Meeting, 12 September 1973, Min (73) SR/Add. 1) Ministerial Meeting, Statements Delivered at the Second Meeting, 12 September 1973, Min (73) SR/Add. 2) Ministerial Meeting, Statements Delivered at the Third Meeting, 13 September 1973, Min (73) SR/Add. 3) GDL.
[161] Ministerial Meeting, Statements Delivered at the Third Meeting, 13 September 1973, Min (73) SR/ Add. 3, GDL.
[162] Ministerial Meeting, Statements Delivered at the Third Meeting, 13 September 1973, Min (73) SR/ Add. 3.
[163] Ministerial Meeting, Statements Delivered at the Second Meeting, 12 September 1973, Min (73) SR/ Add. 2.

heightened protectionist sentiment, direct participation in negotiations was especially important to improve access for commodities where they had a comparative advantage, such as textiles and shoes, and to prevent any backsliding.[164]

While developing countries pushed for radical reform elsewhere, within GATT they concentrated on how to achieve more complete participation in negotiations. Developing countries were aiming to benefit from exports in ways that reinforced traditional GATT activities, especially reducing barriers to trade. This made clear the importance of trade as a catalyst to development. The prosperity of developing countries, according to Peru's minister, was 'to a great extent the result of the dynamic expansion of foreign trade'.[165] Officials also discussed how the structures, rules, and norms of trade created an interdependence that stifled opportunities to expand or transform their economies.

The ministerial declaration prior to the Tokyo round outlined expectations and priorities. There would be no expectation of reciprocity in negotiations involving developing countries. They would strive to improve the GSP. Tropical products were 'a special and priority sector' because many of the exports of developing countries fell into this category. Representatives of developing countries complained that the declaration did not go far enough, but they still had 'faith' that the Tokyo round would bring real change that benefited developing countries. It would be a 'tragic historical error' if the exports of developing countries were not positively affected: GATT 'cannot be an island of selfishness or indifference vis-à-vis the great historical cause of development'. As Peru's representative saw it, the Tokyo round was possibly the last chance 'to inspire within the GATT the conscience of development'.[166]

One after another, representatives of developed countries affirmed the importance of development for the round. Trade as it stood was unequal and unjust. They were willing to employ different tactics to ensure that the Tokyo round served the cause of development and the interests of developing members. They suggested that they had the political will to act unilaterally, guided by principles of justice and equity rather than commercial advantage. But concessions on the basis of historical and

---

[164] Report of the Committee on Trade and Development to the Contracting Parties, 20 November 1975, L/4252; Committee on Trade and Development: Proceedings of the 29th Session, 21 July 1975, COM.TD/97, GDL.

[165] Ministerial Meeting, Statements Delivered at the Third Meeting, 13 September 1973, Min (73) SR/Add.3.

[166] The range of concerns, priorities, and expectations of developing countries were included in their opening speeches from 12–14 September 1973. See Min (73) SR/Add.1-5, GDL.

structural causes of inequality were offset by a persistent belief that the liberalization of trade would bring about peace and prosperity. Japan's Prime Minister Kakuei Tanaka, as host of the round, upheld GATT's traditional aims: to strengthen the 'framework of international trade which can sustain peace and prosperity for all the peoples of the world . . . through the expansion of world trade in a free and open world economy'.[167]

Even though development was a prominent global issue, it was not the priority of the Tokyo round. On the heels of the collapse of Bretton Woods and the increased appeal of protectionism, many feared that the international economic order would collapse. The main challenge for countries such as the USA and Canada was to shore up GATT, not remake it. As Gilbert Winham explains, the point was to make the rules work better and to find ways to protect national economies without sparking retaliation that might cause 'the whole fabric of the trading system so patiently constructed after World War II' to unravel.[168] The aim was preservation and consolidation, not reconstruction.

Like the rounds before it, this one revolved around negotiations among its strongest developed members, especially the USA and the EEC. Developing countries did not participate more directly in actual negotiations. Negotiations still took place between dominant pairs of countries and the effects were then generalized through the application of the MFN principle. Developing countries benefited, but as Winham points out, they were not 'essential to the process and the accords did not directly address their perceived needs'.[169] The total value of tariff reductions affecting developing country exports was valued at US$1.7 billion. The commitment of participants to development-related priorities, such as liberalizing trade on tropical products, was evident. Of the 4,400 requests made for reductions, 3,000 were acted upon.[170]

Despite tariff reductions that would benefit their exports, the second-class status of developing countries in GATT persisted, evident in negotiations on safeguards. The General Agreement of 1947 had built in several provisions to protect domestic economies from the unpredictability and volatility of international trade. With these exceptions, members could introduce freer trade policies knowing that they had recourse to safeguards to offset any dislocating consequences.[171] Safeguards made

---

[167] Summary Record of the Meeting, 28 September 1973, Annex: Opening Address by the Prime Minister Kakuei Tanaka, Summary Record of the Meeting, Min (73) SR. GDL.
[168] G. R. Winham, *International Trade and the Tokyo Round Negotiation* (Princeton: Princeton University Press, 1986), 7.
[169] Ibid., 376.   [170] Ibid., 275–276.
[171] The role of safeguards in the original ITO was explained optimistically, and somewhat naively, in Twenty-Five Questions and Answers in the Proposed International Trade

the incremental and long-term liberalization of global trade possible. As Long explained, 'prospects for a more liberal trading system would be increased if there was a good safeguard system'.[172]

The main safeguard was Article XIX: Emergency Action on Imports of Particular Products.[173] Article XIX was supposed to be applied in a non-discriminatory way, meaning that if a particular industry was threatened, the relevant imports from all countries would be restricted. But some GATT members claimed they could sometimes trace a problem to a particular country – often one in which wages were low – and they wanted to limit the application of safeguards to the offending country. The EEC was the strongest supporter of the selective application of safeguard measures. It produced a revised draft of Article XIX that would permit members to apply safeguards against the specific country or countries that were seen to be causing a market disturbance.

Developing countries feared, for good reason, that they would be at the receiving end of the targeted use of Article XIX, and they wanted safeguards to be applied in a non-discriminatory fashion. What was at stake in this debate over the selective versus non-discriminatory application of safeguards was anticipated domestic dislocation (often leading to industry closure and unemployment) that would result from developing countries being more fully integrated into the global trade system.[174] By insisting on selective application, the EEC privileged stability within the trade system over the creative destruction that would follow if developing countries were allowed to compete fully and fairly in global trade.

The debate on safeguards was not resolved by the end of the round: discussions continued afterwards. By 1979, some developing countries were prepared to compromise as long as there were stringent measures to monitor the use of Article XIX. They paired selectivity with surveillance. They also called for prior consultation, rather than unilateral action and subsequent GATT approval, before an Article XIX measure was put into effect. They suggested a phased approach, bringing in general safeguards first and introducing targeted safeguards only if the general application

Organization, Office of Public Affairs, Department of State, December 1948, Caroline Ware/Box 25/Consumer Materials International Trade Negotiations, FDRL.

[172] *Tokyo Round of Multilateral Trade Negotiations, Report by the Director General.*

[173] The article reads: 'If an operative concession leads unexpectedly to serious injury to a domestic industry, the affected contracting party may invoke this "escape clause" to temporarily withdraw the concession. In the absence of an agreement providing otherwise, the country to which the concession was originally granted is then entitled to withdraw equivalent concession.'

[174] Winham, *International Trade and the Tokyo Round Negotiation*, 246.

was not effective.[175] If it got to the point of implementing selective action, they wanted clear and strict definition of the conditions to allow such actions. The EEC objected: no country or organization could tell them whether, for how long, and in what way they could introduce safeguards to protect their industries. They agreed to notify GATT, but not to give GATT the right to approve such action.[176]

In the end, the safeguard negotiations were not concluded. There was much finger-pointing. Yugoslavia's representative insisted on behalf of developing countries that they had been willing to accept the selective application of Article XIX even though this was 'a serious departure from the rules of GATT'. But their consent had been contingent upon 'clearly defined criteria and conditions ... including a test by an international body'. The EEC refused to be held responsible. They maintained that they had been committed to resolving this issue and had taken an open-minded approach, and that developing countries had not been as flexible as they suggested.[177] The unresolved debate over safeguards was a major failing of the Tokyo round. The GATT secretariat vowed that it would continue to seek a solution to what was 'a matter of urgency'.[178]

Domestic stability was also the principle behind the Multifibre Arrangement (MFA), which came up for renewal during the round. Although the stated purpose of the agreement was to liberalize trade in textiles, which would in theory benefit developing countries, in practice the agreement was used to block their exports so as to prevent market disruptions. Douglas Irwin likens the MFA to 'the biggest piece of protectionist cholesterol, blocking the arteries of world trade'.[179]

The EEC insisted that it must protect its textile sector from competition. Europe had seen significant growth in textile and clothing imports (41 per cent between 1974 and 1975, compared to 3 per cent for the USA),[180] even though demand had slowed. The responsibility to improve market access for textiles from developing countries had been met, but from the EEC's point of view, that growth 'had entailed serious

---

[175] 'GATT Trade Talks: End in Sight', *The Economist* (7 April 1979), 84; 'Trade Talks', *The Economist* (2 December 1978); 'GATT Trade Deal: Yes, But', *The Economist* (28 July 1979), 100.

[176] 'GATT Trade Deal: Yes, But', 100.

[177] Council of Representatives, Report of Work of the 34th session, Addendum, L/4884/Add.1, 26 November 1979, GDL.

[178] *Tokyo Round of Multilateral Trade Negotiations, Report by the Director General.*

[179] D. A. Irwin, *Free Trade Under Fire*, 2nd edition (Princeton: Princeton University Press, 2005), 65.

[180] Heron, *Global Political Economy*, 29. Heron explains that unlike the USA, the EEC had not negotiated bilateral agreements to restrict imports following MFA I.

disruption in markets'.[181] Textile factories across Europe were closing, and over half a million European textile labourers were out of work. According to *The Economist*, the textile industries of the developed world were being 'squeezed in a tightening vice' by developing exporters who were aggressively 'grabb[ing] growing shares of developed markets'.[182] The EEC was willing to renew the MFA as long as the increase in imports went along with stabilization measures to limit 'serious disruption of its market'. The EEC also wanted to freeze textile and clothing imports from Taiwan, Hong Kong, and South Korea, the dominant suppliers, in favour of a redistribution of market share towards smaller developing suppliers.[183] Finally, the EEC indicated that unless its proposal prevailed, they would 'move fast to full-scale protectionism'.[184] Sweden and Canada supported the EEC's claim that textile imports had damaging domestic consequences. The United States did not approve of the EEC's position but could not do much about it.

No one was under the illusion that domestic stability meant anything other than restricting the textile exports of developing countries. A Thai official claimed that what importing nations were really trying to do was 'alter the pattern of international trade in textiles so as to suit their needs and serve their interests'. But there did not seem to be a choice between an MFA and no MFA; as the UK official put it, the absence of the MFA would 'lead to a chaotic situation in world textile trade and to the resurgence of the worst form of protectionism to the detriment of the interests of the weaker exporting countries'.

Developing countries were able to block revisions that would have made the MFA even more restrictive, but the unrevised MFA was renewed for four years. Reactions varied. The EEC asserted that there was a 'secure international legal basis' for the development of this trade. The more relieved US view was that 'the chaos which would, in its absence, reign in the textile trade' had been averted. Developing countries saw it as 'the best of a bad bargain'.[185] The renewal of the MFA without revision made it clear that developed countries would not passively accept the consequences of the growing export competitiveness of developing countries. They protected their own economies – a practice

---

[181] Report of the Meeting of the Committee held on 16–17 March; on 5–7 and on 24 July and 22 December 1977, Com.Tex/W/50, 1 February 1978, GDL.

[182] 'Textiles and Clothing Through the Wringer', *The Economist* (31 December 1977), 87.

[183] Report of the Meeting of the Committee held on 16–17 March; on 5–7 and on 24 July and 3 December 1977, Com.Tex/W/50, 1 February 1978, GDL.

[184] 'Textiles Behind the Maginot Line', *The Economist* (30 July 1977), 75.

[185] Report of the Meeting of the Committee held on 16–17 March; on 5–7 and on 24 July and 22 December 1977, Com.Tex/W/50, 1 February 1978, GDL.

consistent with the implicit understandings of how GATT would work –
but in ways that prevented economic advances in developing countries.

In an effort to end the Tokyo round, which dragged on years longer
than expected, representatives from the major countries in GATT including Austria, Canada, the EEC, Japan, New Zealand, and the USA,
drafted a framework of understanding that included all the elements
necessary for 'a successful conclusion of the negotiations', including
commodity agreements, curbing the use of subsidies, and consultation
and cooperation in order to stop the endless 'political and commercial
confrontations in this highly sensitive sector'. They believed that what
they had achieved would strengthen the trade system and make it more
open than ever. They reverted to the universalist assumption of the early
GATT that within such a system, all would benefit, including developing
countries.[186] But nothing made clearer that developing countries were
not essential to GATT than their exclusion from the framework agreement negotiations. In a collective statement, they listed the missing elements of a successful round: tropical products, safeguards, subsidies for
industrial development, and quantitative restrictions. More generally,
they were uncertain about what actual benefits they would receive.[187]
But they did not denounce GATT or liberalization. On the contrary, they
expressed support for the goal of liberalization and endorsed GATT. For
instance, India's representative affirmed that his government attached
'the greatest importance to maintenance of the integrity and consistency
of the GATT system'.[188] Some even referred to it as the 'new GATT',
which was perhaps more hopeful than accurate.[189]

Developing countries spoke up about their dissatisfaction with the
Tokyo round at the fifth general assembly of UNCTAD in 1979.
There, the G77 explained that the negotiations fell short. First, in some
key areas, such as tropical products, developed countries had made no
reductions. Second, their participation in actual negotiations remained
passive. Structures and principles had not really changed. The commitment to non-reciprocity had not been upheld. The safeguard clause was
left hanging. At the end of the round, the principle of 'differential and
more favourable treatment' as the 'guiding principle on trade relations
between developed and developing countries had not been achieved'.

[186] Statement by Several Delegations of Current Status of Tokyo Round Negotiations,
13 July 1978, MTN/INF/33, 14 July 1978, GDL.
[187] Statement by Delegations of Developing Countries on Current Status of Tokyo Round
Negotiations, 14 July 1978, MTN/INF/38, 17 July 1978, GDL.
[188] For example, see India, Summary Record of the Third Meeting, 28 November 1979,
SR.35/3, 14 December 1979, GDL.
[189] For example, see Brazil, Summary Record of the Third Meeting, 28 November 1979,
SR.35/3, GDL.

Developed countries responded that the Tokyo round made the global economy stronger and more rules-based, and was thereby fighting back protectionist forces – which damaged all countries – and preserving conditions from which all would benefit. They insisted that GATT 'would continue to be an important positive factor for the world economy in the future.'[190]

Despite the dissatisfaction of developing countries, there were no alternatives to GATT. During the Tokyo round, UNCTAD had been involved in its own negotiations over commodities in what was a more direct political confrontation between north and south than what was taking place in GATT. Nothing came of UNCTAD's efforts. Even though the results of the Tokyo round were disappointing, quitting GATT did not seem to be an option.

Protectionism, Development, and the Uruguay Round, 1986–1994

Curbing protectionism had been the main goal for the developed members of GATT. Many praised the results of the Tokyo round for strengthening a rules-based trade system, but there was little confidence that GATT had slain protectionism. As *The Economist* observed, the range of weapons in the 'protectionist armoury' was impressive, including voluntary restraint agreements, orderly marketing agreements, health and sanitation standards, subsidies, bureaucratic delays, and international agreements such as the MFA.[191] They affected a wide range of commodities including cars, steel, shoes, alcohol, and textiles. All GATT members used some protectionist measures. And increasingly, people clamoured for protection: US car workers protested against Japanese imports; people in Hong Kong wanted to retaliate against French bans on watches with a boycott on brandy; US farmers lamented EEC restrictions on soya beans.[192] Protectionist practices also sparked trade disputes, which some people feared would provoke a trade war.[193] Jimmy Carter and Gerald Ford, both former US presidents, made a public

---

[190] Proceedings of the United Nations Conference on Trade and Development, Fifth Session, 7 May – 3 June 1979 (New York: UN 1981), 61–63, accessed 8 July 2016.

[191] '50 Years On the Undertakers are Back', *The Economist* (25 December 1982), 75.

[192] 'On the Brink of a Trade War?', *The Economist* (29 November 1982), 77.

[193] In most years, there were one to three complaints brought before GATT under Article XXIII. These increased to three in 1979, six in 1980, four in 1981, and eight in 1982. Most complaints involved the USA, Canada, Japan, and EEC as either the complainant or the object of complaint. See Negotiating History of Art 18:9 and the treatment of reports of working parties and panels under Art XXIII of the General Agreement, Note by Secretariat, 11 May 1983, SCM/W/48, GDL.

appeal in 1982 in which they acknowledged the attraction of protectionist measures, but pointed out that they damaged political alliances, threatened the liberal global trade order that had 'made possible an unparalleled expansion of trade among nations and stimulated economic growth in most parts of the globe', and ran the risk of a trade war.[194]

Arthur Dunkel replaced Long as director-general in 1979, and he steered GATT through an increasingly protectionist international environment. No one seemed particularly sorry to see Long go. According to Canadian officials, Long lacked the 'dynamic leadership to establish GATT as trade policy institution for 1980s'.[195] Dunkel was a Swiss diplomat and an expert in trade policy and negotiations. His candidacy apparently 'surfaced naturally' and elicited broad-based support, including from developing countries.[196] He has been described as self-effacing and unpretentious, but also determined and a consensus-builder. A colleague and friend likened him to a cat: intelligent, tenacious, clever, and independent.[197] Dunkel was also able to wear down negotiators in all-night meetings. He commanded respect and, according to some, fear. His obituary described him as 'an almost papal presence in the GATT'.[198] His leadership resembled that of Eric Wyndham White: widely respected, proactive, and adept at manipulating circumstances to persuade members to support GATT.

Dunkel knew that 'his stewardship' occurred 'at a point of major strain in international trade relations'.[199] Like Wyndham White before him, he solicited the help of outside experts to study the problems confronting world trade and to propose solutions. In doing so, he acted independently, but not in a way that over-stepped his authority.[200] The experts produced a report in 1987 called 'Trade Policies for a Better Future' (commonly referred to as the Leutwiler Report) in which they warned that protectionism was 'chok[ing]' international trade. The authors insisted that the benefits of protectionism were illusory. The economic

---

[194] J. Carter and G. R. Ford, 'Stop the Drift Toward Economic Anarchy', *The Economist* (21 November 1982), 19.

[195] Telegram, Geneva to External, 9 November 1979, RG19: F-2/5961/8718–1-4 pt. 11, LAC.

[196] Telegram, Geneva to External, 23 November 1979, re GATT: CPs Session: Succession of DirGen and Related Matters and Telegram, Genev to External, 9 November 1979, RG19: F-2/5961/718–1-4 pt. 11, LAC.

[197] J.-P. Delamuraz, 'Arthur Dunkel' in J. Bhagwati and M. Hirsch (eds.), *The Uruguay Round and Beyond: Essays in Honor of Arthur Dunkel* (Ann Arbor: University of Michigan Press, 1998), 5.

[198] 'Arthur Dunkel, Diplomat and Pioneer of the World Trade Organisation', *The Guardian* (16 June 2005), www.theguardian.com/news/2005/jun/16/guardianobituaries.wto

[199] Scenario Brief for Dunkel Visit (1981), RG19: F-2/5931/8718–01 pt. 4, LAC.

[200] Delamuraz, 'Arthur Dunkel', 6.

rationale for protectionism was misguided (for example, it did not save jobs) and caused disputes between nations. Protectionism was a short-term solution, understandably appealing to resolve immediate problems, but ultimately a cop-out that hindered economic growth and change. They warned that GATT and the liberal trade system it oversaw were in jeopardy. Exceptions to the rules were rampant and members had 'abused' GATT's flexibility. The solution was to fortify a liberal trade order by strengthening GATT's oversight authority, tightening the rules for customs unions and free trade areas, reinserting sectors of trade (such as textiles, clothing, and agriculture) into the GATT system, integrating developing countries more fully into world trade, and having more high-level political involvement in the GATT process. Finally, they called for another round of trade negotiations.

Development was demoted as a priority; it was protectionism that threatened the GATT system. Even though GATT had long been on the defensive about its relevance to developing countries and had on occasion acknowledged elements of a postcolonial critique of the institution and the global trade order, in the early 1980s an alternative narrative emerged that recast developing countries as part of the problem confronting GATT. The Leutwiler report maintained that developed countries bore 'the largest responsibility for the functioning of the trade system', but the authors expected developing countries to do their part to ensure the system was safe and well served.[201] Echoing the logic that had prevailed during the Second World War, the authors affirmed the universalist thinking that general conditions of open trade would benefit all and that common interests transcended differences. There really was no choice: 'One road leads to protectionism, distortion of competitive conditions, attempts to avoid change, and economic decline. The other road offers more open trade, observance of mutually accepted trading rules, readiness for change, and the promise of widespread economic growth.'[202]

While most of the recommendations were directed at developed countries, the report also recommended putting an end to special and differential treatment for developing countries, a new legal principle that had been enshrined in the enabling clause. The authors of the Leutwiler report – among them economists from India, Brazil, and Indonesia – observed that special treatment from GATT rules had 'limited value'.

---

[201] GATT, *Trade Policies for a Better Future: The 'Leutwiler Report', the GATT and the Uruguay Round*, with an introduction by A. Dunkel (Dordrecht, Boston, and Lancaster: Martinus Nijhoff Publishers, 1987), 12, 39–40. According to Preeg, Dunkel did not publicize the report because of its critical stand towards developing countries. Preeg, *Traders in a Brave New World*, 52–53.

[202] GATT, *Leutwiler Report*, 39.

They agreed that developing countries needed to be more fully integrated into the global trade system and that this should be done on the basis of their 'competitive strengths'. The least developed among them would need 'additional help'.[203]

The experts' support for another round of negotiations dovetailed with the USA's desire to broaden the scope of trade to include services and intellectual property. There was resistance to a round on these terms: developing countries preferred to address unsolved problems before introducing new sectors of trade that might put them in an ever more disadvantageous position.[204] The USA insisted on holding a vote on another round. Confident that they would get a majority, they proposed a stark choice: participate in the expanded terms or stay away. Dissension slowly crumbled and eventually all members participated. As Wilkinson and Scott make clear, this moment confirmed that although developing countries participated actively in GATT, they were 'largely ignored'.[205] GATT moved towards its longest and final round of trade negotiations.

I leave a fuller discussion of the Uruguay round to the next chapter on agriculture, an area of particular interest to developing countries. Below is a short summary of the results of the round for developing countries. The story resembled previous rounds. It began with a ministerial declaration that once again acknowledged that the interests of developing countries deserved special attention. Developing countries frequently expressed dissatisfaction over the course of the negotiations. The main concern was that negotiations would produce unbalanced results and that issues of particular importance to them would be marginalized. In a collective statement in 1990, they identified textiles, agriculture, and the selective use of safeguards as issues on which insufficient progress was being made. More fundamentally, there was concern that they were being 'deprived' of rights in favour of obligations, 'in disregard of their special need and conditions'.[206]

In 1990, Dunkel produced a draft final agreement in the hope of saving the round. This was an occasion for developing countries to express their dissatisfaction. Argentina's representative went to the heart of the matter. The current deadlock in the round was the result of the failings of developed countries, who lacked the necessary political will to push back against protectionism. Disagreements among the most powerful members delayed

[203] Ibid., 51–52.
[204] P. Low, *Trading Free: The GATT and US Trade Policy* (New York: Twentieth Century Fund Press, 1993), 201–202.
[205] Wilkinson and Scott, 'Developing Country Participation in GATT', 503–504.
[206] Statement by the Informal Group of Developing Countries, 1 March 1990, MTN. TNC/W/18, GDL.

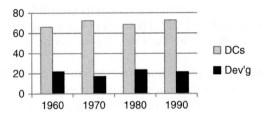

Figure 5.4 Per cent share of world trade (imports and exports combined), 1960–1990: developed and developing countries (DCs and Dev'g)
Source: *UN Yearbook of International Trade Statistics* (1981), pp. 1080–1081; (1992), pp. S2, S3.

consideration of all other issues, including those of greatest importance to developing countries. In contrast, developing countries had made radical changes to their economies to better conform to a liberal trade system, 'often at a high political and social cost'. The imbalance between expectations and contributions – with developed countries offering little, whereas developing countries were expected to make concessions which they could not be sure would encourage their own economic growth – was unacceptable. Subsequent speakers from developing countries endorsed Argentina's statement, including Brazil, Chile, Colombia, and Nicaragua. Bangladesh's representative reminded all of the recent UN declaration that 'it was an "ethical imperative" not to accept the marginalization of the least developed countries as irreversible'. He too endorsed a successful end to the round and noted that Bangladesh's very survival and security would benefit from a successful conclusion. The endorsement of developing countries for the trade negotiations was bolstered by changing trade patterns in the 1980s that saw their share of global exports rise (see Figure 5.4). The remarkable growth of the Asian tigers of Singapore, South Korea, Taiwan, and Hong Kong showed that trade could be an engine of rapid economic growth and rising standards of living. The logic behind their endorsement of the Uruguay round echoed the liberal interdependent reasoning and the internationalist thinking of the 1940s. As Bangladesh's representative put it: 'Success in the Uruguay round is the surest insurance for us all to sail on the boat of multilateralism to a safe and predictable voyage of liberalizing the global trading system and thus make interdependence of nations truly meaningful.'[207]

---

[207] Statement by the Representative of Bangladesh, 26 November 1990, MTN.TNC/W/45, GDL.

The end of the Cold War reinforced the widespread endorsement of lower barriers to trade and GATT's mission to promote an interdependent trading order that was based on non-discrimination and multilateralism.[208] This was a dramatic reversal from the 1989 proclamation of GATT's death as a result of the rise of regional trade groups. The success of liberal trade was evident in the way former communist countries joining GATT began to make economic reforms that brought them into line with a liberal trade order, as I discussed in Chapter 2. It was also evident in the reforms being made in developing countries in response to the neoliberal conception of development. But this apparent convergence of ideas about means and ends did not eliminate all obstacles to agreement in the Uruguay round. As Preeg observes, although GATT had become 'the bellwether for an evolving world economic order ... the bell more often than not rang faintly'.[209] There were forceful entreaties to members to support liberal trade. The consequences, if they did not, were painted in stark terms: plenty or want, peace or conflict, order or chaos.

As the end of the round neared, there were ways in which the interests of developing countries were better served than previously, beginning with the phased removal of the Multifibre Arrangement. The fiction that it served liberalization could not be sustained any longer. The Textile Surveillance Body reported that there were 114 restraint agreements in place, of which 94 were directed against producers in developing countries.[210] GATT members agreed that textiles and clothing should be integrated within the GATT system. Perhaps the most important catalyst to change was the acknowledgement that the MFA was unsustainable and no longer served the economic interests of developed countries.[211] Nonetheless, the EEC sounded a cautious note and insisted that phasing out the MFA and its restrictive devices had to be accompanied by a strengthening of GATT rules and disciplines.[212] Meanwhile other states were unilaterally removing non-tariff barriers on textiles and clothing.[213] Any lingering hesitation was overcome by discussions aimed at putting in place a special safeguard mechanism that GATT members could invoke in the event of further market disruption.[214]

The single greatest result of the round was the establishment of the World Trade Organization (WTO). At last, there was a properly constituted international organization to oversee and guide the global trade

---

[208] Preeg, *Traders in a Brave New World*, 106.   [209] Ibid., 20.
[210] *The Activities of GATT 1989*, 114.   [211] Heron, *Global Political Economy*, 13.
[212] *The Activities of GATT 1989*, 47–48.
[213] Unilateral Trade Liberalization Undertaken by 45 Countries, Reports the Director General of GATT, 18 April 1991, GATT/1509, GDL.
[214] *The Activities of GATT 1990*, 33.

system. Developing countries supported the new organization because it included agriculture and textiles. They were also reassured that they would be accorded special and differential treatment when it came to phasing in the responsibilities of membership.[215] In addition, the WTO reinforced the rules-based approach to global trade. As Peter Sutherland, the final director-general of GATT, explained, the establishment of the WTO was 'a major advance in the rule of law in international economic relations'.[216] Developing countries endorsed a rules-based system. It leveled the playing field by offsetting the use of force or other forms of persuasion as a way to conduct trade relations. As Indonesia's representative put it at the closing ceremony in Marrakesh in 1994, the WTO should be 'the guardian of a rules-based, predictable and non-discriminatory multilateral trading system and the guarantor of the rights of the weaker trading partners against arbitrary and unilateral actions of the strong'.[217] India's minister of commerce drew out the irony that developing countries now endorsed 'the logic of competition based on comparative advantage', whereas the industrial countries were 'shying away from the playing field and seeking a tilt in the rules of the game'.[218]

Conclusions

Most accounts of GATT do not pay sufficient attention to the majority of its members: developing countries. There is a reason for this: the key to the impasses that threatened to derail rounds in the end always came down to US–EEC agreement. But a more comprehensive history, with a focus on the daily work of GATT and on issues other than rounds of negotiations, makes clear that developing countries were essential to the organization's history. Although this chapter focuses on development, developing countries figure prominently across this volume, in connection with the Cold War, the establishment of the EEC, regionalism, and agriculture. Several developing countries stand out as engaged, committed, and vocal members, including Bangladesh, Brazil, India, Mexico, Nigeria, and Peru, to mention only a few. Some scholars have portrayed them as *demandeurs* and free riders, but these characterizations tell more about the attitudes and interests of conservative powers wanting

[215] A. Narlikar, *The WTO: A Very Short Introduction* (New York: Oxford University Press, 2005), 25.

[216] A New Framework for International Economic Relations, Sutherland, Third Hayek Memorial Lecture, 16 June 1994, GATT/1640, GDL.

[217] Statement by H. E. Mr. S. B. Joedano, Minister of Trade, 12 April 1994, MTN.TNC/MIN (94)ST/17, GDL.

[218] Statement by Mr. Pranab Mukherjee, Minister of Commerce, 13 April 1994, MTN.TNC/MIN (94)ST/38, GDL.

to preserve the status quo. Developing countries participated construc-
tively and meaningfully in GATT, even when they asked for exceptional
treatment and especially when they wanted to reform the organization.
Such requests were not in principle objectionable to an organization that
had always considered the specific challenges of its members. The argument for exceptions was credible and consistent with the long-term goals
of GATT: that they needed special treatment temporarily so that they
could be in a position to compete fairly in world trade rather than be
locked into marginal roles. Their support for the use of quantitative
restrictions in the 1954–1955 review also made clear that they only
wanted recourse to practices that other GATT members had employed.
GATT obligations had never been applied rigidly to any members,
including the USA and EEC. But they often did seem to apply unevenly,
a point that developing country representatives made explicitly, such as at
the 1954–1955 review on the question of quantitative restrictions or when
the Argentine ambassador observed that GATT was filled with waivers
'for the benefit of major countries'.[219] Paradoxically, as developing countries became competitive and tried to participate more fully in trade
negotiations, they confronted a host of barriers and impediments to
their exports. Textiles and agriculture are the best examples of this. As
a result, developing countries became strong advocates of a rules-based
trade organization and, at times, they were more staunch champions of
GATT than ostensible leaders such as the USA and Britain. A recent
PEW study of attitudes towards free trade confirms that there has been
a shift of the advocates and opponents of free trade: today, developing
countries believe in free trade most strongly, whereas the alleged economic giants, countries such as France and the USA, equate free trade
with domestic economic instability, in particular unemployment.[220]

The study of development and developing countries also highlights the
way that GATT functioned as a decentralized organization in which
initiatives could be taken by any member. On the question of preferences,
the combined prodding and support of developing countries, the secretariat, and Australia paved the way to acceptance of preferences for the

---

[219] Memorandum of Conversation re GATT Trade Negotiations, between Roberto
Alemann, Argentine Ambassador, and Herter and Norwood, 11 March 1963, Box 10,
file Memoranda of Telephone Conversation, 12/14/62–7/30/63, Herter Papers, JFKL.
[220] Discussion of the Trans-Pacific Partnership in the United States reflects mercantilist
reasoning whereby international trade and specialized production are linked to domestic
unemployment. See Hilary Clinton's acceptance speech at the Democratic National
Convention (July 2016) where she stated that refusing unfair trade deals and standing up
to China were ways to 'support our steelworkers, automakers and homegrown manufacturers': www.politico.com/story/2016/07/full-text-hillary-clintons-dnc-speech-2264
10, accessed 23 May 2018.

purpose of development, despite determined US opposition. Brazil, backed by the secretariat, took the lead in establishing the International Trade Centre, which helped developing countries take part in GATT more fully. These examples support Low's description of a multipolar economic realm.[221] A multipolar assessment of GATT challenges the entrenched view of the United States as the hegemon of the post-1945 global order and as the world's economic leader. Such an assessment does not deny that the USA and EEC were leaders in GATT, but it suggests they were not the only leaders who mattered. Moreover, it questions the association of economic power with leadership, meaning the ability to set the agenda, define priorities, and rally support for goals and preferences. Within GATT, the USA frequently did not get its way. In relation to development, that might be explained in part because it was a lower US priority. Perhaps the USA allowed others to lead on an issue that it considered to be of secondary importance. But given the importance of a growing global economy to the USA's economic well-being and global security, this is not an entirely convincing explanation.

Within an organization that did not have a hegemon or undisputed leader, there was both opportunity and need for the secretariat to lead. This had been especially evident under Eric Wyndham White. He pressed to make GATT more responsive to its developing members, facilitated their accession to GATT (despite US criticism), and orchestrated the inclusion of the development chapter to the General Agreement. However, the absence of a strong and consistent champion among developed members contributed to the fact that development was not a higher priority within GATT.

There had always been critics of liberal trade who doubted claims that it would benefit all countries and all sectors of the economy. Representatives of developing countries repeatedly challenged the confident universalist assumptions on which GATT rested, suggesting instead that GATT reinforced existing global structures, privileging those who were 'already endowed with economic and political power'.[222] At the Marrakesh closing ceremonies for the Uruguay round, Cuba's minister of foreign trade observed that 'today's world offers free trade as our only alternative' even though the goals of development were far from achieved: 'the figures showing the increase in unemployment, extreme poverty, the cruel and paradoxical emergence of a Fourth World,

[221] Low, *Trading Free*, 239.
[222] E. S. Rosenberg, 'Transnational Currents in a Shrinking World' in E. S. Rosenberg (ed.), *A World Connecting, 1870–1945* (Cambridge, MA: Belknap Press of Harvard University Press, 2012), 848. Rosenberg wrote this about the IMF and the World Bank, but it is equally applicable to GATT.

the reduced use of new technologies, and the growing informal sector refute the alleged positive effects of such measures'.[223] Despite GATT's meagre contributions to development, in the mid-1990s the belief in liberal trade was widespread and arguments made in favour of differential treatment and nuanced understanding of the challenges confronting developing countries lost traction. Nonetheless, developing countries continued to hope that GATT, and its successor the WTO, would be helpful to them. They endorsed a global trade order that was competitive and specialized, as well as rules-based. However, the failure of the Doha development round suggests that narrow self-interest and short-term thinking continue to work against connecting trade and development. The trade system cannot easily be used to achieve economic justice. It does not follow from GATT's shortcomings that developing members served GATT, or the liberal trade order, poorly. Normalizing their involvement – for example, by seeing demands for exceptional treatment as consistent with the waivers and exceptions of developed countries – and understanding that they confronted structural disadvantages allows us to see their calls for reform or expressions of dissatisfaction as both reasonable and constructive. It also forces us to ask who was a constant supporter of GATT, who made consistent contributions to trade liberalization, and who always thought in terms of the collective interest. The answer is that no member did all the time, as the chapter on agriculture will make clear.

---

[223] Statement by H. E. Mr. Ricardo Cabrisas Ruíz, Minister for Foreign Trade, 13 April 1994, MTN.TNC/MIN (94)/ST58, GDL.

6 'Agricultural Anarchy'
The Agriculture Challenge to GATT

The history of agricultural production and the history of agricultural trade move in opposite directions. While agricultural production has increased dramatically since the mid-nineteenth century, the proportion of agricultural goods in global trade has decreased sharply in the twentieth century. Before 1930, agricultural goods (cultivated products that can be in primary or manufactured form and are not restricted to food products) comprised roughly half of all trade; by the 1990s its share hovered around 10 per cent.[1] These statistics suggest that global trade did not contribute to the expansion of agricultural production. Governments around the world have taken this logic further, seeing global trade as a threat to domestic agricultural production. The policy implication is that agricultural production required protection, and as a result governments have protected farmers. So while Giovanni Federico characterizes the history of agriculture as 'an outstanding ... success story'[2], Allen Maunder and Alberto Valdés argue that agricultural trade has 'remained an island of protectionism is an increasingly interdependent world economy'.[3] Agriculture stands out as GATT's greatest failure. It was seen this way throughout GATT's history. In 1960, Wyndham White lamented that agriculture 'hung like a cloud over the GATT'.[4] A US assessment from 1972 described the state of affairs as 'agricultural anarchy' and observed that GATT was utterly ineffectual in trying to bring order to this vital sector of trade: 'In no sector has the GATT proved more helpless than in that of agricultural

---

[1] G. Federico, *Feeding the World: An Economic History of Agriculture, 1800–2000* (Oxford and Princeton: Princeton University Press, 2005), 28. According to *International Trade Statistics 2001*, agricultural goods made up 12.2 per cent of total merchandise trade in 1990. See Table IV.1, 95, available at www.wto.org/english/res_e/statis_e/its2001_e/chp_4_e.pdf

[2] Federico, *Feeding the World*, xiii.

[3] A. Maunder and A. Valdés (eds.), *Agriculture and Governments in an Interdependent World: Proceedings of the Twentieth International Conference of Agricultural Economists* (Aldershot: Dartmouth Publishing Company, 1989), 279.

[4] 'Europe in the GATT', address by Wyndham White, Europe House, London, May 1960, WTO.

policies affecting trade.'[5] By the end of the Uruguay round, agriculture was slowly being drawn under the umbrella of a liberal trade regime, but the reversal was incomplete, grudging, and contested.

The challenge of liberalizing trade in agriculture was compounded by the many ways in which agriculture was implicated in domestic politics and meaningful to national identities. The association of agriculture with particular and cherished national characteristics reinforced arguments in favour of protection. As Grace Skogstad and Andrew Cooper point out, farm life has long been linked to national ideology and national values, as in depictions of the integrity of peasant farming in France and the rugged individualism of the American farmer. Agriculture also resonated with the preservation of the family as the core of society. Farming was evidence of pasts that were part of foundation myths or associated with nation-building projects. Agriculture was associated with ways of life and national identities that could not be subject to the rationale of efficient production.[6] Even citizens with no direct experience of farm life nonetheless appreciated rural virtues and values.[7] Agricultural production was often seen as a form of national service. The social wellsprings of agriculture were sometimes openly acknowledged in GATT meetings. As a British official pointed out, 'The rural way of life plays an important part in the British social structure.'[8] The values and characteristics associated with farm life were seen as justifications of protectionism.

The ability of farmers to mobilize politically also influenced government policy, even though their proportion of the workforce was shrinking (see Table 6.1). Farmers in Canada, the USA, Japan, and the EEC lobbied their governments for help; they were 'highly mobilized, vociferous, and persistent in their demands'.[9] There was widespread belief that some people would lose out badly from a liberalization of trade in agriculture. In the case of small or uncompetitive farmers, they stood to lose their livelihood. Given the high stakes, farmers acted to protect their economic interests. Richard Manning suggests that US farmers commanded disproportionate political weight because of the industrialization of agricultural

---

[5] 'Reform of the GATT', First draft by Evans, n.d., RG364: US Trade Representative General Counsel 1962–1975: Box 55, file GATT Reform 1972.

[6] G. Skogstad and A. F. Cooper, 'Introduction' in Skogstad and Cooper (eds.), *Agricultural Trade: Domestic Pressures and International Tensions* (Halifax, NS: Institute for Research on Public Policy, 1990), 5–6. B. Wilson and P. Finkle, 'Is Agriculture Different? Another Round in the Battle Between Theory and Practice' in Skogstad and Cooper (eds.), *Agricultural Trade*, 13–26. Hathaway notes that farmers are generally seen to possess 'superior moral and political values'. D. E. Hathaway, *Agriculture and the GATT: Rewriting the Rules* (Washington, DC: Institute for International Economics, 1987), 69.

[7] Wilson and Finkle, 'Is Agriculture Different?', 17.

[8] Expansion of Trade: Tariff Conference, Report of Committee I: Addendum, 17 November 1959, L/1043/Add. 1, GDL.

[9] Skogstad and Cooper, 'Introduction' in Skogstad and Cooper (eds.), *Agricultural Trade*, 6.

Table 6.1   *Employment in agriculture as a percentage of civilian employment*

	1960	1987	1994
Australia	11.0	5.7	5.1
Belgium	8.7	3.0	2.5
Canada	13.2	4.7	4.1
France	22.5	6.9	4.9
Germany	14.0	4.2	3.3
Italy	32.6	10.5	7.8
Japan	30.2	8.3	5.8
New Zealand	14.6	10.3	10.4
Switzerland	14.5	5.7	4.3
United Kingdom	4.7	2.3	2.1
United States	8.5	3.0	2.9

Based on data from Table 2.9, Employment in agriculture as a percentage of civilian employment, *OECD Historical Statistics 1960–1997* (1999), p. 42, https://read.oecd-ilibrary.org/economics/oecd-historical-statistics-1999_hist_stats-1999-en-fr#page42, accessed 13 June 2019.

production; the farm lobby included multiple economic actors, such as chemists, tractor makers, and migrant labour.[10] Agricultural lobby groups seeking protection were well organized and powerfully motivated. Farm lobbies campaigning for protection could have an influence that was disproportionate to their numbers, for various reasons including electoral considerations and domestic stability.[11] The support for farmers was linked to key geographical areas (such as Quebec in Canada or the midwestern USA) as well as to particular bases of power. In a country such as the United States, in which some farmers were competitive and others were not, the administration could play them off against one another. But this required careful political maneouvring. As the former deputy US trade representative Harald Malmgren put it, agricultural policies were wrapped up in 'votes, regions, and the glue of the community'.[12] As a result, governments either refused to introduce or moved cautiously towards, liberal practices and open markets in agriculture.

Many scholars have examined the importance of domestic factors in shaping trade policy and determining the ability of states to pursue trade

[10] R. Manning, *Against the Grain: How Agriculture Has Hijacked Civilization* (New York: North Point Press, 2004), 96.

[11] D. Kenyon and D. Lee, *The Struggle for Trade Liberalization in Agriculture: Australia and the Cairns Group in the Uruguay Round* (Canberra: Commonwealth of Australia, 2006), 2.

[12] Author interview with Malmgren, 15 May 2008.

liberalization globally. While some scholars claim that domestic factors determine trade policy, others explain trade policy as a product of international goals.[13] Robert Putnam's study of the two-level game acknowledges that domestic and international determinants are both relevant. He dismisses attempts to identify which factor is more influential as 'fruitless'. In reply to the question of whether domestic or international factors matter, he replies sensibly: "'Both, sometimes." The more interesting questions are "When?" and "How?"'[14] The relationship between domestic and international environments, and their combined effect on trade policy, is also an important consideration. In John Ruggie's theory of embedded liberalism, conditions of domestic economic well-being permitted the pursuit of trade liberalization internationally. As he puts it, two goals, not always compatible, were pursued jointly: to 'safeguard and even aid the quest for domestic stability without, at the same time, triggering the mutually destructive external consequences that had plagued the interwar period'.[15] Domestic stability was a precondition for the promotion of trade liberalization and made it easier to absorb the economic dislocation that arose from liberalization. But for embedded liberalism to work, there had to be a balance between domestic and international economic interests and well-being. The case of agriculture shows that domestic policies such as subsidies and trade barriers have tended to skew trade patterns, sustain inefficient production, jeopardize international negotiations, and erode confidence that the global trade system worked to benefit all. A zero-sum dynamic replaced the balanced trade-off that had allowed embedded liberalism to support domestic economic stability and global economic growth. Or, to use Putnam's terminology, international negotiations under GATT failed repeatedly to identify a large enough win-set with respect to global agricultural trade.

Although Putnam, Ruggie, and others draw out the political considerations and aims that informed trade policy, these were not always acknowledged in GATT discussions of specific issues such as agricultural export subsidies. Nonetheless, political considerations are influential, sometimes definitive. Agricultural issues may be highly technical, but as Ann

---

[13] Compare J. Goldstein, 'Trade Liberalization and Domestic Politics' in A. Narlikar, M. Daunton, and R. M. Stern (eds.), *The Oxford Handbook on the World Trade Organization* (New York: Oxford University Press, 2012), 64–84, and Vleuten and Alons, who link French policies of agricultural protection and defence of the CAP to the foreign policy goal of national greatness. A. van der Vleuten and G. Alons, '*La Grande Nation* and Agriculture: The Power of French Farmers Demystified', *West European Politics* 35 (2) (March 2012): 266.

[14] R. D. Putnam, 'Diplomacy and Domestic Politics: The Logic of Two-Level Games', *International Organization* 42 (3) (Summer 1988), 427.

[15] J. Ruggie, 'International Regimes, Transactions, and Change: Embedded Liberalism in the Postwar Economic Order' in S. D. Krasner (ed.), *International Regimes* (Ithaca, NY: Cornell University Press, 1983), 204–210.

Capling notes, they are too political to be left to technocrats.[16] It was certainly the case that agricultural trade often involved high-level meetings of ministers. Little could be achieved without political assent and direction. The case of agriculture exposes the economic and political functions of trade policy, always present, but not always explicit.

Global agricultural trade is also a useful focus in the study of protectionism, and more broadly in examining the way people have thought and talked about trade. Even though most governments reported that the size of the agricultural workforce had been shrinking relative to manufacturing since 1945, they insisted that they had to maintain a domestic agricultural sector and that farming should be a viable way of life. Indeed, the levels of protection were highest in industrial countries where the farm sectors were smallest – and getting smaller.[17] The justification for protection was that agriculture was an exceptional kind of production. Some emphasized the unique circumstances that affected agricultural production, such as soil conditions and the weather. Unpredictability distinguished farmers from other producers.[18] Preserving a domestic agricultural sector through government support was also justified in relation to food security. But not all accepted that agriculture was a special sector. Josling notes that similar cases can be made for other sectors, although he concedes that the rationale for agriculture's exceptionalism was more compelling.[19] The Economist, on the other hand, called out a double standard. If a country introduces a voluntary export restraint on an industrial good – say, cars – then the world will think that country 'slightly wicked'; but if a country introduces quotas or import bans on an agricultural commodity, 'most of the world will swallow the results without turning a hair'.[20] Even though liberalization was generally seen (or at least spoken of) as the default best approach to global trade, protecting agriculture was widely seen as a legitimate, even virtuous, expression of social policy. Not all farmers lobbied for protection and control over the domestic market. Many farmers were efficient producers who wanted access to foreign markets. There were also inefficient farmers who wanted access to foreign markets, which raised questions about fairness. An examination of global trade in agriculture brings to the fore the

---

[16] A. Capling, *Australia and the Global Trade System: From Havana to Seattle* (Cambridge: Cambridge University Press, 2001), 141.

[17] C. L. Davis 'International Institutions and Issue Linkage: Building Support for Agricultural Trade Liberalization', *American Political Science Review* 98 (1) (February 2004), 153.

[18] Skogstad and Cooper (eds.), *Agricultural Trade*, 16.

[19] T. E. Josling, *Agriculture in the Tokyo Round Negotiations* (London: Trade Policy Research Centre, 1977), 11.

[20] 'The Gnat and the Camel', 1 July 1978, *The Economist*, 71.

open-versus-protectionist push-and-pull that had existed since the establishment of GATT and determined the context in which it could, or could not, promote ongoing liberalization. In this case, the protectionist position usually prevailed.

Agriculture is an essential component of GATT's institutional history because it challenged GATT's credibility as a universally relevant organization. Just as it could not withstand accusations of being a rich-man's club, GATT was damaged by lopsided advances in liberalization that favoured manufactured goods over agricultural goods. There were too many agricultural exporting countries in GATT to accept the exemption of agriculture passively. Starting in the early 1960s, the United States pressed for liberalization in agriculture, but its position was compromised by an earlier GATT waiver that allowed it to protect US agricultural producers. Instead, smaller countries such as Australia and New Zealand, joined periodically (and inconsistently) by countries such as Canada, Brazil, and Denmark, pressed for liberalization in agriculture. Their efforts met with determined opposition by large GATT members, including the EEC, the USA, and Japan. Repeated failures and disappointed expectations meant that some agricultural-exporting countries came to see GATT as irrelevant to their interests and possibly even as 'a threat to their well-being'.[21] But attempts to include negotiations on agricultural products in rounds of negotiations also ran the risk of alienating members that were determined to maintain domestic support for farmers. In a memorandum on agricultural trade that Wyndham White prepared in 1973, he commented on the risks to GATT if its efforts to liberalize agricultural trade were thwarted or disregarded: 'Nothing is more destructive to the credibility of international institutions than recommendations which are systematically ignored.'[22] Whether the liberalization of agriculture was pursued or whether agriculture was kept in an exceptional category, GATT's institutional relevance and authority were called into question.

There was no sudden shift to agricultural protectionism following the Second World War. As Dale Hathaway explains, 'Agricultural policies are rooted in national history, often predating World War II and the GATT.'[23] In negotiations to establish GATT, agriculture was granted

---

[21] Hathaway, *Agriculture and the GATT*, 3.

[22] E. Wyndham White, 'Negotiating on Agriculture', March 1973, RG19: F-2/5394/8720/ A278 pt. 5, LAC.

[23] Hathaway, *Agriculture and the GATT*, 2. Evans points out that the USA and Europe had 'extensive machinery for supporting their domestic agricultural production and limiting imports by one device or another' before the GATT was established. J. W. Evans, *The Kennedy Round in American Trade Policy: The Twilight of the GATT?* (Cambridge, MA: Harvard University Press, 1971), 70.

exceptional treatment in response to domestic political and economic realities in industrialized countries, principally the USA, Britain, and western Europe.[24] The result was that governments were able to introduce (or maintain) measures – such as export subsidies and import quotas – to protect farmers. This had long been the case.

But agriculture's special status did not mean that all accepted that GATT negotiations would leave this major sector of trade untouched. Many members expected that markets would be opened to trade in agricultural goods. Perhaps, as John Warley explains, this expectation existed because there was a 'silent promise' in the 1940s that the liberalization of agricultural commodities would only be postponed, not excluded.[25] A GATT study of agriculture from the 1980s concluded that the rules of the General Agreement did not exempt agriculture: 'on their face value [they] relate to agriculture and industry alike'.[26] This report reinforced the mounting frustration of members whose agricultural exports were marginalized in negotiations. My reconstruction confirms a gradual and contested exceptional status for agriculture in the 1950s and 1960s, when the USA sought a waiver to restrict agricultural commodities that threatened domestic producers, and the EEC subsequently introduced the CAP. Many scholars have written about these two moments;[27] the difference here is in making a case that agriculture's exemption was incremental and that this development was challenged and resisted. The story of agriculture in GATT cannot be left to the Uruguay round. There were difficult discussions about agriculture before and during every GATT round.

Frustration over the failure to liberalize agricultural trade reached new heights in the 1980s, with pundits and officials suggesting that a trade war might erupt. GATT repositioned itself as an advocate of consumer interests, in the hope that this would offset protectionist thinking about agriculture. This argument did not elicit much support, in sharp contrast

[24] T. E. Josling, S. Tangermann, and T. K. Warley, *Agriculture in the GATT* (Basingstoke: Macmillan, 1996), 11, 21. Ingersent, Rayner and Hine also note that agriculture was exempt from GATT rules, permitting the use of quantitative restrictions and export subsidies, but they are vague about exactly when this occurred. K. A. Ingerstent, A. J. Rayner, and R. C. Hine (eds.), *Agriculture in the Uruguay Round* (New York: St. Martin's Press, 1994), 1. Kenyon and Lee make a more general claim that the rules concerning agriculture were defined to suit domestic politics rather than international priorities. Kenyon and Lee, *The Struggle for Trade Liberalisation in Agriculture*, 10.

[25] T. K. Warley, 'Agriculture in the GATT: Past and Future' in Maunder and Valdés (eds.), *Agriculture and Governments in an Interdependent World*, 305.

[26] Agriculture in the GATT: Note by the Secretariat, Consultative Group of Eighteen, 20 January 1982, CG.18/W/59/Rev.1.

[27] See, for example, Josling et al., *Agriculture in the GATT*, 26–29 (waiver) and CAP throughout.

to the first farmers' protests against GATT. Before the 1980s, GATT had flown beneath the radar of public opinion. Increased efforts to liberalize trade in agriculture were met with public demonstrations that equated GATT with the destruction of national distinctiveness, established cultural practices, and social values rooted in historical experience.

There is a fair bit of finger-pointing in the literature, blaming particular countries – or groups of countries – as being the obstacles to liberalization. Warley identifies the USA and the EEC as having a defining and negative influence on the liberalization of trade in agriculture.[28] Hoekman and Kostecki single out Japan and the EEC.[29] Although some scholars have made a convincing case that the EEC was a leader within GATT and that its efforts moved liberalization forward on many fronts, with respect to agriculture it is hard not to see it as a formidable obstacle. First, the phasing in of the CAP over ten years (1958–1968) was used to evade scrutiny; once it was in place it was impossible to extract it from the complex politics of European integration. As Des Dinan noted, it was 'a cherished icon of European integration, and especially of Franco-German friendship'.[30] But it was a lightning rod of discontent among GATT members. However, it must be remembered that agricultural protectionism was widespread and that there were few countries whose commitment to liberalization in this sector was unqualified or consistent.

Most studies of agriculture focus on the 'gladitorial contests'[31] between the USA, Japan, and the EEC, with some attention paid to the Cairns Group (discussed later in the chapter) that usefully reveals the ability of smaller countries such as Australia to lead in GATT.[32] Developing countries do not figure prominently, even though products such as tea, coffee, and bananas were sometimes leading exports of developing countries; nor is development much explored in studies of agriculture. Siamwalla notes that developing countries were 'conspicuous by their quiescence on agriculture'.[33] His observation begs the question of why this was the case. This situation arose for several reasons, including the marginalization and structural disadvantages of developing countries in

---

[28] Warley, 'Agriculture in the GATT', 313.

[29] B. M. Hoekman and M. M. Kostecki, *The Political Economy of the World Trading System: From GATT to WTO* (Oxford and New York: Oxford University Press, 1995), 196.

[30] D. Dinan, *Ever Closer Union: An Introduction to European Integration*, 3rd edition (Boulder, CO: Lynne Reiner, 2005), 354.

[31] Warley, 'Agriculture in the GATT', 314.

[32] See Capling, *Australia and the Global Trade System*, and Kenyon and Lee, *The Struggle for Trade Liberalisation in Agriculture*.

[33] A. Siamwalla, 'Agriculture, the Uruguay Round and Developing Countries' in Maunder and Valdes (eds.), *Agriculture and Governments in an Interdependent World*, 324.

negotiations and their relegation to committees that addressed development rather than agriculture. This chapter conveys the frustration of developing countries over agriculture and shows how GATT upheld trade practices that denied them the benefits of a fair global trading system that could advance their economic interest.

The Exemption of Agriculture from Liberalization, 1947–1957

In the construction of the postwar order, responsibility for improving agricultural production fell to the Food and Agriculture Organization. Its two main goals were to increase production, so that food supplies could satisfy global demand, and to raise nutritional standards to combat malnourishment.[34] But there was also a place for agriculture in GATT. The architects of the postwar trade order had assumed that the liberalization of trade applied to all commodities, including agricultural goods.[35] Nonetheless, there were a few exceptions. Article XVI banned export subsidies on all goods except agricultural commodities. At the time, Article XVI was introduced with US domestic agricultural support programmes in mind, although the United States was not alone in subsidizing farmers.[36] The draft charter also permitted the use of commodity agreements to deal with trade in primary products, some of which would affect agricultural products such as sugar, as well as natural resources such as tin and rubber. The exception with respect to agricultural trade were consistent with a managed approach to agricultural exports, a legacy of the Depression.[37] This exception might support the claim that

---

[34] A. L. S. Sayward, *The Birth of Development: How the World Bank, Food and Agriculture Organization, and World Health Organization Changed the World, 1945–1965* (Kent, OH: Kent State University Press, 2006), 64. See W. Way, *A New Idea Each Morning: How Food and Agriculture Came Together in One International Organisation* (Canberra: Australian National University Press, 2013).

[35] GATT, *The Tokyo Round of Multilateral Trade Negotiations, Report by the Director General of GATT* (Geneva: GATT, April 1979), 18. As the report put it, 'When the GATT rules were originally drafted in the 1940s, they were intended to apply to trade in agriculture and industrial products alike.' Sumner and Tangermann also note that agriculture was formally covered by the General Agreement, was included in every round, and was part of day-to-day discussions in GATT. D. A. Sumner and S. Tangermann, 'International Trade Policy and Negotiations' in B. L. Gardner and G. C. Rausser (eds.), *Handbook of Agricultural Economics, Vol. 2B* (Amsterdam and New York: Elsevier, 2002), 2003.

[36] Hathaway, *Agriculture and the GATT*, 103–104.

[37] G. P. Marchildon, 'War, Revolution and the Great Depression in the Global Wheat Trade 1917–1939' in L. Coppolaro and F. McKenzie (eds.), *A Global History of Trade and Conflict since 1500* (Basingstoke: Palgrave Macmillan, 2013), 158–159. Federico writes that the 1930s stand out as 'the key decade of intervention in agriculture'. *Feeding the World*, 196.

agriculture was exempt from the liberalizing project from the start. What they reveal is that no country was ready to embrace liberal trade practices without recourse to safeguards and exceptions, recognizing the dislocating impact of liberalization on the domestic economy. They also show that the General Agreement was based on pragmatic internationalism: the challenge was to make it work, albeit imperfectly.

The expectation that agriculture would be included in the liberalization of world trade was apparent during the first round of tariff negotiations in Geneva in 1947. Countries sought concessions in foreign markets for items such as wheat, rice, cheese, milk, butter, poultry, beef, veal, lamb, eggs, apples, pears, cucumbers, spinach, cotton, tobacco, and wool. In some cases the negotiations were acrimonious, as in the Australia–USA dispute over wool, which threatened to derail the entire conference. But most items were not particularly controversial.[38] Even so, progress in liberalizing trade in agriculture lagged behind that in manufactured goods from the start.[39]

At the Havana conference, additional escape clauses and other measures were introduced to ensure that farmers enjoyed decent standards of living: these measures reinforced the idea that farmers were vulnerable and that agriculture was different from other sectors of global trade. The Havana charter also strengthened the role of commodity agreements for primary products. But no one proposed that agriculture be exempt from the ITO.

The reaction of farming groups also confirmed that agriculture was seen as being included in the overall liberalizing mandate of GATT. Some welcomed this; others objected, strenuously. In the USA, the American Butter Institute denounced tariff cuts as 'ill-conceived, peculiarly ill-timed and detrimental to the morale of milk producers', whereas a spokesman for the American Farm Bureau Federation, as well as the US Secretary of Agriculture Charles Brannan, agreed that US farmers needed open global markets for their well-being.[40] This mixed reaction was not surprising and not specific to the agricultural sector. Some farmers were more competitive than others. There would be winners and losers, and all made their views known.

[38] ITO 47, telegram from Australian Delegation, the ITO Conference, Geneva 26 April 1947, CP434/1 Bundle 15/9402 pt. 2, AA.

[39] Draft Cabinet Agendum on GATT – For Interdepartmental Committee on Trade and Employment meeting on 23 October 1947, A571/61, 1944/1109F pt. 1, AA.

[40] U.S. Public Reaction to the General Agreement on Tariffs and Trade, 5 December 1947, RG43: Records of International Conferences, Commissions and Expositions, Second Preparatory Committee Meeting, 1946–1947, Box 136, file: Trade (Geneva) – Domestic reaction to GATT, NARA. Statement by Secretary of Agriculture Charles F. Brannan before the House Committee of Foreign Affairs in Support of United States Approval of the Charter of an International Trade Organization, 1 May 1950, RG25: 6513/9100-AB -40 pt. 1, LAC.

The critical development that confirmed a special status for agriculture was the USA's request for a waiver for agriculture in 1955. To understand why the United States requested the waiver, one has to go back to 1933, when the US government introduced the Agricultural Adjustment Act. Section 22 of this Depression-era measure stipulated that if domestic farmers were being harmed by imports, then, after investigation by the Tariff Commission, the president must restrict imports. This put domestic legislation at odds with obligations undertaken in the General Agreement. The US government had used Section 22 sparingly, but its incompatibility with GATT obligations stood out in the 1950s, when it was wrapped up with concerns about US sovereignty. The USA's Senator Millikin, a longtime opponent of GATT and the ITO, had also drawn attention to the conflict. If GATT measures prevailed, Millikin argued, 'you have destroyed Section 22'.[41] The USA had to resolve this conflict between domestic legislation and international obligation.

The problem in the USA was exacerbated by surplus production. As prices fell, the government offered support to farmers. Government subsidies not only alleviated the financial hardship caused by the vicissitudes of farming, they also made all agricultural production financially viable. This created a larger problem of over-production. The results were far-reaching: a disconnect between supply and demand; gaps between domestic and world prices that shifted the flow of agricultural goods; limited access to domestic markets; and the dumping of surplus on the world market. Subsidies were also a burden for the US taxpayer. The US government introduced several measures to alleviate the surplus problem, such as reducing the number of acres under cultivation. But it could not side-step its own protectionist laws.

The USA tried to reconcile the conflict by requesting a waiver from GATT. Unlike most waivers, which had fixed terms, the USA wanted a blanket waiver, covering any and all domestically produced agricultural goods for the foreseeable future. Some GATT members suggested that the waiver should be restricted by time, say for five years, by stipulating what items would be affected and asking the US government to report annually to GATT.[42]

---

[41] Attitude of Senator Millikin Toward 'Organizational Provisions' of GATT as Indicated in Hearings Before the Senate Committee on Finance, 8 February 1954, RG59: Office of the Assistant Legal Advisor for Economic Affairs, Records Relating to GATT 1947–66, NARA.

[42] For example, see United States Request for a Waiver: Suggestions by the Delegation of Cuba on the modifications to be introduced in the draft waiver (W.9/170), 9 February 1955, W.9/185, GDL.

Wyndham White feared that the US waiver was filled with 'manifest dangers'. It would introduce a double standard between agricultural and industrial exporters that would divide GATT members.[43] Canadian officials were also alarmed because the USA's request 'would in effect write a piece of United States agricultural legislation, unqualified and virtually unsupervised, into GATT'.[44] They also worried that the waiver would open a floodgate of exceptions to protect agriculture. At a high-powered meeting between Canadian and US officials that included three Canadian cabinet ministers (Pearson – External Affairs; Harris – Finance; and Howe – Trade and Commerce) and their three US counterparts (Dulles – State Department; Humphrey –Treasury; and Morse – Agriculture), the Canadians explained that they could not support the waiver, for many reasons, including that it would weaken GATT. They added that measures such as the waiver sapped support in Canada for GATT. US officials were unmoved. Dulles insisted that overall US trade policy was 'enlightened'. He denied that the waiver would '"bust the GATT wide open" and lead to a trade restriction spiral'. He made clear that the waiver was essential to ongoing Congressional approval of the Trade Agreements Extension Act that would give the US executive the authority to negotiate tariff reductions in GATT. He went on to explain that this was a case where domestic and international obligations clashed and where support for GATT hinged on upholding domestic laws and priorities: 'the issue of executive–legislative powers and the superiority of domestic law would be injected into the debate on the Trade Extension Act unless the U.S. obtained a waiver under GATT that made it crystal-clear that there would be no conflict between the two'.[45]

The Canadians voted against the waiver, even though they acknowledged that its defeat could drive the USA out of GATT, a development they did not believe GATT could survive.[46] Cuba, New Zealand, the Netherlands, and Denmark also voted against it.

Enough members supported the waiver that it was granted. In characteristic fashion, officials lauded a compromise that permitted the USA to remain an active and committed member of GATT. Dana Wilgress, who chaired the session, celebrated GATT's ability to 'regularize an

[43] Letter, Wyndham White to Isbister, 13 April 1954, RG19: F-2/4203/8710–1 pt. 1, LAC.
[44] 'Views on the Proposed Waiver, Note by the Canadian Delegation', 9 February 1955, W.9/186, GDL.
[45] Minutes of Meeting with Canadian Minister on GATT, 6 January 1955, RG59: Box 65/ CF 424 – US, Canadian Ministers Meeting GATT 1955, Executive Secretariat Conference Files 1949–1963, NARA.
[46] High Commissioner in UK to SSEA, tel. 77, 21 January 1955, #110, *DCER* Vol. 21, 1955. Memo from SSEA to Cabinet, 'The Revised GATT', 14 June 1955, *DCER* Vol. 21, 1955, doc #119. Also see documents 100–118 of this volume.

irregular position of long-standing', thereby allowing the United States 'to reaffirm their long-term commitments and the objectives of their policy'.[47] Wilgress's assessment was not just empty spin. He reminded all that GATT was not about the immediate realization of liberal trade or rigid adherence to its principles. His words underlined the difference between ideal and real-world conditions and the incremental way that GATT achieved its goals.

> Thus, we are confronted with a situation whereby we are agreeing on certain ideals and objectives, but are admitting frankly that these are not now fully attainable. We have agreed to work towards the attainment of the ideals and objectives by the progressive removal of the exceptions which necessity has compelled us to permit. We have had to recognize that countries are not yet prepared to go very far in derogating sovereignty for the common good. We must, therefore, for the moment feel our way.[48]

There were three immediate consequences of the waiver for GATT. Because the USA had requested the waiver, it set a precedent for other members. This meant that compliance with GATT norms and rules would become harder to enforce. It solidified the belief that agriculture was different from all other sectors of trade: it 'reinforced the perception that trade in agriculture was subject to its own special standards'.[49] Moreover, it exacerbated tension between those who participated in agricultural trade and those who traded in manufactured goods. There was now an imbalance between the rights and obligations of members exporting manufactured goods and those exporting agricultural commodities. According to Wyndham White, GATT had to 'restore the balance'.[50]

Agricultural Protectionism Entrenched, 1958–1968

The excision of agriculture from GATT, and the proliferation of protectionist practices affecting agricultural production, prompted the GATT secretariat to add agriculture to the 1958 study of global trade by Gottfried Haberler, James Meade, Roberto de Oliveiro Campos, and Jan Tinbergen, in which they also examined the impact of the EEC on trade and the extent to which developing countries were participating in

---

[47] Remarks of the Chairman of the Contracting Parties, Ambassador L. Dana Wilgress, Delivered at the Conclusion of the Ninth Session of the Contracting Parties to the General Agreement on Tariffs and Trade, 8 March 1955, L/348, GDL.

[48] Remarks of the Chairman of the Contracting Parties, 8 March 1955.

[49] Warley, 'Agriculture in the GATT', 306.

[50] Geneva to External, tel. re GATT – Agriculture, 15 July 1958, RG20: A-3/1921/20–28 pt. 6, LAC.

the growth of trade. The economists noted that they could not with certainty measure the impact of protection on agricultural trade. But they could be sure of two things: industrialized countries offered extensive protection to agricultural producers; and as agricultural production increased in industrialized countries, agricultural imports became 'more and more marginal in relation to their total domestic production and consumption'.[51] This was all the justification the GATT secretariat needed to establish a committee (Committee II) to examine the use of non-tariff barriers on agriculture in order to determine their effect on international trade, and to consider the ways in which existing GATT provisions could combat agricultural protectionism.[52] There was an ulterior motive: to influence the implementation of the Common Agricultural Policy of the EEC. It was not yet fully laid out, but many feared it would be unabashedly protectionist.

The committee began meeting in 1959 and investigated the various practices used by members to protect farmers. It also examined specific agricultural commodities, including meat, dairy, wheat, sugar, and fish. This was time-consuming work. Their initial investigations established the scope and complexity of agricultural protectionism. Agriculture was protected everywhere: this was hardly a revelation. Even in countries that boasted of their efficiency in agricultural production and their international competitiveness – New Zealand and Denmark being two examples – the committee identified areas of government intervention that had a protective impact.[53] The representative for Canada noted that Canada's agricultural imports had more than doubled since 1945, and he characterized such practices as price supports, import controls, and farm credits as 'minor exceptions' in an otherwise 'liberal trade policy'. Canada's example was alarming because it was a competitive agricultural producer that was sliding towards protectionism.[54] There were other justifications for agricultural protection. Japan and West Germany claimed to be responding to postwar conditions.[55] Switzerland required a high degree of self-sufficiency with respect to food because of its commitment to

---

[51] GATT, *Trends in International Trade: Report by a Panel of Experts* (Geneva: GATT, October 1958), 87–88.

[52] Committee on Expansion of International Trade: Report of the Drafting Group on Terms of Reference, 13 November 1958, W.13/39, GDL.

[53] Expansion of Trade – Agricultural Policy. Report of Committee II on the Consultations with Denmark on Agricultural Practices, 4 May 1960, L/1176, GDA. Expansion of Trade – Agricultural Policy. Report of Committee II on the Consultations with New Zealand on Agricultural Practices, 7 March 1960, L/1152, GDL.

[54] Expansion of Trade – Agricultural Policy. Report of Committee II on the Consultation with Canada, 4 May 1960, L/1175, GDL.

[55] Expansion of Trade – Agricultural Policy. Report of Committee II on the Consultations with Japan on Agricultural Policies, 29 April 1960, L/1172. Expansion of Trade –

neutrality.[56] India was trying to increase agricultural production because it served an important role in the development of its national economy.[57] France was the most unapologetically protectionist and the Committee described its agricultural system as 'autarchy or near autarchy', noting that French agriculture was 'insulated from world market forces'.[58] Perhaps the greatest disappointment was reserved for the United States, where a gap existed between the government's stated commitment to a liberal and multilateral order and its protectionist agricultural practices, which included price support, quantitative restrictions, and export subsidies. US officials might paint their overall policies as being consistent with an international trade system, but the committee characterized it in terms similar to those used to describe France: there was 'substantial insulation of the American producer from world market forces'. The Canadian committee member harkened back to the 1955 waiver, pointing out that it had 'possibly caused more serious damage to the fulfillment of the Agreement than any other single factor'.[59]

Governments protected agriculture in many ways: export subsidies, loans, centralized marketing boards, price setting, deficiency payments, import restrictions, subsidies for agricultural production, transportation subsidies, technical assistance, and variable import levies. It also became apparent that agricultural policies were shaped by specific conditions and challenges such as Japan's population pressure, Brazil's reliance on coffee as its main export, 1.5 million poor farmers in the USA, small average farm size in France, shortage of convertible currency in India, and limits on urban employment in Belgium. Sustaining domestic agricultural sectors in such varied circumstances made it impossible to identify general rules or prescribe comprehensive norms. Overall, the committee accepted moderate levels of protection that were in place for reasons linked to security and social policy.[60]

Agricultural Policy. Report of Committee II on the Consultations with the Federal Republic of Germany, 21 May 1960, L/1198, GDL.
[56] Expansion of Trade – Agricultural Policy. Report of Committee II on the Consultation with Switzerland, 2 October 1959, L/1052, GDL.
[57] Expansion of Trade – Agricultural Policy. Report of Committee II on the Consultation with India, 24 May 1961, L/1486, GDL.
[58] Expansion of Trade – Agricultural Policy. Report of Committee II on the Consultation with France on Agricultural Policies, 25 April 1960, L/1165, GDL.
[59] Expansion of Trade – Agricultural Policy. Report of Committee II on the Consultation with the United States, 19 May 1960, L/1163, GDL. Telegram, Geneva to Secretary of State from USDel GATT Comm. II, 9 February 1960, RG59: GATT 394.41, 1960–63/ Box 172, file 394.41/2–160, NARA. The telegram reported that the tone of the discussion was friendly but 'questioning was frank and searching'.
[60] 'Suggestions for Draft Progress Report of Committee II: Effect of Protection on Trade', 18 October 1960 RG59: 716/394.41/11–1560, NARA.

Such measures, even if moderate, affected global trade in agriculture. This was particularly problematic for developing countries: 'the maintenance of the present situation ... constitutes a source of great concern, as impediments to the marketing of their products have the effect of discouraging increased production, of intensifying balance of payments difficulties and of delaying their process of economic development'.[61]

Individual GATT representatives also called attention to the inequities in global trade that agricultural protectionism created. Sir John Crawford of Australia observed that agricultural protectionism had now taken 'more extreme and more harmful forms' and, as a result, 'was less subject to fair trade rules than was the protection for secondary industry products'. A New Zealand official lamented that trade in agriculture was not fair; exporters did not have a reasonable chance in foreign markets. This situation had existed for a long time and redress was long overdue. He was hopeful of progress, but that required 'a change in attitude'.[62] Australia, New Zealand, and Denmark – GATT members who believed they were losing out – most loudly denounced protection and called for meaningful action; other representatives on the committee from the USA, the UK, and western Europe were determined to maintain protective measures. As L. V. Castle of New Zealand put it, 'were it not for Australia, New Zealand and Denmark there would be tacit agreement' to evade the issue of agricultural protection and, even worse, to legitimize such practices through more waivers.[63] But as Canadian officials reported, Australia made its case with such force that it lost the support of other agricultural exporting nations.[64]

Julio Lacarte, the representative from Uruguay who spent much of his career working in GATT, lamented that after three years Committee II had not made any recommendations. While its studies were valuable, they masked disagreement among committee members[65] and it was not obvious how it should move forward. The focus on the EEC and the embryonic CAP also impeded the committee's work because the EEC had decided it would not cooperate. A French official outlined the options

---

[61] Third Report of Committee II, 10 May 1961, L/1461, GDL.

[62] Summary record of the fourth meeting, SR. 16/4, 28 May 1960, GDL.

[63] Telegram, New Zealand House, London to Secretary of External Affairs, Wellington, Gatt Committee II, 25 March 1960, RG20: A-3/2529/4–581-50 pt. 2, LAC. Canadians also reported that US officials were not very active on Committee II: the USA was 'so far playing a minor role and does not appear particularly concerned about discrimination as a general trade problem'. Tel, Geneva to External, 17 September 1959, RG20: A-3/2527/ file 4–581-29 pt. 1.1, LAC.

[64] Geneva to External, 23 March 1961, RG25: Vol. 5650/14051–4 pt. 3, LAC.

[65] Statement by the representative of Uruguay, H. E. Mr. J. A. Lacarte, before the council on 27 September 1961, L/1572, GDL.

before the EEC with respect to agricultural trade: apply the rules; ignore the rules; try to reform the rules to make them better suit European goals and circumstances. Given the EEC's refusal to discuss the CAP while it was being set up, they could not initiate any discussion of the rules. So they opted to ignore them.[66] Sending low-ranking officials who had no policy-making responsibilities to attend committee meetings ensured that the committee could not take meaningful action.[67]

Nonetheless, the committee delivered a hard-hitting report in 1961. If agricultural protectionism was justified because of domestic social priorities, the unintended consequence was the distortion of trade patterns. While the committee could not give a precise measure, it insisted that protection had adversely affected world trade. The failure of GATT to maintain a balance between concessions and benefits for agricultural trade threw the credibility and effectiveness of GATT into doubt and sparked restiveness and frustration among GATT members.[68] Wyndham White was discouraged by the 'depressing situation' in agriculture. He doubted that appeals to governments would have any effect. He now wondered whether it might be better to 'shelve' the question until there was greater likelihood of making progress. 'Lengthy and acrimonious discussion of principles will not bring results.'[69]

The CAP was a lightning conductor for growing frustration, even resentment, about agricultural protectionism. In a plenary discussion in 1962, concerns emerged about the CAP's impact on traditional importers and world prices and about its capacity to generate more exports. John Evans, the US representative, pulled no punches when he characterized the CAP as over-protectionist and used the example of US poultry exports to Germany, which he said had virtually ceased. Australia's representative backed Evans up, characterizing the CAP as 'just about as watertight a system of protection as could be devised, at least for certain commodities'. Raul Migone of Argentina went a little further, insisting that the CAP was incompatible with GATT. The representatives of India, Brazil, Uruguay, Poland, and Yugoslavia also expressed their apprehension about the CAP. The community spokesman, Theodorus Hijzen, insisted that it was compatible with GATT but he also gave assurances

[66] Note d'information: Conclusions de la réunion de travail pour les questions concrètes et urgentes de politique commerciale (2 decembre 1960) – Préparations des prochaines travaux du Comité no. II, 14 decembre 1960, BAC007-1968-2 pt. 2, HAEU.
[67] Official Report of the United States Delegation to GATT Committee II on Expansion of Trade, October 6–20, 1960, 21 November 1960, RG59: GATT394.41, 1960–63/Box 716, file 394.41/11–1560, NARA.
[68] Third Report of Committee II, Note by the Chairman, 10 May 1961, L/1461, GDL.
[69] Statement by the Executive Secretary to the Council on 27 September 1961, L/1570/Rev.1, GDL.

that the EEC would take all of these comments seriously as it continued to map out the CAP.[70]

The real test of liberalization would come in tariff negotiations. As early as the Dillon round (1960–1961), there was pressure to liberalize agricultural trade. Australia and New Zealand did not want to take part in the round unless agriculture was included.[71] And one of the main objectives of US officials was to 'stem the tide of protectionism' by preventing the EEC from establishing a position of 'agricultural autarchy'. But US officials understood the intense domestic political pressure that European farmers exerted: they were 'past masters in the riot techniques and all sorts of revolutionary pressure group tactics'.[72] Compelling incentives were needed to convince European governments to open their markets. The timing of the Dillon round was inauspicious for exerting pressure to include agricultural goods in tariff negotiations because the USA was reluctant to criticize the newly formed EEC for reasons linked to the Cold War.[73] Moreover, the USA's negotiating position was weakened by domestic controls that limited their ability to lower tariffs. Negotiations were made even more difficult because the practice at issue was not tariffs but variable levies, and was therefore beyond GATT's scope. The final results of the round were predictably lopsided: the reduction of tariffs on manufactured goods far exceeded reductions affecting agricultural trade.[74] GATT's continued failure to include agriculture in the liberalizing project opened it up to criticism. As a US official noted, 'Probably the most sweeping complaint hurled at the GATT is that it is almost completely worthless with regard to trade in agricultural goods.' Some suggested that GATT should limit itself to industrial trade. This would 'preserve the integrity' of the organization. Others more quietly acknowledged that this was already the case; as a British memo put it, GATT 'was, and remains, the trade instrument of the industrialized countries'.[75]

---

[70] Summary record of the 12th meeting, 16 November 1962, SR.20/12, GDL.

[71] Discussion Paper for briefing meeting with Goldstein and Reifman re their Ottawa trip, 7 April 1959, RG59: Office of the Assistant Legal Adviser for Economic Affairs: Records Relating to GATT 1947–1966, Box 7, file GATT-Agriculture, NARA.

[72] Memorandum from Karl Brandt of the Council of Economic Advisers to the Chairman of the Council on Foreign Economic Policy (Randall), 21 September 1960, *FRUS 1958–60*, vol. IV, 275–276.

[73] Josling et al., *Agriculture in the GATT*, 51.

[74] Statement by the Executive Secretary to the Council on 27 September 1961, L/1570/ Rev.1, GDL.

[75] Draft memo by Norwood, 'Prospectus on GATT Review', 7 January 1963, RG59: Records of the Component Offices of the Bureau of Economic Affairs, 1941–1963/Box 4, file: Foreign Trade 1963. FT7, Tariff Negotiations GATT, NARA; Cabinet: GATT

In 1963, Committee II was replaced by a Committee on Agriculture with a mandate to recommend rules and practices that would both open world markets and increase agricultural trade. Committee members included the most competitive exporters of agricultural commodities (Canada, Australia, New Zealand, and Denmark) as well as the most determined protectionists (the EEC, Japan, and the United States). The only developing countries included were Argentina and Uruguay.[76] This committee met infrequently and accomplished little. Members could not agree on anything and as a result the committee could only make non-binding suggestions.[77]

But pressure to liberalize agricultural trade did not cease. Preparations for the Kennedy round began in 1962. Expectations for this round were sky-high in relation to diplomatic and trade goals. The United States remained committed to supporting the EEC for strategic reasons, but commercial goals had been elevated because the USA's economic position had weakened by the early 1960s.[78] President Kennedy was preoccupied with a balance-of-payments problem; one way to resolve this was to increase exports, especially agricultural exports. The USA needed markets for approximately 15 per cent of its agricultural products.[79] The main markets for US agricultural exports were in Europe, but these were increasingly restricted by the CAP and the introduction of the variable levy to stabilize prices. The chicken war between the USA and the EEC, which began in 1962, made it clear that markets for US agricultural exports (in this case, frozen chickens sold in West Germany) could be restricted and scaled back.[80]

Policy Committee: U.N. Trade Conference – Possible amendments to the G.A.T.T., 3 January 1963, CAB134/1958, TNA.

[76] Committee on Agriculture, 4 October 1963, TN64/2/Rev 1, GDL.

[77] Agriculture Committee, Report to Council, 18 December 1970, L/3472, GDL.

[78] Zeiler has studied the causes of the USA's economic and geopolitical decline and their implications for the Kennedy round negotiations. See T. W. Zeiler, *American Trade and Power in the 1960s* (New York: Columbia University Press, 1992).

[79] Summary Minutes of Meeting of Interdepartmental Committee of Under Secretaries on Foreign Economic Policy, 21 February 1962, RG59: Records of Component Offices of the Bureau of Economic Affairs, 1941–1963/Box 2, file: Interdepartmental Committee of Under Secretaries on Foreign Economic Policy – 1962, NARA. Winham makes the same point: as the US became an agricultural exporter, it pushed for liberalization. G. R. Winham, *International Trade and the Tokyo Round Negotiation* (Princeton: Princeton University Press, 1986), 148.

[80] According to Evans, the USA's chicken exports had increased five times between 1957–1961, reaching a new high value of US$68 million. Roughly three-quarters of those exports were going to West Germany. After 1962, US chicken exports to Europe plummeted. Evans, *The Kennedy Round in American Trade Policy*, 174–175. For an account of the whole chicken war, see Evans, 173–180 or L. Coppolaro, *The Making of a World Trading Power: The European Economic Community (EEC) in the GATT Kennedy Round Negotiations (1963–67)* (Farnham: Ashgate, 2013), 86–90.

The CAP was at the heart of the chicken war. The USA's concerns were expressed at the highest political levels across western Europe. US Secretary of State Rusk sent a formal note to the French Minister of Foreign Affairs, Couve de Murville, to express US opposition to a move towards 'agricultural autarchy'. He added that if the result of EEC policies was to exclude foreign agricultural products from, and sustain inefficient agricultural production in, Europe, this would be 'retrogression of the most serious kind'.[81] Christian Herter, the USA's special representative for trade, denounced EEC agricultural practices including the CAP, for violating GATT rules, to surprised senior EEC officials. Herter told them that the USA was considering retaliation unless there was progress: 'The United States cannot repeat its experience in the Dillon Round, when agriculture was ultimately laid aside.'[82] Herter and the US Under-Secretary of State Ball were equally firm in a meeting with Walter Hallstein, the president of the European Commission: unless there was agreement to include agriculture, 'there would be no tariff negotiations in 1964'.[83] Although some EEC officials urged the Commission to take action to prevent conflict, concern for the state of relations with the USA was not a strong enough consideration to shift the EEC position. Apparently, Couve de Murville dismissed entreaties to address the USA's concerns, saying they 'overdramatiz[ed] the issue and that very little really needed to be done'.[84]

Couve's cavalier attitude misread the importance that the USA attached to agricultural concessions in the Kennedy round. US President Johnson made clear that there was an agricultural bottom line: there would be no agreement in the Kennedy round without progress for 'our farms as well as our factories'.[85] GATT members agreed that agricultural goods would be part of the round. But when the round opened in 1964, they had not even been able to determine rules for negotiations.[86] Internal EEC negotiations over the CAP, which were in turn linked to larger questions about governance, further delayed

---

[81] Message from Rusk to Couve, 'Problems of Agriculture in the Atlantic Community', 7 December 1962, RG84: Paris Embassy General Records 1962/Box 20, file 500 EEC 1962, NARA.

[82] Memorandum of Conversation, 3 May 1963, RG364: Box 49, file Trade Negotiations – Rey-Marjolin Talks, 2–3 May 1963, NARA.

[83] Informal and Uncleared Memorandum for the Files: Notes on Dinner Conversation, 5 June 1963 (prepared by Deane Hinton, 3 July 1963), JMAS/95, HAEU.

[84] Memo of Conversation, Hallstein and Tuthill, 13 July 1963, JMAS-000095, Jean Monnet series, HAEU.

[85] Remarks of the President to the Public Advisory Committee on Trade Negotiations in the Flower Garden, 21 April 1964, RG20: A-3/2528/4/581–29 pt. 4.2, LAC.

[86] Trade Negotiating Committee, Meeting of the Committee at Ministerial Level, Resolution adopted 6 May 1964, TN.64/27, GDL.

progress on negotiations on agricultural goods. As Coppolaro explains, EEC members had various interests with respect to agricultural production and trade. Some members imported agricultural goods, such as grains. Others exported the same commodities. They had incompatible preferences on such matters as price stabilization and access to markets.[87] These internal struggles peaked in 1965, when France refused to attend EEC meetings. No real progress could be made in Geneva until the intra-EEC crisis was resolved, which happened in 1966.

Once negotiations began in earnest, there was another hurdle to clear: reconciling the different visions of the USA and the EEC with respect to agricultural trade. Whereas the USA focused on market access, the EEC, led by France on this issue, sought a comprehensive system of international regulation of agriculture that took into account prices, standards of self-sufficiency, surplus production, and food aid. Coppolaro distinguishes between US officials, who thought in terms of importers and exporters, and EEC officials, who thought 'in terms of a reorganization of world markets by linking domestic policies and international trade'.[88] These very different models were implicated in US–EEC negotiations on grains; it was a test case for other categories of agricultural goods, especially dairy and meat.[89]

Little progress was made in the grains, meat, or dairy commodity groups.[90] Outside these three key groups, there were tariff reductions on individual items including coffee, tea, tobacco and tobacco products, Roquefort cheese, kale, corn, cabbage, fresh or chilled peas, coconuts, and dried bananas, and thousands of other goods.[91] The main industrial countries – the EEC, Japan, Sweden, Switzerland, the UK, and the USA – made concessions affecting US$11.1 billion worth of tropical and non-tropical agricultural products. These concessions took the form of binding tariffs and reductions to tariff rates. But as Preeg explains,

[87] Coppolaro, *The Making of a World Trade Power*, 152–160.   [88] Ibid., 169.

[89] Ibid., 160–162 and 168–170. Preeg also attaches much significance to the grains negotiations because they exposed the implications of the variable levy system of the CAP. He also believed they would determine whether any progress could be made in meat and dairy categories. E. H. Preeg, *Traders and Diplomats: An Analysis of the Kennedy Round of Negotiations under the General Agreement on Tariffs and Trade* (Washington, DC: Brookings Institute, 1970), 151–152.

[90] Evans notes that the negotiations on dairy and meat began in the last six months of the round, because the USA and EEC never really got past preliminary questions, such as a date by which to present firm proposals. Evans, *The Kennedy Round in American Trade Policy*, 243. Coppolaro claims there was never any real interest on the part of either the USA or the EEC in making concessions in these two sectors. Coppolaro, *The Making of a World Trading Power*, 171.

[91] See Office of the Special Representative for Trade Negotiations, *Report on United States Negotiations, General Agreement on Tariffs and Trade, 1964–1967 Trade Conference, Volume I: General Summary; Volume II: List of Tariff Concessions Granted by the United States.*

one could not anticipate how these reductions might affect market access because there were so many non-tariff barriers used to protect domestic production, including quotas, variable levies, and licensing requirements.[92]

Because expectations for progress in agriculture were so low, and because at some points in the round it seemed likely that there would be no agreement at all, some scholars conclude that the results were positive.[93] Several GATT members also put a positive spin on what was achieved: the fact of including agricultural items in the negotiations was an important 'precedent', even a 'turning point'. Not surprisingly, these points were made by members who were among the most determined to protect their agricultural sectors.[94] There was no rush to build on the advances of the Kennedy round. The French representative urged caution and called for members to 'reflect deeply and seriously before embarking on any given path'.[95] New Zealand and Australian representatives disagreed with those who claimed there was no problem with agriculture. To pretend this was to bury one's head, ostrich-like, according to New Zealand's deputy prime minister. Their agricultural producers had been badly harmed, not only by tariff barriers but also by myriad other obstacles in use worldwide. Australia's representative, John McEwen, noted that GATT's failure to bring agriculture under its mandate was a cause of disillusionment and contravened the basic understanding on which Australia had joined in 1947. J. R. Marshall, New Zealand's minister of overseas trade, insisted that GATT must act on agriculture and thereby restore order and justice to the international trade system. To maintain the status quo meant accepting that GATT was only 'a charter for industrial trade' that excluded 'most of the nations of the world'.[96] Most GATT members did not bury their heads in the sand. They understood that agriculture 'lagged' behind the

[92] Preeg, *Traders and Diplomats*, 249–250. See Preeg, Table 15–1 on p. 250 for a summary of concessions affecting tariffs on agricultural goods.

[93] For example, Evans writes that the concessions for agricultural goods 'were greater than had appeared possible in the fall of 1966'. Still, he concluded that the results were 'far from negligible'. Evans, *The Kennedy Round in American Trade Policy*, 290.

[94] Statement by Sir Richard Powell, Permanent Secretary, Board of Trade, UK, 23 November 1967, W.24/42, GDL. Statement by M. J. F. Deniau, Member of the Commission of European Communities, 23 November 1967, W.24/59, GDL.

[95] Statement by M. Roland Nungesser, Secretary of State for Economy and Finance, France, 23 November 1967, W.24/63, GDL.

[96] Statement by the Rt. Hon. J. R. Marshall, Deputy Prime Minister and Minister of Overseas Trade of New Zealand, 23 November 1967, W.24/56; Statement by the Rt. Hon. John McEwen, Deputy Prime Minister and Minister of State for Trade and Industry of Australia, 23 November 1967, W.24/52, GDL.

liberalization of industry. The United States was among this group of well-intentioned but conflicted members.[97]

Wyndham White and the Low Bar of Expectations for Agriculture in Negotiations

Although Wyndham White had stepped down as director-general in 1968, he analysed the problem of agricultural trade while working as an advisor to the Canadian government during the Tokyo round. It is worth taking a moment to explain how he found himself in this role. It is a sad personal story.

During the twenty years when he led GATT, Wyndham White had frequently threatened to resign, usually to persuade recalcitrant members to be more forthcoming and to overcome impasses that might derail GATT. Members became somewhat cynical about these threats. But in 1967, when he announced that he would step down, he meant it. Praise for Wyndham White was fulsome. His leadership was described as inventive, tireless, determined, fertile, wise, and inspiring. He was personally credited with creating GATT and ensuring that it survived.[98] As the deputy prime minister of New Zealand put it, Wyndham White was leaving 'with honours thick upon him'. An editorial in the *New York Times* agreed that Wyndham White was leaving when he was 'still respected – and, more important, trusted by rich and poor nations alike'.[99] Wyndham White admitted that the decision to resign was 'one of the hardest decisions he had ever taken'. He was humbled and gratified that so many wanted him to stay on. The appeals of developing GATT members meant the most to him. Nonetheless, this was the right time to go, for GATT needed to prepare 'for the great challenges of the future'.[100]

[97] Statement by H. E. Mr. Hans Schaffner, Federal Councillor, Head of the Department of Public Economy of Switzerland, 22 November 1967, W.24/34. Statement by the Rt. Hon. William M. Roth, Special Trade Representative, 23 November 1967, W.24/40, GDL.

[98] Author interviews with Lacarte, 20 May 2005, Warren, 18 May 2005, and Reisman, 17 May 2005. Dam was also full of praise for Wyndham White. 'At every major turning point and in every major success in GATT history has figured an imaginative compromise, an unexpected initiative, or a face-saving formula originated by Wyndham White.' K. W. Dam, *The GATT: Law and International Economic Organization* (Chicago: University of Chicago Press, 1970), 339–340.

[99] 'International Civil Servant', *New York Times* (11 November 1967), 32.

[100] Review of the Work of the Contracting Parties and Future Program, Statement by the Rt. Hon. J. R. Marshall, deputy prime minister and minister of overseas trade of New Zealand on 23 November 1967, W.24/56; Summary record of the 19th meeting, 24 November 1967, SR.24/19, GDL.

There was no doubt that he had excelled at the difficult task of persuading an ever-larger body of nations – there were seventy-six contracting parties by 1967 – to work through compromise, concession, and cooperation. His skills had been ideally suited to the organization. But he had not always been happy in his job. He resented that his position as executive secretary had a lower status than his counterparts in other international organizations. His position was only upgraded to director-general in 1965. He did not like the fact that he was less well compensated than his counterparts.[101] He seems to have believed that by moving on, he could also move up the pay scale. At fifty-four, he still had many working years ahead of him. He explained that he hoped to continue the work he had done in GATT in the private sector: 'I hope to be able to make some contribution in finding a new and fruitful basis for relations between Europe and North America and also in the whole vital area of the economic development of the poorer parts of the world.'[102] After his departure, there were some honours – he was knighted in 1968 for service to the international community and he received honorary degrees from universities in Switzerland and the United States – but few professional offers came his way.

In 1970, James Roosevelt, the US Congressman and son of former President Franklin Roosevelt, recruited Wyndham White to join the board of Investors Overseas Service (IOS). IOS was then seeking business, diplomatic, and political luminaries in Europe and the United States to add lustre to its board. Wyndham White was apparently attracted to IOS because of its potential role in promoting economic development. But IOS was a scam and it was on the verge of imploding when Wyndham White joined. He was pushed into leadership roles, becoming president and chairman of the board. Wyndham White tried to establish it as a viable business. Although Wyndham White's probity and integrity were never in doubt, his involvement with IOS tarnished his reputation. He ended his connection with IOS in 1971. One can only surmise that he did not look back on his involvement in IOS with pride; mention of it in his entry in *Who's Who* was expunged.

During the Tokyo round, Wyndham White's friends in the Canadian delegation hired him as a consultant, mostly it seems as a favour to a once

---

[101] Wyndham White was upset that his salary was lower than those of his counterparts in other international organizations. In 1953 he asked the USA whether they could classify the ICITO as an international organization so he would not have to pay taxes on his salary. The answer was 'No.' Carl Corse, chief commercial policy staff, to Eric Wyndham White, 17 November 1953, RG59: Office of the Assistant Legal Advisor for Economic Affairs: Records Relating to GATT 1947–1966, Box 9, file International Organization, NARA.

[102] 'GATT Chief Says He Will Not Stay', *New York Times* (8 November 1967), 94.

towering man who had 'never found himself again' after his departure from GATT.[103] The memorandum that he prepared for the Canadian government was a stock-taking of the current stalemate over agriculture and included suggestions for how to move forward. He insisted that agriculture could not continue to be excluded from negotiations because it was the USA's agricultural sector that most strongly supported liberalization, in contrast to the manufacturing sector. As he put it, farmers now were 'the principal bastion of trade liberalisation' in the United States. Moreover, shifts in US exports towards services and agricultural goods, and their declining share of manufactured items, meant that the USA's interests in trade negotiations would increasingly be linked to agriculture. He also identified other agricultural exporting members of GATT – Argentina, Australia, Canada, New Zealand, and Uruguay – that wanted progress on agricultural trade in the next round of negotiations. At the very least they needed to see 'a determined effort in good faith to remove the irritants and distortions that are the product of ill-advised national agricultural policies'. Although he did not blame the EEC alone for obstructing trade liberalization in this area, the 'sacred CAP' was a big part of the problem and he singled out French thinking and the importance attached to self-reliance as the driving factor in the EEC stand on the CAP. He acknowledged that European countries well understood its 'inherent defects' and knew it was in need of reform. But any change to the CAP had to result from internal decisions; reform could not be forced on the EEC as a result of 'international bargaining'.[104]

Wyndham White was not optimistic about the likelihood of liberalizing trade in agriculture. 'The margin for meaningful negotiation in these circumstances is narrow.' But with 'a considerable effort of imagination', some advances could be made. He recommended that GATT set up a permanent committee on Trade in Agricultural Products. Its terms of reference would have to be defined carefully for it to accomplish anything. The committee should only meet in plenum once a year. The secretariat would draft a report which would be the centrepiece of the committee's work, identifying problem areas where 'adjustments' could be made. Adjustments should be negotiated directly between parties. He advised against making recommendations; if they were ignored, then the institution's credibility would be damaged. Instead the committee could make 'observations' that explained how trade policies helped or hindered the larger aims of liberalization. The hope was that they would be useful to

---

[103] Author interview with Reisman.
[104] Eric Wyndham White, 'Negotiating on Agriculture', March 1973, RG19: F-2/5394/ 8720/A278 pt. 5, LAC.

national officials 'in combating more negative national pressures'. He also tackled the difficult matter of subsidies, which sustained much agricultural production but at the price of global exchange. He proposed that negotiators rethink how they could make progress on subsidies. Rather than trying to conclude an agreement that would advance liberalization, they should focus on smaller, more realistic gains. He also recommended international commodity agreements for grains, sugar, and dairy products.[105]

Wyndham White hoped his suggestions would rebalance domestic-versus-international considerations with respect to agricultural trade. 'It is the best way to ensure that external considerations are kept in the forefront of policy makers' minds as the inevitable adjustment of national policy proceeds over the coming years.'[106] In GATT's early years, governments had made the case that international goals, linked to stability, cooperation, interdependence, and prosperity, were foremost, and this made it possible for governments to agree to liberalization measures even though there would be difficult domestic consequences. By the 1970s, that argument was less convincing as domestic economic problems, such as inflation and unemployment, intensified and the global economy was more volatile, profoundly affected by the oil shocks and the end of the Bretton Woods system. Arguments had always been made in favour of protectionism, but under these conditions they were especially convincing. GATT officials were alarmed at the surge in protectionist sentiment and policies. So were officials worldwide. Harald Malmgren, soon to be appointed deputy US trade representative, warned that protectionism could spark conflict between nations.[107] It was in this volatile environment, with people predicting trade wars and the collapse of the global trade order, that the Tokyo round began.[108]

Liberalization in Agricultural Trade Stalled in the Tokyo Round, 1973–1979

In 1973, GATT members declared their intention to launch another round, at this point called the Nixon round. As Wyndham White had anticipated, the USA insisted that agriculture be included in the negotiations. Trends in agricultural trade were worrying. First, its relative share of global trade was declining, from 34 per cent in 1950 to 14 per cent in

---

[105] Ibid.   [106] Ibid.

[107] H. B. Malmgren, 'Coming Trade Wars? (Neo-Mercantilism and Foreign Policy)', *Foreign Policy* 1 (Winter 1970/71), 116, 120–121, 135–137, 143.

[108] See, for example, statement by Peter Walker, Secretary of State for Trade and Industry, MIN (73) SR/Add. 3, 13 September 1973, GDL.

258   'Agricultural Anarchy'

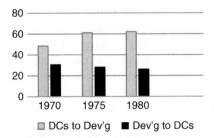

Figure 6.1 Market share of agricultural trade (percentage of total agricultural imports of recipient), 1970–1980, between developed and developing countries (DCs and Dev'g)
Source: calculated from statistical information in 'Trends and Recent Developments in the Agricultural Situation and Agricultural Trade', Note by the Secretariat, September 1981, CG.18/W/55/Rev.1, GDL.

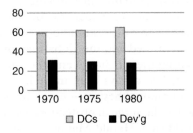

Figure 6.2 Per cent share of world agricultural trade (exports and imports), 1970–1980: developed and developing countries (DCs and Dev'g)
Source: calculated from statistical information in 'Trends and Recent Developments in the Agricultural Situation and Agricultural Trade', Note by the Secretariat, September 1981, CG.18/W/55/Rev.1, GDL.

1976.[109] Second, agricultural exports from developed countries to developing markets were increasing, whereas agricultural exports from the developing countries to developed markets were declining. Third, developed countries' share of global agricultural exports was increasing, whereas that of developing countries fell slightly (see Figure 6.1). In other words, developed countries were exporting more and importing less relatively and developing countries were importing more and exporting less relatively (see Figure 6.2). Although US representatives pushed the issue, concern about agricultural trade was widespread. As a Polish

[109] Winham, *International Trade and the Tokyo Round Negotiation*, 147.

official observed, agriculture was 'one of the darkest – if not the darkest – spots on the international trade scene'.[110]

Concerns about agricultural protectionism invariably turned to the CAP. Previously, the EEC had refused to discuss it on the grounds that it was not fully formed. By the start of the Tokyo round, it had been completely phased in. The EEC's most effective form of protection was subsidies, which resulted in high food prices and production that exceeded demand. The scale of the problem was conveyed in descriptions of mountains of butter, wheat, and sugar and lakes of wine and olive oil in Europe. The EEC also subsidized agricultural exports – sometimes by as much as two-thirds of the price – so that they could compete internationally against agricultural products coming from more efficient agricultural producers in Australia, New Zealand, or the United States. The internal contradictions of the CAP that resulted in expensive over-production were resolved by exporting their subsidized surplus. This was a case of adding insult to injury, and it was no surprise that GATT members complained bitterly about EEC agricultural policy.

The EEC position in the Tokyo round was to preserve the CAP. The French government insisted that the CAP was 'sacrosanct'.[111] Sir Christopher Soames, the EC commissioner for external relations, explained at the opening meeting of the round that the EEC favoured the expansion of agricultural trade, but only in conformity with existing agricultural policies. In case there was any doubt that the CAP was off the table, he added: 'These principles and the mechanisms which support them we consider to be a matter of internal policy and we do not consider them to be the object of international negotiations.'[112]

The EEC made it even more difficult to include agricultural goods by insisting that they be a separate category in the negotiations. The logic behind the EEC position was to prevent linkages between negotiations over agricultural goods and negotiations in other sectors. This was one way to minimize pressure to make concessions on agricultural goods. The EEC view prevailed.[113]

Developing countries wanted freer trade in agriculture, especially for tropical commodities. Even though tropical products had been singled out as a 'special and priority sector' in the declaration that had launched

---

[110] Summary Record of the fifth meeting, 27 February 1970, SR26.5, GDL.

[111] 'The Nine Draw their Gatt Guns', *The Economist* (30 June 1973), 54.

[112] Ministerial meeting Tokyo, 12–14 September 1973, Statements delivered at first meeting, MIN (73) SR/Add.1, GDL.

[113] D. A. Deese, *World Trade Politics: Power, Principles, and Leadership* (London: Routledge, 2008), discusses the leverage that comes from linkages (p. 34). This practice 'increases the stakes' of negotiations.

the Tokyo round, developing country representatives were sceptical that there would be significant progress. Doubts were based on past experience. As the representative from Nigeria put it, 'despite our active participation ... we might at the end be left to pick up the crumbs from the master's table as we did in the Kennedy Round'.[114] His choice of words made clear his belief that GATT and the global trade system sustained conditions of injustice and exploitation. The representative from Indonesia insisted that removing barriers on such goods would be just and effective and would cause little harm to developed countries. Representatives from developing countries objected to privileging industrial commodities and the developed world. The representative for Pakistan noted that the commitment to development had waned since the 1960s; the new decade had been marked by a 'loss of momentum', and initial optimism had been replaced by disillusionment.[115] The Tokyo round was an important chance for GATT 'to dispel the historical impression in the third world that the GATT is a club for the rich'. The developing world might not have been united in their goals or tactics, but the cautious warning sounded by the representative of Fiji struck a chord. Good intentions and 'pious resolutions' would not suffice. The onus rested on the developed countries to act: 'until such time that developed countries sincerely and seriously dedicate themselves to finding ways and means of bridging the gap between the haves and the have-nots – not so much by giving out gifts but by creating conditions whereby because of hard work the have-nots will achieve what is rightfully due to them'.[116]

Developing countries prepared a 'shopping list' of 4,400 agricultural and manufactured items in which they were particularly interested. These lists mostly involved trade with the EEC, Japan, and the USA, as well as Australia, Austria, Canada, Finland, New Zealand, Norway, and Sweden. The items included food products such as tea, coffee, sugar, meat, cocoa, fish, and spices as well as processed and manufactured food commodities. Concessions were made in the agricultural category by lowering tariffs and extending preferential treatment, although some items did not benefit much, including tobacco, fish products, and

[114] Statements delivered at the Fifth Meeting, Ministerial Meeting, Tokyo, 12–14 September 1973, MIN (73) SR/Add. 5, 24 October 1973, GDL.
[115] Ministerial meeting Tokyo, 12–14 September 1973, Statements delivered at first meeting, MIN (73) SR/Add.1. Sayward also identifies the end of the 1960s as the time when people involved in the World Bank lost faith that the gap between rich and poor could be closed. Staples, *The Birth of Development*, 44.
[116] Statements delivered at the Fifth Meeting, Ministerial Meeting, Tokyo, 12–14 September 1973, MIN (73) SR/Add. 5, 24 October 1973, GDL.

sugar.[117] Representatives of the developing countries complained about a lack of progress in the areas most relevant to them.[118] Their complaints were justified. Negotiations did reduce tariff protection on agricultural commodities; the average reduction was by 32 per cent. While this was impressive, it applied to only 30 per cent of all agricultural products and it did not take into account the many non-tariff barriers (NTBs) that affected the flow of agricultural commodities.[119] Furthermore, the problem of subsidies, which enabled inefficient producers to dominate global trade in agriculture, was not resolved. GATT members agreed as a general principle that if a country began to export more than its fair share of a particular agricultural product, it meant that the subsidy was too high.[120] But this was entirely self-regulating and left a lot of room for interpretation.[121]

The delegates also tried to define principles to regulate agricultural trade. A draft text aimed to strike a balance between openness and protection. The draft acknowledged the role of agriculture in stimulating development and the far-ranging commitment to ensuring a decent income for farmers. Rather that pitting domestic and global interests against one another, the draft argued that international cooperation would help to realize domestic agendas with respect to agriculture. The text went on to identify shared goals: assuring food security; expanding agricultural trade in an equitable manner; increasing the efficiency of agricultural production; stabilizing prices; and rationalizing domestic farm policies with international trade. It called for the establishment of an International Agricultural Consultative Council within GATT where members would report changes to their agricultural policies, submit their disputes, and provide data on domestic agricultural production.[122] But there was significant opposition and the draft was shelved. All that was left were empty calls for cooperation. As the chairman of the agricultural group explained, 'the Group had taken its work as far as it could'.[123] That was not very far at all.

---

[117] The results are analysed in GATT, *The Tokyo Round of Multilateral Negotiations*, 156–163.
[118] Developments in the Multilateral Trade Negotiations: Note by Secretariat, 22 March 1979, COM.TD/W/290, GDL.
[119] GATT, *The Tokyo Round of Multilateral Trade Negotiations*, 120.
[120] Developments in the Multilateral Trade Negotiations: Note by Secretariat, 22 March 1979, COM.TD/W/290, GDL.
[121] 'Trade Talks: Paris Willing?' *The Economist* (16 December 1978), 103.
[122] Multilateral Agricultural Framework, Note by the Secretariat, 15 December 1978, MTN/INF/43, GDL.
[123] Meeting of April 1979, Summing up by the Chairman, 3 April 1979, MTN/AG/10, GDL.

US negotiators looked on the bright side of the round. Although the USA would have liked to have seen even more progress in 'resolving the trade problems in the agricultural sector', there had been more progress in this round than earlier ones. The spokesperson for the EEC glossed over agriculture, a telling omission. The representatives of agricultural exporting countries were less happy. New Zealand's spokesperson noted his country's disappointment with the lack of progress in removing either tariff or non-tariff barriers. Australia's representative underlined the underachievement in agriculture, stating that concessions amounted to limited gains. He was disappointed that the best that could be agreed upon was for the director-general to consult with interested parties about ways to cooperate more fully in the future. He highlighted the difference between negotiations over industrial items – with a very specific course of action mapped out for industrial trade after the round, even though 'there were no demonstrable problems' – and the vague generalities and unclear way forward for agriculture, 'where real problems had been in existence for decades'. In the opinion of Australian officials, GATT's treatment of industrial and agricultural goods was inconsistent, and that disparity had widened as a result of the Tokyo round.[124] A new category of haves and have-nots had been created among GATT members: developed industrial states who benefited greatly and agricultural exporters who gained little.

Scholarly assessments were also pessimistic about what had been achieved. Gilbert Winham concludes that agriculture was not one of the many achievements of the round: 'The participating nations ended the Tokyo Round about as far apart on agricultural trade as they were at the beginning of the negotiation.'[125] John Warley echoes this conclusion, 'Agriculture emerged as it entered: the most highly protected major sector in national economies, the most undisciplined area of international commerce, and the cause of some of the most fractious and dangerous frictions in international economic relations.'[126]

Falling Out over Agriculture at the 1982 Ministerial Meeting

Not only had the Tokyo round done little to advance the liberalization of trade in agriculture, but many feared that agricultural protectionism could spark global confrontations and undermine the multilateral basis

---

[124] Summary record of 4th meeting, 28 November 1979, SR.35/4; Summary Record of 5th meeting, 29 November 1979, SR.35/5, GDL.
[125] Winham, *International Trade and the Tokyo Round Negotiation*, 255.
[126] Warley, 'Agriculture in the GATT', 310–311.

of GATT. Winham likens the standoff between developed nations over agriculture to the situation in the Balkans before the First World War: 'it is the place in the system where conflict could most easily touch off a much wider war'.[127] The status quo could not be maintained. As a result, in 1982 Olivier Long charged the Consultative Group of Eighteen (CG18) with the task of evaluating agriculture in 'a general and global manner'.[128] Within the CG18, some members called for decisive action, others supported a more moderate course, and as always there was support for further study, a well-known delaying tactic. While some representatives identified specific problems and proposed solutions, others insisted these same issues were non-negotiable. The committee had to prepare a draft programme and agenda for the ministerial meeting at the end the year. They used an Australian document as the basis for discussion: this included a general checklist of items, such as waivers, surplus production, export subsidies, reconciling national policies with GATT articles, and the creation of a specific Agricultural Committee.[129] But even a general checklist divided GATT members. The committee was unable to 'present an agricultural work programme' to national ministers.[130]

Political will was needed to solve the problems of agricultural protectionism. GATT called a meeting of ministers, the first in over a decade. In the days immediately preceding the meeting, signs were not positive for those wanting a breakthrough in agriculture. The EEC proposed amendments that removed, qualified, or diluted the provisions dealing with liberalizing agricultural trade in the draft ministerial statement. The government of Australia denounced the EEC's proposals.[131] The EEC–Australia clash was becoming a recurring confrontation, but on this occasion the main antagonists were the USA and EEC, in what some predicted could become 'The next transatlantic war'.[132] A Canadian report agreed that the conflict between the two economic superpowers had escalated from 'polite discussions ... to threats of reprisals, boycotts and an outright trade war'.[133]

[127] Winham, *International Trade and the Tokyo Round Negotiation*, 362.
[128] Co-operation on Agriculture in the GATT: Note by the Secretariat, 8 April 1982, CG.18/W/68, GDL.
[129] Agricultural Work Programme: Check-List of Items on Which Clarification is Needed, 21 June 1982, CG.18/W/70, GDL.
[130] Note of the Nineteenth Meeting of the Consultative Group of Eighteen, 26 July 1982, CG.18/19, GDL.
[131] Preparations for the Ministerial Meeting, Communication from the European Communities, 19 November 1982, C/W/404, and Preparations for the Ministerial Meeting, Communication from Australia, 22 November 1982, C/W/405, GDL.
[132] 'The Next Transatlantic War', *The Economist* (20 November 1982), 33.
[133] O. Bertin, 'Farm Policies Under Strain', *Globe and Mail* (22 November 1982).

Trade ministers from eighty-eight countries, supported by thousands of advisers, lobbyists, and politicians, devoted four days to the challenge of agricultural protectionism. But members also recognized that much more was at stake. As the chair of the session explained: their work was to preserve the 'credibility of the GATT system'.[134] Nonetheless, members clashed openly. France's trade minister, Michel Jobert, questioned the purpose of the meeting and attacked the USA and its 'dogmatic liberalism'.[135] US Secretary of State Schultz told France's President Mitterand that he deplored Jobert's obstructionism, after which Jobert apparently became slightly more accommodating.[136] But no agreement was reached. One especially divisive issue concerned agricultural subsidies. The USA wanted to phase out export subsidies for agricultural goods, but the EEC refused to discuss them. Sir Roy Denman, the EEC's main negotiator, called farm subsidies 'a fact of life'.[137] The negotiations seemed doomed, with pundits once more predicting the demise of GATT. In closed all-night meetings, members began to reach compromise positions on other issues, but they remained deadlocked on agriculture. US officials spoke ominously of an imminent farm trade war. A fifth day was added to the meeting, in the hope that outstanding disagreements over agriculture could be resolved.

Alan MacEachen, the Canadian minister of external affairs, chaired the ministerial meeting. He announced that a compromise agreement had been reached. Ministers agreed to more fully integrate agriculture into the multilateral trade system, make GATT rules in this area more effective, regulate export competition, and improve access to foreign markets. In short, they wanted to make global trade in agriculture face fewer obstacles and take place on a more level playing field. The body that would achieve this was a Committee on Agriculture, open to all GATT members.[138]

The backlash was immediate. The Australian spokesman denounced the declaration as little more than 'a package of words that were offering to all contracting parties the license of interpretation'. His criticisms spanned the entirety of the ministers' efforts, but he singled out agriculture as an area where no firm undertaking had been made. The depth of Australia's frustration was evident when the deputy prime minister quit the gathering. Unlike Australia, the EEC endorsed the declaration,

[134] Summary Record of the First Meeting, 22 November 1982, SR.38/1, GDL.
[135] C. Farnsworth, 'Discordant Notes Mar Trade Talks', *New York Times* (25 November 1982), 1.
[136] C. Farnsworth, 'A Reporter's Notebook: Behind the Scenes at the GATT Trade Talks in Geneva', *New York Times* (5 December 1982), 8.
[137] C. Farnsworth, 'GATT Frustrates US So Far', *New York Times* (26 November 1982), 1.
[138] Ministerial Declaration, 29 November 1982, L/5424, GDL.

although with respect to agriculture this was conditional: 'this was not a commitment to any new negotiation or obligation in relation to agricultural products'.[139] In fact, EEC countries were not unified; Britain and Germany accepted codes regulating the use of agricultural subsidies.[140] But that dissent was muted because the EEC spoke through a single representative.

Agricultural Subsidies and the Committee on Trade in Agriculture

Despite doubt about the significance of the compromise agreement, a committee on trade in agriculture was established in 1983.[141] To tackle the problem of agricultural trade, it had to extend GATT's reach into the domestic sphere because domestic agricultural policies directly affected global trade. As the chair of the committee explained, GATT had to uphold 'the permissible or acceptable limits of the impact of domestic agricultural policies on trade'.[142] Predictably, there was opposition. Some pointed out that the relationship between the domestic and international spheres worked in two directions: international trade conditions, which were far from stable, also had an impact on domestic economies. That had to be taken into account when determining whether domestic policy hurt or benefited world trade. More surprisingly, there was support to ensure 'that the internal and external costs of domestic policy were as low as possible, since this would require respect for the interests of other trading partners and observance of some disciplines regarding domestic production policies'.[143] A glimmer of internationalist thinking was appearing in recognition of the damage caused by the dominant national frame of reference in setting agricultural policy.

The committee focused on subsidies, including export subsidies, which were widely used. The rationale behind their use was already well known: subsidies were linked to domestic social policy. No one criticized this purpose. But there were unintended consequences, such as overproduction and deliberate cultivation of marginal land, which

---

[139] Summary record of the Ninth Meeting, Held in the Geneva International Conference Centre, 29 November 1982, SR.38/9, 14 December 1982.

[140] 'Making Sense of the Mad Gatter's Tea Party', *The Economist* (4 December 1982), 75.

[141] The membership of this committee included virtually all members of the GATT. See AG/INF/1, GDL.

[142] Summary of Points Raised during the Meeting from 5 to 8 March 1984: Note by the Secretariat, 16 March 1984, AG/W/6, GDL.

[143] Interestingly, the minutes of the meeting do not identify the speakers. Meeting of Committee at Senior Policy Level: 2–3 April 1984: Note by the Secretariat, 11 May 1984, AG/W/7, GDL.

exacerbated the challenge of opening markets to agricultural exports.[144] The committee identified problems with the way GATT dealt with subsidies: it did so on a case-by-case basis, vague concepts guided their use, and rules only came into effect after a subsidy was in place. Rather than limiting the use of subsidies, the ineffectiveness of GATT rules had actually 'encourage[d] the use of subsidies by an increasing number of countries'.[145] The committee's recommendation was to bring more of these practices under GATT's supervision so that it could enforce its rules. That same approach was applied to other measures, including quantitative restrictions, voluntary export restraints, and state trading practices.[146]

The committee subsequently elaborated on ways to make GATT rules more effective and to achieve a better balance between domestic and international benefits. It proposed banning all direct export subsidies. It tried to clarify vague terms and standards. For instance, it proposed that all countries should make a minimum access commitment for agricultural imports. The suggested minimum was 10 per cent of consumption, which would permit countries to be 90 per cent self-sufficient. In addition, they suggested that all NTBs should be translated into tariffs. Finally, it recommended that the dispute resolution mechanism should be strengthened.[147]

Support evaporated once members were confronted with specific measures. Some of the proposals were criticized on the grounds that they would be ineffective, unworkable, and counter-productive. The committee's efforts to limit their use would, somehow and counter-intuitively, 'perpetuate' and legitimize their use and would therefore not liberalize trade. Other suggestions were deemed to be too sweeping and blunt. For example, the ban on export subsidies was 'too simplistic and idealistic given the divergence of national policies'. Other recommendations were deemed to be unworkable: converting NTBs into tariffs fell into this category. Really there were two underlying objections. First, there was concern that if the committee's recommendations were introduced, then GATT's reach would extend into the domestic sphere. Second, there was a deeply rooted sense that agricultural trade could not be normalized. The

---

[144] See Manning, *Against the Grain* for a thoughtful and critical discussion of the effects of subsidies on agricultural production.

[145] Draft Report of the Committee on Trade in Agriculture: Note by the Secretariat, 13 February 1984, AG/W/5, GDL.

[146] Committee on Trade and Agriculture: Recommendations adopted by the Committee Meeting at Senior Policy Level on 15 November 1984, 16 November 1984, L/5732, GDL.

[147] Recommendations: Draft Elaboration: Note by the Secretariat, Revision, 12 July 1985, AG/W/9/Rev.1, GDL.

way that liberalization applied to manufactured goods 'was not realistically applicable to agriculture'.[148] And yet the exceptional situation in global agricultural trade was clearly not sustainable.

While protectionist agricultural practices and policies were widespread, the EEC stood out as the principal perpetrator of the distorted and iniquitous patterns of agricultural trade. The EEC was becoming the dominant agricultural exporter in the world even though much of its production was not competitive, surpassing producers such as Australia in exports of wheat, meat, and sugar and the United States in exports of wheat. When the EEC sold its exports in developing countries, they undercut local farmers. Because of its increased production, the markets of the EEC were also largely supplied with domestic products. Tensions between the USA and the EEC were acute, and accusations flew across the Atlantic. The EEC proposed that the global agricultural pie should be sliced up, an indication of the extent to which competition and openness had retreated in the thinking and policies of governments. According to *The Economist*, this kind of cure 'was worse than the disease'.[149] Global trade patterns were being distorted, developing countries were being cut out, and international relations were aggravated by agriculture.

The Cairns Group of Fair Trading Nations

Leadership on agricultural liberalization would have to come from members other than the USA and EEC. Australia stepped up.[150] Australia was an exporter of foodstuffs and animal products, but its access to markets was increasingly precarious. Australia's market share in western Europe had declined after the establishment of the EEC. It dropped again when Britain, traditionally their principal market, joined the EEC in 1973. To make matters worse, the EEC's practice of selling its surplus and highly subsidised agricultural production overseas displaced Australian agricultural exports in markets in Southeast Asia. As Australian Prime Minister

---

[148] Summary of Points Raised during the Meeting of the Committee held on 19–21 February 1985: Note by the Secretariat, 26 March 1985, AG/W/12, GDL. Summary of Points Raised during the Meeting of the Committee held on 17–19 September 1985: Note by the Secretariat, 22 October 1985, AG/W/14, GDL. Once again the minutes do not identify individual speakers.

[149] 'Dump the Farmers', *The Economist* (5 March 1983), 19.

[150] Deese describes Australia as one of several 'important secondary players' and identifies Australia and the Cairns Group as structural leaders with respect to agriculture. D. Deese, *World Trade Politics: Power, Principles and Leadership*, 72, 153. Higgott and Cooper call the Cairns Group a 'third force'. R. Higgott and A. F. Cooper, 'Middle Power Leadership and Coalition Building: Australia, the Cairns Group, and the Uruguay Round of Trade Negotiations', *International Organization* 44 (4) (Autumn 1990), 613.

Table 6.2   *The Cairns Group*

	Agriculture as percentage of GDP	Agriculture as percentage of exports
Argentina	13	73
Australia	5	39
Brazil	11	41
Canada	3	18
Chile	–	25
Colombia	20	67
Fiji	–	–
Hungary	17	23
Indonesia	26	21
Malaysia	–	38
New Zealand	11	68
Philippines	26	26
Thailand	17	54
Uruguay	12	58

Source: R. A. Higgott and A. F. Cooper, 'Middle Power Leadership and Coalition Building: Australia, the Cairns Group, and the Uruguay Round of Trade Negotiations', *International Organization* 44 (4) (Autumn 1990), 602.

Bob Hawke explained to an audience in Brussels, Australian farmers were being squeezed.[151] In 1986, Canberra established a coalition from a motley group of agricultural exporting countries – Argentina, Australia, Brazil, Canada, Chile, Colombia, Fiji, Hungary, Indonesia, Malaysia, New Zealand, the Philippines, Thailand, and Uruguay – called the Cairns Group (see Table 6.2). They pushed for fair trade in agriculture. As John Dawkins, Australia's trade minister, put it, the goal was to 'promote a better deal for all our farmers and, we assume, a better deal for farmers everywhere'.[152] There were differences among them in terms of standards of living, political systems, and trade policies. They were not all equally committed to trade liberalization. Brazil, for example, strove for self-sufficiency in food, blocked food imports, and taxed agricultural exports.[153] Canadian support was also qualified. But for all of them, agriculture was critical to national economic activity, and agricultural exports accounted for a sizeable share of their overall exports.[154] The

[151] 'EEC Trade: Beefed Up for a Fight', *The Economist* (9 February 1985), 46.
[152] P. Walters, 'Farming Nations Seek Reforms: Talks in Australia on World Agricultural Reform', *The Guardian* (28 August 1986).
[153] O. Morton, 'Brazil: Consumer Interests and Export Constraints' in Skogstad and Cooper (eds.), *Agricultural Trade: Domestic Pressures and International Tensions*, 141–142.
[154] Higgott and Cooper, 'Middle Power Leadership', 601–604.

group directed its criticisms towards the United States and the EEC and the extensive subsidies that they used, although the EEC was sometimes singled out as the worst offender and more serious obstacle. The president of Uruguay did not mince words when he said: 'The U.S. has passed some bad laws, but Europe is our historical problem.'[155]

The Cairns Group was vocal in the lead-up to the Uruguay round, beginning with the ministerial meeting in Punte del Este, Uruguay, in 1986. Agriculture was not the only controversial item under consideration. Ministerial representatives acknowledged that the world trade regime was at a perilous juncture. Unless GATT could respond to long-standing and pressing problems, it ran the risk of becoming irrelevant. As the US trade representative Clayton Yeutter put it, the decisions made at this meeting would determine whether GATT would remain 'a functional, dynamic institution serving the interests of its members' or deteriorate into 'a static and passive association that is irrelevant to the needs of international trade'.[156] No one denied that the problems confronting agriculture were also urgent. Australia's minister singled out the world's strongest economies in defining the current problems in global agricultural trade. He equated farm subsidies with welfare. He decried the tendency to shelter farmers from the need to adapt in order to remain efficient and competitive. Instead, farmers in the world's richest countries had been 'cocooned ... in a fool's paradise'.[157] The EEC and the USA gave out subsidies worth approximately US$25 billion. One could split hairs over which was the biggest offender, but both had contributed substantially to the 'madness' in global trade in agriculture.[158] Dawkins' words echoed those of Yeutter about the potential irrelevance of GATT, which he said 'now borders on a voluntary agreement for a powerful and privileged few who invoke its provisions only when it suits them to do so'. New Zealand's representative reminded ministers of the impact of current agricultural policies on developing countries. The issue of agricultural trade was bound up in economic justice.[159] The EEC spokesman agreed with many of the general sentiments, but insisted that the fundamental elements of the EEC's agriculture

[155] P. Lewis, 'Food Surplus May Bankrupt European Bloc', *New York Times* (27 December 1986), 1.
[156] US: Statement by Ambassador Clayton Yeutter, 15 September 1986, Min (86)/ST/5, GDL.
[157] Australia: Statement by Hon. J. S. Dawkins, 16 September 1986, MIN (86)/ST/15, GDL.
[158] Developments in the Trading System: April – September 1986, Note by the Secretariat, C/W/502, GDL. See also Kenyon and Lee, *The Struggle for Trade Liberalisation in Agriculture*, 60, for Bob Hawke's characterization of the economic madness pervading agriculture. More generally see Kenyon and Lee, chapter 2.
[159] New Zealand: Statement at the Meeting of the GATT Contracting Parties at Ministerial Level, 16 September 1986, MIN(86)/ST/8, GDL.

policy were not negotiable.[160] France's minister of trade also placed clear limits on negotiations affecting the CAP. He insisted that the approach to a new round must be 'reasonable', which had nothing to do with efficiency or fairness. As he explained: 'With respect to agriculture, to be reasonable implies that some partners must not demand that some other partners should dismantle essential components or instruments of [their] agricultural policy.'[161]

GATT members squared off in familiar and new ways. The USA insisted that agricultural subsidies be included in negotiations. Yeutter suggested that world trade would be plunged into chaos unless there was a breakthrough on agriculture.[162] The EEC refused to include subsidies, primarily because of French opposition, insisting that if subsidies were put on the table the CAP would come under attack. Michel Noir, France's minister of trade, threatened to walk out.[163] With crisis looming, a compromise was reached whereby subsidies would be included on the agenda for the eighth round of negotiations, without necessarily considering their elimination.[164] The compromise wording was celebrated in some quarters. Even Dawkins referred to it as a turning point, although a few days later he likened the current situation in agriculture to an arms race that threatened everyone's security and well-being.[165]

Although several scholars credit the Cairns Group, and Australia in particular, with timely and effective influence in bringing about this preliminary agreement on the round's agenda, the softening EEC position owed much to mounting internal pressure. Simply put, the CAP had become insupportable. The guarantee of high prices encouraged inefficient over-production and by the mid-1980s the cumulative effect was staggering. The food stockpile had reached over twenty million tonnes, mostly comprised of wheat, butter, beef, and milk. Subsidies and other support measures used up approximately two-thirds of the total EEC budget. Sicco Mansholt, a former EC commissioner for agriculture, admitted that the agricultural situation in Europe was 'crazy'.[166]

---

[160] EEC: Statement by Mr. De Lercq, 17 September 1986, MIN (86)/ST/38, GDL.

[161] France: Statement by Mr. Michel Noir, 17 September 1986, MIN (86)/ST/32, GDL.

[162] P. Knox, 'Complex Trade Talks Unravel at Uruguay Meeting', *Globe and Mail* (17 September 1986), A12.

[163] F. Dearden, 'Lyng Criticizes France on Trade', 18 September 1986, *Journal of Commerce*, 2A.

[164] P. Knox, 'GATT Delegates Near Accord on Reducing Food Subsidies', *Globe and Mail* (19 September 1986), A5; P. Knox, 'Big Obstacle Overcome on GATT Guidelines', *Globe and Mail* (20 September 1986), A7.

[165] G. Greene, 'World Trade Talks Give Farmers Some Hope', *The Advertiser* (22 September 1986); 'Dawkins Tells UK to End Farm Trade War', *Sydney Morning Herald* (26 September 1986), 2.

[166] Lewis, 'Food Surplus May Bankrupt European Bloc'.

However, the EEC's willingness to include agriculture in the round of negotiations did not mean that the liberalization of agricultural trade would be straightforward.

Progress and Protests over Agriculture in the Uruguay Round, 1986–1994

The Uruguay round differed from the previous seven rounds in terms of its scope and ambition. Over 100 countries participated, and the mandate was broadened to include services and intellectual property. The complexity of the issues, and the controversy they engendered, dragged out the round over eight years, thirteen if one includes the five preparatory years needed to launch the round. In other ways, the Uruguay round was typical. Pressure ran high, crises were frequent, and accusations of bad conduct were common. It was also characterized by lapsed deadlines, which in turn required renewals of negotiating authority, delays while new administrations got up to speed, and changes in negotiators, all of which slowed progress. There were also distractions that affected the round, such as the end of the Cold War and the First Gulf War. Crisis and deadlines had been instrumental to the success of previous rounds. Stark calculations of gains and losses were made in the capitals of GATT members, often providing just the right pressure to encourage a little more flexibility or a few more concessions so as to make agreement possible.

Negotiations over agriculture contributed to the complexity, controversy, acrimony, and duration of the Uruguay round. Josling, Tangermann, and Warley claim that agriculture was the 'issue above all others' that eluded agreement and dragged out the round.[167] Despite threats, accusations, walkouts, intervention at the highest political level, and repeated warnings that the failure of the round would have cataclysmic effects for global trade, the two main parties – the USA and the EEC – did not budge. The USA insisted on liberalizing agricultural trade. Clayton Yeutter declared that no agreement was better than a bad agreement. He also made it clear that the USA was not without options. It could pursue the bilateral route, as it was then doing in free trade negotiations with Canada. The USA could also fight back: Yeutter threatened retaliatory action.[168] France took the lead for the EEC, insisting that the CAP was not on the table. It was strongly backed by Ireland; other EEC members offered varying degrees of support.

---

[167] Josling, Tangermann, and Warley, *Agriculture in the GATT*, 133.
[168] Details in Preeg, *Traders in a Brave New World*, 81–84.

Although the main impasse was between the USA and EEC, Japan also held back liberalization because of its subsidies to rice farmers. Rice production was a nation-wide activity, done mostly on a small scale. Not only did seven out of eight farmers grow rice, but so did 16 per cent of all Japanese families. Inefficient production required massive subsidies to ensure that rice farmers remained solvent. The effect of subsidies was to raise prices. *The Economist* calculated that Japanese consumers paid six times the world price for rice, and the average person in Japan consumed almost 150 pounds of rice per year – a situation amounting to an US$800 yearly tax on each household. Seventy-two per cent of the income of rice farmers came from government subsidies. The Japanese lobbied for a food security clause, whereby a nation would have the right to ensure access to 100 per cent of domestic demand for staple items such as rice.

Electoral concerns largely explained this position. Despite a long-standing majority in the Diet, the Liberal Democratic Party depended on support from rural areas to stay in power.[169] It relied on farm cooperatives across Japan to deliver votes. Because all political parties in Japan supported agricultural protectionism – specifically the right to produce all food domestically – these cooperatives could easily transfer their support from one party to another.[170] Yeutter countered that consumers should have a choice and that the market should play a larger role in Japanese rice production. Consumers could have security of supply by opening their markets. This argument did not convince many Japanese voters. According to Christina Davis, their primary concerns were not price and choice, but food quality and safety.[171] The common refrain in the early 1980s was that Japan could not import a single grain of rice and the Diet reinforced this hardline stance by passing resolutions in 1980 and 1984 in favour of increasing agricultural self-sufficiency.[172]

The impasse over agriculture contributed to the decision to hold a ministerial meeting in Montreal in 1988. It was optimistically assumed to be a mid-term review. Progress was made on a number of difficult issues, including intellectual property and services. But discussions on agriculture stalled. Yeutter insisted that all trade-distorting subsidies had to be removed. The EEC spokesman denounced US negotiating tactics as bullying and the USA's aims as unrealistic. The EEC negotiator walked out, saying he wanted nothing to do with the US officials.[173] There was

[169] 'Of rice and men', *The Economist* (28 July 1990), 56.
[170] C. L. Davis, *Food Fights Over Free Trade: How International Institutions Promote Agricultural Trade Liberalization* (Princeton and Oxford: Princeton University Press, 2003), 123–124.
[171] Ibid., 126–127.   [172] Ibid., 181.   [173] Preeg, *Traders in a Brave New World*, 86–87.

some indication that the USA and the EEC were in fact willing to agree to disagree. When they emerged from closed meetings, US and EEC officials informed the others that they could go ahead with everything except agriculture. The representative from Brazil – a member of the Cairns Group – said that without an agreement on agriculture, there would be no agreement.[174] Thus, a small but important member of GATT threatened to derail the round unless there was meaningful agreement on the liberalization of agricultural trade.

The meeting in Montreal focused primarily on the USA and EEC, to the relief of Japanese negotiators, who tried to adopt a low profile in the hope of deflecting attention from themselves. But Japanese determination was made clear. The Diet passed a unanimous resolution against opening the market to rice imports.[175]

There was no progress in agricultural discussions until the next ministerial meeting in Brussels in 1990. Arthur Dunkel explained that the Uruguay round was in crisis and that unless rapid success was made to unblock negotiations on agriculture (as well as textiles and services) they would all lose.

The developing countries, including the countries engaged in reforms, would be the main victims. But the major economies would also lose. 'The losses will not suddenly appear overnight. It will be a slow erosion, and that is the danger, because this erosion is difficult to perceive immediately.'[176]

Social protest movements had not been a serious factor affecting GATT's work. That changed in the 1980s with agriculture. In 1988, 2,000 farmers from twenty-four countries gathered to protest the reduction of subsidies at the Montreal meeting. Now, 25,000 farmers gathered in Brussels to protest the reduction of subsidies. They marched into the city centre. They were met by barricades, barbed wire, and mounted riot police. As the marchers advanced, there was vandalism and anxious Belgian police eventually used water cannons and tear gas against the farmers.[177]

People involved in the negotiations predicted that the round would fail, with 'gattastrophic' implications for the global economy. The spectre of the Great Depression of the 1930s was frequently invoked. At the end of the Brussels meeting, Yeutter announced that the round had 'one foot in the grave and the other one almost there'.[178] But rather than cancel the

[174] Ibid., 92, 138–140.   [175] Davis, *Food Fights Over Free Trade*, 185, 186.
[176] 'Arthur Dunkel Warns of Dangerous Erosion of Economic Prospects if Negotiations Fail', GATT/1496, 28 November 1990, GDL.
[177] P. Torday and D. Usborne, 'Farmers Riot as World Trade Talks Head for Collapse', *The Independent* (4 December 1990), 22.
[178] J. Zarocostas, 'No Green Light Yet for GATT Talks: Agriculture Remains the Major Obstacle to Resumption of Suspended Discussions', *Globe and Mail* (15 January 1991).

round, Dunkel suspended it in the hope that he would find a way to get talks back on track. Or, as Dunkel had earlier put it, the death of the old GATT might not be tragic if a new, and better, GATT that included agriculture, textiles, services, and intellectual property rose from its ashes.[179] Dunkel made clear that the success or failure of the round rested with the USA and EEC. He assured them of his belief in their commitment, but he lamented the tendency to let political will evaporate in 'the nitty-gritty of negotiations'. He also disabused them of the belief that their own trade policies were beyond criticism. As neither occupied the high road in trade morality, he gave them stern advice about engaging in sincere and constructive negotiations.

Have it as you will: either the US and the EC are paragons of open trade virtues with just the occasional lapses from the straight and narrow, or they are both rough players whose good points are largely obscured by their frequent reversions to foul play. Whatever the case, there is not much to choose between them. So trade policies and rhetoric which are founded on the idea that one side is all white and the other all black are bound to be both futile and counter-productive. And that goes for agriculture as much as for any other sector. It really is quite a sterile procedure for the major trading nations to throw figures backwards and forwards as if merely winning the numbers argument somehow supplies an answer to the real challenges of the Uruguay Round.[180]

Dunkel subsequently produced a blueprint for a comprehensive final settlement. This was a bold move. At 436 pages, it put forward compromise positions on a broad range of issues, including a possible compromise on agriculture that blended US and European positions.[181] Dunkel also called for a halt on new export subsidies and a 20 per cent reduction of existing subsidies in terms of their scope and amount. He also proposed converting non-tariff barriers into tariffs, thereby making them easier to negotiate away. Dunkel told GATT members that they could take or leave his proposed settlement. They could not accept portions of it.

Dunkel's intervention showed the ability of the director-general to act as broker and facilitator. His methods were not diplomatic. This was reminiscent of Eric Wyndham White, who had used threats and heavy-handed methods to bring about agreement in earlier rounds. His actions also showed that the secretariat had the authority to intervene to offset narrower national interests that obstructed agreement. He was the

[179] E. Greenspon, 'GATT Director is Calm amid The Free-Trade Battle', *Globe and Mail* (18 September 1989).
[180] Speech by Dunkel to the European Atlantic group, London, 15 May 1991, NUR048, GDL.
[181] Preeg, *Traders in a Brave New World*, 135.

champion of the internationalist trade cause. In stepping up, Dunkel also defended the relevance of GATT as an organization.[182]

There was widespread criticism of Dunkel's draft. The French agriculture minister denounced it.[183] The EC president, Joao de Deus Pinheiro, said the proposal was 'virtually impossible to accept'.[184] The Japanese minister of agriculture said 'Japan is unable to accept the paper. It is not based on our discussions.'[185] The representative from Morocco noted that it had 'shortcomings and gaps'. Australia and New Zealand disliked it because it did not go far enough on agriculture. Argentina noted that it was deficient in many areas. India was 'greatly disappointed' with the draft; some opponents burned Dunkel in effigy.[186] Colombia had 'reservations'. Indonesia, on behalf of ASEAN, said it 'fell short of their original expectations'. Even in the USA, which had pushed most strongly for a successful round, Carla Hills, the US trade representative, emphasized that it was only a draft and therefore not binding.[187] However, most governments recognized that Dunkel's draft constituted the only feasible basis for concluding the round.[188]

Farmers around the world also protested. In Japan, the executive director of the Central Union of Agricultural Co-operatives denounced the draft because it was 'biased in favour of exporting nations'. Japanese and South Korean rice farmers objected.[189] At a peaceful protest in Ottawa, the president of the Quebec farmers' union denounced Canadian negotiators as 'a bunch of idiots who don't know a damn thing about farming'.[190]

Dunkel tried to win over the farmers. He explained that the goal was not to cap any country's volume of agricultural exports, but to ensure that they developed according to the principles of fair competition and efficient production. 'It only puts a new name to the game, more competition

[182] J. Tallberg, 'The Power of the Chair: Formal Leadership in International Cooperation', *International Studies Quarterly*, 54 (1) (March 2010), 254, 259. Tallberg notes that the chair acted on behalf of the organization rather than individual state aims.

[183] 'GATT: So Close and Yet So Far', *The Economist* (4 January 1992), 62.

[184] J. Brewer, 'US Farmers Renew Attack on Dunkel Plan', *Lloyd's List* (9 January 1992), 3.

[185] N. Ono, 'Tokyo Calls Dunkel's Draft Unacceptable', *Nikkei Weekly* (4 January 1992), 3.

[186] 'Arthur Dunkel: Diplomat and Pioneer of the World Trade Organisation', *The Guardian* (16 June 2005), www.theguardian.com/news/2005/jun/16/guardianobituaries.wto, accessed 9 June 2018.

[187] S. Greenhouse, 'A Move to Break World Trade Deadlock', *New York Times* (21 December 1991), 33.

[188] Trade Negotiations Committee, Twenty-first meeting, 13 January 1992, MTN.TNC/25, 5 February 1992, GDL.

[189] Because of the extent of state support for Japanese and South Korean farmers, Federico described them as 'all but in name state employees': *Feeding the World*, 200.

[190] 'Farmers to Converge on Ottawa', *Globe and Mail* (7 February 1992).

through efficiency and not through financial power.' The draft did not recommend that farmers should be subject to unmitigated market pressures. Instead, it proposed a new way to deliver government support, by directly supplementing incomes rather than raising prices. As Dunkel told a meeting of world farmers, the measures called for 'a progressive switch from policies that support prices to policies that support people, namely the rural community, which plays such an essential political and social role in every society'. He acknowledged that the draft agreement would require changes in government policy as well as in farming practices. But he insisted that the changes would lead to more stability, certainty, and opportunity for farmers. Moreover, the current practice of subsidization was not working: farmers were not prospering. He made it clear that the choice was not between change and the status quo. Change in agriculture would come with or without a GATT agreement. But change along the lines he proposed would be much smoother and easier than 'unilateral changes that would become unavoidable sooner or later, under the pressure of political and economic necessity'.[191]

Meanwhile, US–EEC trade relations deteriorated, revolving around European treatment of subsidies for oilseed producers. Two GATT dispute resolution panels had sided with the USA. Washington had held off introducing retaliatory measures while there was some promise of redress within the Uruguay round negotiations. They now claimed that that negotiated route was not working and they applied a 25 per cent tariff to European white wine valued at US$300 million. Because the effect of the block on US oilseeds was estimated at US$1 billion, Washington promised that additional retaliatory measures affecting another US$700 million worth of EC trade was forthcoming. The USA's objective was not to give up on the round but to renew it, more likely when all parties confronted the reality of trade hostilities.[192]

Senior US and EC negotiators met in Washington in November 1992 to negotiate a conclusion to the round. They agreed to reduce export subsidies as well as domestic subsidies. Their agreement involved changes to domestic policies and practices that would increase market access for foreign producers. Even more significant, this decision affected domestic practices. As expected, there was a sharp backlash. The French government denounced the terms. French farmers rose up. They demonstrated in front of the National Assembly and stormed the Bourse. They also expressed anti-American sentiments by vandalizing MacDonald's and burning the American flag. But as Davis explains, France found itself

[191] Dunkel speech, 'Trade-Related Agricultural Policies and the Uruguay Round', Quebec City, 1 June 1992, GATT/1543, GDL.
[192] Preeg, Traders in a Brave New World, 143–144.

isolated within the EEC for the first time in relation to agriculture and GATT. Despite relentless efforts to revoke the agreement on agriculture, other EEC members refused to scupper the round.[193]

With the resolution of the US–EEC standoff, attention turned to Japan. The USA demanded that Japan open its market to imported rice. As Yeutter put it, 'They better get the word concession into their vocabulary.'[194] Their request for an exemption for rice was refused; GATT members feared that granting an exemption to Japan would encourage all countries to seek exemptions. This was a replay of the debate in 1955 over the US waiver. In the face of US and GATT determination, the Japanese government's position began to shift. The shift was also a result of more vocal support for rice liberalization in Japan as the necessary price for maintaining GATT and the liberal trade system, which overall worked to Japan's benefit and for which there was no real alternative. As a Ministry of International Trade and Industry (MITI) official put it, 'Japan is a trading state and cannot go forward alone.'[195] As the end of the round loomed, the prime minister announced that Japan would import rice up to 4 per cent of annual consumption. His justification was that Japan could not be blamed for the demise of the round: 'Japan cannot be the criminal that wrecks the Uruguay Round.'[196]

Agreement sparked another wave of protest. French farmers used more aggressive and high-publicity tactics in part because of the appearance of a more militant French farm group, Coordination Rurale. In the international media, they were described as a 'fringe farm group', a 'new extremist group', and a 'rogue farmers body'. Their early supporters numbered only a few thousand, but they commanded disproportionate notice because of their attention-seeking tactics, such as blocking access to EuroDisney.[197] They also blocked road access to Paris, rioted outside the National Assembly, stormed the Bourse, burned effigies of Ray MacSharry, the EC commissioner for agriculture, and Carla Hills, committed acts of vandalism, caused traffic jams, burned hay bales, let off fire crackers and sometimes molotov cocktails, threw cow manure at cabinet ministers, and pelted French riot police with apples, bottles, stones, and whatever else came to hand. Their banners declared that 'GATT equals

---

[193] Davis, *Food Fights Over Free Trade*, 302–306.   [194] Ibid., 188.   [195] Ibid., 192.
[196] Ibid., 196, and also see 188–202.
[197] J. Tomlins, 'Siege of Mickey's Castle', *Daily Mail* (27 June 1992), 9; C. Bremner, 'French Farmers Target British Lorries', *The Times* (London) (25 November 1992); K. Hone, 'Maverick Farmers' Body to Blockade Paris over GATT', *Irish Times* (15 September 1993), 8.

death to the rural world.'[198] Thousands of farmers were involved in the protests. They received support from other European farmers, particularly in Belgium and Ireland, as well as in Canada, Japan, and the USA.[199] The largest, and perhaps most violent, demonstration took place in Strasbourg, with estimates of between 40,000 and 70,000 mostly European farmers, who attempted to march on the European parliament. There were clashes between riot police and the demonstrators. Twenty were injured, including one French farmer who lost his hand in an explosion.[200]

Although the tentative concessions of the Uruguay round triggered agrarian protests, French farmers were really frustrated with their own government and EEC policies and practices. The increasingly gloomy future confronting French farmers, whose numbers were plummeting and whose incomes continued to fall despite US$50 billion in annual subsidies, underpinned these protests. There were several other issues that complicated the situation. Many farmers were frustrated with the CAP because its benefits were not distributed evenly. According to some estimates, 20 per cent of European farms received 80 per cent of the subsidies. There were also concerns about an evolving national identity that divided Parisians, and other urban dwellers, from rural areas. Whereas in Paris there was a belief in an identity that was modern and republican, in rural areas, the identity of the nation was rooted to the land and was epitomized culturally and socially by French farmers.[201]

The French government insisted on changes to the tentative agreement and hinted that they might use a veto. This caused intense strain within the EEC. British Foreign Secretary Douglas Hurd suggested the EEC could not continue to function normally if it wrecked the Uruguay round.[202] By this time, there was a new administration in the USA under President Clinton, and Mickey Kantor was the US trade representative. President Mitterrand, whose popularity at home was dropping,

---

[198] 'Violence Grows as French Blast Trade Pact with US', *Toronto Star* (25 November 1992), A1; 'French, American Farmers Assail US–EEC Accord', *Toronto Star* (21 November 1992), C2.

[199] W. Drozdiak, 'French Set for "Crisis" on Trade: Farmers Press Government to Keep Export Subsidies', *Washington Post* (16 September 1993), A20.

[200] W. Drozdiak, '40,000 Farmers Protest US–European Trade Accord', *Washington Post* (2 December 1992), A33; 'Farmer Hurt in Fierce Riots Against GATT Deal', *Irish Times* (2 December 1992), 1; A. Bell, 'GATT Deal Protest Leaves 20 Hurt', *The Guardian* (2 December 1992), 7.

[201] I. Bell, 'Last Straw for Paysans', *The Herald* (Glasgow) (14 October 1992), 15; G. Crossley, 'Baleful Straws in the Wind', *The Guardian* (27 November 1992), 19.

[202] P. L. H. van den Bossche, 'The European Community and the Uruguay Round Agreements' in J. H. Jackson and A. O. Sykes (eds.), *Implementing the Uruguay Round* (Oxford: Clarendon; New York: Oxford University Press, 1997), 63–64.

insisted that the GATT agreement would have to be assessed as a complete package. Sensing the possibility for a breakthrough, Kantor agreed to a more gradual schedule for phasing out export subsidies. But the real clincher was a US concession affecting French film, another cultural icon. With this last concession, the French government threw its support behind the ratification of the Uruguay round package.

The final terms of the agreement affected agricultural subsidies and non-tariff barriers. Non-tariff forms of protection, such as quotas and levies, were converted into tariffs which would be easier to measure and reduce moving forward. Converting tariffs revealed just how prohibitive the NTBs had been. For example, the new tariff rate on butter in Canada was 351.4 per cent, EC 235.3 per cent, and Switzerland 862.2 per cent; on white sugar, EC 207.1 per cent, Japan 326.7 per cent, and USA 134.7 per cent; on wheat, Japan 422.9 per cent and EC 142.3 per cent; and on beef, EC 96.9 per cent, Poland 162 per cent, and Switzerland 139.7 per cent.[203] There were exceptions to tariffication. Japan and South Korea guaranteed foreign rice access to their markets in terms of a percentage. In Japan, the pledge was to increase market access from 4 per cent to 8 per cent over six years; in South Korea, the increase was from 1 per cent to 4 per cent. There were also safeguard provisions in the event of falling world prices and import surges. Members agreed to reduce export subsidies by 36 per cent and to retract the number of items receiving subsidies by 21 per cent. No new subsidies were allowed. Finally, governments agreed to reduce domestic support to farmers by 20 per cent.[204]

Prior to the Uruguay round, the extent of liberalization of agriculture had been determined by the lowest common denominator. That had been low indeed. Meaningful progress had been unattainable because members could not agree on an agenda or on ways to discuss issues related to agricultural production and exchange. The Uruguay round achievements were notable because they pinned down the two most formidable obstacles to agricultural trade: NTBs and subsidies. Moreover, they moved beyond generalities and laid down specific targets with respect to the reduction of barriers to trade, and they set timelines. Agriculture was now subject to GATT discipline and regulation. Australia's representative believed they had made 'a good start'.[205] But as Sumner and Tangermann describe it, the success of the Uruguay round was more

---

[203] Sumner and Tangermann, 'International Trade Policy and Negotiations', 2015.
[204] Ibid., 2010–2018.
[205] Statement by the Hon. Bob McMullan, Minister for Trade, 14 April 1994, MTN.TNC/MIN (94)/ST/89, GDL.

potential than realized. The results made more far-reaching liberalization possible down the road.[206]

During the Uruguay round, another chronic challenge confronting the organization was resolved: the creation of a permanent organization. Although there had been no discussion about creating an international organization to replace GATT prior to the round, in June 1990 EEC officials proposed the establishment of the Multilateral Trade Organisation (MTO). The EEC's motivation was practical. An institution with a stronger legal foundation was necessary to bring the various agreements together and make them work effectively. There were elements of continuity between the EEC proposal and GATT, particularly in its emphasis on the rights of members rather than their obligations.[207] After forty years of consistently affirming the rights of states within the organization, it would have been a shocking departure if the EEC had proposed to make GATT more powerful vis-à-vis its members.

The government of Canada threw its support behind the EEC proposal. In other quarters, the EEC proposal met with a lukewarm reception and even, from US delegates, outright 'hostility'. Dunkel was not keen on the MTO either, fearing it would divert attention away from pressing trade issues that remained unresolved.[208] Confronted with opposition and lack of interest, the MTO proposal was temporarily dropped. Canada, Mexico, and the EEC raised it again one year later. A bare-bones sketch was produced of an organization that would bring together GATT, GATS (the agreement on services), TRIPS (the agreement on intellectual property), and dispute resolution within one institution. The outline was buried at the end of the Final Draft Act of 1991, the draft that Dunkel put together in the (failed) hope of wrapping up the round. Even though Dunkel's draft lapsed, the MTO proposal remained alive.[209] Washington objected to it, insisting that a new organization was not necessary. US officials chalked up GATT's problems to an absence of political support, not to its incomplete institutional foundation. The USA also repeated earlier objections to arrangements for voting and let it be known that the MTO would create difficulties with Congress. The USA wanted to drop the MTO, but its opposition united MTO supporters. The EEC went so far as to insist on the MTO as a condition for the successful conclusion of the round.[210]

In typical GATT fashion, the MTO came together through compromise. On the crucial issue of voting, members agreed to continue the

[206] Sumner and Tangermann, 'International Trade Policy and Negotiations', 2017–2018.
[207] Croome, *Reshaping the World Trading System*, 273–274.   [208] Ibid., 274.
[209] Ibid., 334–335.   [210] Ibid., 342, 359.

GATT tradition of making decisions by consensus, at least on most questions.[211] Where votes would be taken, a three-quarters majority would be necessary to pass and the terms of the MTO could only be amended through unanimity. Developing countries were won round to the proposal because the new organization would include agriculture and textiles. They were also reassured that they would be accorded special and differential treatment when it came to phasing in the responsibilities of membership.[212] The USA proposed a last-minute name change: they preferred the World Trade Organization. As Kantor explained, the new name 'sounds a lot less bureaucratic and has more gravitas'.[213]

The WTO meant that after almost fifty years and repeated failed attempts there was a properly constituted international organization to direct and manage global trade. According to Peter Sutherland, the WTO would be proactive, rather than a passive forum waiting for members to act.[214] National representatives also praised the WTO. The Canadian trade minister called it the round's 'crowning achievement' and an EC official compared it to 'the new comet that must guide us all in our daily activities'.[215] The celebration was tempered by recognition that the WTO could only be as effective as its members' commitment to it. The representative from Cuba struck a particularly dour note, but nonetheless acknowledged that it was 'a step in the right direction' to counter the 'law of the jungle' that defined international trade relations.[216] The end of the Uruguay round marked a high point for GATT and a defeat for its legion of critics and opponents. As Canada's minister for international trade pronounced: 'Our common achievement is an eloquent answer to those prophets of doom who not long ago were trumpeting that "the GATT is dead".'[217]

---

[211] K. Buterbaugh and R. Fulton, *The WTO Primer: Tracing Trade's Visible Hand through Case Studies* (Basingstoke: Palgrave Macmillan, 2007), 61.

[212] A. Narlikar, *The WTO: A Very Short Introduction* (New York: Oxford University Press, 2005), 25.

[213] R. Cohen, 'The World Trade Agreement; The Overview; GATT Talks End in Joy and Relief', *New York Times* (16 December 1993), D1.

[214] Address by Mr. Peter Sutherland, Director-General of GATT, 12 April 1994, MTN. TNC/MIN (94)/4, GDL.

[215] Statement by the Honourable Roy MacLaren, Minister for International Trade, 12 April 1994, MTN.TNC/MIN (94)/ST/2; Statement by His Excellency Mr. Theodorus Pangalos, Deputy Minister for Foreign Affairs of Greece on behalf of the Presidency of the Council of the European Communities, 12 April 1994, MTN. TNC/MIN (94)/ST/4, GDL.

[216] Statement by H. E. Mr. Ricardo Cabrisas Ruíz, Minister for Foreign Trade, MTN. TNC/MIN (94)/ST/54, GDL.

[217] Statement by the Honourable Roy MacLaren, Minister for International Trade, 12 April 1994, MTN.TNC/MIN (94)/ST/2, GDL.

But at the signing ceremony of the Uruguay round in Marrakesh in April 1994, not all was celebration. Fights over agriculture resurfaced. Behind the scenes, France and Germany were at loggerheads over bananas.[218] Canada and the United States were locked in a battle over wheat subsidies. Australia accused Canada of reneging on a commitment for its beef exports. There was also a last blast from farmers, who protested the final agreement. Five thousand famers took to the streets of Tokyo. Prime Minister Hosawaka was accused of treason and deceit.[219] In South Korea, 20,000 protestors carried banners with messages such as 'Rice imports will kill 6 m of our farmers' and 'Don't destroy rice farmers'.[220] The concessions to GATT stuck, but the president of South Korea resigned.[221] French farmers also objected. Christian Leplus of the Fédération nationale des syndicats d'exploitants agricoles (FNSEA) directed his displeasure at the globalization of agricultural trade: 'GATT means we'll buy our wheat from Canada, our meat from New Zealand and our cars from South Korea. And what will that leave France? Just tourism.'[222] But the prospect of a final agreement did not spark protests on the scale of the 1992 protests, and France stuck by the agreement.[223] In their closing remarks in Marrakesh, national representatives praised free trade, criticized the uneven distribution of benefits among rich and poor countries, celebrated the dawn of a new trade era, and called for constant vigilance against the threats of regionalism, unilateralism, and protectionism. Most national representatives had little to say in praise of the agricultural agreements and concessions.[224]

Conclusions

Agricultural trade was never a technical or commercial subject. Debates and negotiations over agriculture were shaped by fundamental questions

[218] France wanted to maintain a preference for the banana exports of former colonies, whereas Germany extended a preference for the larger type of banana grown in Latin America. They did not resolve their dispute. Rather they agreed to shelve it temporarily.
[219] 'Farmers Lash Out at Rice Ruling', *Courier-Mail* (15 December 1993), 29; A. Pollack, 'Tokyo Journal: For the Rice Lobby the Bowl of Plenty Dries Up', *New York Times* (13 December 1993), A4.
[220] 'Seoul Protest', *Lloyd's List* (17 November 1993), 14; M. Breen, 'S. Koreans Protest Rice Imports', *Washington Times* (6 December 1993), A11.
[221] Preeg, *Traders in a Brave New World*, 168–176.
[222] K. Hone, 'Farmers Protest in the Rain at GATT Deal', *Irish Times* (16 September 1993), 6.
[223] K. Hone, 'France Celebrates "A Great and Fine Victory" for European culture', *Irish Times* (15 December 1993), 7.
[224] Statement by Mr. Pranab Mukherjee, Minister of Commerce, 13 April 1994, MTN. TNC/MIN (94)/ST/38; Statement by Mr. Guido Di Tella, Minister for Foreign Affairs, International Trade and Religion, 14 April 1994, MTN.TNC/MIN (94)/ST/94, GDL.

about the authority and limits of global governance, whether or not trade should uphold national history and traditions or deepen conditions of interdependence among states, and whether or not states should, or could, balance a responsibility to the well-being of national electorates as well as that of a global citizenry. Agricultural issues made clear that the domestic and international spheres were mutually constitutive. International negotiations over agriculture also spilled over into questions about global order. Debates over agricultural trade elicited fundamental questions about the purpose and forms of international association and cooperation. It raised an alternative set of priorities and conditions that challenged the beliefs and goals that had informed the internationalist thinking out of which the UN system had emerged. Before national trade officials could get down to nitty-gritty negotiations over agricultural commodities, their political leaders had to sort through these intractable and basic problems. Their answers could have profound implications not only for GATT, but for the whole global system. The possibility of a breakdown in negotiations over agriculture was seen as portentous, imperiling conditions of peace and the survival of the global community: 'Costly trade wars, poisoned political relationships, and more difficult cooperation in other areas of international economic policy could have followed.'[225] The stakes over agriculture were high and would affect far more than farmers.

The tension between nationalist and internationalist thinking was not limited to the agricultural sector, but it was most explicit and pronounced in relation to agriculture. From its beginning, membership in GATT required that members cede a piece of sovereignty and consider international well-being alongside national interests. Members accepted an obligation to adhere to the rules and obligations of GATT and this could, and did, have implications for domestic practices and policies. When national interests or laws and international obligations and rules clashed – as they did for the USA in the mid-1950s –a waiver permitted deviation from the rules. Because GATT lacked a strong enforcement mechanism – and members might never have joined if a stricter enforcement mechanism had been in place – there was really no option but to grant the waiver. But many members lamented this outcome. GATT's so-called flexibility revealed the limits of its authority and the threshold of support for internationalist action. Some anticipated that the waiver would give blanket permission to all members to protect domestic agriculture. But the fact that the US government sought a waiver also showed an acceptance of accountability to the organization and its members. There was a symbolic

[225] Josling, Tangermann, and Warley, *Agriculture in the GATT*, 134.

significance that upheld the legitimacy of GATT as the defender of a collective well-being, even as the waiver highlighted its limitations and its dependence on the willingness of its members to work within it. In the Uruguay round, the tension between sovereignty over domestic policies and international accountability continued to play out. For example, the decision to cap subsidies and slowly roll them back involved a recalibration of the domestic–international dynamic, with more consideration of international regulation and oversight. The debate about agricultural trade revealed the limits of internationalism in practice, and forced a recognition of the dangers of following a narrow nationalist approach to involvement in world affairs.

Although the establishment of GATT shortly after the war seemed to represent the triumph of liberal economic ideas about efficient production, open markets, and economic interdependence, the story of agriculture within the GATT reveals the persistent appeal of protectionist and nationalist thinking. The mandate of GATT was based on the assumption that the trade of all states would rise and fall together. The lesson from the Great Depression was that no country could insulate itself from global economic forces and that policies devoted to national economic well-being impeded global recovery and growth. But not everyone accepted these liberal axioms or the internationalist logic that flowed from them. To many, including farmers seeking protection, global trade was harmful. The appeal of protectionism revealed the persistence of mercantilist thinking that was based on beliefs that global trade was zero-sum and that it created winners and losers. Drawing this thinking to a logical conclusion, GATT, and the liberal ideas on which it was based, were understood to be iniquitous and oppressive. By the end of GATT's independent existence, that view was becoming more widespread. It challenged the universalist assumption that liberal trade was in the best collective interest of all in the long run. But the nationalist backlash did not come out with full force until after GATT had been subsumed within the WTO.

In 1963, the US official Myer Rashish described agriculture as GATT's Achilles heel.[226] Agriculture exposed many of GATT's weaknesses: its lack of enforcement mechanisms, its inability to do more than the lowest common denominator, the limited appeal of liberal trade ideas and practices, and the way real people experienced and reacted to global trade. Agriculture was a divisive subject that GATT could not evade.

---

[226] Myer Rashish, Memo For Discussion at Meeting of Trade Negotiations Subcommittee, 29 October 1963, Herter Papers, Box 7, file Committee for Economic Development 5/63–11/63, JFKL.

To ignore it would have alienated agricultural exporters, cast doubt on GATT's relevance, and undermined a rules-based global order; on the other hand, pressing for liberalization provoked bitter fights between its strongest members, raised concerns that the organization was over-stepping its authority, and weakened support for an internationalist ideology. But the story of agriculture within GATT also reveals GATT's resilience and scope for independent action. The organization could generate information that shaped the priorities and problems that member countries addressed. The rules, even if breached, continued to have symbolic power. And the directors-general, Dunkel in particular, called leading GATT members to account and spoke directly to citizens – often angry farmers – to point out errors in their thinking. Moreover, the deadlock between the USA and the EEC created both the space and the need for alternative leadership regarding the liberalization of trade in agriculture. The Cairns Group filled the breach, revealing the agency, power, and relevance of smaller actors, especially when acting collectively, to facilitate and force agreement on controversial issues.

Conclusion
The Embattled History of GATT

Despite GATT's inauspicious beginnings, it became the established and accepted steward and defender of a liberal trade order. Many scholars agree that it was highly successful, 'near the top'[1] of all international organizations, possibly even 'the most important and authoritative of all the current international organizations and regimes'.[2] There are many reasons why GATT can be considered a success. Its membership grew from twenty-three original members in 1948 to 122 by 1995. It concluded eight rounds of ever more complicated negotiations and scaled back many barriers to trade. Perhaps GATT's most remarkable achievement was that it survived at all, until it was subsumed within the World Trade Organization. It did so despite critics who called for it to be shut down or replaced; trade negotiations that included dramatic walkouts, accusations of bad faith, and hard bargaining; growing opposition to liberalization and free trade; and public demonstrations that denounced GATT as an enemy of farmers, the environment, labour, national sovereignty, and cultural distinctiveness. But the purpose of this book has not been to celebrate its success. Rather, GATT's story is important because it provides concrete historical evidence about the workings of a key institution of the postwar liberal order, explains why nations work within international organizations despite their many shortcomings, draws out the importance of trade in relations between states, unpacks the way that people and governments think about trade, and considers the significance

---

[1] K. W. Dam, *The GATT: Law and International Economic Organization* (Chicago: University of Chicago Press, 1970), 335.

[2] D. Deese, *World Trade Politics: Power, Principles and Leadership* (London and New York: Routledge, 2008), 13. Josling, Tangermann, and Warley, experts on agricultural trade, praise the GATT as 'one of the more influential and respected of the post-war international organizations'. T. E. Josling, S. Tangermann, and T.K. Warley, *Agriculture in the GATT* (Basingstoke: Macmillan, 1996), 8. Blackhurst, a former member of the GATT secretariat, agrees with this view, claiming that GATT was 'widely considered to have been one of the most successful – if not the most successful – of the post-war international economic organizations'. R. Blackhurst, 'The Role of the Director-General and the Secretariat' in A. Narlikar, M. Daunton, and R. M. Stern (eds.), *The Oxford Handbook on the World Trade Organization* (Oxford: Oxford University Press, 2012), 149.

of the cooperative–competitive trade dynamic for the global community. These insights are particularly important at a time when the global trade order, including the network of trade agreements that have been negotiated in and beyond GATT, is under attack.

Members mattered to GATT, and some members seemed to matter more than others.[3] Certainly, GATT depended on its members to participate in its activities, especially rounds of trade negotiations, and to ratify and implement decisions, and in so doing to affirm the legitimacy of the organization. However, our understanding of what it means to be a member-driven organization, and of the role of the most powerful members, should be refined. The USA and the EEC receive the most attention in GATT studies, and the conventional wisdom is that they upheld the global trade order and determined its scope and limits. Although the USA and the EEC were leaders, their commitment to the organization was neither complete nor constant. The EEC pushed liberalization forward in some sectors and blocked it in others. Although scholars typically identify US leadership as decisive, it was sometimes evident and sometimes absent; US officials were by turns silent and outspoken, opposed and followed, and even, on occasion, marginalized. US engagement may have been essential to GATT's creation, but not to its subsequent operations. Many nations stepped up to lead, including Australia, Brazil, Canada, India, Japan, and Mexico, at different times and on different issues. Individual members pushed for items to be included on the agenda and forced other members to discuss – and even make decisions about – contentious questions of trade policy. Leadership in GATT was fluid and opportunistic, and the engagement and support of small and mid-sized members helped to sustain GATT's momentum and legitimacy.

The secretariat was much more than a pacifying bystander among national members. It was proactive in promoting trade liberalization, shoring up support for an organization and a cause that frequently fell out of favour, and responding to challenges and opportunities. Because the support of individual members varied over time and by issue, and with no country standing out as a constant champion of the organization or trade liberalization, the secretariat, and the directors-general in particular, had to defend the organization. It did so in several ways. The secretariat worked closely with national officials to cultivate support and coordinate tactics that subsequently played out in GATT. The directors-

---

[3] Blackhurst, 'The Role of the Director-General and the Secretariat', 151. Kock concludes that 'GATT is what the member countries make out of it.' K. Kock, *International Trade Policy and the GATT, 1947–1967* (Stockholm: Almqvist and Wiksell, 1969), 302.

general pushed the liberalizing mandate forward, striving to reconcile the different interests of members and to reach compromises that upheld the overall and long-term promotion of trade liberalization, and lobbying for the enduring relevance of a liberal trade order. The secretariat was quick to raise alarms about the devastating consequences that would follow from failure. This was a negative kind of pressure, but it helped members overcome impasses and reach agreements that allowed liberalization to advance. GATT also had to adjust from its low visibility early on to becoming a magnet for critics. The organization needed a public relations strategy to sell liberal trade; the directors-general made the case for GATT before organized and staunch critics, including at UNCTAD and at meetings of farmers. Behind the high-minded commitment to an international ideal associated with peace and prosperity, institutional insecurity fuelled the secretariat's activism and vigilance.

Its capacity to adapt to a changing international environment was essential to GATT's continued relevance.[4] The changes in world affairs from 1947 to 1995 were dramatic: the Cold War began and ended, regional alliances flourished and failed, wars were waged, the global economy boomed and stagnated, new states emerged as formal empires shut down, norms evolved, and centres of economic power shifted. Many initiatives to maintain GATT's relevance began with the secretariat, including extending membership to communist countries, adding a development chapter to the General Agreement, and bringing more areas of trade, such as agriculture, under the umbrella of GATT. It was not always successful, as the case of agriculture reveals. Regardless of the outcome, GATT officials rarely drew attention to their lobbying, coordinating, and cajoling for fear they might trigger a backlash against the ambition and reach of GATT into national spheres.

Throughout its history, GATT was praised for its flexibility, meaning not insisting on strict compliance with its own rules. Flexibility that acknowledged long-term goals without being rigid about means to achieve them was necessary. But flexibility ran the risk of subverting GATT's mission and institutional authority. Members did not flaunt their transgressions; they justified deviations in terms of reconstruction priorities, implementing social welfare measures, ensuring full employment, overcoming the legacy of imperialism, and modernizing industrial bases. GATT also put a positive spin on departures and transgressions, suggesting that they were compatible (regional trade agreements), or

---

[4] Winham says that adapting to changing circumstances was 'a prerequisite for survival in any institution'. G. R. Winham, *International Trade and the Tokyo Round Negotiation* (Princeton: Princeton University Press, 1986), 22.

temporary (preferences as a short-term measure leading to liberal trade practices), or that they demonstrated the goodwill of members (the exception made for the ECSC). Some members justified departures in evolutionary terms. World conditions in the 1980s or 1990s were not the same as those following the Second World War, and as a result new policies and practices were needed. But the non-compliance of members ran the risk of making GATT's rules meaningless and was a worrying and telling trend. Members only ever upheld norms and rules in part, and they generally emphasized rights over obligations.

Privileging rights over obligations shows that the liberal promise of GATT was not convincing. Neither people nor governments believed that freer trade, the collective good, long-term economic growth, and the logic of interdependence was the best, right, or only way to think about trade. As a result, GATT members did not pursue their interests exclusively within a universal framework and through a multilateral process. The regional approach to trade appealed widely because GATT did not do enough for its members. Regional trade agreements seemed a viable and necessary alternative in which to promote their trade interests. But GATT was in a near-constant beleaguered state because these alternatives also seemed to foreshadow the end of the organization. There were occasional, and usually short-lived, outbursts of celebration, such as at the end of a round of trade negotiations. But even when GATT most convincingly showed what it could do, there were critics – the rounds did not go far enough and left out key sectors of trade, and concessions were not distributed evenly.

The reaction to GATT was polarized throughout the whole of its existence. GATT was held up simultaneously as a destructive agent of globalization and as a force for global stability and prosperity. That trade produces winners and losers is an often-repeated claim. The so-called losers were more vocal, and often more sympathetic, than the more restrained winners of global trade. In the eyes of GATT sceptics and free-trade critics, GATT sustained the interests of big business, destroyed local cultures, caused unemployment, and undermined national sovereignty and well-being. It was a destructive force, like Pandora unleashing a slew of ills and plagues on the world. Advocates, on the other hand, insisted that GATT stood for law, rules, and fairness and that lower barriers to trade were the most effective way to stimulate economic growth and reinforce a world that was stable, interdependent, and peaceful. In the long run, everyone would win, although deferred benefits did not offset losses that were felt 'instantly' and 'devastatingly'.[5] Both views

---

[5] 'A Future that Does Not Work', *The Economist* (25 December 1982), 90.

are right and wrong. Trade has consequences that benefit some people, groups, and communities while others must adapt to dislocation and change. At its heart, there was a clash between those who had faith in free trade and those who feared it.

Given the polarized attitudes to trade, it comes as no surprise that liberalization was never easily achieved. Trade negotiations were characterized by clashing priorities, compromise and consensus, deadlocks and breakthroughs, flexibility and rigidity, long-term planning and short-term calculations.[6] But this is only surprising if one believes in the logic of liberal economic thought. If a country is genuinely committed to free trade, it should dismantle barriers to trade unilaterally and without compensation because the act of freeing trade should generate its own rewards. This was not how tariffs, and other trade barriers, were lowered in GATT. National negotiators weighed concessions offered and received, and insisted on a balanced exchange, receiving as much as they gave in return. There was an enduring zero-sum calculus, consistent with a mercantilist outlook in which exports were desirable, imports less welcome. Negotiations also left out (completely or in part) many large sectors of the global trade system, such as oil, weapons, textiles, and agriculture. Trade has been compared to many things, including a bicycle that must keep moving forward or fall over and a natural disaster such as a hurricane. The global trade system can also be thought of as a winding river that carves out space amid natural barriers, sometimes moving forward, sometimes deflected when it comes up against an insurmountable obstacle. Overall, liberalization advanced and global trade expanded between 1948 and 1995, but progress was imperfect and gradual.

One might reasonably wonder why countries stayed in GATT and why ever more countries chose to join. GATT represented a vision of a cooperative and integrated world order that claimed to benefit all members, even though it fell short in practice. A rules-based organization was valued because it required compliance from all its members, no matter their strength or weakness. When deviations occurred, there was an accountability that kept members more or less aligned. Because of what GATT symbolized, the restraint and oversight that it provided, and the possibilities that it promised, countries wanted in. For those members that felt ill-served or under-served by GATT, the alternative was to quit, an option some members considered but few chose. It was riskier to be

---

[6] L. Coppolaro and F. McKenzie, 'Trading Blocs and Trading Blows: GATT's Conflictual Path to Trade Liberalisation, 1947–1967' in L. Coppolaro and F. McKenzie (eds.), *A Global History of Trade and Conflict since 1500* (Basingstoke: Palgrave Macmillan, 2013), 163–187.

outside the organization than inside. Repeated failures to establish a permanent organization until the establishment of the WTO, and the shortcomings of other trade organizations such as UNCTAD, showed that there were no other real options. GATT had become part of the global governance structure and nations had little choice but to work with it. Members chafed at GATT, but they never rejected it outright.

GATT's role in stabilizing international relations has been proclaimed by liberal trade theorists, who argue that a more economically interdependent world would be more peaceful and prosperous.[7] The increase in global trade has contributed to an overall rise in standards of living, but not everyone has benefited. For the 800 million people today who subsist on less than US$2 a day, for people whose conditions of life have been set back by the transformative and dislocating effects of trade, as well as for people who lose their jobs and livelihoods, the liberal promise has yet to bear fruit. There is a vibrant political economy literature about whether trade between states prevents armed conflicts.[8] But even with the abundance of GATT statistics, it is not possible to quantify the impact of GATT in promoting world peace. There may be a correlation, but GATT's causal role cannot be specified. Its contribution should be assessed instead in relation to its normative influence and symbolic role, upholding an international ideal and facilitating multilateral processes.

GATT's history shows how even a supposedly technical organization was 'deeply entangled in politics'.[9] Yet it is easy to understand why politics have been downplayed in many historical accounts of GATT. Political influences and goals have been embedded in discussions about dumping, subsidies, sanitary provisions, health and safety standards, and preferences. They were also masked by the economic vernacular spoken

---

[7] Jackson believes that the liberal international economic order could support 'the avoidance of armed conflict'. J. H. Jackson, *Restructuring the GATT System* (London: Royal Institute of International Affairs, 1990), 2. Winham also maintains there is a link between trade and peace because trade promotes prosperity and prosperity is conducive to cooperation. Winham, *International Trade and the Tokyo Round Negotiation*, 402–403.

[8] Oneal and Russett demonstrate that economically significant trade and democracy have 'substantively significant pacific benefits'. J. R. Oneal and B. Russett, 'Clear and Clean: The Fixed Effects of the Liberal Peace', *International Organization* 55 (2) (Spring 2001), 471, 474. They conclude that democracy reduces the likelihood of conflict by 44 per cent, whereas trade reduces it by 22 per cent. When challenged, they have revised their calculations, for example by taking distance and size into account, but continue to find 'clear evidence for the liberal peace'. H. Hegre, J. R. Oneal, and B. Russett, 'Trade Does Promote Peace: New Simultaneous Estimates of the Reciprocal Effects of Trade and Conflict', *Journal of Peace Research* 47 (6) (2010), 771. See also H. Dorussen and H. Ward, 'Trade Networks and the Kantian Peace', *Journal of Peace Research* 47 (1) (January 2010), 41.

[9] E. Roehrlich, 'State of the Field Essay on the History of the UN and its Organizations', H-Diplo Essay No. 153 (20 April 2018), 13, http://tiny.cc/W153.

at GATT. To openly admit that political concerns or interests were driving one's position at GATT was not acceptable, even though all members thought this way.[10] For example, the USA and Czechoslovakia rarely referred to Cold War tensions to explain their stands on European integration. French officials did not explain that they were trying to restore French greatness by protecting agriculture or subverting the Kennedy round. Governments did not admit that they were protecting farmers because they wanted their votes. Politics was thought to debase the economic mandate of GATT. But political considerations were pervasive and inescapable, obscured rather than absent. There are always multiple layers of meaning in discussions about commodities, the formulation of trade policies, and participation in trade negotiations. Scratch the surface and the political significance of economic policies and international trade negotiations is revealed.

Political considerations were present from the start, when trade policies were defined, to the end, when governments ratified trade agreements. Officials with highly specialized knowledge negotiated fine points of trade practice, and their instructions were informed by wide-ranging domestic and international considerations, including protecting vulnerable workers, winning over potential voters, defending national sovereignty, preventing global economic downturn, and strengthening alliances. The results of trade negotiations also had to have political backing – and enjoy sufficient public support – to come into effect. Economic reason did not win the day in rounds of negotiations. Trade policy and trade negotiations could also be instruments of foreign policy and could communicate foreign policy ideas or goals. Trade became an increasingly prominent strand of foreign policy, foreign relations, and world affairs. In the early postwar years, the issues that were considered high diplomacy related to national security, such as nuclear weapons, whereas trade was considered a matter of low diplomacy. Part-way through GATT's existence, the distinction between low policy and high policy vanished: trade was seen to be essential to national welfare and national security, and a globalized economy intensified connections that were implicated in the larger workings of the international community. The centrality of trade to global affairs is starkly evident today as governments exchange punitive trade measures, scupper trade negotiations, dismantle long-standing agreements, and use access to their markets to achieve political goals – such as stopping the flow of migrants – that have nothing to do with trade, all of which spreads

---

[10] Gilpin observes that liberals see economics as 'progressive', whereas politics are seen as 'retrogressive', which might explain why political objectives or concerns were couched in GATT discourse. R. Gilpin, *The Political Economy of International Relations* (Princeton: Princeton University Press, 1990), 30.

alarm throughout the world. Separating trade and politics makes a false distinction. It is more productive to think in terms of hybrid (economic–political) categories, rather than narrow or exclusive ones, and a porous continuous space (domestic–international), rather than distinct spheres.

This study also shows that our view of the main actors and priorities of post-1945 international relations needs rethinking. Take the Cold War. It turned GATT into a subset of the western alliance, but the history of GATT also reveals the limits of the Cold War as the defining issue of the postwar era. The creation of the EEC draws attention to the logic and appeal of regional forms of association and engagement, the basis of which suggested a very different geopolitical organization from the bipolar order. Or take the nation-state. While many studies of international relations focus on great powers and assume that they largely direct the course of world affairs, this study shows that smaller powers can effectively contest their leadership and direction and can step up as leaders in their own right. Furthermore, the experiences of the greatest powers do not explain what matters to other states or define their experiences in world affairs. This study also makes clear how international negotiations in Geneva affected conditions of everyday life. Trade negotiations connect decisions by elites and a seemingly technical process with conditions that people experienced on a daily basis. We need to think about farmers, labourers, consumers, producers, citizens, and voters as meaningful, and powerful, actors in world affairs and connect board rooms in Geneva to homes, streets, workplaces, and communities around the world. All of this becomes apparent when we see GATT as being positioned more centrally within the international community.

Finally, GATT's history complicates our understanding of the postwar liberal order, in several ways. First, the liberal order that stood for law, cooperation, tempered sovereignty, and collective well-being had to be reconciled with the fact that nations remained the principal actors in a system where power and interests sometimes clashed with rules and norms. But if the history of GATT confirms the resilience of the nation-based order, it also shows that there was an interlocking of national–international conceptions of global order. The balance between them shifted over time, but both had legitimacy and set expectations for appropriate behaviour. Individual nations had to promote their economic interests, but not if the toll was too high for others. Zero-sum thinking went too far. Measures to promote international well-being that caused too much dislocation or dissatisfaction for nations, or that delayed or interfered with domestic plans, also went too far. GATT upheld the logic of internationalist thinking without downgrading the importance of national and local interests and well-being. National governments had to observe international baselines, and international organizations had to be mindful of national bottom lines.

Second, the liberal order of which GATT was a key part could not presume to be the best kind of order. It always had to demonstrate its relevance and prove its worth. Legitimacy was earned over and over. Moreover, claims about what the liberal order delivered – that it supported peace and prosperity from which all benefited – obscured other consequences of that same order: privileging some nations, some sectors of the economy, and some people over others. Many scholars explain the postwar order as a Pax Americana. This study does not entirely reject that interpretation, but it does show that the Pax Americana worked best for the USA and other industrial, democratic, and capitalist countries. And yet it did not work well enough even for them, and GATT's greatest beneficiaries found fault with the organization, deviated from its rules, and sought other options to advance their commercial interests.

Third, stability and predictability were goals of the postwar trade system, but these laudable objectives translated into rigidity and made GATT a conservative organization. It was no surprise that GATT inspired critics and opponents and sparked alternative visions of order – such as the New International Economic Order or regional associations.

Finally, GATT's mandate could at times be malleable and partisan, as was evident during the Cold War, when GATT was implicated in the struggle between communism and capitalism. The internationalist argument on which GATT rested was never entirely refuted or rejected, but nor was it ever completely or whole-heartedly accepted. A do-gooding organization, GATT was never good enough.

References

Primary Sources

Archives and Libraries

CIA Freedom of Information Act Electronic Reading Room
Central Intelligence Bulletins

FDRL: Franklin Delano Roosevelt Library, Hyde Park, New York
Berle Papers
Morgenthau Diary

Foreign Affairs Oral History Collection of the Association for Diplomatic Study and Training, Library of Congress, USA
Ionnes Interview, www.loc.gov/collections/foreign-affairs-oral-history/about-this-collection/

GDL: GATT Digital Library
http://gatt.stanford.edu/page/home

HAEU: Historical Archives of the European Union, Florence
BAC: Fonds of the EEC and ECSC Commissions
CEAB: High Authority of the Coal and Steel Community Series
JMAS: Jean Monnet Series
JMDS: Jean Monnet Duchêne Series
MAEF: Olivier Wormser Papers, Ministère des affaires étrangères français

HI: Hoover Institution, Stanford University
Papers of Will Clayton

HL: Houghton Library, Harvard University, Cambridge, Massachusetts
Christian Herter Papers
Time Magazine Dispatches, 1st series (1942–1955); 2nd series (1956–1968)

JFKL: John F. Kennedy Library, Boston, Massachusetts
Ball Papers
Herter Papers

LAC: Library and Archives of Canada, Ottawa
MG30-E91: Herbert Kemp Papers
MG30-E144: Arnold Heeney Papers
MG30-E163: Norman Robertson Papers
MG31-E6: D. V. LePan Papers
MG31-E9: Leolyn Dana Wilgress Papers
MG31-E84: Louis Couillard Papers
MG32-B41: Mitchell Sharp Papers
RG2: Privy Council Office
RG19: Department of Finance
RG20: Department of Trade and Commerce
RG25: Department of External Affairs

LSE: London School of Economics Archive, London
Papers of James Meade

MAE: Ministère des affaires extérieures, Paris
Affaires économiques et financières (series)
    Cooperation économique 1945–60
    Cooperation économique 1961–66

NAI: National Archives of India, Delhi
Ministry of Commerce and Industry
Ministry of External Affairs

NARA: National Archives Records Administration, College Park, Maryland, USA
RG43: Records of the United States Trade Representative
RG59: State Department
RG84: Records of the Foreign Service Posts of the United States
RG364: Special Trade Representative

NATO Archives Online
http://archives.nato.int/

NMML: Nehru Memorial Museum and Library, Delhi
Papers of the Indian Merchants' Chamber, Bombay

TL: Truman Library, Independence, Missouri
Clayton-Thorp Papers
Edminster Papers
White House Central Files

TNA: The National Archives, Richmond, UK
BT: Board of Trade
CAB: Cabinet Records
DO: Dominions Office
FCO: Foreign and Commonwealth Office
FO: Foreign Office

WTO: World Trade Organization, Geneva
CP: Contracting Parties Series
E. Wyndham White: Speeches and Articles 1948–1964
L Series: General Records
MTN: Ministerial Series
Secret Series

Interviews with the Author

Bruce Brown, 18 July 2005
Confidential interview, 13 July 2006
Richard Cooper, 12 February 2013
Rodney de C. Grey, 12 January 2005
Sir Frank Holmes, 17 July 2005
John Jackson, 17 November 2004
Julio Lacarte, 20 May 2005
Harald Malmgren, 15 May 2008
John Martin, 18 July 2005
Hugh McPhail, 19 July 2005
James Meade, 24 May 1993
Richard Nottage, 18 July 2005
Terence O'Brien,19 July 2005
Sylvia Ostry, 2 July 2009
Simon Reisman, 17 May 2005
Alan Renouf, 8 May 2008
J. H. Warren, 18 May 2005
John Weekes, 21 March 2013

Author's Correspondence

Alan Renouf, 3 March 2008

Published Primary Documents

Cavell, J., M. D. Stevenson, and K. Spooner (eds.). *Documents on External Relations, 1959, Vol. 26, 1959* (Ottawa: Department of External Affairs, 2006).
Crawford, J., N. Anderson, and M. G. N. Morris (eds.). *Australian Trade Policy 1942–1966: A Documentary History* (Canberra: Australian National University Press; Toronto: University of Toronto Press, 1968).

Donaghy, G. (ed.). *Documents on Canadian External Relations, 1955, Vol. 21* (Ottawa: Department of External Affairs, 1999).

Foreign Relations of the United States 1949, Vol. I: National Security Affairs, Foreign Economic Policy (Washington, DC: United States Government Printing Office, 1976).

Foreign Relations of the United States 1950, Vol. I: National Security Affairs, Foreign Economic Policy (Washington, DC: United States Government Printing Office, 1977).

Foreign Relations of the United States 1951, Vol. I: National Security Affairs; Foreign Economic Policy (Washington, DC: United States Government Printing Office, 1979).

Foreign Relations of the United States 1952–1954, Vol. I: General: Economic and Political Matters, Part 1 (of 2) (Washington, DC: United States Government Printing Office, 1983).

Foreign Relations of the United States 1955–1957, Vol. IX: Foreign Economic Policy; Foreign Information Program (Washington, DC: United States Government Printing Office, 1987).

Foreign Relations of the United States 1958–1960, Vol. IV: Foreign Economic Policy (Washington, DC: United States Government Printing Office, 1992).

Foreign Relations of the United States 1961–1963, Vol. IX: Foreign Economic Policy (Washington, DC: United States Government Printing Office, 1995).

Food and Agriculture Organization of the United Nations (FAO). *The State of Food and Agriculture 1995* (Rome: FAO, 2002–).

GATT. *The Activities of GATT* (1959/60, 1960/61, 1961/62, 1964/65, 1967/68, 1973, 1975, 1978, 1979, 1987, 1989, 1990, 1992).

GATT. *The Tokyo Round of Multilateral Trade Negotiations: Report by the Director General of GATT* (Geneva: GATT, April 1979).

GATT. *Trade Policies for a Better Future: The 'Leutwiler Report', the GATT and the Uruguay Round*, with an introduction by A. Dunkel (Dordrecht, Boston, and Lancaster: Martinus Nijhoff Publishers, 1987).

GATT. *Trends in International Trade: Report by a Panel of Experts* (Geneva: GATT, October 1958).

Howson, S. (ed.). *The Collected Papers of James Meade, Vol. III* (London: Unwin Hyman, 1988).

Lipgens, W. (ed.). *Documents on the History of European Integration, Vol. 4* (Berlin and New York: De Gruyter, 1985).

Office of the Special Representative for Trade Negotiations. *Report on United States Negotiations. The General Agreement on Tariffs and Trade, 1964–1967 Trade Conference, Geneva, Switzerland, Vol. I: General Summary; Vol. II: List of Tariff Concessions Granted by the United States.*

Proceedings of the United Nations Conference on Trade and Development, 23 March – 16 June 1964, Vol. I: Final Act and Report; Vol. II: Policy Statements; Vol. V: Financing and Invisibles, Institutional Arrangements (New York: United Nations, 1964).

Proceedings of the United Nations Conference on Trade and Development, Fifth Session, 7 May – 3 June 1979 (New York: United Nations 1981).

Newspapers and Magazines

'A Future that Does Not Work', *The Economist* (25 December 1982), 90.

'Arthur Dunkel, Diplomat and Pioneer of the World Trade Organisation', *The Guardian* (16 June 2005), www.theguardian.com/news/2005/jun/16/guardiano bituaries.wto.

Bell, A. 'GATT Deal Protest Leaves 20 Hurt', *The Guardian* (2 December 1992), 7.

Bell, I. 'Last Straw for Paysans', *The Herald* (Glasgow) (14 October 1992), 15.

Bertin, O. 'Farm Policies Under Strain', *Globe and Mail* (22 November 1982).

Breen, M. 'S. Koreans Protest Rice Imports', *Washington Times*, 6 December 1993), A11.

Bremner, C. 'French Farmers Target British Lorries', *The Times* (London) (25 November 1992).

Brewer, J. 'US Farmers Renew Attack on Dunkel Plan', *Lloyd's List* (9 January 1992), 3.

Carter, J., and G. R. Ford. 'Stop the Drift toward Economic Anarchy', *The Economist* (21 November 1982), 19.

'Clubland', *The Economist* (29 March 1986), 58.

Cohen, R. 'The World Trade Agreement; The Overview; GATT Talks End in Joy and Relief', *New York Times* (16 December 1993), D1.

Crossley, G. 'Baleful Straws in the Wind', *The Guardian* (27 November 1992), 19.

'Dawkins Tells UK to End Farm Trade War', *Sydney Morning Herald* (26 September 1986), 2.

Drozdiak, W. '40,000 Farmers Protest US–European Trade Accord', *Washington Post* (2 December 1992), A33.

Drozdiak, W. 'French Set for "Crisis" on Trade: Farmers Press Government to Keep Export Subsidies', *Washington Post* (16 September 1993), A20.

'Dump the Farmers', *The Economist* (5 March 1983), 19.

'EEC Trade: Beefed Up for a Fight', *The Economist* (9 February 1985), 46.

'Expect Other Pacts Will Follow Geneva', *Financial Post* (22 November 1947), 1.

'Farmer Hurt in Fierce Riots Against GATT Deal', *Irish Times* (2 December 1992), 1.

'Farmers Lash Out at Rice Ruling', *Courier-Mail* (15 December 1993), 29.

'Farmers to Converge on Ottawa', *Globe and Mail* (7 February 1992).

Farnsworth, C. 'A Reporter's Notebook: Behind the Scenes at the GATT Trade Talks in Geneva', *New York Times* (5 December 1982), 8.

Farnsworth, C. 'Discordant Notes Mar Trade Talks', *New York Times* (25 November 1982), 1.

Farnsworth, C. 'GATT Frustrates US So Far', *New York Times* (26 November 1982), 1.

'50 Years on the Undertakers are Back', *The Economist* (25 December 1982), 75.

'Freeish Trade', *The Economist*, (29 December 1979), 44.

'French, American Farmers Assail US–EEC Accord', *Toronto Star* (21 November 1992), C2.

'French Communists Aim Attacks on Tariff Pacts', *Christian Science Monitor* (17 November 1947), 15.

'GATT Chief Says He Will Not Stay', *New York Times* (8 November 1967), 94.

'GATT Pulls Back from the Brink', *The Economist* (30 November 1982), 1.

'Gatt: So Close and Yet So Far', *The Economist* (4 January 1992), 62.

'GATT's Trade Talks', *The Economist* (17 June 1978), 86.

'GATT Trade Deal: Yes, But', *The Economist* (28 July 1979), 100.

'GATT Trade Talks: End in Sight', *The Economist* (7 April 1979), 84.

'Geneva Pact to Prod Australian Trade? Expansion of Markets' *Christian Science Monitor* (20 November 1947), 6.

Greene, G. 'World Trade Talks Give Farmers Some Hope', *The Advertiser* (22 September 1986).

Greenhouse, S. 'A Move to Break World Trade Deadlock', *New York Times* (21 December 1991), 33.

Greenspon, E. 'GATT Director is Calm amid the Free-Trade Battle', *Globe and Mail*, 18 September 1989).

Hoffman, M. 'Britain Proposes World Trade Plan', *New York Times* (9 November 1954), 1, 10.

Hoffman, M. 'French Irk Allies with Trade Stand', *New York Times* (30 November 1954), 17.

Hoffman, M. 'Tariff Body Opens Key Geneva Talks', *New York Times* (29 October 1954), 2.

Hone, K. 'Farmers Protest in the Rain at GATT Deal', *Irish Times* (16 September 1993), 6.

Hone, K. 'France Celebrates "A Great and Fine Victory" for European Culture', *Irish Times* (15 December 1993), 7.

Hone, K. 'Maverick Farmers' Body to Blockade Paris over GATT', *Irish Times* (15 September 1993), 8.

'International Civil Servant', *New York Times* (11 November 1967), 32.

Knox, P. 'Big Obstacle Overcome on GATT Guidelines', *Globe and Mail* (20 September 1986), A7.

Knox, P. 'Complex Trade Talks Unravel at Uruguay Meeting', *Globe and Mail* (17 September 1986), A12.

Knox, P. 'GATT Delegates Near Accord on Reducing Food Subsidies', *Globe and Mail* (19 September 1986), A5.

Lewis, P. 'Food Surplus May Bankrupt European Bloc', *New York Times* (27 December 1986), 1.

Lyne, P. 'Britain Takes Lead for Freer Trade', *Christian Science Monitor* (2 November 1954).

'Making Sense of the Mad Gatter's Tea Party', *The Economist* (4 December 1982), 75.

Nossiter, B. D. 'Poles Make Western Trade Bid', *Washington Post* (19 June 1964), A21.

'Of Rice and Men', *The Economist* (28 July 1990), 56.

Ono, N. 'Tokyo Calls Dunkel's Draft Unacceptable', *Nikkei Weekly* (4 January 1992), 3.

'On the Brink of a Trade War?', *The Economist* (29 November 1982), 77.

'Paris and Geneva', *The Economist* (27 September 1947), 505–506.

Passell, P. 'The World: Regional Trade Makes Global Deals Go Round', *New York Times* (19 December 1993).

Pollack, A. 'Tokyo Journal: For the Rice Lobby the Bowl of Plenty Dries Up', *New York Times* (13 December 1993), A4.

'Prelude to Geneva', *The Economist* (29 March 1947), 444.

'Regionalism and Trade: The Right Direction?', *The Economist* (16 September 1995), 23.

Samuelson, R. 'Why GATT Isn't Boring', *Washington Post* (22 December 1993), A21.

'Seoul Protest', *Lloyd's List* (17 November 1993), 14.

'Tariffs and Trade', *The Economist* (22 November 1947), 828.

'Textiles and Clothing Through the Wringer', *The Economist* (31 December 1977), 87.

'Textiles Behind the Maginot Line', *The Economist* (30 July 1977), 75.

'Texts Placed on Sale', *New York Times* (18 November 1947), 16.

'The Gnat and the Camel', *The Economist* (1 July 1978), 71.

'The New Tariff Agreement', *Los Angeles Times* (23 November 1947), A4.

'The Next Transatlantic War', *The Economist* (20 November 1982), 33.

'The Nine Draw their Gatt Guns', *The Economist* (30 June 1973), 54.

'Threaten to Curb Reciprocal Pacts', *New York Times* (20 November 1947), 3.

Tomlins, J. 'Siege of Mickey's Castle', *Daily Mail* (27 June 1992), 9.

Torday, P., and D. Usborne. 'Farmers Riot as World Trade Talks Head for Collapse', *The Independent* (4 December 1990), 22.

'Trade-Block Folly', *The Economist* (20 April 1991), 13.

'Trade Talks', *The Economist* (2 December 1978).

'Trade Talks: Paris Willing?', *The Economist* (16 December 1978), 103.

Varga, E. 'The Geneva Trade Talks', *New Times*, No. 20 (16 May 1947).

'Violence Grows as French Blast Trade Pact with US', *Toronto Star* (25 November 1992), A1.

Walters, P. 'Farming Nations Seek Reforms: Talks in Australia on World Agricultural Reform', *The Guardian* (28 August 1986).

Zarocostas, J. 'No Green Light Yet for GATT Talks: Agriculture Remains the Major Obstacle to Resumption of Suspended Discussions', *Globe and Mail* (15 January 1991).

Statistics

Food and Agriculture Organization of the United Nations, Statistics Division. FAOstat, http://faostat3.fao.org/home/E.

Kravis, I. B., A. W. Heston, and R. Summers. *International Comparisons of Real Product and Purchasing Power* (United Nations International Comparison Project, Phase II, produced by the Statistical Office of the United Nations and the World Bank) (Baltimore: Johns Hopkins University Press, 1978).

Kravis, I. B., Z. Kenessey, A. W. Heston, and R. Summers. *A System of International Comparisons of Gross Product and Purchasing Power* (United Nations International Comparison Project, Phase One, produced by the Statistical Office of the United Nations, the World Bank, and the International Comparison Unit of the University of Pennsylvania) (Baltimore: Johns Hopkins University Press, 1975).

Mitchell. B. R. *International Historical Statistics, Africa, Asia and Oceania, 1750–2000,* 4th edition, OECD Historical Statistics 1960–1997 (Paris: OECD, 1999).

Mitchell, B. R. *International Historical Statistics, Europe 1750–1988* (New York: Palgrave Macmillan, 1992).

Mitchell, B. R. *International Historical Statistics, The Americas 1750–1988* (New York: Palgrave Macmillan, 1993).

Pew Research Centre. 'Faith and Skepticism about Trade, Foreign Investment', Pew Research Centre Report (September 2014), www.pewresearch.org/global/ 2014/09/16/faith-and-skepticism-about-trade-foreign-investment/

United Nations. *Yearbook of International Trade Statistics* (1980).

United Nations. *Yearbook of International Trade Statistics* (1981).

Books and Journal Articles

Aaronson, S. A. *Taking Trade to the Streets: The Lost History of Public Efforts to Shape Globalization* (Ann Arbor: University of Michigan Press, 2001).

Aaronson, S. A. *Trade and the American Dream: A Social History of Postwar Trade Policy* (Lexington: University of Kentucky Press, 1996).

Ajulo, S. B. 'Lomé Convention: A Review', *Journal of African Studies* 13 (4) (Winter 1986), 142–152.

Alkema, Y. 'European-American Trade Policies, 1961-1963' in D. Brinkley and R. T. Griffiths (eds.), *John F. Kennedy and Europe* (Baton Rouge: Louisiana State University Press, 1999), 212–234.

Allison, G. 'The Myth of the Liberal Order: From Historical Accident to Conventional Wisdom', *Foreign Affairs* 97 (4) (July/August 2018), 124–133.

Amrith, S., and G. Sluga. 'New Histories of the United Nations', *Journal of World History* 19 (3) (September 2008), 251–274.

Angell, N. *The Great Illusion: A Study of the Relation of Military Power to National Advantage* (London: Heinemann, 1912).

Aslund, A. 'The New Soviet Policy Towards International Economic Organisations', *World Today* 44 (February 1988), 27–30.

Auffret, D. *Alexandre Kojève: La Philosophie, l'état, la fin de l'histoire* (Paris: Grasset, 1990).

Ayoob, M. 'The Third World in the System of States: Acute Schizophrenia or Growing Pains?', *International Studies Quarterly* 33 (1) (March 1989), 67–79.

Baldwin, D. A., and H. V. Milner (eds.). *East-West Trade and the Atlantic Alliance* (New York: St. Martin's Press, 1990).

Barbieri, K. *The Liberal Illusion: Does Trade Promote Peace?* (Ann Arbor: University of Michigan Press, 2002).

Barbieri, K., and G. Schneider. 'Globalization and Peace: Assessing New Directions in the Study of Trade and Conflict', *Journal of Peace Research* 36 (4) (July 1999), 387–404.

Barnett, M. N., and M. Finnemore. 'The Politics, Power, and Pathologies of International Organizations', *International Organization* 53 (4) (Autumn 1999), 699–732.

Bellefroide, D. de. 'The Commission pour l'Étude des Problèmes d'Après-Guerre (CEPAG), 1941-1944' in M. Conway and J. Gotovitch (eds.), *Europe in Exile: European Exile Communities in Britain, 1940–1945* (New York and Oxford: Berghan Books, 2001), 121–134.

Bernstein, W. J. *A Splendid Exchange: How Trade Shaped the World* (New York: Atlantic Monthly Press, 2008).

Bevir, M., and F. Trentmann (eds.). *Governance, Consumers and Citizens: Agency and Resistance in Contemporary Politics* (Basingstoke: Palgrave Macmillan, 2007).

Bhagwati, J. *Protectionism* (Cambridge, MA and London: MIT Press, 1988).

Bhagwati, J. *Termites in the Trading System: How Preferential Agreements Undermine Free Trade* (Oxford: Oxford University Press, 2008).

Bhagwati, J., and M. Hirsch (eds.). *The Uruguay Round and Beyond: Essays in Honor of Arthur Dunkel* (Ann Arbor: University of Michigan Press, 1998).

Bhagwati, J., P. Krishna, and A. Panagariya (eds.). *Trading Blocs: Alternative Approaches to Analyzing Preferential Trade Agreements* (Cambridge, MA and London: MIT Press, 1999).

Bhalla, A. S., and P. Bhalla. *Regional Blocs: Building Blocks or Stumbling Blocks?* (Basingstoke: Macmillan Press Ltd; New York: St. Martin's Press, 1997).

Blackhurst, R. 'The Role of the Director-General and Secretariat' in A. Narlikar, M. Daunton, and R. M. Stern (eds.), *The Oxford Handbook on the World Trade Organization* (Oxford: Oxford University Press, 2012), 146.

Borgwardt, E. *A New Deal for the World: America's Vision for Human Rights* (Cambridge, MA: Belknap Press of Harvard University Press, 2005).

Brzezinski, Z. *The Soviet Bloc: Unity and Conflict* (New York: Praeger, 1961, 1965).

Bundy, H. 'An Introductory Note', *International Organization* 1 (1) (1947), 1–2.

Buterbaugh, K., and R. Fulton. *The WTO Primer: Tracing Trade's Visible Hand Through Case Studies* (Basingstoke: Palgrave Macmillan, 2007).

Cain, F. *Economic Statecraft During the Cold War: European Responses to the US Trade Embargo* (London and New York: Routledge, 2007).

Capling, A. *Australia and the Global Trade System from Havana to Seattle* (Cambridge: Cambridge University Press, 2001).

Chan, S. 'Taiwan's Application to the GATT: A New Urgency with the Conclusion of the Uruguay Round', *Indiana Journal of Global Legal Studies, Symposium: Global Migration and the Future of the Nation-State* 2 (1) (Fall 1994), 275–299.

Clavin, P. *Securing the World Economy: The Reinvention of the League of Nations, 1920–1946* (Oxford: Oxford University Press, 2013).

Clavin, P. *The Great Depression in Europe, 1929–1939* (Basingstoke: Macmillan, 2000).

Connelly, M. *Fatal Misconception: The Struggle to Control World Population* (Cambridge, MA: Belknap Press of Harvard University Press, 2008).

Cooper, R. N. 'Trade Policy is Foreign Policy', *Foreign Policy* 9 (1972/73), 18–36.

Coppolaro, L. 'A Power Without Leadership: The EC in the GATT Trade Regime' in U. Krotz, K. K. Patel, and F. Romero (eds.), *Europe's Cold War Relations: The EC Towards a Global Role* (London: Bloomsbury Academic, 2019), 127–144.

Coppolaro, L. *The Making of a World Trade Power: The European Economic Community (EEC) in the GATT Kennedy Round Negotiations 1963–1967* (Farnham: Ashgate, 2013).

Coppolaro, L., and F. McKenzie (eds.). *A Global History of Trade and Conflict since 1500* (Basingstoke: Palgrave Macmillan, 2013).

Croome, J. *Reshaping the World Trading System: A History of the Uruguay Round* (Geneva: World Trade Organization, 1995).

Cullather, N. 'Development? It's History', *Diplomatic History* 24 (4) (Fall 2000), 641–653.

Curzon, G., and V. Curzon. 'GATT: A Trader's Club' in R. W. Cox and H. K. Jacobson (eds.), *The Anatomy of Influence: Decision Making in International Organization* (New Haven, CT, and London: Yale University Press, 1974), 298–333.

Dam, K. W. *The GATT: Law and International Economic Organization* (Chicago: University of Chicago Press, 1970).

Davis, C. L. *Food Fights Over Free Trade: How International Institutions Promote Agricultural Trade Liberalization* (Princeton and Oxford: Princeton University Press, 2003).

Davis, C. L. 'International Institutions and Issue Linkage: Building Support for Agricultural Trade Liberalization', *American Political Science Review* 98 (1) (February 2004), 153–169.

Deese, D. *World Trade Politics: Power, Principles and Leadership* (London and New York: Routledge, 2008).

Destler, I. M. *American Trade Politics*, 4th edition (Washington, DC: Institute for International Economics, 2005).

Deudney, D., and G. J. Ikenberry. 'Liberal World: The Resilient Order', *Foreign Affairs* 97 (4) (July/August 2018), 16–24.

Devuyst, Y. 'European Union Trade Policy after the Lisbon Treaty: The Community Method at Work' in N. Witzleb, A. M. Arranz, and P. Winand (eds.), *The European Union and Global Engagement: Institutions, Policies and Challenges* (Cheltenham: Edward Elgar, 2015), 138–158.

Dinan, D. *Ever Closer Union: An Introduction to European Integration*, 3rd edition (Boulder, CO: Lynne Reiner, 2005).

Dormael, A. van. *Bretton Woods: Birth of a Monetary System* (London: Macmillan, 1978).

Dorussen, H., and H. Ward. 'Trade Networks and the Kantian Peace', *Journal of Peace Research* 47 (1) (January 2010), 29–42.

Dosman, E. J. *The Life and Times of Raúl Prebisch, 1901–1986* (Montreal: McGill-Queen's University Press, 2008).

Dryden, S. *Trade Warriors: USTR and the American Crusade for Free Trade* (New York: Oxford University Press, 1995).

Dunkley, G. *The Free Trade Adventure: The WTO, the Uruguay Round and Globalism – A Critique* (London and New York: Zed Books, 2000).

Eckes, A. E. Jr. 'In Globalization, People Matter: Eight Who Shaped the World Trading System', *Global Economy Quarterly* 1 (4) (2000), 303–314.

Eckes, A. E. Jr. (ed.). *Revisiting U.S. Trade Policy: Decisions in Perspective* (Athens, OH: Ohio University Press, 2000).

Edsall, N. C. *Richard Cobden: Independent Radical* (Cambridge, MA: Harvard University Press, 1986).

Edwards, R. D. *The Pursuit of Reason: The Economist, 1843–1993* (London: Hamish Hamilton, 1993).

Ekbladh, D. *The Great American Mission: Modernization and the Construction of an American World Order* (Princeton: Princeton University Press, 2010).

Ellison, J. *Threatening Europe: Britain and the Creation of the European Community, 1955–1958* (Basingstoke: Macmillan Press; New York: St Martin's Press, 2000).

Escobar, A. *Encountering Development: The Making and Unmaking of the Third World* (Princeton: Princeton University Press, 2011).

Evans, J. *The Kennedy Round in American Trade Policy: The Twilight of the GATT?* (Cambridge, MA: Harvard University Press, 1971).

Fallenbuchl, Z. M. 'The Council for Mutual Economic Assistance', *International Journal* 43 (Winter 1987/8), 106–126.

Federico, G. *Feeding the World: An Economic History of Agriculture, 1800–2000* (Oxford and Princeton: Princeton University Press, 2005).

Ferguson, N., C. S. Maier, E. Manela, and D. J. Sargent (eds.). *The Shock of the Global: The 1970s in Perspective* (Cambridge, MA: Belknap Press of Harvard University Press, 2010).

Finlayson, J. A., and M. W. Zacker. 'The GATT and the Regulation of Trade Barriers: Regime Dynamics and Functions' in S. D. Krasner (ed.), *International Regimes* (Ithaca, NY: Cornell University Press, 1983), 273–314.

Finney, P. *Palgrave Advances in International History* (Basingstoke and New York: Palgrave Macmillan, 2005).

Forsberg, A. 'The Politics of GATT Expansion: Japanese Accession and the Domestic Political Context in Japan and the United States, 1948-1955', *Business and Economic History* 27 (1) (Fall 1998), 185–195.

Frank, A. G. *Capitalism and Underdevelopment in Latin America: Historical Studies of Chile and Brazil* (New York: Monthly Review Press, 1967).

Gaddis, J. L. *We Now Know: Rethinking Cold War History* (Oxford: Clarendon Press; New York: Oxford University Press, 1997).

Gallup, G. H. *The Gallup Poll: Public Opinion 1935–1971, Vol. One: 1935–1948; Vol. Two: 1949–1958; Vol. Three: 1959–1971* (New York: Random House, 1972).

Gallup, G. Jr. *The Gallup Poll: Public Opinion 1994* (Wilmington: Scholarly Resources, 1995).

Gardner, R. *Sterling–Dollar Diplomacy in Current Perspective: The Origins and Prospects of Our International Economic Order* (New York: Columbia University Press, 1980).

Gillingham, J. *Coal, Steel and the Rebirth of Europe 1945–1955: The Germans and French from Ruhr Conflict to Economic Community* (Cambridge and New York: Cambridge University Press, 1991).

Gilman, N. 'The New International Economic Order: A Reintroduction', *Humanity: An International Journal of Human Rights, Humanitarianism, and Development* 6 (1) (Spring 2015), 1–16.

Gilpin, R. *The Political Economy of International Relations* (Princeton: Princeton University Press, 1987).

Glendon, M. A. *A World Made New: Eleanor Roosevelt and the Universal Declaration of Human Rights* (New York: Random House, 2001).

Goldstein, J. 'The United States and World Trade: Hegemony by Proxy?' in T. C. Lawton, J. N. Rosenau, and A. C. Verdun (eds.), *Strange Power: Shaping the Parameters of International Relations and International Political Economy* (Aldershot and Burlington: Ashgate, 2000), 249–272.

Grazia, V. de. *Irresistible Empire: America's Advance through 20th-Century Europe* (Cambridge, MA: Belknap Press of Harvard University Press, 2005).

Grosbois, T. 'La Belgique et le Benelux: De l'universalisme au régionalisme' in M. Dumoulin, G. Duchenne, and A. Van Laer (eds.), *La Belgique, les petits états et la construction européenne* (Bern: Peter Land, 2004), 59–91.

Hart, M. 'Almost but Not Quite: The 1947–1948 Bilateral Canada–U.S. Negotiations', *American Review of Canadian Studies* 19 (1) (Spring 1989), 25–58.

Hart, M. *Also Present at the Creation: Dana Wilgress and the United Nations Conference on Trade and Employment at Havana* (Ottawa: Centre for Trade Policy and Law, 1995).

Hart, M. *A Trading Nation: Canadian Trade Policy from Colonialism to Globalization* (Vancouver: University of British Columbia Press, 2002).

Hart, M., C. Robertson, and B. Dymond. *Decision at Midnight: Inside The Canada–US Free Trade Negotiations* (Vancouver: University of British Columbia Press, 1994).

Haslam, J. 'The UN and the Soviet Union: New Thinking?', *International Affairs* 65 (4) (Autumn 1989), 677–684.

Hathaway, D. E. *Agriculture and the GATT: Rewriting the Rules* (Washington, DC: Institute for International Economics, 1987).

Haus, L. H. *Globalizing the GATT: The Soviet Union's Successor States, Eastern Europe, and the International Trading System* (Washington, DC: Brookings Institution, 1992).

Hearden, P. J. *Architects of Globalism: Building a New World Order during World War II* (Fayetteville: University of Arkansas Press, 2002).

Hegre, H., J. R. Oneal, and B. Russett. 'Trade Does Promote Peace: New Simultaneous Estimates of the Reciprocal Effects of Trade and Conflict', *Journal of Peace Research* 47 (6) (2010), 763–774.

Helleiner, E. *Forgotten Foundations of Bretton Woods: International Development and the Making of Postwar Order* (Ithaca, NY: Cornell University Press, 2014).

Helleiner, E. 'The Development Mandate of International Institutions: Where Did it Come From?', *Studies in Comparative International Development* 44 (3) (September 2009), 189–211.

Hennessy, P. *Never Again: Britain 1945–51* (London: Jonathan Cape, 1992).

Heron, T. *The Global Political Economy of Trade Protectionism and Liberalization: Trade Reform and Economic Adjustment in Textiles and Clothing* (Abingdon and New York: Routledge, 2012).

Herter, C. A. 'U.S. Aims in the Kennedy Round', *Atlantic Community Quarterly* 2 (2) (Summer 1964), 240–246.

Higgott, R. A., and A. F. Cooper. 'Middle Power Leadership and Coalition Building: Australia, the Cairns Group, and the Uruguay Round of Trade Negotiations', *International Organization* 44 (4) (Autumn 1990), 589–632.

Hirschman, A. O., J. Adelman, E. Rothschild, and A. Sen. *The Essential Hirschman* (Princeton: Princeton University Press, 2013).

Hobson, J. M. 'Re-Embedding the Global Colour Line Within Post-1945 International Theory' in A. Anievas, N. Manchanda, and R. Shilliam (eds.), *Race and Racism in International Relations: Confronting the Global Colour Line* (London: Routledge, 2015), 81–97.

Hoekman, B. M., and M. M. Kostecki. *The Political Economy of the World Trading System: from GATT to WTO* (Oxford and New York: Oxford University Press, 1995).

Howe, A., and S. Morgan (eds.). *Rethinking Nineteenth-Century Liberalism: Richard Cobden Bicentenary Essays* (Aldershot: Ashgate, 2006).

Howse, R. 'Kojève's Latin Empire', *Policy Review* 126 (August/September 2004), 41–48.

Howson, S. *Lionel Robbins* (Cambridge: Cambridge University Press, 2011).

Hudec, R. E. *Developing Countries in the GATT Legal System* (Cambridge: Cambridge University Press, 2011).

Hull, C. *The Memoirs of Cordell Hull* (New York: Macmillan, 1948).

Ikenberry, G. J. *After Victory: Institutions, Strategic Restraint, and the Rebuilding of Order After Major Wars* (Princeton: Princeton University Press, 2001).

Ikenberry, G. J. 'A World Economy Restored: Expert Consensus and the Anglo-American Postwar Settlement', *International Organization* 46 (1) (Winter 1992), 289–321.

Ingersent, K.A., A. J. Rayner, and R.C. Hine (eds.). *Agriculture in the Uruguay Round* (New York: St. Martin's Press, 1994).

Iriye, A. *Global and Transnational History: The Past, Present and Future* (Basingstoke: Palgrave Macmillan, 2013).

Iriye, A. *Global Community: The Role of International Organizations in the Making of the Contemporary World* (Berkeley: University of California Press, 2002).

Irwin, D. A. *Against the Tide: An Intellectual History of Free Trade* (Princeton: Princeton University Press, 1996).

Irwin, D. A. *Clashing over Commerce: A History of US Trade Policy* (Chicago: University of Chicago Press, 2017).

Irwin, D. A. *Free Trade Under Fire*, 2nd edition (Princeton: Princeton University Press, 2005).

Irwin, D. A., P. C. Mavroidis, and A. O. Sykes. *The Genesis of the GATT* (New York and Cambridge: Cambridge University Press, 2008).

Jackson, J. H. *Restructuring the GATT System* (London: Royal Institute of International Affairs, 1990).

Jackson, J. H. 'The Case of the World Trade Organization', *International Affairs* 84 (3) (May 2008), 437–454.

Jackson, J. H. *World Trade and the Law of GATT: A Legal Analysis of the General Agreement on Tariffs and Trade* (Indianapolis: Bobbs Merrill, 1969).

Jackson, J. H., and A. O. Sykes. *Implementing the Uruguay Round* (Oxford: Clarendon Press, 1997).

Jackson, I. *The Economic Cold War: America, Britain and East-West Trade, 1948–63* (Basingstoke: Palgrave Macmillan, 2001).

Jackson, S., and A. O'Malley (eds.). *The Institution of International Order: From the League of Nations to the United Nations* (London and New York: Routledge, 2018).

Jacobson, H. K., and M. Oksenberg. *China's Participation in the IMF, the World Bank, and GATT: Toward a Global Economic Order* (Ann Arbor: University of Michigan Press, 1990).

Jervis, R. L., F. Gavin, J. Rovner, and D. Labrosse (eds.). *Chaos in the Liberal Order: The Trump Presidency and International Politics in the Twenty-First Century* (New York: Columbia University Press, 2018).

Jolly, R., L. Emmerij, D. Ghai, and F. Lapeyre. *UN Contributions to Development Thinking and Practice* (Bloomington: Indiana University Press, 2004).

Josling, T. E. *Agriculture in the Tokyo Round Negotiations* (London: Trade Policy Research Centre, 1977).

Josling, T. E., S. Tangermann, and T. K. Warley. *Agriculture in the GATT* (Basingstoke: Macmillan, 1996).

Judt, T. *Postwar: A History of Europe Since 1945* (New York: Penguin Press, 2005).

Kenyon, D., and D. Lee, *The Struggle for Trade Liberalisation in Agriculture: Australia and the Cairns Group in the Uruguay Round* (Canberra: Commonwealth of Australia, 2006).

Keohane, R. O. *After Hegemony: Cooperation and Discord in the World Political Economy* (Princeton and Oxford: Princeton University Press, 1984).

Kim, S. Y. *Power and the Governance of Global Trade: From the GATT to the WTO* (Ithaca, NY: Cornell University Press, 2010).

Kimball, W. F. *The Juggler: Franklin Roosevelt as Wartime Statesman* (Princeton: Princeton University Press, 1991).

Kirshner, O. (ed.). *The Bretton Woods-GATT System: Retrospect and Prospect after Fifty Years* (Armonk, NY: M. E. Sharpe, 1996).

Kock, K. *International Trade Policy and the GATT, 1947–1967* (Stockholm: Almqvist and Wiksell, 1969).

Kott, S. 'Fighting the War or Preparing for Peace? The ILO During the Second World War', *Journal of Modern European History* 12 (3) (August 2014), 359–376.

Krugman, P. 'Does the New Trade Theory Require a New Trade Policy?', *World Economy* 15 (4) (July 1992), 423–442.

La Barca, G. *The US, the EC and World Trade from the Kennedy Round to the Start of the Uruguay Round* (London: Bloomsbury Academic, 2016).

Leffler, M. P., and O. A. Westad (eds.). *The Cambridge History of the Cold War: Vol. I, Origins* (Cambridge: Cambridge University Press, 2010).

Liang, W. 'China's WTO Negotiation Process and Its Implications', *Journal of Contemporary China* 11 (33) (2002), 683–719.

Long, O. *International Trade Under Threat: A Constructive Response* (London: Trade Policy Research Centre, 1978).

Low, P. *Trading Free: The GATT and US Trade Policy* (New York: Twentieth Century Fund Press, 1993).

Ludlow, N. P. 'The Emergence of a Commercial Heavy-Weight: The Kennedy Round Negotiations and the European Community of the 1960s', *Diplomacy & Statecraft* 18 (2) (July 2007), 351–368.

Ludlow, N. P. *The European Community and the Crises of the 1960s: Negotiating the Gaullist Challenge* (London and New York: Routledge, 2006).

Mackenzie, D. *ICAO: A History of the International Civil Aviation Organization* (Toronto: University of Toronto Press, 2010).

Mahan, E. R. *Kennedy, de Gaulle, and Western Europe* (Basingstoke: Palgrave Macmillan, 2002).

Maier, C. S. 'The World Economy and the Cold War in the Middle of the Twentieth Century' in M. Leffler and O. A. Westad (eds.), *The Cambridge History of the Cold War, Vol. I: Origins* (Cambridge: Cambridge University Press, 2010), 44–66.

Malmgren, H. B. 'Coming Trade Wars? (Neo-Mercantilism and Foreign Policy)', *Foreign Policy* 1 (Winter 1970/71), 115–143.

Manning, R. *Against the Grain: How Agriculture Has Hijacked Civilization* (New York: North Point Press, 2004).

Mansfield, E. D., and H. V. Milner. 'The New Wave of Regionalism', *International Organization* 53 (3) (Summer 1999), 589–627.

Marceau, G. (ed.). *A History of Law and Lawyers in the GATT/WTO: The Development of the Rule of Law in the Multilateral Trading System* (Cambridge: Cambridge University Press, 2015).

Maunder, A., and A. Valdés (eds.). *Agriculture and Governments in an Interdependent World: Proceedings of the Twentieth International Conference of Agricultural Economists, held at Buenos Aires, Argentina, 24–31 August 1988* (Aldershot: Dartmouth Publishing Company, 1989).

Mazower, M. *Governing the World: The History of an Idea, 1815 to the Present* (New York: Penguin Press, 2012).

McKenzie, F. 'Eric Wyndham White' in B. Reinalda and K. Kille (eds.), *The Biographical Dictionary of Secretaries-General of International Organizations* (2012), www.ru.nl/fm/iobio

McKenzie, F. 'Imperial Solutions to International Crises: Alliances, Trade, and the Ottawa Imperial Economic Conference of 1932' in J. Fisher, E. Pedaliu, and R. Smith (eds.), *The Foreign Office, Commerce and British Foreign Policy in the Twentieth Century* (London: Palgrave Macmillan, 2017), 165–188.

McKenzie, F. *Redefining the Bonds of Commonwealth: The Politics of Preference, 1939–1948* (Basingstoke: Palgrave Macmillan, 2002).

McKenzie, F. 'Where was Trade at Bretton Woods?' in G. Scott Smith and S. Rofe (eds.), *Global Perspectives on the Bretton Woods Conference and the Post-War World Order* (Basingstoke: Palgrave Macmillan, 2017), 163–180.

McMahon, R. J. *Dean Acheson and the Creation of an American World Order* (Washington, DC: Potomac Books, 2009).

Meade, J. E. *The Economic Basis of a Durable Peace* (London: George Allen & Unwin, 1940).

Mélandri, P. 'The Troubled Friendship: France and the United States 1945-1989' in G. Lundestad (ed.), *No End to Alliance: The United States and Western Europe: Past, Present and Future* (Basingstoke: Macmillan, 1998), 112–133.

Morgan, K. O. *Labour in Power 1945–1951* (New York: Oxford University Press, 1984).

Muirhead, B. 'Canada, the United States and the GATT Review Session 1954–55: A Clash of Perceptions', *Canadian Historical Review* 73 (4) (December 1992), 484–506.

Narlikar, A. *The WTO: A Very Short Introduction* (New York: Oxford University Press, 2005).

Narlikar, A., M. Daunton, and R. M. Stern. *The Oxford Handbook on the World Trade Organization* (Oxford: Oxford University Press, 2012).

Nuenlist, C., A. Locher, and G. Martin (eds.). *Globalizing de Gaulle: International Perspectives on French Foreign Policy 1958–1960* (Lanham, MD: Lexington Books, 2010).

Oatley, T. 'The Reductionist Gamble: Open Economy Politics in the Global Economy', *International Organization* 65 (2) (Spring 2011), 311–341.

Oestreich, J. E. (ed.). *International Organizations as Self-Directed Actors: A Framework for Analysis* (Abingdon: Routledge, 2012).

Oneal, J. R., and B. Russett, 'Clear and Clean: The Fixed Effects of the Liberal Peace', *International Organization* 55 (2) (Spring 2001), 469–485.

Ostry, S. 'Looking Back to Look Forward: The Multilateral Trading System after 50 Years' in WTO Secretariat (ed.), *From GATT to the WTO: The Multilateral Trading System in the New Millenium* (The Hague, London, and Boston: Klumer Law International and World Trade Organization, 2000), 97–112.

Painter, D. S. *The Cold War: An International History* (London and New York: Routledge, 1999).

Pedersen, S. *The Guardians: The League of Nations and the Crisis of Empire* (New York: Oxford University Press, 2015).

Perlow, G. H. 'The Multilateral Supervision of International Trade: Has the Textiles Experiment Worked?' *American Journal of International Law* 75 (1) (January 1981), 93–133.

Pollard, R. A. *Economic Security and the Origins of the Cold War, 1945–1950* (New York: Columbia University Press, 1985).

Pomeranz, K., and S. Topik. *The World that Trade Created: Society, Culture and the World Economy, 1400 to the Present* (Armonk, NY: M. E. Sharpe, 1999).

Prebisch, R. *The Economic Development of Latin America and its Principal Problems* (New York: Economic Commission for Latin America, 1950).

Preeg, E. H. *Traders and Diplomats: An Analysis of the Kennedy Round of Negotiations under the General Agreement on Tariffs and Trade* (Washington, DC: Brookings Institute, 1970).

Preeg, E. H. *Traders in a Brave New World: The Uruguay Round and the Future of the International Trading System* (Chicago and London: University of Chicago Press, 1995).

Pressnell, L. S. *External Economic Policy Since the War, Vol. I: The Post-War Financial Settlement* (London: Her Majesty's Stationery Office, 1986).

Putnam, R. D. 'Diplomacy and Domestic Politics: The Logic of Two-Level Games', *International Organization* 42 (3) (Summer 1988), 427–260.

Qin, Y. 'China and GATT: Accession Instead of Resumption', *Journal of World Trade* 27 (2) (Spring 1993), 77–98.

Reinisch, J. 'Internationalism in Relief: The Birth (and Death) of UNRRA', *Past & Present* 201 (6) (January 2011), 258–289.

Reves, E. *The Anatomy of Peace* (New York and London: Harper & Brothers, 1945).

Ridgeway, G. *Merchants of Peace: Twenty Years of Business Diplomacy through the International Chamber of Commerce 1919–1938* (New York: Columbia University Press, 1938).

Rittberger, V., B. Zangl, and M. Staisch. *International Organization: Polity, Politics and Policies*, translated by A. Groom (Basingstoke: Palgrave Macmillan, 2006).

Robertson, C. 'The Creation of UNCTAD' in R. Cox (ed.), *International Organisation, World Politics, Studies in Economic and Social Agencies* (London and Toronto: Macmillan, 1969), 258–274.

Roehrlich, E. 'State of the Field Essay on the History of the UN and its Organizations', H-Diplo Essay No. 153 (20 April 2018), http://tiny.cc/E153

Rose, A. K. 'Do We Really Know that the WTO Increases Trade?' *American Economic Review* 94 (1) (March 2004), 98–114.

Rose, A. K. 'Do We Really Know that the WTO Increases Trade? Reply', *The American Economic Review*, 97 (5) (December 2007), 2019–2025.

Rosenberg, E. S. 'Transnational Currents in a Shrinking World' in E. S. Rosenberg (ed.), *A World Connecting, 1870–1945* (Cambridge, MA: Belknap Press of Harvard University Press, 2012).

Rosenboim, O. *The Emergence of Globalism: Visions of World Order in Britain and the United States, 1939–1950* (Princeton: Princeton University Press, 2017).

Rostow, W. W. *The Stages of Economic Growth: A Non-Communist Manifesto*, 2nd edition (Cambridge: Cambridge University Press, 1971).

Ruggie, J. G. 'International Regimes, Transactions, and Change: Embedded Liberalism in the Postwar Economic Order' in S. D. Krasner (ed.), *International Regimes* (Ithaca, NY: Cornell University Press, 1983), 195–232.

Sanchez-Sibony, O. *Red Globalization: The Political Economy of the Soviet Union from Stalin to Khrushchev* (New York: Cambridge University Press, 2014).

Sander, H. 'Multilateralism, Regionalism, and Globalisation: The Challenges to the World Trading System' in H. Sander and A. Inotai (eds.), *World Trade After* the Uruguay Round: Prospects and Policy Options for the Twenty-First Century (London and New York: Routledge, 1996), 17–36.

Sargent, D. J. A Superpower Transformed: The Remaking of American Foreign Relations in the 1970s (Oxford: Oxford University Press, 2015).

Sauvant, K. P., and H. Hasenpflug (eds.). The New International Economic Order: Confrontation or Cooperation between North and South (Boulder, CO: Westview Press, 1977).

Sayward, A. L. The United Nations in International History (London and New York: Bloomsbury, 2017).

Sayward, A. L. S. The Birth of Development: How the World Bank, Food and Agriculture Organization, and the World Health Organization Changed the World, 1945–1965 (Kent, OH: Kent State University Press, 2006).

Schaller, M. The American Occupation of Japan: The Origins of the Cold War in Asia (New York and Toronto: Oxford University Press, 1985).

Schild, G. Bretton Woods and Dumbarton Oaks: American Economic and Political Postwar Planning in the Summer of 1944 (New York: St. Martin's Press, 1995).

Schlesinger, S. C. Act of Creation: The Founding of the United Nations: A Story of Superpowers, Secret Agents, Wartime Allies and Enemies and Their Quest for a Peaceful World (Boulder, CO: Westview Press, 2003).

Schonberger, H. B. Aftermath of War: Americans and Remaking Japan, 1945–52 (Kent, OH, and London: Kent State University Press, 1989).

Schroeder, P. W. 'International History: Why Historians Do It Differently than Political Scientists' in D. Wetzel, R. Jervis, and J. S. Levy (eds.), Systems, Stability and Statecraft: Essays on the International History of Modern Europe (Basingstoke and New York: Palgrave Macmillan, 2004), 285–296.

Schultz, S. 'Regionalisation of World Trade: Dead End or Way Out?' in M. P. van Dijk and S. Sideri (eds.), Multilateralism versus Regionalism: Trade Issues After the Uruguay Round (London and Portland, OR: Frank Cass in association with European Association of Development Research and Training Institutes, 1996), 20–39.

Schutts, R. 'Born Again in the Gospel of Refreshment?: Coca-Colonization and the Re-Making of Postwar German Identity' in D. F. Crew (ed.), Consuming Germany in the Cold War (Oxford: Berg, 2003), 121–150.

Sen, A. Development as Freedom (New York: Anchor Books, 2000).

Shangming, D., and W. Lei. 'China and GATT' in P. Zhang and R. Huenemann (eds.), China's Foreign Trade (Lantzville, BC, and Halifax, NS: Oolichan Books and Institute for Research on Public Policy, 1987), 68–77.

Shephard, B. The Long Road Home: The Aftermath of the Second World War (New York: Alfred A. Knopf, 2011).

Siamwalla, A. 'Agriculture, the Uruguay Round and Developing Countries', in A. Maunder and A. Valdés (eds.), Agriculture and Governments in an Interdependent World: Proceedings of the Twentieth International Conference of Agricultural Economists, held at Buenos Aires, Argentina, 24–31 August 1988 (Aldershot: Dartmouth Publishing Company, 1989), 320–332.

Skidelsky, R. John Maynard Keynes, Vol. Three: Fighting for Britain 1937–1946 (Basingstoke and Oxford: Papermac, 2001).

Skogstad, G., and A. F. Cooper (eds.). *Agricultural Trade: Domestic Pressures and International Tensions* (Halifax, NS: Institute for Research on Public Policy, 1990).

Slobodian, Q. *Globalists: The End of Empire and the Birth of Neoliberalism* (Cambridge, MA: Harvard University Press, 2018).

Sluga, G. 'UNESCO and the (One) World of Julian Huxley', *Journal of World History* 21 (3) (September 2010), 393–418.

Sluga, G., and P. Clavin (eds.). *Internationalisms: A Twentieth Century History* (Cambridge: Cambridge University Press, 2017).

Smith, A. *An Inquiry into the Nature and Causes of the Wealth of Nations* (Oxford: Oxford University Press, 1993).

Souza Farias, R. de. 'Brazil and the Origins of the Multilateral Trading System', *International History Review* 37 (2) (March 2015), 303–323.

Souza Farias, R. de. 'Mr. GATT: Eric Wyndham White and the Quest for Trade Liberalization', *World Trade Review* 12 (3) (July 2013), 463–485.

Srinivasan, T. N. *Developing Countries and the Multilateral Trading System: From the GATT to the Uruguay Round and the Future* (Boulder, CO: Westview Press, 1998).

Steil, B. *The Battle of Bretton Woods: John Maynard Keynes, Harry Dexter White, and the Making of a New World Order* (Princeton and Oxford: Princeton University Press, 2013).

Strange, S. 'Protectionism and World Politics', *International Organization* 39 (2) (Spring 1985), 233–259.

Sumner, D. A., and S. Tangermann. 'International Trade Policy and Negotiations' in B. L. Gardner and G. C. Rausser (eds.), *Handbook of Agricultural Economics, Vol. 2B: Agriculture and Food Policy* (Amsterdam and New York: Elsevier, 2002), 1999–2055.

Takeda, H. *Attainment of Economic Self-Support, Vol. III* in M. Sumiya (ed.), *A History of Japanese Trade and Industry Policy* (Oxford: Oxford University Press, 2000), 253–388.

Tallberg, J. 'The Power of the Chair: Formal Leadership in International Cooperation', *International Studies Quarterly* 54 (1) (March 2010), 241–265.

Thurow, L. C. 'GATT is Dead; the World Economy as We Know It is Coming to an End, Taking the General Agreement on Tariffs and Trade With It', *Journal of Accountancy* 170 (3) (September 1990), 36–39.

Tomz, M., J. L. Goldstein, and D. Rivers. 'Do We Really Know that the WTO Increases Trade? Comment', *American Economic Review* 97 (5) (December 2007), 2005–2018.

Tooze, A. *The Wages of Destruction: The Making and Breaking of the Nazi Economy* (New York: Viking, 2007).

Toye, R. 'Developing Multilateralism: The Havana Charter and the Fight for the International Trade Organization, 1947–1948', *International History Review* 25 (2) (June 2003), 282–305.

VanGrasstek, C. *The History and Future of the World Trade Organization* (Geneva: World Trade Organization, 2013).

Viner, J. *The Customs Union Issue* (New York: Carnegie Endowment for International Peace; London: Stevens & Sons United, 1950).

Vleuten, A. van der, and G. Alons. '*La Grande Nation* and Agriculture: The Power of French Farmers Demystified', *West European Politics* 35 (2) (March 2012), 266–285.

Wagnleitner, R. *Coca-Colonization and the Cold War: The Cultural Mission of the United States in Austria after the Second World War*, translated by D. M. Wolf (Chapel Hill: University of North Carolina Press, 1994).

Walt, S. M. 'Why I Didn't Sign Up to Defend the International Order', *Foreign Policy* (1 August 2018), https://foreignpolicy.com/2018/08/01/why-i-didnt-sign-up-to-defend-the-international-order/

Warley, T. K., 'Agriculture in the GATT: Past and Future' in A. Maunder and A. Valdés (eds.), *Agriculture and Governments in an Interdependent World: Proceedings of the Twentieth International Conference of Agricultural Economists, held at Buenos Aires, Argentina, 24–31 August 1988* (Aldershot: Dartmouth Publishing Company, 1989), 304–319.

Way, W. *A New Idea Each Morning: How Food and Agriculture Came Together in One International Organisation* (Canberra: Australian National University Press, 2013).

Weiss, J. 'E. H. Carr, Norman Angell, and Reassessing the Realist-Utopian Debate', *International History Review* 35 (5) (August 2013), 1156–1184.

Wertheim, S. 'Paeans to the "Postwar Order" Won't Save Us' (6 August 2018), War on the Rocks website, https://warontherocks.com/2018/08/paeans-to-the-postwar-order-wont-save-us/

Wiener, J. *Making Rules in the Uruguay Round of the GATT: A Study of International Leadership* (Aldershot: Dartmouth Publishing Company, 1995).

Wilkinson, R., and J. Scott. 'Developing Country Participation in GATT: A Reassessment', *World Trade Review* 7 (3) (July 2008), 473–510.

Winand, P. *Eisenhower, Kennedy, and the United States of Europe* (Basingstoke: Macmillan, 1993).

Winham, G. R. *International Trade and the Tokyo Round Negotiation* (Princeton: Princeton University Press, 1986).

Yoneyuki, S. *Pitfall or Panacea: The Irony of U.S. Power in Occupied Japan, 1945–1952* (New York: Routledge, 2003).

Zeiler, T. W. *American Trade and Power in the 1960s* (New York: Columbia University Press, 1992).

Zeiler, T. W. *Free Trade, Free World: The Advent of GATT* (Chapel Hill: University of North Carolina Press, 1999).

Zhang, S. G. *Economic Cold War: America's Embargo against China and the Sino-Soviet Alliance, 1949–1963* (Washington: Woodrow Wilson Centre Press; Stanford, CA: Stanford University Press, 2001).

Index

agriculture: *see also* Cairns Group; by individual country; developing countries; EEC, CAP
  ministerial meeting 1982, 264–265
  protectionism, 120, 121, 149, 232, 233, 237–238, 239, 245–246, 247, 248, 249
  rules, 238, 246, 247–248
  Tokyo round, 257–262
Angell, N.
  Carr's critique, 28
  trade and international politics, 28
Argentina, 79
  agriculture, 250, 256
  Cairns Group, 268
  CAP, 248
  Dunkel draft, 275
  Havana Charter, 181
  Uruguay round, 225–226
Arusha agreements, 153
Atlantic Charter 1941, 35
Augenthaler, Z., 72–73
Australia
  agriculture, 237, 247, 249, 250, 253, 256, 262, 264, 279
  Cairns Group, 267–270
  communist members of GATT, 87
  Dunkel draft, 275
  EEC, 118, 124, 126, 128, 263
  GATT review 1954–1955, 112
  Geneva conference 1947, 44
  IMF and GATT, 188
  imperial preferences, 50
  ITO, 182
  leadership in GATT, 239, 267
  Polish accession, 91
  PRC accession, 98
  preferences for developing countries, 202, 211
  ratification of GATT, 54
  reaction to GATT, 50–51
  regional trade, 155, 167

regional trade agreement with New Zealand, 149–150
selection of director-general, 212
support for GATT, 60–61
trade and employment, 41
trade and international politics, 41
trade policy, 50–51

Ball, G.
  agriculture, 251
  de Gaulle, 133
  Dillon round, 128
  LTA, 198
  UNCTAD, 206–207
bananas, 282
  developing countries, 239
Bangladesh
  developing country rivalry, 177
  liberal trade, 226
  PRC accession, 98
  Uruguay round, 226
Bhagwati, J.
  GATT, 145
  Great Depression, 29
  regional trade agreements, 143, 144
  USA, 161, 170
Brazil, 79
  agriculture, 237, 268
  Cairns Group, 268
  CAP, 248
  characterization of, 43, 203
  development, 192–193
  EEC, 117
  end of Cold War, 96
  International Trade Centre, 201, 230
  leadership of developing countries, 177
  Part IV, 203
  preferences for developing countries, 202
  quitting GATT, 58
  regional trade, 155
  selection of chairs, 190
  support for UNCTAD, 204